Critical Essays on Richard Wright

Critical Essays on Richard Wright

Yoshinobu Hakutani

G. K. Hall & Co. • Boston, Massachusetts

c. 1

Library of Congress Cataloging in Publication Data
Main entry under title:

Critical essays on Richard Wright.

  (Critical essays on American literature)
  Includes index.
  1. Wright, Richard, 1908–1960—Criticism and interpretation— Addresses, essays, lectures. I. Hakutani, Yoshinobu, 1935–
II. Series.
PS3545.R815Z62   813'.52   81–7227
ISBN 0–8161–8425–9   AACR2

CRITICAL ESSAYS ON AMERICAN LITERATURE

This series seeks to collect the most important previously published criticism on writers and topics in American literature along with, in various volumes, original essays, interviews, bibliographies, letters, manuscript sections, and other materials brought to public attention for the first time. Yoshinobu Hakutani's volume on Richard Wright fulfills these objectives nobly. In addition to gathering previously published articles by James Baldwin, Ralph Ellison, Irving Howe, Blyden Jackson, Houston A. Baker, Jr., and other notable writers and scholars, it contains original essays by Donald B. Gibson, Fred L. Standley, Michel Fabre, John M. Reilly, Nina Kressner Cobb, and Robert Tener. In addition, Professor Hakutani's long introduction is a complete and sensitive overview of Wright's career and the history of scholarly reaction to it. We are confident that this collection will make a permanent and significant contribution to American literary study.

JAMES NAGEL, GENERAL EDITOR

Northeastern University

CONTENTS

INTRODUCTION

In discussing the importance of Richard Wright, Irving Howe has said, "The day *Native Son* appeared, American culture was changed forever." It would appear, from the intensive commentary of the past forty years since Wright published his earliest works, that the significance of his writings comes not so much from his technique and style, but from the particular impact his ideas and attitudes have made on American life. To assess his achievement in such terms would require a broad study, not only of his art, but also of the social and cultural backgrounds of his work. His early critics' first consideration was that of race. They were unanimous in the view that if Wright had not been black his work would not have been so significant. As his vision of the world extended beyond the United States, his quest for solutions expanded from problems of race to those of politics and economics in the emerging Third World. Finally, his long exile in France gave his national and international concerns a universal dimension. Thus, Wright's development was marked by an ability to respond to the currents of the social and intellectual history of his time.

Wright was a remarkably resilient thinker and writer. His successes are beyond dispute, his failures understandable. He has fascinated not only literary critics, but also philosophers, psychologists, sociologists, and historians. Though many of his works failed to satisfy the rigid standards of the New Criticism, his evolution as a writer has excited readers the world over. Michel Fabre is right in speculating that toward the end of his life Wright "was once again going through a period of ideological change which, had its course been completed, might have caused him to start writing in a new vein. It is highly probable that the civil rights and Black Power movements would have given him a second wind, had he lived another five years."

Needless to say, Wright's literary reputation was firmly established by his early works. *Uncle Tom's Children*, *Native Son*, and *Black Boy* alone have made him the greatest black writer in America and accorded him the label of a major American novelist. His emergence as a black writer was a phenomenon, as *Black Boy* clearly demonstrates, for not only did he endure oppression and lack of freedom in the South and the North, but he triumphed over them. His successful transformation of that experience into enduring art has been recognized by readers of different races. Before Wright, the black American writer primarily addressed himself to the black audience. (If he had written for a white audience, he would have been expected to present stereotyped pictures of Negroes.) Exceptions like W. E. B. DuBois and Charles W. Chesnutt went largely unheeded, because Negroes, as Wright said, "possessed deep-seated

1

resistance against the Negro problem being presented, even verbally, in all its hideous dullness, in all the totality of its meaning." It was, therefore, somewhat miraculous that both blacks and whites believed what they read in *Native Son* and *Black Boy*, in which Wright destroys the white myth of the patient, humorous, subservient black man.

Some readers, notably James Baldwin, have regarded Wright as a protest writer, while some critics have gone so far as to attribute Wright's wide appeal to the sensationalism in his work. One cannot deny the terrifying suspense Bigger Thomas' actions generate, but Baldwin, for example, accuses Wright of distorting the otherwise complex Negro character. Other readers have disagreed: Robert Bone, arguing that Bigger is one of the Negro's "roles," felt that Wright did not simplify the complexity of black life. Though many of Wright's fictional works appear to be protest literature, they poignantly dramatize the themes of alienation, fear, and guilt that had not successfully been treated by Wright's predecessors.

It has generally been taken for granted that Wright was schooled in the tradition of American literary naturalism. In *Black Boy* Wright tells us how he was inspired by Theodore Dreiser's *Jennie Gerhardt* and *Sister Carrie*: "It would have been impossible for me to have told anyone what I derived from these novels, for it was nothing less than a sense of life itself. All my life had shaped me for the realism, the naturalism of the modern novels, and I could not read enough of them." Such testimony, however, only indicates Wright's youthful taste in books; it hardly proves that he became a doctrinaire naturalist in his writing. Indeed, to what extent he is part of American naturalism has become one of the central questions about Wright's work. In *Native Son*, for instance, does he subscribe to the novel's implicit assumption that American social conditions are directly responsible for the degradation of blacks? Recent criticism has modified or refuted this assumption, suggesting that Wright went beyond naturalism. The pessimistic determinism often associated with literary naturalism had taught the young Wright the meaning of racial oppression. A victim of oppression himself, Wright by necessity directed his energy toward rebellion. While he escaped the pessimistic outlook of naturalism, his respect for the philosophy helped him develop his own individualism and endow his characters with self-determination. Self-pity and rage alone would not have impressed modern readers. As Wright moved beyond anger and protest, he developed a new concern for character and literary discipline, seeking a deeper involvement in the world of art and philosophy. Naturalism taught him how to determine man's position in the world; existentialism taught him how to liberate man from the strictures imposed on him.

The assessment of a writer's achievement cannot be complete without considering his influences upon other writers. Black literary history clearly indicates that after the publication of *Native Son* and *Black Boy*, quaintness and idealized folksiness disappeared from Negro literature. Instead, writers like Chester Himes and William Gardner Smith wrote on the agonizing effects of the urban ghetto environment. During the forties emerged many examples of the so-called "problem novel": Wright's influences can be detected in such works as Chester Himes' *If He Hollers Let Him Go*, William Gardner Smith's *Last of the Conquerors*, Ann Petry's *The Street*, Willard Motley's *Knock on Any Door*, and Willard Savoy's *Alien Land*, to mention a few. In the fifties black literature came to occupy a permanent place in contemporary American literature. Despite disclaimers to the contrary by the authors themselves, Ralph Ellison's *Invisible Man* (1952) and James Baldwin's *Notes of a Native Son* (1955) would not have enjoyed the critical acclaim without the road Wright had paved a decade earlier. Like Wright, Ellison was deeply involved with the problem of race, but with the help of his creative imagination succeeded in making what is racial and regional into what is universal. Likewise, Baldwin, with the sharpest rhetorical skills of any black writer, describes his work as a concern with "the depthless alienation from oneself and one's people—this is the sum of the American experience."

I   GENERAL COMMENTARIES

The magnitude of Wright's achievement and importance is indicated by the numerous biographical studies, three of book length, made since the forties. Constance Webb's *Richard Wright: A Biography* is a long, passionate account by a personal friend of Wright's.[1] Despite Webb's access to Mrs. Wright's notes, letters, and other original materials, the book lacks the coherence and chronology critics need. Though it provides useful information, it falls far short of a definitive biography of a major writer, such as Mark Schorer's *Sinclair Lewis: An American Life* or W. A. Swanberg's *Dreiser*. John A. Williams' *The Most Native of Sons: A Biography of Richard Wright*, though dismissed by Michel Fabre as a juvenile book, provides an intimate account of the psychological makeup of a black novelist by a black novelist.[2] Although Williams persuasively demonstrates that the central theme of Wright's work is race, he hypothesizes that Wright would have established his reputation earlier and more easily had he not been a black writer. Michel Fabre's *The Unfinished Quest of Richard Wright* ranks with the biographies of Lewis and Dreiser mentioned above for its scope and organization,[3] the only difference being that, despite Fabre's intention to exclude criticism, he fails to do so in many parts of his book. The reason for this failure can be explained partly by his statement of principle: "Literature and politics were two equally indispensable tools in the service of humanism. This is why I insist upon judging Wright's work as a whole, not separating his writing from its ideological framework, and not making a split, only artificially justified by his exile, in the unfolding of his career."[4]

The earliest book-length critical study was attempted by Edward

Margolies: *The Art of Richard Wright*.[5] Unlike some critics, who regard Wright as merely a proletarian writer, Margolies successfully demonstrates Wright's themes of fear and alienation, though he admits that Wright "seldom achieved his fullest measure of artistic promise."[6] Far from a critical study, *The Example of Richard Wright*, by Dan McCall, attempts to show the link between the author's personality and work, but McCall is surely handicapped by his failure to use all of the biographical data available to him.[7] In *Richard Wright: An Introduction to the Man and His Works* Russell C. Brignano organizes his study not by the chronology of Wright's writing, but by a focus on Wright's themes and topics.[8] One of Brignano's unique contributions to Wright criticism is his attempt to discuss Marxism. Brignano argues, as does Michel Fabre in his biography, that Wright was essentially a humanist and thus naturally collided with Communist Party doctrine. In *The Emergence of Richard Wright* Keneth Kinnamon explains convincingly that Wright faced more formidable obstacles in his youth than any other American writer.[9] Kinnamon accounts for Wright's extraordinary accomplishment with well-annotated evidence. Referring to the emotional depravity the young Wright felt in his fanatically religious family and racially prejudiced community, as well as the occasional release he felt in reading fiction, Kinnamon carefully demonstrates how Wright converted his anger into creativity. Robert Bone's pamphlet *Richard Wright* attempts to explain Wright's attraction to existentialism by noting his "tendency to make a virtue out of rootlessness, to conceive of the human condition as a kind of cosmic exile."[10]

The positive effect of Wright's early life on his creativity is well summarized by Houston A. Baker, Jr., in "Racial Wisdom and Richard Wright's *Native Son*" (reprinted in this volume).[11] Baker maintains that Wright criticism has been hampered by tenets of the New Criticism that overemphasize analysis of the work itself at the expense of examining the creator's life. Yet it was Wright's fight for survival in early life, Baker points out, that contributed to the success of his early works. This phenomenon, Baker argues, continued after Wright had left the South and even the United States. On the other hand, Saunders Redding, a noted black critic and writer, observes that in describing his experience in Europe and Africa, Wright "turns precious and arty; honesty deserts him; dedication wilts; passion chills."[12] The dangers inherent in exile are cogently explained by Richard Kostelanetz in "The Politics of Unresolved Quests in the Novels of Richard Wright."[13] Kostelanetz suggests that Wright's emphasis on collective action in his earlier works is modified by his later themes of alienation. This reaction against leftist political activity—Wright himself broke with the Communist Party—led to dangers unexpected in his vision as an exile. In "Richard Wright's Complexes and Black Writing Today," Cecil Brown proposes that, tragically, Wright had to exile himself "because his definition of 'Negro life' was too narrow, too confining, too puny, and too dependent on White Society."[14]

Among the studies focusing on Wright's relations to the Communist Party, John A. Williams's biography (mentioned earlier) is the most perceptive and sympathetic in its discussion of Wright's youth. As a black American novelist, Williams appreciates the strong attraction Communist politics had for the young Wright in the depth of the Depression. The most comprehensive history of the latter's association with the Communist Party is provided by Daniel Aaron in "Richard Wright and the Communist Party."[15] Aaron traces Wright's connection with the actual or would-be Communist world from the early thirties: his initial involvement with the Chicago John Reed Club in 1932, then his membership in the American Communist Party, which concluded with the end of his literary apprenticeship, by 1940. Aaron's survey contains many facts of interest; for instance, the chairman of the first national conference for the John Reed Club held in Chicago in 1932 was a man named Jan Wittenber, the model for Jan Erlone in *Native Son*. The policy of Black self-determination, to which Wright must have been attracted, was maintained between 1928 and 1934, but played down during the Popular Front period (1934–1939). As Aaron points out, by the mid-thirties Wright legitimately felt that "the Party oversimplified Black experience." It would be difficult to determine exactly how Wright felt about Black self-determination, or the Black Republic, at this time, but Aaron believes that the Marxist lawyer's statement on American Blacks in *Native Son* may provide an important clue: "They are not simply twelve million people; in reality, they constitute a separate nation, stunted, stripped, and held captive within this nation." Wright's growing disenchantment with the Communist Party is also suggested by his making fools of Jan and Mary, the insensitive Communists in the novel. Wright left the Party, Aaron concludes, because he was unable to reconcile Black nationalism, in which he had faith, with Marxist universalism, to which he paid lip service. A new account of Wright's relations with the Communist Party is provided by Alvin Starr's "Richard Wright and the Communist Party —The James T. Farrell Factor."[16] Starr points out that Farrell's address to the Writers' Congress held in 1935 influenced Wright not to subordinate to aesthetic concerns.

As for the literary tradition Wright followed, most critics view him as a naturalist writer. In his review of *Lawd Today*, "Dreiser to Farrell to Wright," Granville Hicks maintains that Wright "could scarcely have failed to be influenced by James T. Farrell who was just beginning to have a strong effect on American fiction. As Farrell had learned something about documentation from Dreiser, so Wright had learned from Farrell."[17] Michel Fabre, however, argues in "Richard Wright: Beyond Naturalism?" that Wright, far from being deterministic and concerned with detail, seeks intensity of feeling.[18] Wright, Fabre says, is akin to Frank Norris, who viewed naturalism as a type of romanticism; reality must be twisted from the ordinary. Fabre bases his argument on "Blueprint for Negro Writing," in which Wright contends: "The presentation of their lives should be simple, yes; but all the complexity, the strangeness, the magic, the wonder of life that plays like a bright sheen over the most sordid existence should be there. To borrow a phrase from the Russians, it should have a *complex simplicity*."

Discussion of Wright's relations with his literary contemporaries has focused on James Baldwin, who is well known to have regarded Wright as his mentor, but soon rebelled against him. In "Everybody's Protest Novel" Baldwin calls Bigger Thomas a descendant of Uncle Tom.[19] In "Many Thousands Gone" (reprinted in this volume) Baldwin asserts that *Native Son* "suggested a revolution of racial conflict that was merely the liberal dream of good will in which blacks would obliterate their personalities and become as whites." Michel Fabre maintains that although Baldwin was helped by his mentor, he was afraid the American public would not recognize his originality, and "had, therefore, leaned over backwards to assert their differences."[20] To Baldwin, Wright's treatment of the problem of race seems to be directed toward the fictional but realistic presentation of his rage. Though sympathetic to the rage, Baldwin sees a basic flaw in Wright's technique, contending that the novelist must analyze raw emotion and transform it into an identifiable human experience. Baldwin cannot approve of Wright's use of violence, which he regards as "gratuitous and compulsive because the root of the violence is never examined. The root is rage."[21] In "Wright, the Protest Novel, and Baldwin's Faith," Kichung Kim advances the theory that the difference between Wright and Baldwin arises from the two different concepts of man.[22] Kim explains that the weakness Baldwin sees in Wright and other protest writers "is not so much that they had failed to give a faithful account of the actual conditions of man but rather that they had failed to be steadfast in their devotion . . . to what man might and ought to be. Such a man . . . will not only survive oppression but will be strengthened by it." Fred L. Standley's essay " '. . . Farther and Farther Apart': Richard Wright and James Baldwin" (presented in this volume) examines their relationship in four major aspects: Wright as Baldwin's "spiritual father," Baldwin's betrayal of friendship, their concepts of "protest literature," and their interpretations of Bigger Thomas. Relying on a precise chronology of the events that occurred between them, Standley offers well-annotated evidence that their attitudes toward each other came from "the deep and irreconcilable differences" in their philosophies of life and theories of literature.

Interestingly enough, the controversy over the Wright-Baldwin relationship has involved other black writers. In recent decades Baldwin's audience of American readers has displeased black militants; Eldridge Cleaver has called Baldwin one of the "Stepin Fetchits" of our age. Cleaver attacks Baldwin personally, claiming that his criticism of *Native Son* stems from an envy of Wright's masculinity. Furthermore, Cleaver despises Baldwin's work because in it he finds "the most grueling, agonizing, total hatred of the blacks, particularly of himself, and the most shameful, fanatical, fawning, sychophantic love of the whites that one can find in the writings of any black American writer of note in our time."[23] Amiri Baraka, another 'militant writer, predictably shares this point of view.[24] Baraka accuses Baldwin of failure to become involved in the racial struggle: "Men like Baldwin and [Peter] Abrahams want to live free from such 'ugly' things as 'the racial struggle' because (they imply) they simply cannot stand what it does to men." Baldwin and Baraka believe in two fundamentally different principles of love and hate. Baldwin, discovering that hatred has the power to destroy, has invested his absolute faith in the redemptive role of blacks in American society through love; Baraka, observing that hatred of whites is the natural result of being black in America, has sanctioned hatred as the only reasonable reaction to oppression. Baraka is also critical of Wright's treatment of race in his fiction. Wright's work, as well as black literature in general, has become a white literature written in imitation of "the useless, ugly inelegance of the stunted middle-class mind." As long as the black writer refuses to look around him and "tell it like it is," Baraka warns, he will be just another dead, mediocre writer. Wright, Baldwin, and Ellison can be compared to Maugham, not Joyce or Melville.[25]

Baraka's disparaging remarks about Wright's achievement notwithstanding, the general estimate of Wright's work by white writers and critics is higher than for any other black writer. As a writer and reader, Gerald Green in "Back to Bigger" claims that what really excites the modern sensibility is well-constructed social fiction like *Native Son*.[26] For Green, Wright's novel, more than anything else, informs the reader what it means to be black in America. Richard Wright's Bigger Thomas, Green confesses, "still has the power to scare me silly . . . Baldwin has never frightened me the slightest." Green concludes this general essay by mourning "what a falling off, from Richard Wright, say, to LeRoi Jones, from Sean O'Casey to Edward Albee." In "Art and Act: The Example of Richard Wright" Barry Gross asserts, as many have, that *Black Boy* is the portrait of the artist as a young man and *Native Son* is the portrait of the artist in action.[27] Gross, however, makes a far-fetched comparison between Bigger and Melville's Ahab, the white world in *Native Son* and the white whale in *Moby-Dick*. Finally, Donald B. Gibson, in "Richard Wright: Aspects of His Afro-American Literary Relations" (presented in this volume), advocates that Wright differs with other black novelists chiefly in his endowment of his characters with power. Another difference is his adherence to both naturalism and Marxism; while Wright is aware of the forces that control man's behavior, he believes that life can be changed by man. Racism in Charles Chesnutt and Paul Dunbar, as Gibson shows, differs from that in Wright, who views discrimination not merely on the basis of race, but also on the basis of political, economic, and social considerations.

II   CRITICISM OF FICTION

Uncle Tom's Children

The initial critical reception of *Uncle Tom's Children*, Wright's first work of fiction, was generally favorable. James T. Farrell, appreciative of Wright's direct and realistic style, remarked in *Partisan Review* that *Uncle Tom's Children* serves as an exemplary refutation for those who wished to write "such fancy nonsense about fables and allegories."[28] In response to such reviewers as Granville Hicks and Alan Calmer, who wanted Wright to pace more steadily in his narrative and delve more deeply into his material, Farrell argued that Wright effectively employs simple dialogue "as a means of carrying on his narrative, as a medium for poetic and lyrical effects, and as an instrument of characterization." Most reviewers, both black and white, praised Wright's first work without reservation: Herschel Brickell in the *New York Evening Post*, Lewis Gannett in the *New York Herald Tribune*, and Sterling Brown in *The Nation*, all respected Wright for breaking away from stereotypes.[29] Malcolm Cowley found these stories "heartening, as evidence of a vigorous new talent, and terrifying as the expression of a racial hatred that has never ceased to grow and gets no chance to die."[30] Cowley considered legitimate the communist slogan to unite black and white and regarded racial violence in the South as inevitable. Many critics were impressed by Wright's language and art. Marvel Cooke, writing in the *New York Amsterdam News*, thought Wright's use of black dialect superb.[31] Robert Van Gelder compared Wright to Hemingway; Allen Maxwell likened his style to Steinbeck's.[32]

Both Van Gelder and Charles Poore were antagonistic to Wright's racial views.[33] As if in return for Wright's unfavorable review of her novel *Their Eyes Were Watching God*, the black novelist Zora Neale Hurston categorized *Uncle Tom's Children* as a chronicle of hatred with no act of understanding and sympathy.[34] She too opposed Wright's politics, arguing that his stories fail to touch the fundamental truths of black life.

The earliest extended critical analysis of Wright's short fiction was "The Art of Richard Wright's Short Stories" by Edwin Berry Burgum.[35] Burgum confirms Wright's skill in structuring his stories in the form of modern tragedy, in which the hero's awareness of individualism directly collides with the external forces of society. For example, Wright skillfully illustrates a black man's rebellion against society in the heroism of Silas, the protagonist in "Long Black Song." Burgum also finds Wright's style extremely congenial to his material, claiming that his style in the short stories was influenced by Hemingway: both writers use short sentences to describe surface activities; whereas Hemingway disguises the confusions beneath the surface, Wright clarifies them.

Later estimates of the book concur with Burgum's. In a chapter on *Uncle Tom's Children* and *Eight Men* in *The Art of Richard Wright*, (reprinted in this collection) Edward Margolies observes that one of the successes of *Uncle Tom's Children* is Wright's use of Marxism for didactic purposes. Portraying conflicts that are true to the facts of life in the South, his stories usually succeed by their integration of plot, imagery, character, and theme. Wright also renders his stories sometimes in Biblical terms. Rev. Taylor and Aunt Sue, for example, arrive at their moments of truth not through communistic or religious ideals, but as a result of "their peculiar Negro folk mysticism." Margolies concludes his study by pointing out the sweep and magnitude of Wright's stories "suffused with the author's impassioned convictions about the dignity of man." That the dignity of man is a central issue in Wright's fiction is echoed by a black critic's analysis of "Big Boy Leaves Home," Wright's earliest fictional effort. Blyden Jackson ("Richard Wright in a Moment of Truth") explains that "Big Boy Leaves Home," instead of showing the quality of the Negro will to survive oppression, demonstrates the lynching of Bobo as a symbolic rite of castration, "the ultimate indignity that can be inflicted upon an individual."[36] In "Richard Wright's Successful Failure: A New Look at *Uncle Tom's Children*," James R. Giles detects a shift from Wright's concern with youth and adults who meet lonely deaths to his treatment of Sue in "Bright and Morning Star," who dies "martyred to Communism, and thus triumphs over all the forces that have limited the characters in the first four stories."[37] Not surprisingly, the estimates of individual stories in the collection vary widely among the critics.

Native Son

Native Son, Wright's first novel, achieved phenomenal success with critics as well as readers. As a Book-of-the-Month-Club selection it became at once a best-seller, a popularity accorded to no other black novelist before him. Sterling Brown, a black reviewer for *Opportunity* was quick to recognize the book's revolutionary status. Brown felt that if a single book could awaken the conscience of the whole nation, that book would be *Native Son*. Bigger's characterization, not the revolutionary setting, nor the thrilling narrative, was regarded as Wright's greatest achievement. Unlike Big Boy, Bigger is able to contend with destructive forces and is determined not to leave home as Big Boy does. Brown saw Bigger as the first character in American fiction to exhibit "a psychological probing of the consciousness of the outcast, the disinherited, the generation lost in the slum jungles of American civilization."[38] As Irving Howe was to note later, *Native Son* would destroy once and for all the misconception of white readers who had seen "the Negro as one peculiarly endowed to bear the burdens and suffer the shame without rancor, without bitterness, and without essential humanity."[39]

The favorable reviews are too numerous to mention; a few will suffice.[40] Jonathan Daniels praised Wright's depiction of Bigger's terror. Edward Skillin, Jr., regarded the Communist characters in the book as genuine sympathizers for the Negro cause in American society. Margaret Marshall called Bigger's actions in the novel authentic. Significantly, *Native Son* received unanimously sympathetic attention from leftist publications like *New Masses*. Malcolm Cowley and Ben Davis, Jr., compared *Native Son* to *The Grapes of Wrath*, the most popular proletarian novel published in the previous year. Clifton Fadiman wrote, "*Native Son* does for the Negro what Theodore Dreiser in *An American Tragedy* did a decade and a half ago for the bewildered, inarticulate American white."[41] In "A Tragic Novel of Negro Life in America" Peter Monro Jack found in both *Native Son* and *An American Tragedy* the problems of social maladjustment, environmental influence, and subsequently of crime and punishment. Jack also noted differences: the injustice in *Native Son* is obviously racial, not simply social; the plot in *Native Son* is simple and melodramatic, whereas in *An American Tragedy* Dreiser broods slowly and patiently over the fate of Clyde Griffiths.[42] In his review mentioned above, Edward Skillin, Jr. also likened Wright's novel to Dreiser's. And James W. Ivy compared Bigger with Raskolnikov or one of the Brothers Karamazov, all of whom produce the effects of the catharsis of Greek tragedy.[43]

The harshest review came from David L. Cohn who accused Wright of distorting fact and argued that the kinds of social problems Wright dealt with could not be solved.[44] In "Negro Novel and White Reviewers" Burton Rascoe objected to Bigger's proneness to violence.[45] One of the weaknesses some reviewers found was Wright's overwriting Bigger into a social symbol, as the leftist critic Ben Davis, Jr., pointed out in the *Sunday Worker*. Malcolm Cowley, generally very positive about the novel, deplored Max's courtroom plea for Bigger's life as thematically weakening. That plea would be quite meaningful on behalf of the whole black population, Cowley argued, but Bigger must die to stand as an individual, not a symbol. The most constructive criticism was offered by the British critic David Daiches, who recognized the validity of Bigger's action, but objected that "Wright is trying to prove a normal thesis by an abnormal case."[46] Daiches saw as pure melodrama a plot that involves the hero's hacking off the head of an innocent white girl, sticking her body into the furnace, and bashing the head of his black sweetheart; consequently, the novel as a valid interpretation of life unnecessarily suffers. Likewise, Howard Mumford Jones admitted the power of the plot at first reading, but lamented the melodrama, lacking in subtlety and complexity, that greatly undermines the otherwise significant thesis of the book.[47]

The most controversial analysis of *Native Son* is James Baldwin's "Many Thousands Gone," (mentioned earlier and reprinted in this volume). Baldwin adamantly opposes Wright's characterization of Bigger as a monster who does not embody a true Negro feeling. Failing to recognize humanity and the genuine struggle of Negro life, the author merely records "that fantasy Americans held in their minds when they speak of the Negro." Bigger is a misrepresentation of the Negro because he "has no discernible relationship to himself, to his life, to his own people, nor to any other people . . . and his force comes, not from his significance as a social (or anti-social) unit, but from his significance as the incarnation of a myth." The serious limitation Baldwin sees in Bigger's character is not Wright's use of Bigger as a symbol, but the absence of the social and human relations that underlie that symbol. Baldwin would treat Bigger's story differently: "To tell his story is to begin to liberate us from his image and it is, for the first time, to clothe this phantom with flesh and blood, to deepen, by our understanding of him and his relationship to us, our understanding of our selves and all men." What Baldwin fails to discover behind the symbol, Keneth Kinnamon tries to fill in ("*Native Son*: The Personal, Social, and Political Background"; reprinted in this collection). Trying to distill the essence of Bigger's character, Kinnamon traces in substantial detail the personal, social, and human experiences reflected in the novel. The evidence his study presents is convincing; as Wright explains in "How 'Bigger' Was Born," the character of Bigger is a composite of many individual Negroes Wright knew in his life. Kinnamon also shows that the slum condition of Chicago described in the novel "had been the daily reality of a decade in Wright's life (1927–1937). . . The details of the Chicago environment in the novel have a verisimilitude that is almost photographic." Also, Bigger's pattern of fear and frustration was supported by the sociological research of Wright's friend, Horace R. Cayton, as well as the Robert Nixon case. Kinnamon adds that the success of the novel derives from a proper balance of objective and subjective detail.

Partly in response to Baldwin's criticism, Donald B. Gibson ("Wright's Invisible Native Son") reads *Native Son* as psychological rather than social fiction.[48] Baldwin has charged that Max's speech at the end of the novel fails to clarify Bigger's humanity, "the relationship in which he stands to all other Americans—and, by implication, to all people." Gibson, on the other hand, citing quotations from Book III, shows that Bigger at the end of the book is trying to come to terms with himself rather than with society. A similar view is voiced by Edward Margolies in *Native Sons: A Critical Study of Twentieth-Century Negro American Authors*.[49] *Native Son*, Margolies suggests, is a psychological as well as sociological novel, which not only shocks the reader's conscience, but also raises "questions regarding the ultimate nature of man."

The third part of the novel has been given close scrutiny by many critics. Robert Bone, mentioned earlier, calls it a failure because Bigger cannot be an advocate of Communism. As a result, there is no appropriate action for the thesis in Book III. In contrast, Malcolm Cowley asserts that this part is the best, since "the case of Bigger Thomas is not the author's deepest concern." Rather, Wright has a larger mission: "Because he does speak for and to the nation, without ceasing to be a Negro, the book has more force than any other American novel by a member of his race."[49A] Edward Kearns argues that despite the abstractness of Bigger's speech, the third section of the novel "is a logical and necessary extension of Wright's thematic strategy, because once Bigger has acted and begun to establish his identity, he must conceptualize the meaning of his act if it is to have any value."[50] Paul N. Siegel, on the other hand, argues against such white critics as Howe, Kazin, Bone, McCall, Margolies, and Brignano, who he charges have misread the ending of the novel.[51] Max's long speech in the courtroom, Siegel suggests, does not have a party-line defense; Max hands the case to a judge, thereby rejecting a trial by an all-white jury. Phyllis R. Klotman, borrowing Wayne Booth's term "moral distancing," interprets Book III as Wright's way of shifting the burden of Bigger's guilt to society.[52]

Critics of *Native Son* have not neglected to study Wright's technique and style. James A. Emanuel demonstrates that Bigger's consciousness of life is presented in a series of images such as those of light, dark, blurs, closure, walls, and curtains.[53] In "Images of 'Vision' in *Native Son*" (reprinted in this collection) James Nagel observes that the novel is not only a solid sociological study of the Negro's life in the United States but also a work of art that "transcends the limitation of sociological prose." The most significant artistic element is Wright's use of the imagery of blindness. Through his killing of a white girl, Bigger is able to see himself as an individual; this scene becomes "the pivotal point for not only the structure and theme, but the imagery as well: it is a moment of 'recognition' in the classical sense." Furthermore, Bigger's act of killing results in a change of vision for other characters in the novel. Bessie now sees her relationship to Bigger in a different light; Max "sees most brilliantly and explains Bigger's plight to the court, though ironically he fails to see Bigger as an individual." Covering much the same ground as Nagel's study, Thomas LeClair explains that Bigger, suffering from different degrees of blindness, can only begin to see clearly at the end of the novel. And Lloyd W. Brown maintains that at the beginning of the novel Bigger's vision is a reflection of white perception, but as the story progresses he acquires his own vision.[54]

The Outsider

Orville Prescott's *New York Times* review was a typical reaction to *The Outsider*.[55] The hero of the novel is a Negro in name only; not only is his plight unreal, but all the incidents and characters turn out to be ill-digested ideas and clumsily constructed symbols. With due respect for Wright's previous successes, Prescott politely insisted that Wright must have deplored Cross Damon's moral weakness and irrational behavior at the end of the book. Prescott further remarked, "That men as brilliant as Richard Wright feel this way is one of the symptoms of the intellectual and moral crisis of our times." Much the same opinion was expressed by a host of reviewers: James N. Rhea found Cross Damon "pathetically insane, despite Wright's efforts to give him great intellectual powers"; Melvin Alshulter entitled his review "An Important, but Exasperating Book"; Roland Sawyer felt that the ill-designed book might be a reflection of the author's "fringe thinking"; Max Eastman considered the existentialism in the book a racket, because the philosophy is used for making art rather than providing guidance for the hero to follow.[56]

·Black reviewers were bewildered by *The Outsider*, not because of Wright's novel philosophy, but because he seemed to have lost contact with his native soil.[57] In the *Baltimore Afro-American* Saunders Redding noted that Wright's brand of existentialism, instead of being a device for the representation of truth, "leads away from rather than toward reality." Arna Bontemps, in the *Saturday Review*, was even sarcastic: "The black boy from Mississippi is still exploring. He has had a roll in the hay with the existentialism of Sartre, and apparently he liked it." Lloyd L. Brown not only found the novel to be "fictional failure," but saw as naive in the extreme the activities of Cross Damon, who goes such a long distance to discover that "life is an incomprehensible disaster."

For the first time in Wright's career his work received predominantly negative reviews. Most of the initial reactions indicate that Wright's characterization was unconvincing; Cross Damon is simply an embodiment of a half-baked philosophy. Granville Hicks, however, was sympathetic, describing *The Outsider* as Wright's "most valiant and successful effort to come to terms with his feelings about the human conditions.[58] Similarly, Gilbert Highet found the book moving; Cross Damon, a man of solitude and remorse, reminded him of the hero of *Light in August* and Ishmael in *Moby-Dick*.[59] To Highet, however, Wright's transformation of a distracted, lustful postal clerk into a Nietzschean philosopher was unconvincing. Thomas D. Jarrett saw a "more advanced, intellectualized Bigger Thomas" in Cross Damon.[60] The most favorable review was Harvey Curtis Webster's "Richard Wright's Profound New Novel," which ranked Wright with masters of modernist fiction such as Hemingway, Mann, Gide, and Faulkner.[61] In none of the three previous masterpieces—*Uncle Tom's Children*, *Native Son*, and *Black Boy*—did Webster find "the faltering brilliance" he discovered in *The Outsider*. Ralph De Toledano was equally enthusiastic; the novel indicated Wright's mature ability for fusing the novel of violence with the novel of ideas.[62]

Despite the cold reception this novel encountered in the beginning, except for *Native Son*, none of Wright's other books have received such intensive critical attention. Many of the early critics regard Wright's philosophy in the book as nihilistic. Charles I. Glicksberg, in "Existentialism in *The Outsider*" and "The God of Fiction," sees parallels between Wright and Camus in treatment of the metaphysical rebel, and calls Cross Damon's philosophy most consistently nihilistic.[63] Likewise, Kingsley Widmer ("The Existential Darkness: Richard Wright's *The Outsider*") observes that Cross Damon descends into the darkness of defiant nihilism.[64] The hero, finding himself alienated racially as well as metaphysically, fails to assert himself and ends in an ambiguous notion of self. This intellectual plight of Damon's is interpreted by Addison Gayle, Jr., as a warning against "a nation incapable of putting its ideals into practice."[65] Such a nation would naturally produce Cross Damons who sought "their manhood through a nihilistic attempt to negate the very structure of democracy itself."

Much of the struggle and ambiguity that accompany Damon's characterization may have derived from Wright's own experience. Nathan A. Scott suggests that Wright, unlike his American contemporaries, shared an existential view of man with his European writers even prior to *The Outsider*. Scott, however, believes that Wright's fictionalization of his own metaphysical quest in *The Outsider* is a failure, chiefly because Wright lacks knowledge in "the labyrinthine interiorities of the human soul."[66] Wright's failure is also analyzed by Darwin T. Turner through a comparison of *The Outsider* with *Native Son*.[67] Turner maintains that despite the difference in character between Bigger and Damon, the two novels have parallel themes. Bigger is economically poor and uneducated; Damon is a middle-class black and an intellectual. Both, through murder, achieve manhood, but are destroyed by an organized institution—Bigger by a capitalistic society and Damon by Communists. In *The Outsider*, Turner argues, Wright succeeds intellectually, but fails artistically. The economically poor and uneducated Bigger elicits sympathy, but the self-sufficient Damon "does not evoke the sentimentality which can be showered on those judged to be socially and economically inferior."

More recently, the definition of *The Outsider* as a purely existentialist novel has been challenged. In *Richard Wright: An Introduction to the Man and His Works* (mentioned earlier) Russell C. Brignano argues that *The Outsider* indicates Wright's "rejection of existentialism." In portraying a destructive man like Cross Damon who has walked outside of society, Wright is "really asking man to be responsible for others as well as for himself" so that man can eventually discover "a way out of a history of injustices and irrationalities." Lewis A. Lawson's "Cross Damon: Kierkegaardian Man of Dread" is an effort to read *The Outsider* as a Christian rather than an atheistic, existential novel, for at the end of the book Cross's acceptance of guilt frees him to seek atonement.[68] Raman K. Singh argues that by secularizing the concept of original sin, Wright has unnecessarily endowed the mediocre Cross Damon with the inflated confidence in himself.[69] Finally, Michel Fabre, in "Richard Wright, French

Existentialism, and *The Outsider*" (included in this collection), points out that Wright, Sartre, and de Beauvoir are less concerned with aestheticism than Camus. Thus Fabre finds *The Outsider* full of passion and feeling, whereas Camus's style in *The Stranger* strikes him as impersonal. In Fabre's view, Damon's revelation that his disregard for others weakens his capacity for change comes from de Beauvoir, who has stated, "To be free consists in being able to transcend the given towards an open future." Fabre discovers that while the French existentialists are concerned with social survival by upholding humanism and morality, in *The Outsider* Wright calls for "a negation of all societal norms." As a result, Damon's resolution at the end of his journey is a reflection of his dread rather than an independently reached choice.

Savage Holiday

One reason why *Savage Holiday*, Wright's third novel, received no reviews is his exclusive treatment of white characters and his concern with nonracial matters. The anomaly of this novel is further reflected by the scantiness of the critical attention it has received. In *The Art of Richard Wright*, Edward Margolies maintains that while Wright's other novels study the social and psychological pressures imposed on blacks, *Savage Holiday* experiments with the similar pressures society imposes on whites. Although Margolies finds some of Wright's best prose in the first part, "Anxiety," he considers the novel far short of genuine artistic achievement. Not only are the author's psychological interpolations too condescending, but Fowler's character is patterned too strictly on a Freudian principle; consequently, the plot becomes contrived, coincidental, and hackneyed. Though Margolies considers the psychological determinism valid, he believes Wright fails to give it much artistic support in this novel. Fowler is too weak a character; he has "neither the stature nor the potential strength to put up the good fight with his irrational passions." In contrast, John M. Reilly reads the book as a thriller as well as a psychological novel.[70] Accordingly, he analyzes it as a dual narrative: on the one hand, Fowler's character is well portrayed by action and dialogue; on the other, the plot is developed strictly for the purposes of detecting the crime.

The Long Dream

Despite Wright's efforts to portray his bitter experiences in the rural South, as he did so successfully in *Uncle Tom's Children* and *Black Boy*, *The Long Dream* betrayed a distinct decline in his creative power. Saunders Redding, who had earlier detected a danger inherent in Wright's exile, observed that in *The Long Dream* Wright "has cut the emotional umbilical cord through which his art was fed, and all that remains for it to feed on is the memory, fading, of righteous love and anger."[71] In "A Long Way from Home" Nick Aaron Ford, another black critic, concurred with Redding that Wright had lost touch with his native soil and the swiftly changing racial currents in the United States.[72] Agreeing with Redding and Ford, Maxwell Geismar ("Growing Up in Fear's Grip") remarked that while *Uncle Tom's Children, Native Son,* and *Black Boy* were "solid, bitter, savage, almost terrifying fictional studies of the Negro mind," *The Long Dream* turned out to be "a surrealistic fantasy of paranoid and suicidal impulses, veiled in political terminology."[73] For Granville Hicks, what Wright had thought realism in *The Long Dream* was merely a surface realism. Fishbelly Tucker "is not merely alienated from the culture in which he has been born; he is alienated from reality."[74]

The lack of depth many reviewers deplored had some appeal for others, who considered *The Long Dream* with an eye for the social dimension provided in the novel.[75] Roi Ottley argued that the novel provided "a social document of unusual worth" with a catalog of lynching, police brutality, and race riot in a Southern town. Writing in *Best Sellers* Paul Kiniery found a value in Wright's depiction of black characters as amoral and as "interested in practically nothing but irregular but frequent sexual relations." Kiniery, however, cautioned that "this is in reality blamed on the white people." Charles Shapiro compared *The Long Dream* with *Native Son* for its treatment of the problem of race directly, not by analogy, and also with well-established social novels like *An American Tragedy* and *The Grapes of Wrath.*

The Long Dream, like *Savage Holiday*, has received insufficient critical attention. The most sympathetic, but discerning analysis is provided by Edward Margolies in *The Art of Richard Wright*. He considers Wright's characterization impeccable, except toward the end of the book, where Wright allows Fishbelly to remove himself from the black world, go to jail, and then travel to Paris "to seek his dream." What is lacking at the crucial point in Fishbelly's development is his "physical survival in a concrete, known setting." Insisting that any dream must be related to an authentic environment, Margolies concludes that "Fishbelly's removal from that environment somehow alloys the dream." Similarly, Katherine Sprandel interprets the novel in terms of Wright's own life. Sprandel's observation is valuable, since she cogently relates the hero's quest to what actually happened to Wright. "As early as his childhood," says Sprandel, "Wright could find little love in his own people, and he surely found little in whites. It is not surprising . . . that Wright leaves his last hero literally up in the air."[76]

Eight Men

Saunders Redding characteristically dismissed *Eight Men* as the work of a declining author.[77] Though all the stories in the collection indicated distress with his rootlessness, Wright's long exile, Redding theorized, somehow lightened "his anguish," which was "the living substance of his best books." For Redding, even the most impressive story, "The Man Who Lived Underground," seemed "a first-class Gothic tale." Despite the extraordinary vividness and stylistic innovations, Redding observed, "It is as if Gabriel, brandishing his trumpet and filling his lungs with air to blow the blast of doom, managed only a penny whistle's pipe." In a similar vein, Richard Gilman ("The Immediate Misfortunes of Widespread Literacy") found the collection of stories inept, "dismayingly stale and dated."[78] Wright's attempts at humor, at tragedy, at pathos, "all fail."

The most sympathetic notice was by Irving Howe, Wright's consistent champion, in a long review, "Richard Wright: A Word of Farewell."[79] *Eight Men* pleased Howe for its signs of Wright's continuous experimentation, despite uneven results. Howe found in "Big Black Good Man" "a strong feeling for the compactness of the story as a form. . . . When the language is scraggly or leaden there is a sharply articulated pattern of event." Furthermore, such a story as "Big Black Good Man" is sustained by "Wright's sardonic humor, the humor of a man who has known and released the full measure of his despair but finds that neither knowledge nor release matters in a world of despair." In the better-known "The Man Who Lived Underground" Howe found not a congenial expression of existentialism, as other critics did, but an effective narrative rhythm, "a gift for shaping the links between sentences so as to create a chain of expectation." In sum, Wright thrives on naturalism, for when he moves from his naturalistic sytle to "a more supple and terse instrument," he goes astray. His experiments with stories constructed entirely in dialogue or Freudian symbolism are failures. For Howe, Wright's naturalistic detail is as "essential to his ultimate effect of shock and bruise" as understatement to Hemingway's effect of irony and loss. In "Articulated Nightmare" Gloria Bramwell similarly rejected "The Man Who Lived Underground" as Wright's failure in using existentialism, just as he "failed to blend Communism convincingly with his work."[80] The result would not even rank with Ralph Ellison's similar treatment in *Invisible Man*; Ellison's hero "adopts consciously the fate thrust upon him," while Wright's hero "performs the deeds of theft and murder" as a rebellious child. "This inverse paternalism," Bramwell argued, "constitutes a major weakness of Wright's as an artist."

Later critical estimates of this short story collection are decidedly more favorable. Even James Baldwin, in "The Survival of Richard Wright,"considers the work a reflection of Wright's authentic rage.[81] Baldwin writes that "Wright's unrelentingly bleak landscape was not merely that of the Deep South, or of Chicago, but that of the world, of the human heart." The most intensive critical analysis of *Eight Men* is provided by Edward Margolies in a chapter of his book (reprinted in this volume). Margolies notices a distinct change of tone in *Eight Men* by comparison with *Uncle Tom's Children*; the earlier racial hatred is replaced by racial understanding in a story like "Big Black Good Man." As for "The Man Who Lived Underground," Margolies interprets Fred Daniels' adventures as suggestive of Wright's own feelings after ten years in the Communist underground.

Recent criticism of the collection has concentrated on "The Man Who Lived Underground." William Goede argues that though many critics consider Wright's story the chief source for Ellison's *Invisible Man*, the works differ in that "nothing has happened in any significant way" to Wright's hero, while Ellison's "endures, and, if we can believe him, is on his way back to us, a man of wisdom and hope."[82] David Bakish regards this novella as Wright's finest accomplishment because it is an intellectualized story based upon an authentic experience.[83] Wright himself lived underground, "struggling with an ambiguous identity," and like Daniels, found it difficult to separate dream and reality. Michel Fabre testifies to the authenticity of the story in "Richard Wright: The Man Who Lived Underground," showing that it derives not from Dostoevski, but from an account in *True Detective* (August 1941) of Herbert C. Wright, a Los Angeles white man who lived underground and robbed businesses in 1931 and 1932.[84] Fabre reads it as an "existential parable" presenting the humanist message that while an individual can impose masks upon himself, he "acquires his identity from other men." In his biography Fabre notes the differences between Wright's story and Dostoevski's *Notes from Underground*. Dostoevski's underground is spiritual and unreal, unlike Wright's, where Fred Daniels must traverse a maze of sewers. Fred is rather like Bigger, his situation symbolic of Black America; he is both part and not part of American society.

Lawd Today

Granville Hicks ("Dreiser to Farrell to Wright") affectionately defended *Lawd Today*, calling it less powerful than *Native Son* and *Black Boy*, but uniquely interesting.[85] What interested Hicks is that although Wright was an avowed Communist at the time he wrote the novel, he did not make a Communist out of Jake Jackson. Jake even despised Communism and refused to become a victim of the capitalist system, either. He was delineated as uneducated, frustrated, and "erring but alive." Hicks thus agreed with James Baldwin's observation that Wright's "great forte, it now seems to me, was an ability to convey inward states by means of externals."

In general, those opposed to naturalism in modern fiction were not appreciative of *Lawd Today*.[86] Nick Aaron Ford ("The Fire Next Time?: A Critical Survey of Belles Lettres by and about Negroes Published in 1963") could not believe that *Lawd Today* was written by Richard Wright. Objecting to Wright's concept as well as his technique, Ford deplored the book's melodramatic and disjointed pattern "with a multitude of hackneyed episodes." Lewis Gannett thought that the novel lacked the tension of *Native Son* because of its monotonously overdrawn dialogue and absence of the overtones. Doris Grumbach, while recognizing Wright's painfully direct and honest rendition of a racial victim, faulted Wright's excessive use of realism.

Even though the theme of the novel is directly related to the author's racial views, *Lawd Today* has failed to attract sufficient critical attention. Edward Margolies regards it as an interesting treatment of the anti-hero. Keneth Kinnamon ("The Pastoral Impulse in Richard Wright") considers it a satire against mechanized urban society, in contrast to the pastoral tranquility that dominates *Uncle Tom's Children*. In "*Lawd Today*: Richard Wright's Apprentice Novel," Kinnamon praises Wright's realistic portrayal of black life on Chicago's South Side in the Depression years, but maintains that the novel is flawed by its failure to integrate social themes into Jake's story.[87] Critics generally agree on Wright's authentic presentation of detail. Michel Fabre, in *The Unfinished Quest of Richard Wright*, shows that Wright's own experiences in Chicago as a holder of menial jobs and later a postal worker closely correspond to those in the novel. John M. Reilly suggests that "in writing *Lawd Today*, Wright found the demand of naturalism upon his narrative manner revealed the inadequacy of naturalistic assumptions."[88]

The most sympathetic, but revealing study is Lewis Leary's "*Lawd Today*: Notes on Richard Wright's First/Last Novel" (reprinted in this collection). Leary persuasively argues that *Lawd Today*, though an apprentice work, is a superb novel that portrays accurately and humorously what human life in urban society is. Much like George F. Babbitt and Studs Lonigan before him, Jake Jackson is caught between "a badly focussed dream and a reality which zooms in mercilessly to reveal every pore and pimple." On one level Jackson is an American black who knows what it is like to be black in America; on another level the novel alludes to "what it means to be white, colorless, ubiquitous." If Jackson is a caricature, Leary argues, he caricatures "the white world which tempts with more than it dares to offer." Wright's hero is neither black nor white; he is a symbol of all men "whose hunger for an unidentified good life . . . is not satisfied by the small mouthfuls allowed them."

III   CRITICISM OF NONFICTION

12 Million Black Voices

An anonymous reviewer for the *Sunday Worker* found great value in Wright's painstaking retrospect on the neglected race in America at a time when the nation was devoting her energy to world politics.[89] Horace R. Cayton, a black sociologist, defined the book as counterpart to *Native Son* in that it describes the habit, the milieu, the social matrix from which the personage of Bigger Thomas emerged.[90] L. D. Reddick, a black critic, in *The Jewish Survey* reminded readers of the significant parallels between the Jewish and Negro people. "Black folk from Georgia appreciate the Jim Crow of German Jews."[91]

Most black reviewers for white audiences were not as enthusiastic as the black reviewers quoted above. George Streator objected in *Commonweal* to Wright's predominantly Marxian voice in the book, charging that "Mr. Wright speaks words related to Toussaint L'Ouverture and the black slaughter of whites and mulattoes in Haiti that marked the first sharp break between the New World and the Old."[92] Streator, "a plain light-skinned Negro of legally married light-skinned Negro parentage," seemed to abhor even the slight hint of racial separatism in the book. Charles Curtis Muntz interpreted the book not as a folk history of the Negro in the United States as the subtitle suggests, but as a manifesto declaring that the New Negro, "the Embattled Negro," has arrived and now stands at the grave of Uncle Tom.[93]

The only notable critical analysis of *12 Million Black Voices* is provided by Edward Margolies who (in *The Art of Richard Wright*) reads the work not as a historical document, but as "a kind of prose-poem account of the lives of simple folk in their own voice." *12 Million Black Voices* anticipates Wright's autobiography *Black Boy*, since the book shows Wright's personal reaction to life in the South and immigration to the North. One of the chief differences between the two books is that Wright in *12 Million Black Voices* identifies his voice with that of the black masses, whereas in *Black Boy* the masses are unconsciously his enemy. Wright's thesis is that the black experience from the family-oriented tribal life to city life represents the American experience. "If America's Negroes perish," Margolies suggests, "then America will perish because the Negro experience is what America is."

Black Boy

George Streator, who had earlier opposed the concept of racial separatism in *12 Million Black Voices*, appreciated *Black Boy* for Wright's unique power in telling American blacks, American Jews, and Irish Catholics what real oppression means.[94] In Streator's assessment, the book's chief value lies in leading the nation on the road to emancipation. Sinclair Lewis, writing for *Esquire*, entitled his brief review "Gentlemen, This Is Revolution."[95] Of all the reviews, Lionel Trilling's "A Tragic Situation" was most thorough.[96] Granted, *Black Boy* is an accurate account of misery and oppression, but Trilling maintained that the book does not let its readers make "the moral 'escape' that can be offered by accounts of suffering and injustice." What underlies the power and effect of the book is not Wright's personal experience, but his moral and intellectual power. Trilling suggested that Wright "does not make himself that different kind of human being, a 'sufferer.' He is not an object, he is a subject; he is in the same kind of person as his reader, as complex, as free." This is why reading *Black Boy* led Amy H. Croughton to observe, "There is little in the picture of the child and youth of *Black Boy* to make understandable the present-day author of *Native Son*."[97] Lewis Gannett asked why this black boy escaped the bitter darkness and seized the opportunity to write as he did.[98] Likewise, Lillian Smith asked, "What early experiences of warmth and tenderness and human world did he have that convinced him of his own dignity, that tied him to reality and kept him from totally rejecting the good with the bad?"[99]

Favorable reactions were expressed by several of the black reviewers.[100] Wright's friend Horace Cayton in an extended essay, "Frightened Children of Frightened Parents," praised his mastery of the tools of school psychology in covering "the debased masses of the Negro people." Cayton observed that Wright carefully introduces the device of "Lords of the Land" and contrasts it with the "Bosses of the Buildings," thereby translating "into literary form the popular types of social organization: the anthropological concepts of Robert Redfield . . . and the sociological concepts of Louis Wirth." James W. Ivy, in an essay entitled "American Hunger," refuted those who called Wright's childhood atypical, and confirmed the direct and unpalatable truths presented in the book. Ivy held that Wright "does not play up nor glorify Negro virtues, and he is thoroughly unabashed in recounting our vices and shortcomings."

Negative reviews by black critics were as numerous as the positive ones, with several criticizing *Black Boy* for its unrepresentativeness. In the *Chicago Defender* Ben Burns rejected the book as "a study in sadism" without a redeeming light of hope; Wright fails "to see that the clock of history is moving ahead, not backward." Similarly W. E. B. DuBois found *Black Boy* to be fiction, rather than simply a record of life: while parts of Wright's story seem autobiographical and believable, the total picture is utterly unconvincing. Beatrice M. Murphy quibbled that the power of pen Wright boasted in the autobiography was used in turn "as a sword to stab his own race in the back."[101] Murphy's objection to the book as autobiography was also based on various discrepancies she found between Wright's accounts in the book and "The Ethics of Living Jim Crow." For example, *Black Boy* tells of a fight between Wright and a group of white boys in which he was injured behind the ear and later rushed to a doctor by his mother, whereas in his "Ethics of Living Jim Crow," Wright relates, ". . . a kind neighbor saw me and rushed me to a doctor, who took three stitches in my neck." Some white reviewers were equally antagonistic.[102] R. L. Duffus, in "Deep-South Memoir," could not see how Wright's grim experience in the South had fostered his creative power. Duffus's question was prophetic: "But what would Richard Wright have been in a more genial social climate? In France, perhaps?" W. T. Winston, though pointing to Wright's vivid re-creation of his childhood and youth, accused Wright of "naive egotism" and disregard for the historical background that accounted for racial prejudice in the South.

Later critics were unanimous in celebrating Wright's extraordinary achievement in *Black Boy*, not merely as a record of his early life, but as a work of art. Ralph Ellison's "Richard Wright's Blues" (reprinted in this volume) demonstrates that Wright's depiction of black fears is grounded in the Blues. According to Ellison, blacks repressed their individuality as a defense mechanism to counter white reprisals. For Ellison, Wright's assertion means that "Negro sensibility is socially and historically conditioned; that western culture must be won, confronted." Wright, says Ellison, is one of the very few blacks who could convey this confrontation in terms of the wounds he had received. Thus, his stories take the form of the Blues, expressing "both the agony of life and the possibility of conquering it through sheer toughness of spirit." Wright's critics mostly concurred with Ellison. Hugh M. Gloster, one of the pioneer black critics, underscores Wright's sociological concerns in *Black Boy*.[103] Charles I. Glicksberg treats *Black Boy* as the testimony of a black who renounced black violence and devoted his energy to creative work.[104] David Riesman's "Marginality, Conformity, and Insight" echoes Glicksberg's reaction.[105] *Black Boy* and "I Tried to Be a Communist," says Riesman, record the processes in which Wright converted his minority status and refusal to conform into affirmative and creative living.

Later critics have been ecstatically appreciative of Wright's power in *Black Boy*.[106] Among them, Blyden Jackson, in "Richard Wright: Black Boy from America's Black Belt and Urban Ghettos" (reprinted in this volume), gives the intimate account of Wright's Southern background that only a black critic can. Albert W. Vogel reads the book as a testimony of the segregationist education by which blacks' desire for knowledge was suppressed. John M. Reilly describes *Black Boy* as Wright's attempt to create a self-image, rather than as a realistic record of his youth. Gayle Gaskill examines Wright's perception of "power and knowledge in blackness, repression and impotence in whiteness." Finally Claudia C. Tate attempts to find differences between this self-portrait and Wright's actual experiences, finding the book as a conscious portrait of an artist rather than an account of his childhood.

Black Power

One reason *Black Power* was unfavorably received was its appearance immediately after *The Outsider*, which was considered by most critics intellectually confusing and emotionally tortuous. Thus Saunders Redding, who was highly critical of Wright's existentialism, called *Black Power* a confused book.[107] The reader would be bewildered, he said, not by the dark complexity of the Gold Coast, but by Wright's own dark philosophical ambivalence. Wright had recently repudiated both communism and existentialism and *Black Power* drifted between wishful Marxist politics and fragile Western democracy. Michael Clark found the book unbalanced in its appraisal of the African nation.[108] Wright, Clark pointed out, discusses "pre-Christian Africa" with nostalgia, more taken with Mohammedanism than Christianity. The same reservation was expressed by R. T. Horchler, who questioned the reliability of Wright's analysis of a highly religious and spiritually oriented African nation, given his inadequate knowledge of Chrisitianity and religion in general, as well as the "materialistic bias of Wright's mind."[109]

Other reviewers were not so negative.[110] Walter White evaluated Wright's reporting in superlative terms, though he pointed out some inaccurate assumptions. One was Wright's attributing Nkrumah's skill and success to the training he had received from British Communists; rather, Nkrumah had learned a great deal in the United States while a student there. Also, Wright was ignorant of a diversity among African cultures, psychologies, and religions, tending to think all Africans would think and act identically. John Chapman found Wright's description vivid and his scrutiny close, but criticized his "anti-British chip on his shoulder." The latter assessment was strongly refuted by Joyce Cary, a writer and a veteran of the British Foreign Service. For Cary, Wright had presented a most judicious picture of "an extraordinary situation." Cary concurred with Wright on almost all aspects of life in the Gold Coast: for example, in seeing tribal paganism as more genuinely religious than the bourgeois Christian church, or in criticizing the British for educating Africans at the expense of shattering their tribal culture.

Although many reviewers were not satisfied with the objectivity of Wright's reporting, they were still impressed by his forceful imagination and art.[111] Margot Jackson even found the book "funny and frank, rich in descriptions and interpretations." An anonymous reviewer for *The Reporter* saw the book's power coming from "the colorful, almost photographic portraiture of villages and market places." William Hugh Jansen emphasized Wright' skill as artist, pointing out that he never fails to state "his own point of view and his own perplexity." Jansen's point was prophetic, because if *Black Power*'s value lies in Wright's unique quality as journalist as well as artist, the book is perhaps one of the pioneer works in the development of what is now called "nonfiction fiction" or "New Journalism."

The most comprehensive critical appraisal for *Black Power*, as for most of his nonfiction works, is Edward Margolies' *The Art of Richard Wright*. Margolies' thesis is that both Wright's fiction and nonfiction reveal a pattern in which his central interest in social oppression is replaced by an argument for self-determination and, ultimately, freedom. Thus the central theme in *Black Boy, 12 Million Black Voices, Black Power,* and *Pagan Spain* is the fractured personality, whereas in *The*

Color Curtain and *White Man, Listen!* it is the shattered civilization. Another significant study of Wright's nonfiction work is John M. Reilly's "The Self-Creation of the Intellectual: *American Hunger* and *Black Power*" (presented in this volume). Aside from *Black Power*'s concern with the historical phenomenon of the Gold Coast, the work, Reilly suggests, provides a vision of Wright's self-created persona. Wright's journalistic observations are adapted to "*a priori* conceptions that will explain what Africa means to him as well as to his readers."

The Color Curtain

Reviews of *The Color Curtain* were more favorable than those of *Black Power*, since in it Wright takes a less anticolonial and more pro-West stance. Furthermore, he is decidedly anticommunist, admonishing the elites of the Third World against sympathizing with World Communism in developing their nations. In the *New York Times Book Review* Tillman Durdin, himself an "elite" of Indonesia, where the 1955 Bandung Conference was held, concurred with Wright's conclusion: the crucial question facing Asians is whether Asia will be dominated by communism or by democracy.[112] Guy Wint also agreed with this conclusion.[113] Even Abner W. Berry, a leftist critic for the *New York Daily Worker* found it difficult to disagree with Wright's anticommunism.[114] In *Masses and Mainstream* Charles Wisley strongly endorsed Wright's message that Imperialism is dead in the Third World.[115] Ellen Logue was also appreciative of Wright's "rational and imaginative" approach to the development of the emerging Third World.[116] A. T. Steele thought Wright's warning of the communist danger in Asia and Africa was convincing in the light of his own experience with the American Communist Party.[117] Paula Snelling, who had lived in Indonesia, found Wright's account of "the myth of white superiority upon Asia and Africa" illuminating, even though she admitted that his knowledge of the philosophical and cultural history of these people was inadequate.[118]

According to Margolies (*The Art of Richard Wright*), Wright's major point in *The Color Curtain* is that the issue of race determines the cultural climate of emerging nations in Asia and Africa. For Wright, race has bound these people together despite their obvious differences in culture, religion, and custom. It does not seem to occur to Wright, however, that "possibly their new leaders use race simply to maintain themselves in power. But practically all of Wright's political views are derived ultimately from his observations of the characterological efforts of racism among those who have been directly or indirectly involved in the colored areas of the world." In "Richard Wright and the Third World" (presented in this collection) Nina Kressner Cobb agrees with Margolies. Wright, Cobb explains, concluded from the Bandung Conference that the national movements in Asia and Africa could not be analyzed in the context of left and right politics.

Pagan Spain

After two successful nonfiction works on the Third World, Wright followed Gertrude Stein's suggestion to visit one of the oldest Western cultures. *Pagan Spain* is unique in Wright's canon, because race is not a primary issue in his report. Reviewers were unanimous in their praise for Wright's taking on this new challenge in writing. Herbert L. Matthews predicted that the book would offend the Franco regime and most Roman Catholics who read the book.[119] For Matthews, *Pagan Spain* proved that Spaniards were not race-conscious. As other books had done, *Pagan Spain* reported that Spain was deeply rooted in religion and sex. Wright's observation that "Spain seemed one vast brothel," for instance, made the book sensational, provocative, and disturbing to many. And his assertion that "all was religion in Spain . . . but Spain was not yet even Christian" was not factual; Wright's contention betrayed more about himself. For this reason Granville Hicks dismissed Wright's statement as invalid, declaring, "What Toynbee calls fossilization has taken place in Spain, but I suspect that Wright has misdated the fossil."[120]

Detractors of *Pagan Spain*, in fact, identified Wright's personality in the book with its weakness.[121] In "He Should Stick to Fiction" Roi Ottley called Wright's reporting of a bullfight glaringly inferior to Hemingway's: "But we actually do not see a bullfight. We are only privy to Wright's emotional agonies." Similarly, an anonymous reviewer for the *Washington Star* observed, "Wright's patent bias and prejudice weaken all his findings." Harry J. Carman, while recognizing the strength of the book in its interviews with various Spaniards, regretted that Wright's facts are "often inaccurate and his point of view is entirely personal."

Edward Margolies in his book agrees with the reviewers who maintained that *Pagan Spain* is as much a personal document as an objective analysis. Yet he does not consider Wright's view of Christianity in Spain invalid; there is clearly a parallel between Wright's own oppressive Seventh Day Adventist upbringing and the role of the church in Spain. Despite the "rambling, discursive, impressionistic" style on the surface, the book has the unity of purpose. And in *Pagan Spain*, as in his best fiction, Wright succeeds in conveying "in vivid visual terms violence, suspense, movement, and action."

White Man, Listen!

White Man, Listen! was received with respect by the reviewers mainly because by 1957 Wright had firmly established his reputation as an authority on social oppression. James W. Ivy quoted Wright's well-proven statement on the psychological reactions of oppressed people: that "oppression oppresses, that oppression takes its toll, that it leaves a mark behind."[122] Ivy's reaction to the book was typical, noting Wright's emphasis upon the crucial role Western-educated leaders of the nations were playing in bridging the Western and non-Western worlds. Paula Snelling heeded Wright's warning that if this "tragic elite" lose their leadership in their own countries, the Third World would eventually reject the whole Western world.[123] Stanley Plastrik similarly described the elite of the new nations Wright had dealt with as the " 'lonely outsiders' existing on the margins of many cultures."[124] For Joseph F. Maloney, Wright emphasizes the Western contributions these elites made: "not a particular political or economic system, but freedom of speech, the secular state, the independent personality and the autonomy of science."[125] The central question of *White Man, Listen!*, observed Oscar Handlin, is whether the West would be able to encourage the elite in working out "a creative accommodation," rather than remaining a promoter of Western technology.[126] The same view was expressed by Saville R. Davis: Wright proposes "that the West must support the western-trained elite in these countries, not by dictating to them, but by trusting them . . . even if their methods sometimes seem offensive to the West."[127]

Harold R. Isaacs argues that Wright's disbelief in religion and his status as an outsider in his own country gave him a unique vantage point to assess the Third World independently.[128] In his introduction to *White Man, Listen!*, John A. Williams attributes Wright's success to his "fantastic sense of perception," and regards his writing as prophetic, as great writing should be.[129] For Edward Margolies (*The Art of Richard Wright*), Wright's point in *White Man, Listen!*, as elsewhere, is that "the achievement of freedom is an individual and private matter." This is why, even though *White Man, Listen!* deals with the problem of race, it is also a book about Wright himself—"how he liberated his mind from the terrible circumstances of his home and environment, how he discovered himself an outsider, and how he tried to change the world in which he lived." Likewise, Nina Kressner Cobb ("Richard Wright and the Third World") believes that his experience as a black man in America influenced the basic concepts underlying his later nonfiction works.

American Hunger

Most of the reviewers of *American Hunger* regarded it as a record of Richard Wright as an emerging artist. Michael Harrington considered it not a political tract, but the sensitive work of an artist and psychologist.[130] For Bob Greenlee, the book captured the feelings of a great writer sensitively responding to the spirit of the times.[131] "*American Hunger*," Theodore Rosengarten wrote, "is the testimony Wright would have given in defense of himself. Brilliant in its indictment of racism and of White America's 'lust for trash,' it would have been a proof of the organizing power of imaginative works."[132]

While *American Hunger* was interpreted as the artist's self-portrait, it also cast light on Wright's relations with the Communist Party. About this aspect of Wright's life, Roy E. Perry perceived Wright's "efforts to maintain his individuality and integrity as an artist," which were in conflict with being a communist propagandist.[133] Harrington, in his review mentioned above, explained that Wright's break with the Communist Party "was not a disagreement over their positions but rather his comrades' inability to understand him as a writer." Wright's involvement with communism, however, could be interpreted differently: Kenneth Walker suggested that whereas *Black Boy* ends with the promise of success, *American Hunger* ends with a cynicism "more appropriate for a black American Communist with a ninth grade education in Chicago during the Great Depression."[134] George Breitman also noted that Wright then "had a prickly personality, and the frictions between him and the CP could not have come all from one side."[135] Likewise, Jack Conroy noted that the sign of hope pervading the ending of *Black Boy* "as Richard enters the promised land of Chicago soon is muted in *American Hunger*."[136]

Michel Fabre, in the afterword to his edition of *American Hunger*, concurs with the reviewers who have noted a contrast between this work and *Black Boy*.[137] *American Hunger*, says Fabre, not only gives a gloomy outlook of life in contrast to the hopeful *Black Boy*, but "constitutes a more profound questioning of man's predicament in a mass consumption society whose daily practice negates its humanistic pretenses." While *Black Boy* addresses itself to the materialism of the South, the United States overall, and the West, *American Hunger* "speaks to the whole of mankind in calling for radical awareness and change." In this sense, Fabre contends, the book resembles "the Nietzschean reaches" of *The Outsider*. In "Richard Wright's *American Hunger*," Gerian Steve Moore's analysis is shallower, showing that the autobiography indicates Wright's total alienation from the black community and his brainwashing by the Communist Party.[138]

IV   COMMENTARIES ON POETRY

Wright first attracted critics' attention as a proletarian writer in the John Reed Club with his "Yale and Harvard." Edward Clay, himself a club member and poet, in his article "The Negro and American Literature," compared Wright's apprentice poems with the poetry of Langston Hughes and Sterling Brown.[139] Since none of Wright's poems have been collected as a unit, they have not received reviews. One of the earliest commentaries on Wright's poetry is by Russell C. Brignano in his *Richard Wright: An Introduction to the Man and His Works*. Wright's Marxist poetry in the thirties, Brignano says, has a poetic subtlety rather than a propagandistic voice; "Old Habit and New Love," for example, suggests his interest in poetic creation, not political dogma. For Brignano, "Transcontinental" is Wright's finest poem; amidst the noisy and ugly name-callings and violent actions for revolution, the poem recreates the sensation of a moving automobile on the poet-speaker's journey across the country. In such an effort Brignano sees the young novelist exploring the possibilities of language.

The earliest critical appraisal of Wright's poetry is Keneth Kinnamon's "Richard Wright: Proletarian Poet" (reprinted in this volume). The article suggests that much of the weakness in his poetry stems from the quasi-metaphysical conceits that are not incorporated into the Whitmanesque tone apparent in it. Kinnamon, however, considers "Between the World and Me" successful, because it is "an intensely felt and potently realized poem in which the theme of human solidarity in suffering goes far beyond the excessive subjectivity of another lynching poem, 'Obsession.' " Art and ideology do not mix well in Wright's works, but "the ideology of his proletarian poems was a basic, even essential, motive force" of his art. In the most comprehensive treatment ("The Poetry of Richard Wright," reprinted in this book), Michel Fabre traces Wright's development from the violent Marxist poems of the thirties to the tranquil haiku poems of the late fifties. The major theme in his early poems is obviously the suffering of the black American; one of the most successful poems to Fabre (as to Kinnamon) is "Between the World and Me," in which the suffering of the victim is identified with that of the reader. Wright's communist poems, though diametrically opposed to religious intentions, nonetheless have Biblical references, thereby producing a paradoxical effect. Wright, Fabre suggests, combines two traditions in his poetry: the lyrical and rhetorical gifts of MacLeish and Eliot and the robust simplicity of Sandburg and Whitman.

Finally, Wright scholars have known for some time that Wright tried his hand at composing haiku in English toward the very end of his life. Out of some four thousand of these haiku, however, only twenty-three have appeared in print, whose merits Fabre makes some attempt to discuss. The most thorough analysis of the published poems is a long essay by Robert Tener, entitled "The Where, the When, the What: A Study of Richard Wright's Haiku" (presented in this volume). Himself a poet and critic, Tener closely examines the backgrounds and sources of Wright's effort, particularly the four volumes of R. H. Blyth's *Haiku*, from which Wright learned the history and technique of the Japanese form. Many of his haiku, such as

> Make up your mind snail!
> You are half inside your house
> And half out!

are considered failures. In this poem, Tener suggests, Wright violates the union between the creature and its environment, though humor is provided; in Zen there must be a fusion of animate and inanimate objects in nature. Some of Wright's haiku achieve what those of the Zen poet Basho did. "At his best," Tener concludes, "Wright was clearly capable of perceiving the peaceful and temperate aspects of nature and avoiding the confused and violent elements in man and in nature . . . when man needs to know where he is . . . and what he will be when that happens."

Although no efforts are apparent among Wright scholars to publish the rest of Wright's haiku, further discussion of his poetry must deal with this entire body of work. With respect to his prose works, only recently have some been published as books for the first time: *Eight Men* (1961), *Lawd Today* (1963), and *American Hunger* (1977). Clearly, most of these works, including his poetry, have received insufficient critical attention. The future study of Richard Wright seems to be taking two directions. On the one hand, Wright's later works will be closely examined on the basis of the rigorous scholarship produced in the seventies. On the other, a reassessment of Wright's life and work is under way. For example, Addison Gayle, Jr.,'s forthcoming book may contain new information relating to actions by and against Wright on the part of the investigative agencies of the U.S. Government. Also there will be a special Modern Language Association session, "Richard Wright's Novels: A Revaluation," which is scheduled to be held in Houston in December 1980. As this survey of criticism indicates, however, too little attention has been paid Wright's nonfiction. Even *Black Boy*, while hailed as one of the finest autobiographies written by an American, has not been analyzed for its artistry with the same acumen as *Native Son* and *Uncle Tom's Children*.

The most comprehensive bibliography of Wright's works is provided in Michel Fabre's *The Unfinished Quest of Richard Wright*. Keneth Kinnamon is preparing an annotated bibliography of criticism on Wright to be published by G. K. Hall. John M. Reilly's "Richard Wright: An Essay in Bibliography" is another useful tool for Wright scholarship.[140] Equally useful is his *Richard Wright: The Critical Reception*, a well-organized collection of all the major reviews of Wright's books (which made it unnecessary to include any reviews in this volume).[141] For the preparation of this book, I am deeply indebted to previous writers on Wright, and especially to the publications of Michel Fabre and John M. Reilly. Finally, thanks are due my wife, who has helped me with typing and proofreading.

YOSHINOBU HAKUTANI

Kent State University
Spring 1980

Notes

1. Constance Webb, *Richard Wright: A Biography* (New York: Putnam, 1968).

2. John A. Williams, *The Most Native of Sons: A Biography of Richard Wright* (Garden City, N.Y.: Doubleday, 1970).

3. Michel Fabre, *The Unfinished Quest of Richard Wright* (New York: William Morrow, 1973).

4. Fabre, pp. 527–28.

5. Edward Margolies, *The Art of Richard Wright* (Carbondale: Southern Illinois Univ. Press, 1969).

6. Margolies, p. 167.

7. Dan McCall, *The Example of Richard Wright* (New York: Harcourt, Brace & World, 1969).

8. Russell C. Brignano, *Richard Wright: An Introduction to the Man and His Works* (Pittsburgh: Univ. of Pittsburgh Press, 1970).

9. Keneth Kinnamon, *The Emergence of Richard Wright* (Urbana: Univ. of Illinois Press, 1972).

10. Robert Bone, *Richard Wright* (Minneapolis: Univ. of Minnesota Press, 1969).

11. Houston A. Baker, Jr., "Racial Wisdom and Richard Wright's *Native Son*," in *Long Black Song* (Charlottesville: Univ. Press of Virginia, 1972), pp. 122–41.

12. Saunders Redding, "The Alien Land of Richard Wright," in *Soon, One Morning*, ed. Herbert Hill (New York: Knopf, 1963), pp. 50–59.

13. Richard Kostelanetz, "The Politics of Unresolved Quests in the Novels of Richard Wright," *Xavier University Studies*, 8 (Spring 1969), 31–64.

14. Cecil Brown, "Richard Wright's Complexes and Black Writing Today: The Lesson and the Legacy," *Negro Digest*, 18 (Dec. 1968), 45–50, 78–82.

15. Daniel Aaron, "Richard Wright and the Communist Party," *New Letters*, 38 (Winter 1971), 170–81.

16. Alvin Starr, "Richard Wright and the Communist Party—The James T. Farrell Factor," *CLA Journal*, 21 (Sept. 1977), 41–50.

17. Granville Hicks, "Dreiser to Farrell to Wright," *Saturday Review*, 46 (30 March 1963), 37–38.

18. Michel Fabre, "Richard Wright: Beyond Naturalism?" in *American Literary Naturalism: A Reassessment*, eds. Yoshinobu Hakutani and Lewis Fried (Heidelberg: Carl Winter Universitätsverlag, 1975), pp. 136–53.

19. James Baldwin, "Everybody's Protest Novel," *Partisan Review*, 16 (June 1949), 578–85; rpt. in *Notes of a Native Son* (Boston: Beacon Press, 1955).

20. Fabre, *The Unfinished Quest of Richard Wright*, p. 362.

21. James Baldwin, "Alas, Poor Richard," in *Nobody Knows My Name* (New York: Dial Press, 1961), p. 151.

22. Kichung Kim, "Wright, the Protest Novel, and Baldwin's Faith," *CLA Journal*, 17 (March 1974), 387–96.

23. Eldridge Cleaver, "Notes on a Native Son," in *Soul on Ice* (New York: McGraw-Hill, 1968), p. 99.

24. Amiri Baraka, "Brief Reflections on Two Hot Shots," in *Home: Social Essays* (New York: William Morrow, 1966), p. 120.

25. Amiri Baraka, "The Myth of a 'Negro Literature,' " *Saturday Review*, 46 (20 April 1963), 19–21, 40.

26. Gerald Green, "Back to Bigger," *Kenyon Review*, 28 (Sept. 1966), 521–39.

27. Barry Gross, "Art and Act: The Example of Richard Wright," *Obsidian*, 2 (Summer 1976), 5–19.

28. James T. Farrell, "Lynch Patterns," *Partisan Review*, 4 (May 1938), 57–58.

29. Herschel Brickell, *New York Evening Post*, 25 March 1938; Lewis Gannett, *New York Herald Tribune*, 25 March 1938, p. 17; Sterling Brown, "From the Inside," *The Nation*, 146 (16 April 1938), 448.

30. Malcolm Cowley, "Long Black Song," *New Republic*, 194 (6 April 1938), 280.

31. Marvel Cooke, "Prize Novellas, Brave Stories," *New York Amsterdam News*, 9 April 1938, p. 16.

32. Robert Van Gelder, "Four Tragic Tales," *New York Times Book Review*, 13 April 1938, pp. 7, 16; Allen Maxwell, *Southwest Review*, 23 (April 1938), 362–65.

33. Charles Poore, *New York Times*, 2 April 1938, p. 13.

34. Zora Neale Hurston, "Stories of Conflict," *Saturday Review of Literature*, 17 (2 April 1938), 32.

35. Edwin Berry Burgum, "The Art of Richard Wright's Short Stories," *Quarterly Review of Literature*, 1 (Spring 1944), 198–211.

36. Blyden Jackson, "Richard Wright in a Moment of Truth," *Southern Literary Journal*, 3 (Spring 1971), 3–17.

37. James R. Giles, "Richard Wright's Successful Failure: A New Look at *Uncle Tom's Children*," *Phylon*, 34 (Fall 1973), 256–66.

38. Sterling Brown, *Opportunity*, 18 (June 1940), 185–86.

39. Irving Howe, "Black Boys and Native Sons," *Dissent*, 10 (Autumn 1963), 353–68; rpt. in this volume, pp. 39–47.

40. Jonathan Daniels, *Saturday Review of Literature*, 21 (2 March 1940), 5; Edward Skillin, Jr., *Commonweal*, 31 (8 March 1940), 438; Margaret Marshall, *The Nation*, 150 (16 March 1940), 367–68.

41. Clifton Fadiman, *New Yorker*, 16 (2 March 1940), 52–53.

42. Peter Monro Jack, "A Tragic Novel of Negro Life in America," *New York Times Book Review*, 3 March 1940, pp. 2, 20.

43. James W. Ivy, *The Crisis*, 47 (April 1940), 122.

44. David L. Cohn, *Atlantic Monthly*, 165 (May 1940), 659–61.

45. Burton Rascoe, "Negro Novel and White Reviewers," *American Mercury*, 50 (May 1940), 113–16.

46. David Daiches, *Partisan Review*, 7 (May–June 1940), 245.

47. Howard Mumford Jones, "Uneven Effect," *Boston Evening Transcript*, 2 March 1940, Book Sec., p. 1.

48. Donald B. Gibson, "Wright's Invisible Native Son," *American Quarterly*, 21 (Winter 1969), 728–38.

49. Edward Margolies, *Native Sons: A Critical Study of Twentieth-Century Negro American Authors* (Philadelphia: Lippincott, 1968).

49A. Malcolm Cowley, *New Republic*, 102 (18 March 1940), 382–83.

50. Edward Kearns, "The 'Fate' Section of *Native Son*," *Contemporary Literature*, 12 (Spring 1971), 146–55.

51. Paul N. Siegel, "The Conclusion of Richard Wright's *Native Son*, *PMLA*, 89 (May 1974), 517–23.

52. Phyllis R. Klotman, "Moral Distancing as a Rhetorical Technique in *Native Son*: A Note on 'Fate,' " *CLA Journal*, 18 (Dec. 1974), 284–91.

53. James A. Emanuel, "Fever and Feeling: Notes on the Imagery in *Native Son*," *Negro Digest*, 18 (Dec. 1968), 16–24.

54. Thomas LeClair, "The Blind Leading the Blind: Wright's *Native Son* and a Brief Reference to Ellison's *Invisible Man*," *CLA Journal*, 13 (March 1970), 315–20; Lloyd W. Brown, "Stereotypes in Black and White: The Nature of Perception in Wright's *Native Son*," *Black Academy Review*, 1 (Fall 1970), 35–44.

55. Orville Prescott, *New York Times*, 28 Feb. 1945, p. 21.

56. James N. Rhea, *Providence Sunday Journal*, 22 March 1953; Melvin Alshulter, *Washington Post*, 22 March 1953; Roland Sawyer, *Christian Science Monitor*, 30 April 1953, p. 11; Max Eastman, *The Freeman*, 3 (4 May 1953), 567–68.

57. Saunders Redding, *Baltimore Afro-American*, 19 May 1953; Arna Bontemps, *Saturday Review*, 36 (28 March 1953), 15–16; Lloyd L. Brown, "Outside and Low," *Masses and Mainstream*, 6 (May 1953), 62–64.

58. Granville Hicks, "The Portrait of a Man Searching," *New York Times Book Review*, 22 March 1953, pp. 1, 35.

59. Gilbert Highet, "Mind-forged Manacles," *Harper's Magazine*, 206 (May 1953), 97–98.

60. Thomas D. Jarrett, "Recent Fiction by Negroes," *College English*, 16 (November 1954), 85–91.

61. Harvey Curtis Webster, "Richard Wright's Profound New Novel," *The New Leader*, 36 (6 April 1953), 17–18.

62. Ralph De Toledano, *Classic Features*, 22 March 1953.

63. Charles I. Glicksberg, "Existentialism in *The Outsider*," *Four Quarters*, 7 (Jan. 1958), 17–26; "The God of Fiction," *Colorado Quarterly*, 7 (Autumn 1958), 207–20.

64. Kingsley Widmer, "The Existential Darkness: Richard Wright's *The Outsider*," *Wisconsin Studies in Contemporary Literature*, 1 (Fall 1960), 13–21.

65. Addison Gayle, Jr., "Richard Wright: Beyond Nihilism," *Negro Digest*, 18 (Dec. 1968), 4–10.

66. Nathan A. Scott, "Search for Beliefs: Fiction of Richard Wright," *University of Kansas City Review*, 23 (Autumn 1956), 19–24; "The Dark and Haunted Tower of Richard Wright," *Graduate Comment*, 7 (July 1964), 93–99.

67. Darwin T. Turner, "*The Outsider*: Revision of an Idea," *CLA Journal*, 12 (June 1969), 310–21.

68. Lewis A. Lawson, "Cross Damon: Kierkegaardian Man of Dread," *CLA Journal*, 14 (March 1971), 298–316.

69. Raman K. Singh, "Wright's Tragic Vision in *The Outsider*," *Studies in Black Literature*, 1 (Autumn 1970), 23–27.

70. John M. Reilly, "Richard Wright's Curious Thriller, *Savage Holiday*," *CLA Journal*, 21 (Dec. 1977), 218–23.

71. Saunders Redding, "The Way It Was," *New York Times Book Review*, 26 Oct. 1958, pp. 4, 38.

72. Nick Aaron Ford, "A Long Way from Home," *Phylon*, 19 (Winter 1958), 435–36.

73. Maxwell Geismar, "Growing Up in Fear's Grip," *New York Herald Tribune Book Review*, 16 Nov. 1958, p. 10.

74. Granville Hicks, "The Power of Richard Wright," *Saturday Review*, 41 (18 Oct. 1958), 13, 65.

75. Roi Ottley, "Wright's New Novel Isn't for Squeamish," *Chicago Sunday Tribune Magazine of Books*, 26 Oct. 1958; Paul Kiniery, *Best Sellers*, 18 (1 Nov. 1958), 296–97; Charles Shapiro, "A Slow Burn in the South," *New Republic*, 139 (24 Nov. 1958), 17–18.

76. Katherine Sprandel, "*The Long Dream*," *New Letters*, 38 (Winter 1971), 88–96.

77. Saunders Redding, *New York Herald Tribune Book Review*, 22 Jan. 1961, p. 33.

78. Richard Gilman, "The Immediate Misfortunes of Widespread Literacy," *Commonweal*, 28 (April 1961), 130–31.

79. Irving Howe, "Richard Wright: A Word of Farewell," *New Republic*, 144 (13 Feb. 1961), 17–18.

80. Gloria Bramwell, "Artistic Nightmare," *Midstream*, 7 (Spring 1961), 110–12.

81. James Baldwin, "The Survival of Richard Wright," *The Reporter*, 24 (16 March 1961), 52–55; rpt. as "Eight Men," *Nobody Knows My Name*, pp. 181–89.

82. William Goede, "On Lower Frequencies: The Buried Men in Wright and Ellison," *Modern Fiction Studies*, 15 (Winter 1969), 483–501.

83. David Bakish, "Underground in an Ambiguous Dreamworld," *Studies in Black Literature*, 2 (Autumn 1971), 18–23.

84. Michel Fabre, "Richard Wright: The Man Who Lived Underground," *Studies in the Novel*, 3 (Summer 1971), 165–79.

85. Hicks, "Dreiser to Farrell to Wright," pp. 37–38; cf. Baldwin, *Nobody Knows My Name*, p. 150. Baldwin's response refers to Wright's characterization of Cross Damon in *The Outsider*, whose prototype is Jake Jackson: Cross begins as an uneducated, frustrated worker in the Chicago post office, exactly as Jake does.

86. Nick Aaron Ford, "The Fire Next Time?: A Critical Survey of Belles Lettres by and about Negroes Published in 1963," *Phylon*, 25 (Summer 1964), 129–30; Lewis Gannett, *New York Herald Tribune Books*, 5 May 1963, p. 10; Doris Grumbach, *The Critic*, 21 (June–July 1963), 82.

87. Keneth Kinnamon, "The Pastoral Impulse in Richard Wright," *Midcontinent American Studies Journal*, 10 (Spring 1969), 41–47; "*Lawd Today*: Richard Wright's Apprentice Novel," *Studies in Black Literature*, 2 (Summer 1971), 16–18.

88. John M. Reilly, "*Lawd Today*: Richard Wright's Experiment in Naturalism," *Studies in Black Literature*, 2 (Autumn 1971), 14–17.

89. "Richard Wright's Powerful Narrative Beautifully Illustrated in New Book," *Sunday Worker*, 9 Nov. 1941, p. 22.

90. Horace R. Cayton, "Wright's New Book More than a Study of Social Status," *Pittsburgh Courier*, 15 Nov. 1941.

91. L. D. Reddick, "Negro and Jew," *The Jewish Survey*, 2 (Jan. 1942), 25.

92. George Streator, *Commonweal*, 25 (28 Nov. 1941), 147–48.

93. Charles Curtis Muntz, "The New Negro," *The Nation*, 153 (13 Dec. 1941), 620.

94. George Streator, *Commonweal*, 46 (23 March 1945), 568–69.

95. Sinclair Lewis, "Gentlemen, This Is Revolution," *Esquire*, 23 (June 1945), 76.

96. Lionel Trilling, "A Tragic Situation," *The Nation*, 160 (7 April 1945), 391–92.

97. Amy H. Croughton, *Rochester Times-Union*, 3 March 1945.

98. Lewis Gannett, *New York Herald Tribune*, 28 Feb. 1945, p. 17.

99. Lillian Smith, "Richard Wright Adds a Chapter to Our Bitter Chronicle," *PM*, 4 March 1945, p. m15.

100. Horace Cayton, "Frightened Children of Frightened Parents," *Twice-a-Year*, 12–13 (Spring–Summer/Fall–Winter 1945), 262–69; James W. Ivy, "American Hunger," *The Crisis*, 52 (April 1945), 117–18.

101. Ben Burns, *Chicago Defender*, 3 March 1945, p. 11; W. E. B. DuBois, "Richard Wright Looks Back," *New York Herald Tribune Weekly Book Review*, 4 March 1945, p. 2; Beatrice M. Murphy, *Pulse*, 3 (April 1945), 32–33.

102. R. L. Duffus, "Deep-South Memoir," *New York Times Book Review*, 4 March 1945, p. 3; W. T. Winston, *Best Sellers*, 5 (15 March 1945), 219–20.

103. Hugh M. Gloster, *Negro Voices in American Fiction* (Chapel Hill: Univ. of North Carolina Press, 1948).

104. Charles I. Glicksberg, "Negro Fiction in America," *South Atlantic Quarterly*, 45 (Oct. 1946), 477–88; "The Alienation of Negro Literature," *Phylon*, 11 (Spring 1950), 49–58.

105. David Riesman, "Marginality, Conformity, and Insight," *Phylon*, 14 (Fall 1953), 241–57.

106. Albert W. Vogel, "The Education of the Negro in Richard Wright's *Black Boy*," *Journal of Negro Education*, 35 (Spring 1966), 195–98; John M. Reilly, "Self-Portraits by Richard Wright," *Colorado Quarterly*, 20 (Summer 1971), 31–45; Gayle Gaskill, "The Effect of Black/White Imagery in Richard Wright's *Black Boy*," *Negro American Literature Forum*, 7 (Summer 1973), 46–48; Claudia C. Tate, "*Black Boy*: Richard Wright's 'Tragic Sense of Life,' " *Black American Literature Forum*, 10 (Winter 1976), 117–19.

107. Saunders Redding, *Baltimore Afro-American*, 23 Oct. 1954.

108. Michael Clark, "A Struggle for the Black Man Alone?" *New York Times Book Review*, 26 Sept. 1954, p. 3.

109. R. T. Horchler, *Best Sellers*, 14 (1 Oct. 1954), 97.

110. Walter White, *New York Herald Tribune Book Review*, 26 Sept. 1954, p. 1; John Chapman, "Beware of the West, Negro Writer Warns Africans," *Minneapolis Star*, 1 Oct. 1954; Joyce Cary, "Catching Up with History," *The Nation*, 179 (16 Oct. 1954), 332–33.

111. Margot Jackson, "*Black Power* Is Strong Work," *Akron Beacon Journal*, 24 Oct. 1954; "*Native Son* in Africa," *The Reporter*, 11 (4 Nov. 1954), 48; William Hugh Jansen, "Pretentious Is the Term," *Lexington Herald Leader*, 7 Nov. 1954.

112. Tillman Durdin, *New York Times Book Review*, 18 March 1956, p. 1.

113. Guy Wint, "Impatience of the East," *The Nation*, 172 (14 April 1956), 324.

114. Abner W. Berry, "Richard Wright's Report on Bandung," *New York Daily Worker*, 15 May 1956, p. 5.

115. Charles Wisly, *Masses and Mainstream*, 9 (June 1956), 50–53.

116. Ellen Logue, *Books on Trial*, 14 (April–May 1956), 351–53.

117. A. T. Steele, "Color of Asia," *New York Herald Tribune Book Review*, 22 April 1956.

118. Paula Snelling, "Import of Bandung," *The Progressive*, 19 (June 1956), 39–40.

119. Herbert L. Matthews, "How It Seemed to Him," *New York Times Book Review*, 24 Feb. 1957, p. 7.

120. Granville Hicks, "Richard Wright: Spain the Fossil," *New York Post*, 29 Feb. 1957.

121. Roi Ottley, "He Should Stick to Fiction," *Chicago Sunday Tribune Magazine of Books*, 3 March 1957, p. 10; "Spain Today," *Washington Star*, 24 Feb. 1957; Harry J. Carman, "Richard Wright in Spain," *New York Herald Tribune Book Review*, 10 March 1957, p. 8.

122. James W. Ivy, "Promise and Failure," *The Crisis*, 64 (Dec. 1957), 640.

123. Paula Snelling, "Warning Voice," *The Progressive*, 20 (Dec. 1957), 42–43.

124. Stanley Plastrik, "Lonely Outsider," *Dissent*, 5 (Spring 1958), 191–92.

125. Joseph F. Maloney, *Best Sellers*, 17 (15 Nov. 1957), 280.

126. Oscar Handlin, "Patterns of Prejudice," *New York Times Book Review*, 20 Oct. 1957, p. 3.

127. Saville R. Davis, "Wright Speaks His Mind," *Christian Science Monitor*, 17 Oct. 1957, p. 11.

128. Harold R. Isaacs, "Five Writers and Their African Ancestors," *Phylon*, 21 (Fall 1960), 243–65, 317–36.

129. John A. Williams, Introd., *White Man, Listen!* (Garden City, N.Y.: Doubleday, 1964), pp. ix–xii.

130. Michael Harrington, *Chicago Sun-Times Book Week*, 29 May 1977, p. 7.

131. Bob Greenlee, *New Haven Register*, 19 June 1977, p. D-3.

132. Theodore Rosengarten, *Washington Post Book World*, 19 June 1977, p. K-1.

133. Roy E. Perry, *Nashville Banner*, 14 May 1977.

134. Kenneth Walker, *Washington Star*, 5 June 1977, p. F-19.

135. George Breitman, *International Socialist Review*, 38 (5 August 1977), 12.

136. Jack Conroy, *Kansas City Star*, 15 May 1977, pp. D1-2.

137. Michel Fabre, Afterword, *American Hunger* (New York: Harper and Row, 1977), pp. 136-46.

138. Gerian Steve Moore, "Richard Wright's *American Hunger*," *CLA Journal*, 21 (Sept. 1977), 79-89.

139. Edward Clay, "The Negro and American Literature," *International Literature*, No. 6 (June 1935).

140. John M. Reilly, "Richard Wright: An Essay in Bibliography," *Resources for American Literary Study*, 1 (Autumn 1971), 131-80.

141. John M. Reilly, *Richard Wright: The Critical Reception* (New York: Burt Franklin, 1978).

GENERAL ESSAYS

Black Boys and Native Sons

Irving Howe*

James Baldwin first came to the notice of the American literary public not through his own fiction but as author of an impassioned criticism of the conventional Negro novel. In 1949 he published in *Partisan Review* an essay called "Everybody's Protest Novel," attacking the kind of fiction, from *Uncle Tom's Cabin* to *Native Son*, that had been written about the ordeal of the American Negroes; and two years later he printed in the same magazine "Many Thousands Gone," a tougher and more explicit polemic against Richard Wright and the school of naturalistic "protest" fiction that Wright represented. The protest novel, wrote Baldwin, is undertaken out of sympathy for the Negro, but through its need to present him merely as a social victim or a mythic agent of sexual prowess, it hastens to confine the Negro to the very tones of violence he has known all his life. Compulsively re-enacting and magnifying his trauma, the protest novel proves unable to transcend it. So choked with rage has this kind of writing become, it cannot show the Negro as a unique person or locate him as a member of a community with its own traditions and values, its own "unspoken recognition of shared experience which creates a way of life." The failure of the protest novel "lies in its insistence that it is [man's] categorization alone which is real and which cannot be transcended."

Like all attacks launched by young writers against their famous elders, Baldwin's essays were also a kind of announcement of his own intentions. He wrote admiringly about Wright's courage ("his work was an immense liberation and revelation for me"), but now, precisely because Wright had prepared the way for all the Negro writers to come, he, Baldwin, would go further, transcending the sterile categories of "Negroness," whether those enforced by the white world or those defensively erected by the Negroes themselves. No longer mere victim or rebel, the Negro would stand free in a self-achieved humanity. As Baldwin put it

*Reprinted from *A World More Attractive*, pp. 98–110, by Irving Howe. Copyright © 1963, by permission of the publisher, Horizon Press, New York. The essay originally appeared in *Dissent*, 10 (Autumn 1963), 353–68.

some years later, he hoped "to prevent myself from becoming *merely* a Negro; or even, merely a Negro writer." The world "tends to trap and immobilize you in the role you play," and for the Negro writer, if he is to be a writer at all, it hardly matters whether the trap is sprung from motives of hatred or condescension.

Baldwin's rebellion against the older Negro novelist who had served him as a model and had helped launch his career, was not of course an unprecedented event. The history of literature is full of such painful ruptures, and the issue Baldwin raised is one that keeps recurring, usually as an aftermath to a period of "socially engaged" writing. The novel is an inherently ambiguous genre: it strains toward formal autonomy and can seldom avoid being a public gesture. If it is true, as Baldwin said in "Everybody's Protest Novel," that "literature and sociology are not one and the same," it is equally true that such statements hardly begin to cope with the problem of how a writer's own experience affects his desire to represent human affairs in a work of fiction. Baldwin's formula evades, through rhetorical sweep, the genuinely difficult issue of the relationship between social experience and literature.

Yet in *Notes of a Native Son*, the book in which his remark appears, Baldwin could also say: "One writes out of one thing only—one's own experience." What, then, was the experience of a man with a black skin, what *could* it be in this country? How could a Negro put pen to paper, how could he so much as think or breathe, without some impulsion to protest, be it harsh or mild, political or private, released or buried? The "sociology" of his existence formed a constant pressure on his literary work, and not merely in the way this might be true for any writer, but with a pain and ferocity that nothing could remove.

James Baldwin's early essays are superbly eloquent, displaying virtually in full the gifts that would enable him to become one of the great American rhetoricians. But these essays, like some of the later ones, are marred by rifts in logic, so little noticed when one gets swept away by the brilliance of the language that it takes a special effort to attend their argument.

Later Baldwin would see the problems of the Negro writer with a greater charity and more mature doubt. Reviewing in 1959 a book of poems by Langston Hughes, he wrote: "Hughes is an American Negro poet and has no choice but to be acutely aware of it. He is not the first American Negro to find the war between his social and artistic responsibilities all but irreconcilable." All but irreconcilable: the phrase strikes a note sharply different from Baldwin's attack upon Wright in the early fifties. And it is not hard to surmise the reasons for this change. In the intervening years Baldwin had been living through some of the experiences that had goaded Richard Wright into rage and driven him into exile; he too, like Wright, had been to hell and back, many times over.

II

Gawd, Ah wish all them white folks was dead.

The day *Native Son* appeared, American culture was changed forever. No matter how much qualifying the book might later need, it made impossible a repetition of the old lies. In all its crudeness, melodrama and claustrophobia of vision, Richard Wright's novel brought out into the open, as no one ever had before, the hatred, fear and violence that have crippled and may yet destroy our culture.

A blow at the white man, the novel forced him to recognize himself as an oppressor. A blow at the black man, the novel forced him to recognize the cost of his submission. *Native Son* assaulted the most cherished of American vanities: the hope that the accumulated injustice of the past would bring with it no lasting penalties, the fantasy that in his humiliation the Negro somehow retained a sexual potency—or was it a childlike good-nature?—that made it necessary to envy and still more to suppress him. Speaking from the black wrath of retribution, Wright insisted that history can be a punishment. He told us the one thing even the most liberal whites preferred not to hear: that Negroes were far from patient or forgiving, that they were scarred by fear, that they hated every moment of their suppression even when seeming most acquiescent, and that often enough they hated *us*, the decent and cultivated white men who from complicity or neglect shared in the responsibility for their plight. If such younger novelists as Baldwin and Ralph Ellison were to move beyond Wright's harsh naturalism and toward more supple modes of fiction, that was possible only because Wright had been there first, courageous enough to release the full weight of his anger.

In *Black Boy*, the autobiographical narrative he published several years later, Wright would tell of an experience he had while working as a bellboy in the South. Many times he had come into a hotel room carrying luggage or food and seen naked white women lounging about, unmoved by shame at his presence, for "blacks were not considered human beings anyway . . . I was a non-man . . . I felt doubly cast out." With the publication of *Native Son*, however, Wright forced his readers to acknowledge his anger, and in that way, if none other, he wrested for himself a sense of dignity as a man. He forced his readers to confront the disease of our culture, and to one of its most terrifying symptoms he gave the name of Bigger Thomas.

Brutal and brutalized, lost forever to his unexpended hatred and his fear of the world, a numbed and illiterate black boy stumbling into a murder and never, not even at the edge of the electric chair, breaking through to an understanding of either his plight or himself, Bigger Thomas was a part of Richard Wright, a part even of the James Baldwin who stared with horror at Wright's Bigger, unable either to absorb him into his consciousness or eject him from it. Enormous courage, a discipline of self-conquest, was required to conceive Bigger Thomas, for this was no eloquent Negro spokesman, no admirable intellectual or formidable proletarian. Bigger was drawn—one would surmise, deliberately—from white fantasy and white contempt. Bigger was the worst of Negro life accepted, then rendered a trifle conscious and thrown back at those who had made him what he was. "No American Negro exists," Baldwin would later write, "who does not have his private Bigger Thomas living in the skull."

Wright drove his narrative to the very core of American phobia: sexual fright, sexual violation. He understood that the fantasy of rape is a consequence of guilt, what the whites suppose themselves to deserve. He understood that the white man's notion of uncontaminated Negro vitality, little as it had to do with the bitter realities of Negro life, reflected some ill-formed and buried feeling that our culture has run down, lost its blood, become febrile. And he grasped the way in which the sexual issue has been intertwined with social relationships, for even as the white people who hire Bigger as their chauffeur are decent and charitable, even as the girl he accidentally kills is a liberal of sorts, theirs is the power and the privilege. "We black and they white. They got things and we ain't. They do things and we can't."

The novel barely stops to provision a recognizable social world, often contenting itself with cartoon simplicities and yielding almost entirely to the nightmare incomprehension of Bigger Thomas. The mood is apocalyptic, the tone superbly aggressive. Wright was an existentialist long before he heard the name, for he was committed to the literature of extreme situations both through the pressures of his rage and the gasping hope of an ultimate catharsis.

Wright confronts both the violence and the crippling limitations of Bigger Thomas. For Bigger white people are not people at all, but something more, "a sort of great natural force, like a stormy sky looming overhead." And only through violence does he gather a little meaning in life, pitifully little: "he had murdered and created a new life for himself." Beyond that Bigger cannot go.

At first *Native Son* seems still another naturalistic novel: a novel of exposure and accumulation, charting the waste of the undersides of the American city. Behind the book one senses the molding influence of Theodore Dreiser, especially the Dreiser of *An American Tragedy* who knows there are situations so oppressive that only violence can provide their victims with the hope of dignity. Like Dreiser, Wright wished to pummel his readers into awareness; like Dreiser, to overpower them with the sense of society as an enclosing force. Yet the comparison is finally of limited value, and for the disconcerting reason that Dreiser had a white skin and Wright a black one.

The usual naturalistic novel is written with detachment, as if by a scientist surveying a field of operations; it is a novel in which the writer withdraws from a detested world and coldly piles up the evidence for detesting it. *Native Son*, though preserving some of the devices of the naturalistic novel, deviates sharply from its characteristic tone: a tone Wright could not possibly have maintained and which, it may be, no Negro novelist can really hold for long. *Native Son* is a work of assault rather than withdrawal; the author yields himself in part to a vision of nightmare. Bigger's cowering perception of the world becomes the most vivid and authentic component of the book. Naturalism pushed to an extreme turns here into something other than itself, a kind of expressionist outburst, no longer a replica of the familiar social world but a self-contained realm of grotesque emblems.

That *Native Son* has grave faults anyone can see. The language is often coarse, flat in rhythm, syntactically overburdened, heavy with journalistic slang. Apart from Bigger, who seems more a brute energy than a particularized figure, the characters have little reality, the Negroes being mere stock accessories and the whites either "agit-prop" villains or heroic Communists whom Wright finds it easier to admire from a distance than establish from the inside. The long speech by Bigger's radical lawyer Max (again a device apparently borrowed from Dreiser) is ill-related to the book itself: Wright had not achieved Dreiser's capacity for absorbing everything, even the most recalcitrant philosophical passages, into a unified vision of things. Between Wright's feelings as a Negro and his beliefs as a Communist there is hardly a genuine fusion, and it is through this gap that a good part of the novel's unreality pours in.

Yet it should be said that the endlessly-repeated criticism that Wright caps his melodrama with a party-line oration tends to oversimplify the novel, for Wright is too honest simply to allow the propagandistic message to constitute the last word. Indeed, the last word is given not to Max but to Bigger. For at the end Bigger remains at the mercy of his hatred and fear, the lawyer retreats helplessly, the projected union between political consciousness and raw revolt has not been achieved—as if Wright were persuaded that, all ideology apart, there is for each Negro an ultimate trial that he can bear only by himself.

Black Boy, which appeared five years after *Native Son*, is a slighter but more skillful piece of writing. Richard Wright came from a broken home, and as he moved from his helpless mother to a grandmother whose religious fanaticism (she was a Seventh-Day Adventist) proved utterly suffocating, he soon picked up a precocious knowledge of vice and a realistic awareness of social power. This autobiographical memoir, a small classic in the literature of self-discovery, is packed with harsh evocations of Negro adolescence in the South. The young Wright learns how wounding it is to wear the mask of a grinning niggerboy in order to keep a job. He examines the life of the Negroes and judges it without charity or idyllic compensation—for he already knows, in his heart and his bones, that to be oppressed means to lose out on human possibilities. By the time he is seventeen, preparing to leave for Chicago, where he will work on a WPA project, become a member of the Communist Party, and publish his first book of stories called *Uncle Tom's Children*, Wright has managed to achieve the beginnings of consciousness, through a slow and painful growth from the very bottom of deprivation to the threshold of artistic achievement and a glimpsed idea of freedom.

III

Baldwin's attack upon Wright had partly been anticipated by the more sophisticated American critics. Alfred Kazin, for example, had found in Wright a troubling obsession with violence:

> If he chose to write the story of Bigger Thomas as a gro-
> tesque crime story, it is because his own indignation and the
> sickness of the age combined to make him dependent on
> violence and shock, to astonish the reader by torrential scenes
> of cruelty, hunger, rape, murder and flight, and then en-
> lighten him by crude Stalinist homilies.

The last phrase apart, something quite similar could be said about the author of *Crime and Punishment*; it is disconcerting to reflect upon how few novelists, even the very greatest, could pass this kind of moral inspection. For the novel as a genre seems to have an inherent bias toward extreme effects, such as violence, cruelty and the like. More important, Kazin's judgment rests on the assumption that a critic can readily distinguish between the genuine need of a writer to cope with ugly realities and the damaging effect these realities may have upon his moral and psychic life. But in regard to contemporary writers one finds it very hard to distinguish between a valid portrayal of violence and an obsessive involvement with it. A certain amount of obsession may be necessary for the valid portrayal—writers devoted to themes of desperation cannot keep themselves morally intact. And when we come to a writer like Richard Wright, who deals with the most degraded and inarticulate sector of the Negro world, the distinction between objective rendering and subjective immersion becomes still more difficult, perhaps even impossible. For a novelist who has lived through the searing experiences that Wright has there cannot be much possibility of approaching his subject with the "mature" poise recommended by high-minded critics. What is more, the very act of writing his novel, the effort to confront what Bigger Thomas means to him, is for such a writer a way of dredging up and then perhaps shedding the violence that society has pounded into him. Is Bigger an authentic projection of a social reality, or is he a symptom of Wright's "dependence on violence and shock?" Obviously both; and it could not be otherwise.

For the reality pressing upon all of Wright's work was a nightmare of remembrance, everything from which he had pulled himself out, with an effort and at a cost that is almost unimaginable. Without the terror of that nightmare it would have been impossible for Wright to summon the truth of the reality—not the only truth about American Negroes, perhaps not even the deepest one, but a primary and inescapable truth. Both truth and terror rested on a gross fact which Wright alone dared to confront: that violence is a central fact in the life of the American Negro, defining and crippling him with a harshness few other Americans need suffer. "No American Negro exists who does not have his private Bigger Thomas living in the skull."

Now I think it would be well not to judge in the abstract, or with much haste, the violence that gathers in the Negro's heart as a response to the violence he encounters in society. It would be well to see this violence as part of an historical experience that is open to moral scrutiny but ought to be shielded from presumptuous moralizing. Bigger Thomas may be enslaved to a hunger for violence, but anyone reading *Native Son* with mere courtesy must observe the way in which Wright, even while yielding emotionally to Bigger's deprivation, also struggles to transcend it. That he did not fully succeed seems obvious; one may doubt that any Negro writer can.

More subtle and humane than either Kazin's or Baldwin's criticism is a remark made by Isaac Rosenfeld while reviewing *Black Boy*: "As with all Negroes and all men who are born to suffer social injustice, part of [Wright's] humanity found itself only in acquaintance with violence, and in hatred of the oppressor." Surely Rosenfeld was not here inviting an easy acquiescence in violence; he was trying to suggest the historical context, the psychological dynamics, which condition the attitudes all Negro writers take, or must take, toward violence. To say this is not to propose the condescension of exempting Negro writers from moral judgment, but to suggest the terms of understanding, and still more, the terms of hesitation for making a judgment.

There were times when Baldwin grasped this point better than anyone else. If he could speak of the "unrewarding rage" of *Native Son*, he also spoke of the book as "an immense liberation." Is it impudent to suggest that one reason he felt the book to be a liberation was precisely its rage, precisely the relief and pleasure that he, like so many other Negroes, must have felt upon seeing those long-suppressed emotions finally breaking through?

The kind of literary criticism Baldwin wrote was very fashionable in America during the post-war years. Mimicking the Freudian corrosion of motives and bristling with dialectical agility, this criticism approached all ideal claims, especially those made by radical and naturalist writers, with a weary skepticism and proceeded to transfer the values such writers were attacking to the perspective from which they attacked. If Dreiser wrote about the power hunger and dream of success corrupting American society, that was because he was really infatuated with them. If Farrell showed the meanness of life in the Chicago slums, that was because he could not really escape it. If Wright portrayed the violence gripping Negro life, that was because he was really obsessed with it. The word "really" or more sophisticated equivalents could do endless service in behalf of a generation of intellectuals soured on the tradition of protest but suspecting they might be pigmies in comparison to the writers who had protested. In reply, there was no way to "prove" that Dreiser, Farrell and Wright were not contaminated by the false values they attacked; probably, since they were mere mortals living in the present society, they were contaminated; and so one had to keep insisting that such writers were nevertheless presenting actualities of modern experience, not merely phantoms of their neuroses.

If Bigger Thomas, as Baldwin said, "accepted a theology that denies him life," if in his Negro self-hatred he "*wants* to die because he glories in his hatred," this did not constitute a criticism of Wright unless one were prepared to assume what was simply preposterous: that Wright, for all his emotional involvement with Bigger, could not see beyond the limitations of the character he had created. This was a question Baldwin never seriously confronted in his early essays. He would describe accurately the limitations of Bigger Thomas and then, by one of those rhetorical leaps at which he is so gifted, would assume that these were also the limitations of Wright or his book.

Still another ground for Baldwin's attack was his reluctance to accept the clenched militancy of Wright's posture as both novelist and man. In a remarkable sentence appearing in "Everybody's Protest Novel," Baldwin wrote, "our humanity is our burden, our life; we need not battle for it; we need only to do what is infinitely more difficult—that is, accept it." What Baldwin was saying here was part of the outlook so many American intellectuals took over during the years of a post-war liberalism not very different from conservatism. Ralph Ellison expressed this view in terms still more extreme: "Thus to see America with an awareness of its rich diversity and its almost magical fluidity and freedom, I was forced to conceive of a novel unburdened by the narrow naturalism which has led after so many triumphs to the final and unrelieved despair which marks so much of our current fiction." This note of willed affirmation—as if one could *decide* one's deepest and most authentic response to society!—was to be heard in many other works of the early fifties, most notably in Saul Bellow's *Adventures of Augie March*. Today it is likely to strike one as a note whistled in the dark. In response to Baldwin and Ellison, Wright would have said (I virtually quote the words he used in talking to me during the summer of 1958) that only through struggle could men with black skins, and for that matter, all the oppressed of the world, achieve their humanity. It was a lesson, said Wright with a touch of bitterness yet not without kindness, that the younger writers would have to learn in their own way and their own time. All that has happened since, bears him out.

One criticism made by Baldwin in writing about *Native Son*, perhaps because it is the least ideological, remains important. He complained that in Wright's novel "a necessary dimension has been cut away; this dimension being the relationship that Negroes bear to one another, that depth of involvement and unspoken recognition of shared experience which creates a way of life." The climate of the book, "common to most Negro protest novels . . . has led us all to believe that in Negro life there exists no tradition, no field of manners, no possibility of ritual or intercourse, such as may, for example, sustain the Jew even after he has left his father's house." It could be urged, perhaps, that in composing a novel verging on expressionism Wright need not be expected to present the Negro world with fullness, balance or nuance; but there can be little doubt that in this respect Baldwin did score a major point: the posture of militancy, no matter how great the need for it, exacts a heavy price from the writer, as indeed from everyone else. For "Even the hatred of squalor / Makes the brow grow stern / Even anger against injustice / Makes the voice grow harsh . . ." All one can ask, by way of reply, is whether the refusal to struggle may not exact a still greater price. It is a question that would soon be tormenting James Baldwin, and almost against his will.

Richard Wright: Black Boy
from America's Black Belt
and Urban Ghettos

Blyden Jackson*

Richard Wright was born in Mississippi, in a rural setting some twenty-five miles from the town of Natchez, on September 4, 1908. His father, whose given name was Nathan, has been variously described as a sharecropper and a mill worker. This is a distinction very much without a difference. For, wherever he went, whatever he did, essentially Nathan Wright was always and utterly a sharecropper. Essentially, moreover, any mill in which he labored would have been like him, as integral a part of the South's agrarian economy as a field of cotton or as any, and all, of the highly regional towns in Arkansas and Mississippi where his son, in an important adjunct of that son's progress toward a precocious manhood, acquired an intimate clinical knowledge of the fundamental nature of color caste in America.

Wright's father apparently was one of those Negroes about whose ethnic identity there can be little question. His skin was rather dark than light. He was also an absolute illiterate, never having set foot inside a school room in his entire life. In formal training, then, as well as in complexion, he differed from the young woman christened Ella Wilson whom he took in marriage. She was, Edwin Embree tells us, "light brown, good looking, [and] possessed a few years of book learning."[1] The relative lightness of her skin is understandable. She had a mother who was constantly being mistaken for white, as well as other Negro relatives equally lacking in discernible evidences of their Negro blood. Her good looks may have borrowed something from an Indian, added to a white and Negro, ancestry. Her son, our Wright, was to be "good" looking, too, with a cast of feature in which, as in his genealogy, Caucasian, Mongol and African would seem to blend, and with a skin more brown than black.

Any crossings of racial strains in Wright's genealogy, however, were not to be duplicated in his early experience of life. That was to be, until

*Reprinted from *CLA Journal*, 12 (June 1969), 287–309, by permission of the author and the journal.

his most impressionable years were quite over, exclusively American Negro. It would seem, indeed, almost as if some tutelary spirit were presiding over his destiny, charged with strict obedience to an injunction from the Fates, "This boy must learn, comprehensively and powerfully, exactly what it means to be a Negro. Not a Negro of the black bourgeoisie who might go to Fisk (or even to an Eastern college) and join a Negro college fraternity, and perhaps journey every August to the Negro tennis 'nationals' and every Christmas holiday with his wife to her Negro sorority convention. No! This boy must be Negro as the masses of Negroes have been Negro. He must know at first hand their peasantry in the South, so pastoral in fable, so bitter in the fact, their groping folk exoduses to the North and West, the grubbiness of their existence in the ghettos of America's greatest cities above the Mason and Dixon line. He must emanate directly from the anonymous black throng, and what that throng has been forced to do, he must be forced to do also."

And so Wright's personal history does begin, as according to such an injunction it should, deep within the world of the folk Negro in the cotton-growing Delta, the world of all American worlds, when Wright was born, closest in form and substance to the plantation world of the ante-bellum South. Somewhere in the atavistic Delta countryside, probably in more than one sharecropper cabin—for sharecroppers have compulsively tended toward nomadism in their search for the ideal tenancy— Wright must have spent his very earliest years. His earliest published recollections, however, in *Black Boy*, his own account of his youth, place his family in Natchez. Wright then was four years old, with a brother, the only brother or sister Wright ever mentions, a year younger than himself. One can well imagine, at this still probationary stage in their lives, what must almost surely have been his parents' shared sentiments. They were young, and youth is notoriously buoyant. Undoubtedly they must have cherished some of those sanguine dreams of making things better for their children which tend to unite parents of every moment and milieu. And so these parents gathered their children and themselves and went up the big river (did they think of their many slave forebears who had come down the same stream?) to mount as it were, an assault on Memphis. They found, in Memphis, living quarters in a one-story brick tenement. The father found a job, as a night porter in a Beale Street drug store. But he found also, and all too soon, a temptress like the Circes of scriptural Babylon, an other woman, unattached, who quickly blotted out from his mind whatever conventional plans he may have brought with him to Memphis. Before Wright was old enough to go to school, this father had completely forsaken the wife and the two small sons for whose presence in alien territory he was largely accountable. He left them just as they were in the one-story brick tenement. His person and all of his support he transferred to the other woman.

The three Wrights thus marooned were in parlous condition. There were whole days after the father's departure when they ate nothing simply because they had no money with which to purchase food. Wright's mother, on occasion, had taught school in the Delta. But Memphis was not the Delta and her formal training, after all, was meager by any standards. She took, therefore, the first job she could obtain, as a cook, while she dispatched to her relatives urgent appeals for funds which would enable her, with her sons, to retreat from Memphis. At the same time she did not neglect her sons' claims upon their father's interest. She haled the father into court on a petition for aid to these sons. A judge, who may have been more percipient than the mother, in her bitterness, supposed, accepted the father's stubborn avowal that he was doing all he could. She did not rest, however, with this rebuff from the law. Over Wright's strenuous objections she persuaded him to accompany her on an expedition which, virtual infant that he still was, yet seemed to him both shameful and futile. The two confronted her husband in the room which he was occupying with the woman who had supplanted her. Wright recreated the encounter in *Black Boy*, referring there to his father's mistress as the "strange woman." Wright's mother put her pride aside to beg her husband for money, not, she was careful to point out, to relieve her own distress, but to pay for the transportation of their two boys to a sister of hers in Arkansas. The father laughed in her face as he rejected her plea. And the "strange woman," true to her role, witting or not, of the ruthless siren from secular Negro folk song, threw her brazen arms possessively around the father's neck.

With Memphis Wright's mother was hardly more successful than with her husband. She had trouble not only in keeping a job. For she was already beginning to show a disposition toward invalidism. She found it difficult also, on the low-paying jobs which were the only means of gainful employment available to her, to provide even the mere creature necessities and the proper supervision for her boys. For a time, indeed, while he was barely six, Wright became a drunkard, enticed into daily tipsiness by the Negro clientele of a nearby saloon for their own ribald sport. Wright's mother put a period to this drunkenness by placing Wright, during the hours of the day while she was away from him, as she had to be, at work, under the strict surveillance of an older woman who lived near the Wrights. Yet Wright's mother still had the problem of a woefully insufficient income. She could not make ends meet. To avoid the rent she could not pay eventually she put her two sons in an orphanage. But it was an orphanage which traduced every principle of Good Samaritanism. Its queasy food was doled out in starvation rations. The unfortunate inmates did little except pull grass, a curious chore they were encouraged to perform because the orphanage could not afford to pay for the mowing of its lawns. To cap everything for Wright, the spinster in charge, whose very appearance and manner set Wright's teeth on edge, doted heavily on him and wanted to adopt him. Small wonder that Wright ran away from this Dickensian horror, albeit not for long. His deliverance came through his mother's relatives. They sent her, at last, the money to withdraw, with her sons, to that sister of hers in Arkansas.

The Wrights' trip to Arkansas was preceded by a stop in Jackson. The parents of Wright's mother lived there now, in a fairly large house of two stories given to them by one of their sons. If any dwelling in which Wright lived until he became a man could be called his home—and none could—this was to be it. In this dwelling he was to spend six years, his last six years of dependence, or semi-dependence, on anyone other than himself. But first he was taken to Arkansas, where he was to stay for four years interrupted only by one return to Jackson of short duration. His mother's sister in Arkansas had married prosperously. Her husband owned a thriving saloon in Elaine. The three Wrights were comfortable with him and well fed. But he was shot to death not long after the Wrights joined his household, Wright avers by whites who coveted the business he would not relinquish, and his wife and the three Wrights, in dread of what might happen further, fled Elaine, under cover of the dark of night, for West Helena, another Arkansas town not far away. The four fugitives stayed in West Helena for a time, went back to Jackson, then retraced their steps to West Helena. The two women took menial jobs. Wright was even able to attend school with some regularity. He was in school in West Helena when the Armistice of 1918 was announced. But another night of terror came. When it passed, Wright's aunt was gone, vanished like a wraith along a trail that led into the fabled north, with a companion, only a vague figure to Wright, the man who had attached himself to her in West Helena. Behind them the escapees left a darksome shadow of something sinister and violent, perhaps dangerously inter-racial, that Wright never penetrated. In West Helena it now became as it had once been in Memphis. Wright's mother, left alone, found herself more than hard-put to try to provide for herself and two sons. Then came a morning of another kind of terror. Wright's brother shook Wright out of his sleep. The younger lad was frightened and frustrated, tremulous, and bewildered. He wanted Wright to look at their mother. Wright did, and called the neighbors, who summoned a doctor. The mother was paralyzed. Now the two boys, neither yet in his teens, were effectively alone. Within days they were back in Jackson with a mother who would never be able to fend for herself, or for them, again.

In Jackson new dispensations were arranged. Wright's brother was sent north to rejoin the aunt with whom the Wrights had lived in Arkansas. Wright was given a choice of residence with any of his other maternal aunts and uncles. He elected the uncle at Greenwood, Mississippi, nearest to his mother in Jackson. But he could not endure life with this uncle and the uncle's wife, kind though the couple tried their best to be. Soon Wright entrained once more for Jackson. He was returning to the house where his afflicted mother at least could give him some feeling of belonging.

The house in Jackson was dominated by his grandmother, a

matriarch whose husband's only interest was his fantastic feud with Washington over a Civil War pension his right to which he had vainly tried for half a century to establish. The matriarch herself was a Seventh Day Adventist and like a member of a persecuted sect in the intensity of her zeal for the true faith. Her house was grim with the grimness of a genteel hopeless poverty. But it was even grimmer with the requirements of the matriarch's devotional austerities. Worse yet, protest as Wright would, he was forced into attendance at a Negro Seventh Day Adventist school in Jackson. Wright did not like the school. He vastly preferred the competitive environment of public education. He liked even less the teaching. This emanated from the sole instructor, a young aunt of Wright's, domiciled under the same roof with him, unsure of herself in her first professional assignment, and cherishing for Wright a temperamental detestation, intensified and enlarged by their teacher-pupil relationship, which he heartily reciprocated. Wright knew he could not continue at this school. Only when he threatened almost hysterically to leave his family altogether was he able, however, to wring from his grandmother permission to transfer from Seventh Day Adventist tutelage to the public schools. In Memphis he had had some months of primary training. He had spent perhaps more than a year all told in school in West Helena. He did not finish a term in Greenwood. His one consecutive experience of formal education that lasted long enough to be considerable came now in Jackson from 1921 to 1925. When, in June of the latter year, he had gone as far as he could go in the schools of Jackson and had finished their highest grade, a ninth grade which he noted constituted a review of the eighth, his formal education was completed.

Jackson offered Wright no future which Wright could accept with equanimity. He was a Negro in the South. He was trained to do nothing of the slightest consequence. Besides—and here was for him the greater rub—since he had first had whispered to him when he was eight or nine, by a girl schoolteacher boarding at his grandmother's, the story of Bluebeard, there had been, firm and unshakeable in his will, the resolution to become a writer. Indeed he had already had a story published in the Jackson Negro weekly newspaper, a tale called "The Voodoo of Hell's Half-Acre," and had been rebuked by his grandmother for the language of the title as well as for the added sinfulness of telling, for any reason whatever, anything but the "truth." And still, he never seems to have thought seriously of any other permanent vocation but that of writing. Until, however, he could write, he had to live. He tried his hand at some of the "Negro" jobs available to him in Jackson. Not only were they leading him nowhere; he sensed, too, a danger in them. He sensed that, in his manner of performing the servile tasks associated with them, he was not acting "right." He was not conducting himself as a Negro should. An opportunity came for him to make a windfall in a petty swindle. He seized it, and supplemented his ill-gotten gains with the proceeds from his one excursion into burglary. Now through with crime for the rest of his days, and saying farewell only to his mother, he stealthily quitted Jackson in the autumn of 1925 for Memphis. In Memphis for two years he worked at another, but better, Negro job with a large optical firm. His best job in Jackson had been also with an optical firm. He managed to re-unite with himself his mother and his brother as well as his aunt from his Arkansas days, who had lost, somewhere along her way, the vaguely figured companion with whom she had departed from West Helena. He saved some money. He began to read avidly on his own. He had access gratis to magazines and newspapers around the building in which he worked. Procuring books was not nearly so easy. He solved that problem with the help of a white employee of the optical firm. He would present himself at the public library with a list of books ostensibly from the employee, and with this employee's card, and thus acquire for his own use the loan of books he wanted to read. But, of course, Memphis was still not the environment for him. He broke one day, as diffidently as he could, to his employers at the optical firm the news that he was leaving, since he was in the position of being "forced" to "accompany" his aunt and his paralyzed mother to Chicago. He had arrived at the end of a first stage in his own life. Behind him was an impressionable youth spent in an urgent roving commission that had immersed him in the folk life of the American Negro at its very base even while it bereft him of any semblance of a normal childhood, a protected environment, or any convenient fantasies about the nature of social truth. Ahead of him, he hoped, would be a chance to learn to write.

Chicago by 1927 may have come to constitute the ideal spot for a Negro writer who wanted thoroughly and reliably to understand the Negro as an American phenomenon. It is even doubtful whether Harlem, always the largest and greatest, and the best known, of American Negro ghettos,[2] was truly quite as representative of American Negro life between the two World Wars as the Black Belt of the South Side. For Harlem evinced, here and there in what it was able to compound with, a strangeness, an easygoing toleration of cosmopolitanism, that was not always American. And the Negro is the most wistfully American of all Americans. He wants to be accepted, on American terms by American people. From Harlem, for example, in the 'twenties a Negro of very sable hue, one Marcus Garvey, intoned his dream of black nationalism, a united Africa, every inch of it governed by black men in the interest, and with the support, of black people everywhere. "Up, you mighty race," he exhorted. And the black masses of America did respond to his exhortation. But it is instructive to examine dispassionately, indeed cynically, the nature of their response. They did not go to Africa. They never have, in sizable numbers to stay, under any persuasion. They long ago learned to want, with the rest of immigrant America, the best of two worlds, a respectable past in some distant overseas and a respectable here and now, or the reasonable hope of it, among their American neighbors.

Provisional Orders of the Black Legion, provisional duchies in Kenya and Uganda as hereditary rights, possessed a psychological value, on this side of the Atlantic, for Negroes who were bowed down beneath the weight of honorific European pasts to which they could lay no claim. The Black Belt of Chicago in the 'twenties, therefore, a teeming wedge within Chicago's South Side, extending seven miles south from Chicago's Loop, almost uniformly more than a mile wide, and growing like any good American boom town in everything except, significantly, its geographical boundaries, its 44,000 Negro inhabitants in 1910 having become 109,000 in 1920 and moving on to become the 237,000 of 1930 did not attract its large inpouring of Negroes from the South[3] because of any thirst those Negroes had for foreign conquest or Pan-Africanism. Chicago in the 'twenties had its own exhorter to black America. He was as sable of hue as Marcus Garvey. But Garvey was from Jamaica in the British West Indies. The mind of the American Negro was never quite in fact an open book to him. Robert S. Abbott, on the other hand, was, like most of Chicago's Negroes, from the American South, in his own case from Georgia. He had made his way to the Illinois eldorado through the classrooms of Hampton Institute, where he acquired a mastery of printing. He had started, on the South Side in the early 1900's, a weekly newspaper, the *Chicago Defender*, which by the 1920's called itself the World's Greatest Weekly, and which did carry its message by then, in some form or other, into virtually every nook and cranny of Negro America. The "Up, you mighty race," which Abbott advocated was Negro migration from the South, and when he stood on his Mount Pisgah and crooned down to the Negro masses his telescopic view of the promised land which Negroes were to seek one had only to eliminate Abbott's references to race to hear in accents pure the booster's voice of George F. Babbitt. Abbott came, indeed, at about the very time that Wright was settling in Chicago, to the campus of a Negro university and there told the undergraduates, in convocation assembled, but still agape from the epiphanic vision of Abbott's emergence from the plush recesses of a chauffeur-driven Rolls Royce, that in Chicago his money was enabling him to pass for white. He spoke not gloatingly, but as an Old Testament prophet dutifully expounding holy writ. His audience listened in a hush of unfeigned reverence.[4] For his audience knew of Jesse Binga, the Pullman porter who became president of one of Chicago's two Negro banks, of Oscar DePriest, the Negro who was to go to Congress from the South Side in 1928, of Daniel Hale Williams, the Chicago Negro surgeon who had operated on the human heart. With Abbott, indeed, this audience shared a black nationalism which began and ended only as a protest against the exclusion of the Negro from full participation in American life as the most conformist of Americans would have defined that life in the era of Harding and Coolidge. Abbott typified for this audience, therefore, what it truly dreamed of, or almost so. For, truth to tell, Abbott himself died without actually ever really "passing for white." Abbott belonged, really, only to a black bourgeoisie. And so, for that matter, did Binga and DePriest and Dr. Williams. What Abbott did have was a certain ease in the externalia of affluence. He did not have the psychological gratifications or the communal privileges of the elect. And still he, and his kind, were relatively fortunate. The vast bulk of Negroes in America in the 'twenties belonged to no kind of bourgeoisie. If they were not peasants on the land they were members of an urban proletariat.[5] The migrant Wright in 1927, a nineteen-year-old boy with no well-placed friends on the South Side, or anywhere else in Chicago, and no acquisitions in training or property that would invest him with economic or social power, had to become an addition to black Chicago's urban proletariat. Ten years of living with Chicago Negroes in the mass—Wright was to leave for New York in 1937—were to make him privy to the intimate condition of the black Chicagoan as nineteen years of residence in the upper region of the Mississippi Delta and its hinterland had made him privy to the intimate condition of the Southern Negro in that Negro's native habitat. He did not merely view the anonymous Negro masses of Chicago with a novelist's eye for material or a scientist's trained detachment. He existed for years as one of them. It may be hard to define the typical American Negro. It would certainly be impossible to define him, particularly as he was before the 1950's, without taking into account both the Negro of the agrarian and the small-town South and his often pathetically impotent cousin in the industrial North. For twenty-nine years of his life Wright never passed through a whole day without rubbing a fraternal shoulder with one, or both, of these Negroes.

His first job in Chicago was as a porter in a white delicatessen. He found this job by the simple expedient of getting on a street car, riding on it until he was out of the Black Belt, dismounting from his conveyance, and then trudging the cold winter streets until he saw a sign anouncing that a porter was wanted. His next job was as a dishwasher in a white restaurant. He had taken, while he was portering, the Civil Service examination for the Chicago Postal Service. In 1929 he received a substitute clerkship in the Chicago Post Office. He tells of remembering the cries of newsboys hawking the story of the great stock-market crash to the Chicagoans past whom he was proceeding as he savored the contents of the letter which had brought him notice of his appointment. Work in the Post Office not only relieved him of menial labor. It gave him time and left him energy for reading and practice at writing. But the cries of the newsboys, had he but known it, had been at least as much of an omen for his life in Chicago as his letter. The Depression came and deepened. Through another examination he had raised his postal rating, but the mails were feeling the effects of the times. He was laid off at the Post Office, and again looking for any job he could find. A stint of duty as agent for various Negro insurance firms improved his knowledge of the Black Belt, but did not solve his problem of caring for the household for which he considered himself responsible. He went on relief and for a while swept streets as a relief worker at thirteen dollars a week. But after the relief authorities placed him as a worker at the South Side Boys' Club—with its provision of close, continuous scrutiny of young Negroes from the Black Belt streets, a job peculiarly appropriate for the writing he was now soon to accomplish—the tasks he performed for subsistence moved ever closer to the things he wanted to do as a matter of self-expression. He was transferred from the boys' club to an assignment as publicity agent for the Federal Negro Theater. Then, still with WPA, he was transferred, again as publicity agent, to a white Federal Experimental Theater. Finally he came, still through the ranks of WPA, to the Federal Writers' Project, with which he became an acting supervisor of essays before he left Chicago.

So his life went through much of the 1930's. And yet his life was much more vivid, much fuller of the play of incident, once incident is conceived of as happenings in an inner, as well as an outer world, than any running account of it can suggest. For one thing he was reading, making himself into something of an intellectual, and talking, no longer to the unread, but to people, many of them keen youngsters like himself—in their keenness, at least, although they tended to be white—for whom the life of the mind carried far beyond the Philistias of an Abbott or a Garvey. For another thing, he was trying his hand at writing, practicing at the learning of a craft too exacting for dilettantes and amateurs, devoting long hours to the business of constructing sentences, a mystery he found that exposed itself only to relentless pursuit, and charging himself for the big job of writing a novel, in the spirit, it would seem, of Keats as Keats approached the parallel necessity, for him, of doing the long poem, *Endymion*. And for a final thing he had encountered Communism, an experience by no means unusual for the intellectually curious during the era of the Great Depression.

Wright has had his say about his bout with Communism in the essay he contributed to the symposium, *The God That Failed.* He made his acquaintance with it through the intermediation of the Chicago John Reed Club, an organization of left-wing writers and painters to which he was attracted by the recommendation of a young Jewish friend. He came home from his first evening at the club too excited to sleep. He read the magazines that had been pressed upon him there far into the night and, near the dawn, wrote a free-verse poem to exorcise his tumultous reactions.

When he was elected executive secretary of the club, in 1932, he joined the Communist Party. He says he tried to be a good Communist. He had not been drawn to the Party by "the economics of Communism, nor the great power of trade unions, nor the excitement of underground politics . . . , . . . [his] attention was caught by the similarity of the experience of workers in other lands, by the possibility of uniting scattered but kindred peoples into a whole."[6]

But the Party did not class him as a worker. It labeled him an intellectual, and he discovered that the Party was suspicious of all intellectuals; that it was, indeed, suspicious of Richard Wright. In his own Party unit, a segregated cell located in the Black Belt of the South Side, even his black comrades seemed to consider him, as an intellectual, a curio.

The Party interfered with his writing, and he had joined it as a writer; had, in fact, had published in Party magazines some of his poetry and in the *New Masses* an article about Joe Louis. He held that a writer should write. The Party held that a writer at best should combine writing with political activity; but, failing that, should never shirk his assignments at the barricades. How very much in dead earnest the Party was in its proscription of art for politics Wright came to know, moreover, by direct experience. He had started on his novel, his major undertaking, when the Party communicated to him its decision that he was to organize a committee on the high cost of living. He expostulated, citing his novel. The Party was adamant, and the novel suffered while he organized.

Nor was the Party, for all of its uniting of peoples, free of color prejudice. In 1935 Wright was sent as a delegate to a writers' congress in New York. The white delegates were lodged without incident through a local committee on arrangements. Wright had to shift for himself to find a place to sleep. One night he spent in the kitchen of a white couple who seemed to be friends of one of his white fellow Chicago Communists. He ended, the next night, in Harlem at the YMCA branch there.

Indeed, when all was taken into account Wright could not fail but notice a certain Gilbert-and-Sullivan derangement of the reasonable in much that the Party said and did. Only, the derangement was not intentional. It was not the consequence of levity or carelessness or, even, a spirit of high jinks. It was the result of solemn effort by solemn people unconsciously acting as addled as lunatics. It was actually true that a man who claimed to be a painter did, on one occasion, appear from out of the void to join the Chicago John Reed Club while Wright was serving as its executive secretary, suggest that he had powerful connections within the Party, cause a great furore with extravagant and palpably unjustified charges against one of the club's most respected members, and then, disappear with the club still somewhat intimidated by him before this tribune of the people was discovered to be nothing more nor less than a lunatic from Detroit somehow free of his usual confinement. How could this happen? It was because of the way "normal" operations were actually conducted in the Party. And the Party could suit its words to its deeds. It could talk as fantastically as it behaved. It could, and did, prate of "counter-revolutionary activity," "incipient Trotskyites," "bastard intellectuals," "anti-leadership attitudes," and something called "seraphim tendencies," a phrase which Wright came to discover signified, within the Party, "that one has withdrawn from the struggle of life and finds himself infallible."

It was, Wright could hardly avoid observing, the good Communists who thought themselves infallible. If the Party had tagged Albert Einstein a "bastard intellectual," to a good Communist so Einstein would have been, despite the inescapable originality of some of his best-known feats of intellect. And all these things were of a piece with a Communist practice that, perhaps, nettled Wright most, the imputation by a Party leader to a lesser light of damaging remarks which the lesser light (and less powerful comrade) had actually never uttered.

In one reflective moment Wright concluded of the Party that much of its both startling and maddening tendency to act in a most unreal fashion before obvious realities was attributable to its history in Russia. Under the czars the Russian Communists were conspirators. They had to be suspicious of everything, for the police were unremittingly in hot pursuit of them. And conventionally conditioned American Communists were behaving in the America of the 1920's as did their ideological forebears in czarist Russia.

The Communists, Wright felt, had given him some good things. He felt that he had found among them his first sustained human relationships. His early years, then, with no father since before he started to school, a mother too soon invalided, only relatives of lesser consanguinity with whom he invariably bickered, and a largely malicious environment outside this none too congenial family circle, may well have been even lonelier than he was ever to care to admit. Certainly he felt that he had learned from the Communists. They had made, he believed, the first organized search for the truth about the oppressed, and he never seems to have lost his respect for the Communist knowledge-in-detail of the lives of the workers of the world nor to cease to appreciate the magnitude of the capacity with which Communism would make "men feel the earth and the people on it."

For Communist social science, then, apparently he retained always an intellectual's regard. So, too, he apparently remained always grateful to the Party for its tonic effect on some of his early writing. Given, he believed, a new knowledge of the great world by Communist materials and a new elevation of spirit by Communist ideals, he produced some of his first work which seemed to him to express what he wanted to say. But, in the final analysis, too much of Communist practice outraged both his sense of independence and his sense of sanity. He had declared himself inactive in the Party well before May Day of 1936, not without some unpleasant reactions from the Party which he avers he tried to avoid. Apparently, his formal severance of membership from the Party did not come until 1944.

But by 1944 Wright was no longer living in Chicago. We may have seen that some poetry of his had been published. So, too, in 1936, had a novella of his in *New Caravan*. And we have seen, too, that he was planning, and trying to work, on a novel. This novel had become for him the something that must be done. And so in May of 1937 he went east. Nor did he go, moreover, without the knowledge that he was taking a risk which was all of his own making. He had taken a third Civil-Service examination on which he had achieved virtually a perfect score. Just now, when he was nerving himself for the great *Putsch* at writing, notice reached him of the appointment to a permanent clerkship in the Chicago Post Office at $2100 annually, a magnificent stipend in 1937. Like Cortez at Vera Cruz, however, he chose to burn his bridges behind him and he hitchhiked for the second time to New York City.

In New York he worked again with the Federal Writers Project. But he also worked at his writing and at trying to peddle his stories. He was not to be successful at selling his individual stories, but his novella "Big Boy Leaves Home," in 1937 won a prize in *Story* for the best story of the year, and Harper's printed four of his stories in *Uncle Tom's Children*. The book was a success. In 1939 Wright received a Guggenheim award to free him for creative work. In October, 1939, *Native Son*, his novel, was published, a dual selection of the Book-of-the Month Club. The novel sold well instantly and brought him recognition as well as profit. The Spingarn Medal, annual award of the NAACP to an American Negro for preeminent achievement, was presented to him in 1940. In 1941 *Native Son* was made into a play, Wright collaborating with Paul Green in the transformation, and produced on Broadway under the direction of Orson Welles. The late Canada Lee took the lead role of Bigger Thomas, and the play had a run of fourteen weeks in the metropolis before it was taken on the road. There could be no doubt, Wright's lean years were over.

The lean years of his personal life were over too. In 1940 Wright had married Ellen Poplar, a Jewish girl of New York City. Their first child was a daughter, Julia, born in 1942, the same year in which Wright's third book, *12 Million Black Voices*, was published. He and this wife were living now in Brooklyn, although Wright, accompanied by his first wife, had spent some time in 1940 in Mexico working on a second novel related to life in New York City which he apparently never finished.[7] He did finish, however, his own account of his early years, *Black Boy*, which was published in 1945. But World War II was ending now. Wright had hoped the peace would bring greater changes in the treatment of minorities in America than he was able to discern. An invitation to reside in France was extended to him by the Government of France. With his wife and Julia, he forsook Greenwich Village, to which the Wrights had moved from Brooklyn, and went to Paris. It was 1946 and the second stage of his life, his stage of residence in the North had run its course.

He never returned, except for one visit, to the United States. Gertrude Stein had found for him, in the Latin Quarter, a large apartment. He settled down in a city where he was free to go and come as he had never been in the United States. This Paris became his home, although France never became the land of his citizenship. He was an expatriate American, never a naturalized Frenchman. Nor was he ever a sedentary boulevardier. Before he left America, he had spent some time in Mexico, but also, in 1945, in Quebec. First, now, he lived, in 1950, on his third continent, South America, where he went to the Argentine for the making, from the novel, *Native Son*, of a movie in which he played, without proving himself an actor, but also, only after having been drafted to do it, the role of Bigger Thomas. In Ghana in 1953 he lived for weeks on his fourth continent, Africa. His coverage of the Bandung Conference in 1955 carried him to Asia. He had set foot, then, on all the major land masses of the world except Australia. And he did move around, also, in western Europe. He lectured, and visited, at various times, in Italy, Holland, Germany, Denmark and the Scandinavian peninsula, and he made two extended trips to Spain for the writing of his *Pagan Spain*. Yet he made only one serious attempt really to detach himself from his acquired Parisian background. In 1958 Julia was looking forward to going to college. A brilliant student with a most impressive scholastic record, the best in the lycée for her year, she received bids from Oxford and Cambridge. She chose Cambridge, but it was not deemed advisable for her to go there alone. Wright and his wife had a second child in 1947, another daughter, born in France and speaking only French, whom they named Rachel. Ellen Wright and Rachel left Wright alone in France to accompany Julia to England. Wright had now to himself both the apartment in the Latin Quarter and a farm house near the village of Ailly on the river Eure in Normandy which he had bought in 1957 as a place to which he could retire from his exposed position in sociable Paris and have the solitude and leisure a working writer tends to need. It took him, who had been for long a grown man before he acquired a felicitous domesticity, little time to make the decision to sell both the apartment and the house and cross the channel to London. He received, of course, from the English the customary tourist's visa. But when he applied for the residence visa which would have permitted him to live in England with his wife and Rachel and thus join them in their propinquity to Julia he was surprised with a rejection. Friends of his in England interceded with the Home Office. He went himself there in person. The residence visa was not forthcoming. Convinced that the British did not truly want Negroes in Britain, although they also wanted not to seem not to want them, Wright returned to France, taking now an apartment in the rue Regis smaller than the one he had surrendered in anticipation of a transfer of his residence to England.

He had worked hard and published much during his years abroad: the three novels, *Savage Holiday*, a "white" novel not about the race problem which was brought out as a paperback original, *The Outsider* and *The Long Dream*; four books that were not fiction, *Black Power*, *Pagan Spain*, *The Color Curtain* and *White Man, Listen!*; as well as prepared for publication the collection of short stories, *Eight Men*, which would appear very shortly after his death. He had lectured before audiences in Europe, seen and unseen. He was beginning to write radio dramas for German radio. He had learned about the special Japanese poetic form, Hai-Kai and was experimenting with the application of this Oriental aesthetic discipline to Negro material. He was even, following an invitation from Nicole Barclay, committed to the writing, for her Barclay's Disques, a French record company, of the comment to accompany some of the recordings of jazz to be issued under that firm's name. Even without his family his days were full. For he was no recluse. He did more than write. He had helped in the organization of the Société Africaine de Culture. He was interested in its magazine, *Presence Africaine*. He had friends and visitors, many of both undoubtedly eminent. Some were French like Sartre. Some were Americans living in Paris, as with his good companion, Ollie Harrington, whose cartoon character, Bootsie, may be the finest satire of its kind yet conceived by a Negro. Some were visiting foreigners, if any person of an intellectual or aesthetic bent can be called a foreigner in Paris. Some were very much like himself, Negro writers, but Negro writers who were remaining in America. Indeed, on an autumn day in 1960 Langston Hughes arrived to visit him and found him in his apartment fully clothed, but lying on a bed under cover. The spectacle before Hughes seemed to require a witticism and Hughes laid under contribution an echo from the familiar vocabulary of the Negro evangelical faiths. "Man," he said, "You look like you're going to glory." Wright explained. There was no cause for alarm. In Africa, some years previously, he had contracted intestinal amoeba. Occasionally, therefore, it became wise for him to submit himself to a rather routine physical examination. He was merely waiting to be taken to the Eugene Gibez Clinic, had dressed for his journey, and had decided to rest while waiting for his transportation. Hughes seems to have been Wright's last visitor. On Monday night, November 28, 1960, Wright was still in the Clinic, but awaiting his scheduled release to return to his apartment in the morning. His nurse had left him and he was alone when his night bell sounded. When the nurse responded, she found him dead. Death had claimed him suddenly and from a rather unexpected quarter. He had had a heart attack, not a fatal onslaught of the complaint which accounted for his presence in the hospital. He must have died almost instantaneously, conceivably even before the full portent of this final seizure from which there could be no appeal was apparent to him.

His body was cremated, and his ashes quietly interred in a locker at the famed cemetery Pere La Chaise. It is a far cry from a Negro hovel in the Mississippi Delta to the inner haunts of an international aristocracy of talent in Paris, that *bon vivant's* elysium of the Western artist-intellectual. Indeed, it is a cry so very "far" in a certain sense of psychic distance as thus alone to constitute a fairly reliable index of the dauntlessness of Richard Wright's resolution and of the indefatigibility of his enterprise—as well as, it may be added, of the extraordinary range of his overt experience of life. For the Richard Wright whom Hamlet's fell sergeant arrested so prematurely at such a great remove from his ancestral roots had achieved a miracle of sorts. He had conquered as his own Odysseus much more than land and sea, in the literal sense. He had really conquered, in effect, a succession of social worlds, and the truly significant pilgrimage he had managed to negotiate had been his migration in progressive stages of advance from the despised universe of the American Folk Negro across formidable barriers of custom and privilege into virtually a white man's status in a particularly privileged enclave of the white man's world.

Hence, undoubtedly we should give a most attentive ear to Wright when, in *Black Boy*, apropos the confrontation which became eventually his final meeting with his father (as it was, at its occurrence on a Mississippi plantation, his first in almost precisely a quarter of a century), after speaking of his father "standing alone upon the red clay . . . a sharecropper, clad in ragged overalls, holding a muddy hoe in his gnarled, veined hands,"[8] he proceeds to declare:

> [when] I tried to talk to him [my own father] I realized that, though ties of blood made us kin, though I could see a shadow of my face in his face, though there was an echo of my voice in his voice, *we were forever strangers, speaking a different language, living on vastly distant planes of reality* [italics mine].[9]

We should, that is, note carefully Wright's own insistence, in terms that brook of no equivocation, upon the great and irreconcilable cultural abyss between himself and his unreconstructed parent. We should acknowledge, too, the ample apparent warrant for the lack of compromise in Wright's depiction of his position relative to his father. After all, Wright had written one book about Spain, another about a country in Africa, a third which dealt with the Bandung Conference, of which he had been an eye witness. Some of his short stories have European settings. One of his novels, even though it is his poorest, departs altogether from racism and its pitifully circumscribed areas of preoccupation. He clearly could not have written what he did write had he lived a life too much like that of his father's. Nor could he, for that matter, have married as he married, or talked as he came to talk, or thought as he came to think. An immensity of cultural variation did sunder him from his father, a whole buoyant mass of learned responses in concepts and behavior, for the assimilation of which he had, in all their blooming welter, discovered a more or less various capacity, but of the nature and uses of which his father had virtually not the slightest inkling. And yet ours is, when everything is said and done, a curious and inconsistent world in which, as an aspect of its sometimes inscrutably organic complexity, it is possible for two propositions which seem mutually to cancel each other out in their abstract logic not only both to be empirically true, but also, each to make the other, empirically, even truer. Just so, as there does seem to be incontrovertibly, good reason to aver of Wright and his father that they ended by becoming, toward each other, in all obvious respects, like total strangers, and evidence just as compelling for the contention that their alienation from each other was the almost unavoidably inescapable consequence of differences in the worlds into which they were cast as their lives continued, so it seems equally valid to maintain that they were, on the other hand, linked together by a bond which could never be severed and to argue that, in spite of the noticeable impact upon Wright of conditioning factors from the white worlds into which he had been able to insinuate himself, this bond was forged out of Wright's fellowship with his father in the world of the American Negro masses.

That fellowship dated, of course, from the moment Wright drew his first breath. It extended on Wright's side, however, actively only through the years of his youth, the formative years for any individual born into the human family, the plastic years during which all creatures so originated tend to acquire the deep-seated basic reactions which shape their characters for the remainder of their lives. Such years obviously are of no little import in the personal history of every person ever socialized. In the development of creative writers, whose trade depends to a considerable extent upon exceptional receptivity to the stimuli from an external world, these very years are probably even more than ordinarily meaningful. Certainly, James Baldwin, who knew Wright on two continents and for more than half of Wright's adult life, found a special significance in those years where Wright was concerned. For Baldwin once observed of Wright—in comparing, incidentally, Wright's sense of reality with the fondness of Sartre and Sartre's circle for ideal speculation—"I always sensed in Richard Wright a Mississippi pickaninny, mischievous, cunning and tough. This seemed to be at the bottom of everything he did, like some fantastic jewel buried in high grass."[10] And while it is true that Baldwin here is making no issue of race, but merely playing upon a racial epithet to heighten the impression he wishes to convey of a Wright educated early, and lastingly, in a particularly bitter school of hard knocks, it is also true that Baldwin's contention opposes any conception of Wright as a creature totally emancipated from the world to which Wright's father still belonged when the father and son faced each other as we have been told they did in Wright's *Black Boy*. If we are to credit Baldwin, even at this last meeting Wright and his father were not total strangers. They did not live on vastly different planes of reality. It may have seemed that they did, and in much that was most perceptible, even to Wright himself, no other conclusion may have appeared as reasonable. Yet Baldwin's phrase may haunt us, may tease us into further thought.

Mississippi pickaninny! It is an apt phrase. And it is even apter if we read it with a keen awareness both of its implications of Wright's indestructible affinities with his own youth and of his membership, which was irrevocable, in a peculiarly racial world. We may wish then, perhaps, to ponder deeply Redding's words, written soon after Wright's death, "In going to live abroad, Dick Wright had cut the roots that once sustained him; the tight-wound emotional core had come unravelled; the creative center had dissolved . . . ,"[11] and to add thereto Redding's veritable extension of those remarks a year later, "His heart's home [Wright's] and his mind's tether was in America. It is not the America of the moving pictures, nor of Thomas Wolfe, John P. Marquand and John O'Hara's novels, nor of the histories of the Allan Nevins and C. J. H. Hayes. It is the America that only Negroes know: a ghetto of the soul, a boundary of the mind, a confine of the heart."[12] For it may well be that Baldwin and Redding, in their separate fashions, have both pointed the way to the indispensable prelude for an understanding of Richard Wright, conceivably as a person, and certainly as a literary artist. It may well be that the picture of Wright which one should bear most in mind is not that of a Wright so visibly grown away from his father as to seem a visitor from another world as the father and the son finally encounter each other for a strained brief moment under a Southern sun, but rather the child described by Baldwin, and confirmed as a presence by Redding, who lurked always at the center of Wright's mind and heart, the child whose only real abode was the "America that only Negroes know," and whose only real release came in the fictive world of Wright's creation closest to the actual world that Wright had known in the Negro sub-culture of his youth.

Notes

1. Edwin Embree, *13 Against the Odds* (New York, 1944), p. 26. "Good looking," it should be remembered, in American parlance almost invariably connotes "good" according to an Aryan standard of right and wrong in personal appearance.

2. And, all through the 'twenties virtually, in ferment with the Harlem, or Negro, Renaissance.

3. As late as the early 1940's St. Clair Drake and Horace Cayton in their careful study of the Negro in Chicago, *Black Metropolis* (New York, 1945), were to find (on p. 99) that over eighty out of every one hundred "Chicago" Negroes had been born in the South.

4. The campus was that of Wilberforce University in southern Ohio. The date is uncertain. I was a contributor to the reverent hush.

5. On the basis of the occupational distribution of Negroes, E. Franklin Frazier stipulates that, in the four northern cities containing, in 1940, Negro communities numbering 100,000 or more, a bourgeoisie element constituted a little more than a fifth of the total Negro population. Cf. Frazier, *Black Bourgeoisie* (Glencoe [Ill.], 1957), pp. 46–47. Chicago was, of course, among these four cities. A Negro bourgeoisie was certainly proportionately no greater in the 1920's than in the 1940's.

6. Richard Wright, "Richard Wright," in Richard Crossman, ed., *The God That Failed* (New York, 1952), p. 106.

7. This seems to have been the book which he also sometimes described as a novel about the status of woman.

8. Richard Wright, *Black Boy* (New York, 1945), p. 30.

9. *Black Boy*, p. 30.

10. James Baldwin, *Nobody Knows My Name* (New York, 1961), p. 184.

11. J. Saunders Redding, "Richard Wright: an Evaluation," *Amsac Newsletter*, 3 (December 1940), 6.

12. Redding, "Home Is Where the Heart Is," *The New Leader* (December 11, 1961), p. 24.

Racial Wisdom and Richard Wright's
Native Son

Houston A. Baker, Jr.*

I

It is impossible to comprehend the process of transcribing cultural values without an understanding of the changes that have characterized both the culture as a whole and the lives of its individual transcribers. In the case of black American culture the principal shift was from a rural to an urban environment; similarly, the patterns in the life of Richard Wright modulated from Mississippi youth to Parisian manhood. Black American literature has a human immediacy and a pointed relevance which are obscured by the overingenious methods of the New Criticism, or any other school that attempts to talk of works of art as though they had no creators or of sociohistorical factors as though they did not filter through the lives of individual human beings. The study of biography, in the case of Richard Wright and his most famous novel, *Native Son*, is a necessity, for the autobiographical element is strong in all of Wright's work, and it is impossible to understand the aspirations, turnings, and contradictions of his work without some understanding of his life.

Diversity and complexity were present from the outset in the fair-skinned, literate and retiring Ella Wilson and the powerful, dark, and uneducated sharecropper from Mississippi's Upper Delta, Nathan Wright, who were married in 1907. A year later, on September 4, when Nathan found himself deeper in debt to the plantation owner who furnished the essentials of his tenancy, Richard Wright was born. His birthplace was Natchez, but his life was more influenced by his early migrations than by any one specific place. According to Blyden Jackson, the character of Wright's life proceeded from the masses of America's "Black Belt," a dense Southern body that has thinned since the turn of the century and became the mass of America's urban ghettos.[1] During his first nineteen years, Wright was nurtured on the values, modes of adaptation,

*Reprinted from Houston A. Baker, Jr., *Long Black Song* (Charlottesville: Univ. Press of Virginia, 1972), pp. 122–41, by permission of the author and the publisher. Copyright © 1972 by the Univ. Press of Virginia.

66

patterns of social and religious organization, bitterness, aspirations, and violence of the Southern black American folk. And during these years he moved from Natchez to Memphis, from Memphis to Jackson, from Jackson to Elaine, Arkansas, and from Elaine back to Jackson, where he completed the ninth grade of Smith-Robertson Public School in 1925. The next move was to Memphis, and here the young boy worked until he had earned enough money to depart from the southern black folk and join the northern in the Promised Land of the American city. It is a dynamic, flowing pattern, which Wright reduced to its essentials in *Black Boy*, an autobiography published in 1945.

Hunger, fear, a father who deserted the family, the violence of whites who killed one of his uncles in order to take over his property, the malignity of a sporting "professor" who was courting his aunt and who murdered a white woman with whom he was having an affair and burned the house that contained her lifeless body—these were but a few of the grim elements of Wright's early life. There was also the domineering Uncle Tom who once advanced on his young relative with a switch:

> "I've got a razor in each hand!" I warned in a low, charged voice. "If you touch me, I'll cut you, so help me God!"
> He paused, staring at my lifted hands in the dawning light of morning. I held a sharp blue-edge of steel tightly between thumb and forefinger of each fist.
> "My God," he gasped.[2]

Violence was omnipresent: there were beatings by whites, black women raped, black men ("bad niggers") fighting back, some of them castrated and lynched. Squalor, fanaticism, and fear characterized the decaying black tenements of southern cities. And a grandmother's overzealous devotion to the Seventh-Day Adventist Church left as much of an imprint on Wright's early years as the custom-ridden relations between black men and white women. The primary element of his life, however, and of all black lives in America, in the words of Stephen Henderson, was "survival motion."[3]

The principal of Smith-Robertson considered Wright an outstanding student, and the editor of Jackson's *Southern Register* accepted a melodramatic short story, "The Voodoo of Hell's Half-Acre," in 1924 and encouraged the author to continue writing; these were two bright spots in a world of leanness and neglect. The young man left the South, however, with more than he conceived. From his first screams in a sharecropper's cabin to his stealthy departure by night from Jackson, he had been immersed in the culture of the black American folk; he rode a night train to Chicago, a man imbued with the concepts, skills, arts, and institutions of America's black folk population.

The northern phase of Wright's life did nothing toward the deculturation of the young man of twenty who arrived in Chicago on a chill December day and made his way to an enclave of black urban culture. His experiences in Chicago and New York for the next twenty years simply reinforced the fundamental attitudes and assumptions he had acquired in the South. Here in the North he also found hunger, "Negro jobs," excessive black population density, intra- and interracial violence, decaying tenements, resentful blacks, and prejudiced whites. The environment altered the modes of adaptation of the folk, but the primary goal and driving impetus of black life was the same as in the South—survival, by any means necessary.

Of course, there is no need to minimize the genuine broadening that Wright underwent in social, intellectual, artistic, and economic spheres during the thirties and forties. The process of self-education that he had begun while working for an optical firm in Memphis continued when he moved to Chicago. Here he did not have to borrow a white man's library card or forge a note saying, "Dear Madam: Will you please let this nigger boy have some books by H. L. Mencken?"[4] but he did have to move beyond the boundaries of his own ghetto environment in order to obtain the type of intellectual stimulation he desired. The John Reed Club of Chicago (an organization of radical artists and writers) and the Communist Party of America seemed to promise this stimulation. The John Reed Clubs were nationally organized by the Communist Party in 1932, and by March of the following year Wright was not only executive secretary of the Chicago branch, but also an official member of the Party. The writers associated with these clubs throughout the country were some of the most noted in white and black American literature—John Dos Passos, Langston Hughes, Theodore Dreiser, Malcolm Cowley, and others. Under the auspices and tutelage of the John Reed Club and the Party, Wright produced poetry, essays, and fiction dedicated to the melioration of world social conditions. His intellectual and social vision expanded to include the lowly and oppressed from all points of the compass, and he genuinely believed (and there are "many thousands gone" who did likewise) that the Communist Party was committed to the cause of civil rights for the black man in America.

The Communist experience for Wright, however, was more than dedication and social vision. Early in his encounters with the Party, he felt that he could enjoy warm and sincere human relationships for the first time in his life. Jan Wittenberger (surely the model for Jan Erlone in Native Son), who recruited Wright for the John Reed Club, was undoubtedly the person who reinforced this view of human relations in the Party.

Considering his life as a whole, one can see that communism was, in fact, an ideology that fit Wright's fundamental cultural assumptions rather than a political camp for which he had to remold his life and values. A communal or collectivistic ethos has always characterized black culture in America, distinguishing it unequivocally from white American culture. The latter endorses individualism and self-help as roads to advancement, but black Americans have long known (as David Walker's *Appeal* [1829] and Henry Highland Garnet's "Address to the Slaves of the United States" [1843] demonstrate) that there can be no advancement of the black individual until the social, economic, and political codes of society have been altered in a manner that makes possible the upward mobility of the entire body of black Americans. Seldom, for all too patent reasons, have black Americans viewed society as a protective arena in which the individual can work out his own destiny.

It is essential to understand the basis in black culture for Wright's "natural allegiance" to the Communist Party. This helps to elucidate the theme and structure of both *Uncle Tom's Children* and *Native Son* to a greater degree than does a critical perspective grounded in Marxist ideology. The group which provided (in Sainte-Beuve's phrase) "all the maturing and value" for Richard Wright, also suggested the strategies of survival and conditioned the world view that Wright set forth in literature. In one of the most ideological stories in *Uncle Tom's Children*, "Fire and Cloud," it is not communism that wins the day for Reverend Taylor and his congregation; it is rather a fused strength based on black religion and reinforced by the belief that not God but "the black people" should receive one's sincerest tributes.[5] In the other stories of *Uncle Tom's Children*, this same sense of fused strength is evident; there is the same affirmation of the positive good to be derived from the unification of black people to overcome their oppressors. The theme of the volume, that "freedom belongs to the strong," certainly implies that Wright believed a united black community stabilized by shared cultural assumptions had the greatest chance of achieving freedom.

In *Native Son*, Bigger Thomas dreams of a strong black man who will emerge to unite the mass of black people. The fulfillment of his dream, of course, is Bigger himself. He accepts the whole way of life that is his culture, and at the end of the novel he emerges as the same type of existential character we see in autobiographical accounts of black American slaves. A case in point is the *Narrative of William Wells Brown, a Fugitive Slave*. One of the most memorable sequences in this narrative records the stages of Brown's physical and psychological movement away from his owners and across the state of Ohio to freedom. Having reclaimed the name of "William," which his master took from him, and having repudiated "trust" and "honor" as they have been defined by his master ("Servants, obey your masters"), he sits cold and alone by a makeshift fire, eating stolen ears of corn, but feeling "all right." Bigger's movement from bondage to freedom follows the same course: he repudiates white American culture, affirms the black survival values of timely trickery and militant resistance, and serves as a model hero—a strong man getting stronger, to use Sterling Brown's words—for all readers of *Native Son* who possess the culture which provided maturation and value for Richard Wright.

An important distinction must be made between the works of

Richard Wright and the works of the Proletarian School of the thirties and forties. While it is true that Wright was influenced by the naturalism and the polemical concerns of contemporary writers, it is also true that his use of naturalism was not the ideologically and literarily self-conscious choice made by such men as John Dos Passos, Mike Gold, and John Steinbeck. Comparing Wright's life with that of almost any of Emile Zola's protagonists, one immediately recognizes the similarity. Wright's existence in the Black Belt and in the urban ghettos of America was one in which events seemed predetermined by heredity (the simple fact of melanin), and the environment seemed under divine injunction to destroy. Wright's choice of communism on an ideological plane and his adoption of naturalism on a literary plane were, in part, culturally determined, and they led to works that mark a high point in the black American literary tradition. One cannot apply critical censures designed for American proletarian literature to Wright's work without just reflection. The following statement by Nathan Scott serves to illustrate:

> And, however robust our respect may still be for the Dos Passos of the *U.S.A.* trilogy or the Steinbeck of *The Grapes of Wrath* or the Wright of *Native Son*, we find them today to be writers with whom it is virtually impossible any longer to have a genuinely reciprocal relation, for the simple fact is that the rhetoric of what once used to be called "reportage" proves itself, with the passage of time, to be a language lacking in the kind of amplitude and resonance that *lasts*. This may not be the precise judgment which the cunning of history, in its ultimate justice, will sustain, but it is, at any rate, *ours*.[6]

Without entertaining the "ultimate," it seems apparent that such a generalized formula is not applicable to Richard Wright. Wright's most significant niche is scarcely to be found in the Proletarian School.

When his comrades in the Communist Party increased his anxieties by ominous hints of purges in Moscow and talk of the fate of "bastard intellectuals" and "incipient Trotskyites" in their midst, Wright realized that he did not belong in the Marxist gallery. In 1937 his "Fire and Cloud" had won *Story* magazine's prize for the best short story of the year; 1939 brought him a Guggenheim fellowship; and in 1940, *Native Son* was chosen as a Book-of-the-Month Club selection and Wright was awarded the Spingarn Medal by the National Association for the Advancement of Colored People. As an established author, Wright asserted his artistic prerogatives and was more than miffed when the Party criticized *Native Son* for—of all things—its individualism and its failure to portray the black and white masses of America. In the early forties the Party also shifted its policies toward the American Negro; no longer was the granting of the rights of full citizenship to black Americans to be a goal. By the end of 1943, therefore, Wright had withdrawn from the Party. In 1944 he published "I Tried to Be a Communist," and five years later he contributed a piece to Richard Crossman's *The God That Failed*, a collection of essays reflecting the disenchantment of former communist supporters.

During the early forties Wright had made even more fundamental shifts in his status. In 1940 he married a ballet dancer, whom he divorced after they had spent an extended (but, for Wright, all too "bourgeois") season in Mexico, and in 1941 he married Ellen Poplar, a Polish member of the Communist Party in New York. In effect, the dream with which he leaves his readers at the end of *Black Boy* had come true: he had achieved fame and stability as a writer (the earnings from his writings totalled thirty thousand dollars), he had married the woman he loved, and his daughter Julia, born in 1942, was moving into a beautiful and precocious childhood. But living in New York has never been easy for a black man, and when an invitation to visit France was extended by the French government, Wright promptly accepted.

Soon after his return from Paris in 1947, while walking the streets of Greenwich Village one day and marvelling at the abundance of America, he paused before a small store's display, then decided to buy some fruit to take home. While he was making his selection, the Italian owner rushed out of the store and brusquely asked, "Whudda yuh want, boy?" With the question, Wright's feeling of a moment before—"It's like Christmas! Just like Christmas!"—vanished, and once again he was suffering the "old and ancient agonies" at the hands of his white American neighbors. One individual from what Ellison calls "the waves of immigrants who have come later and passed us by" had made Wright acutely aware of his true culture. His white neighbors on Charles Street were not the least bit kinder; on occasions, the word "nigger," spoken distinctly and loudly enough for him to hear, drifted from a group of white gossipers as he climbed the steps to his home. After a short and frustrating stay in the United States, therefore, Wright departed once more for France and never again saw his native land.

The last thirteen years of his life were full ones; they were charged with new experiences, interesting friendships, accolades as well as indifference for his works, hope for an emerging Africa and a dying colonialism, feelings of awe before an advanced technology, interest in French existentialism (which accorded with Wright's modes of interpreting experience), new world leaders, and his own possessive involvement with his family—the brilliant Julia, energetic Rachel (a second daughter, born in 1949), and devoted Ellen. In "Alas, Poor Richard," James Baldwin characterizes Wright's Paris years as a time of disillusionment and surliness, but one does not receive the same impression from Constance Webb's *Richard Wright*.[7] An understanding of Baldwin's Oedipal rage and unhappiness because Wright, his artistic *paterfamilias*, could not be easily purged from his psyche somehow leads one to place more faith in Miss Webb's assessment.

The works of the last years, from *The Outsider* (a novel, 1953) to *Eight Men* (a collection of short stories prepared for publication in 1960 but published posthumously in 1961), reflect Wright's attempts to continue his self-education and to order in some way the swiftly changing world around him. Africa and Asia seemed to Wright (as they had to W. E. B. DuBois more than half a century earlier) to hold both a threat and a promise for the modern world, and he explored the complexities of the color line and the new "tragic elite" (leaders of former colonial territories) in *Black Power*, a report on his visit to the Gold Coast in 1954, and in *The Color Curtain*, a report on the Asian Bandung Conference in 1956. Spain also was an attractive yet baffling country to Wright, and following his instincts and curiosity he visited it twice in an attempt to order his reactions; *Pagan Spain* (1956) was the result. Ever since the Civil War of the thirties, Spain had proved a fertile subject for contemporary writers. Wright's own view was characteristically conditioned by his own background. He understood the mentality of the Spanish peasant, and this, coupled with his knowledge of the social, theological, and economic patterns of an industrial world, make *Pagan Spain* an insightful and provocative book.

The creative works of the last years include *Savage Holiday* (1954) and *The Long Dream* (1958). Both novels examine the condition of the contemporary man in an exploitative world, but neither met with even a mild critical success. In part this cool reception (indifferent in the case of *Savage Holiday*) was justified. The books are not candidates for rave reviews, and in both there is a tension between a metaphysical rebellion (which was much more forceful in Wright's cathartic years of the thirties and forties than in the early fifties) and a broad, humanistic view of the Western world. The attempted unity is ambitious and commendable, but finally the tension is neither sustained nor resolved in the fine artistic manner displayed in the author's best fiction. Another novel, *Lawd Today* (begun in 1934 but published posthumously), has done little to enhance his reputation. The later works, however, are at times exciting, and they deserve more critical attention than they have received from black and white American critics, who curiously seem to feel that the end of Wright's artistic life coincides with his departure from the United States in 1947.

On November 28, 1960, after three days of tests at the Clinique Chirurgicale Eugéne Gibez in Paris, Richard Wright, like his most famous protagonist, was feeling "all right." According to the tests, his health was apparently fine. During the early evening he had read all of the newspapers, but after placing the book that he was reading on the bedside table, he felt a sharp pain and reached for the signal light.

> Three minutes later the floor nurse came out of another patient's room, looked up the hallway and saw Richard's light. She walked quietly in her rubber-soled shoes to his room and entered. Richard lay on his back, his head turned toward the door, an apologetic smile on his lips as though to excuse himself

for disturbing her. Before he could speak he simply seemed to fall away, his face smoothed of lines. Richard Wright was dead at fifty-two years of age.[8]

Possibly Wright's strange smile had as much to do with the absurdity of dying when he had so many plans as with his feelings toward the nurse. An ambitious, searching, and strong man, his works seldom manifest anything like a Freudian death urge; his protagonists are always committed to a life lived fully and wholly. There are always obstacles in their path, and they are often destroyed as a result of their commitment, but the title of a long work planned shortly before his death captures the mood of his fiction. The proposed title was "Celebration." Wright's works are generally celebrations of life, particularly the complex life lived by black Americans. Wright repeatedly declares that blacks are affirmers: every imaginable pressure has been exerted against them while they have continued to assert the principles of humanity vested in the American Constitution and the Bill of Rights more fully and effectively than any other group on the continent. The native son, in his eyes, could only be the black American. Bigger Thomas's history is the history of black American culture, which coincides precisely with the founding and duration of the United States. From 1619 to the present, black American culture has grown and flourished, and *Native Son* irrefutably demonstrates that Richard Wright was one of its finest artists and most sensitive chroniclers.

II

For thirty years criticism and commentary on *Native Son* have mounted: positive and negative, insightful and absurd, respectful and racist—the criticism seems to reflect the fundamental reactions of America to its own history. The aim of the protagonist has been fulfilled: ". . . he wished that he could be an idea in their minds; that his black face and the image of his smothering Mary and cutting off her head and burning her could hover before their eyes as a terrible picture of reality which they could see and feel and yet not destroy."[9] Bigger Thomas struck America's most sensitive nerve; he attacked the white female, its "symbol of beauty" (p. 155). There is little mystery about *Native Son*'s ability to attract successive generations of American readers; the great taboo of American culture is shattered in the book, and human beings, like Ralph Ellison's Mr. Norton in *Invisible Man*, possess a fateful desire to look upon chaos without being destroyed. It is Trueblood in *Invisible Man*, however, who actually has vision, and in Wright's novel it is Bigger Thomas. Mr. Norton remains sightless, and those surrounding Bigger (Mrs. Dalton and even the sympathetic lawyer, Boris Max) persist in their blindness.[10]

There is some irony in the fact that critics—black and white—search the novel's image clusters, dialogue, point of view, ideology, and allusions for the source of its power. Those who have undertaken such structural safaris have often shared Mr. Norton's and Mrs. Dalton's fate; they have remained blind to one of the most essential sources of power. Codes restricting the alliance of blacks and whites in colonial America, a Civil War, antimiscegenation laws, thousands of lynchings, the murder of Emmett Till—all point to one reason for *Native Son*'s force; these manifestations of American culture reinforce Bigger's belief that Mary Dalton and her kin are "the flowers" of American civilization, the symbols of purity and innocence which the country has sought to protect. A young white female suffocated, decapitated, and cast into a roaring furnace by a twenty-year-old black man who glories in his act—this is the image that remains fixed in the reader's mind. And the image is not merely melodrama or sensationalism.

Melodramatic and sensational impulses usually proceed from the exploitative regions of an author's soul; they are composed of clichés, set formulas, and exaggerations designed to manipulate the emotions of the reader. The genesis of *Native Son* goes deeper; the book comes from a region where only truth will suffice, a region into which the unpleasant facts of history intrude for honest scrutiny, a realm where myths and stereotypes dissolve and a genuine folk heritage shines forth. When Bigger forces Mary's body into the flames, his act is no more terrifying than a slave's slapping his white mistress to frighten away an opponent. Bigger's swing of the hatchet to take off Mary's head is no more awesome than the decisive stroke with which Nat Turner took the life of his white mistress. Stackolee's fearful acts, which stop the white sheriff from coming after him, are no less daring than Bigger's resistance to the white mob that comes seeking his life, and Brer Rabbit and the hero of the "John Cycle"—both accomplished tricksters—would have been proud of Bigger's handling of the obtuse detective Britten and the voyeuristic reporters who come to the Dalton home in search of melodrama and sensation.

Bigger's culture is that of the black American race, and he is intelligible as a conscious literary projection of the folk hero who embodies the survival values of a culture. Tales of the trickster animal who overcomes his stronger opponents, of John, the slave who outwits his master, of the "bad nigger" (Shine, Stackolee, Dupree) who rebels against an oppressive system—all of these contribute to an understanding of Wright's protagonist. Tales of pillage and plunder, accounts of black men inflicting pain and humiliation on white women with impunity, and stories of injustices suffered by black Americans are plentiful in black folklore, and a tale such as the following helps to illuminate the perspective of *Native Son*:

> In a little Southern town, a mob was fixing to lynch a man when a very dignified old judge appeared. "Don't," he

pleaded, "put a blot on this fair community by hasty action. The thing to do," he insisted, "is to give the man a fair trial and then lynch him."[11]

The story is Bigger Thomas's, and if a representative tale from the white-woman genre is considered, the perspective becomes even clearer:

> You take in the South, they always have one strong colored guy on all the plantations. He's given a lot of consideration by the boss—usually he be foreman. Can put two or three of the others in his back pocket.

The story goes on to tell of two such men whose masters arranged for them to fight one another. On the day of the fight, Jim, one of the combatants, in an attempt to frighten John, his adversary, has his boss attach him to an iron chain staked in the ground. But John arrives at the battling grounds, slaps his own boss's wife in the face, and watches Jim run away:

> So the loser, Jim's master, had to pay off John's boss the three or four thousand dollars they'd put in a bag. Still, John's boss got mad about his wife being slapped. He asked John, "What was the idea slapping my wife?" "Well, Jim knowed if I slapped a white woman I'd a killed him, so he run."[12]

John's concluding words bring to mind the fate of Bessie Mears. When we combine tales of injustice and white-woman tales with stories of the bad-man hero, the picture is complete. A white sheriff responds to Billy Lyons's mother:

> Sheriff said, My name might begin with an *s* and end with an *f*,
> But if you want that bad Stackolee you got to get him yourself.

Black folklore includes countless examples of strong black men giving "a faint, wry, bitter smile," or the final, destructive thrust to the revered symbols of white America, and Bigger Thomas's act is simply a continuation of this heritage.

Why, then, have Bigger's character and action, which are built of so many traditional elements, aroused such concern? The answer is not far to seek. Genuine black folklore has seldom been considered valid literary or historical evidence by our cultural custodians. The arts of the black American folk (rural and urban) have been largely ignored, caricatured, or exploited by white America. Black music was transformed into the distorted croons of the minstrel tradition. The forceful idioms of black folk speech were converted into the muddled syntax and thick-lipped jargon of "Negro jokes." Bessie Smith and Louis Armstrong wailing and transcending in the cabarets of Harlem became Paul Whiteman and George Gershwin harmonizing in theatres downtown. In short, the art of black folk culture (like the art of other American subcultures, such as the Irish, Italian, and Jewish) has been adjusted to suit the needs of white America—to reinforce stereotypes and sometimes even to justify the victimization of the black American. America at large has seldom taken an honest look at its black citizenry.

Since black Americans were kept illiterate by the laws of the land during much of their history, they could not challenge the general American view of the black man in poetry or prose. And when black writers did take pen in hand, polemical demands (the need to castigate slavery and caste in America) and the bare formal requirements of their craft exerted pressures that relegated the true folk heritage to a somewhat minor role. This does not mean that the folk heritage was forgotten; James Weldon Johnson's *The Autobiography of an Ex-Colored Man*, Jean Toomer's *Cane*, Langston Hughes's *Not without Laughter*, and Arna Bontemps's *Black Thunder* all rely on the folk experience. But Richard Wright's *Native Son* was the first black novel that captured its full scope and dimension.

Wright's message to America was that black Americans are a unique people who have produced heroes who hate and wish to destroy those contrived symbols of white culture that insure our victimization. Bigger says to his lawyer:

> "What I killed for must've been good! . . . It must have been good! When a man kills, it's for something. . . . I didn't know I was really alive in this world until I felt things hard enough to kill for 'em. . . . It's the truth, Mr. Max. I can say it now, 'cause I'm going to die. I know what I'm saying real good and I know how it sounds. But I'm all right. I feel all right when I look at it that way. . . ."[13]

The voices of David Walker, Nat Turner, Frederick Douglass, Martin Delaney, and a dishevelled group of black forced laborers singing "Lookin' fer Jimbo/Don' say nothin'/Go 'head Jimbo/Don' say nothin' " resound through Bigger's words.[14] The message is simple: reverberating through black folk culture it says, "Mean mean mean to be free."[15] Wright's theme and his hero were drawn from the folk history to which he was heir. America's attraction to *Native Son* has been the response of the curious to the unknown, the guilty to the reason for guilt, the deceitful to exposure, the sympathetic to the oppressed, the learned to new evidence, and the perceptive to works of genius. No cultural historian (a role that Wright self-consciously assumed the year following *Native Son* in *12 Million Black Voices: A Folk History of the Negro in the United States*) could have hoped to evoke more response than *Native Son* did.

Irving Howe has presented a just assessment of Wright's achievement: "The day *Native Son* appeared, American culture was changed forever. No matter how much qualifying the book might later need, it made impossible a repetition of the old lies."[16] Wright brought to consummation the black artist's struggle to express a folk heritage in unequivocal terms; neither polemical demands nor the requirements of his craft distorted his portrayal of the conditions of blackness in America. In short,

Native Son accomplished the task begun by the black intelligentsia (including Paul Laurence Dunbar, Charles Chesnutt, James Weldon Johnson, and W. E. B. DuBois) at the turn of the century; Wright successfully translated the values of an oral tradition into written form. And the reading public's overwhelming reaction to his novel has been one of praise and discovery, shock and genuine appreciation; in the midst of white America is a culture—a whole way of life—with values in many ways antithetical to those of the larger society, values symbolized by and epitomized in a five-foot, nine-inch black man following the example of his folk predecessors by pushing a cherished white symbol into oblivion.

III

To view Wright as a historian of black folk culture, however, raises several problems for the study of *Native Son*. In "How 'Bigger' Was Born" (1940) and again in *Black Boy*, the author seems to deny (or, at least, to disregard) the life-enhancing aspects of black American culture. In "How 'Bigger' Was Born," he implies that his hero has no integral relation to black folk culture: "First, through some quirk of circumstance, he had become estranged from the religion and the folk culture of his race."[17] This statement makes one recall the conclusions about Coleridge reached by John Livingston Lowes, who after searching many possible sources of the poet's creative works was forced to admit that he could not determine precisely how these sources were transmuted into art.[18] Likewise, the manner in which Wright's experiences were transmuted into art remains unexplained even by himself. When Wright speaks of Bigger's estrangement from black folk culture and religion there is a high degree of critical myopia involved; he reduces folk culture to little more than folk religion. Hence, in *Native Son*, Bigger is estranged from Mrs. Thomas and Reverend Hammond (her minister), who embody the author's perception of his own folk religion. Wright knew that black folk culture was more than otherworldly hymns and humble Hebraism, but in an attempt to explain the genesis of *Native Son* he did not reveal his broader wisdom.

A religious, passive, escapist way of life is presented as the essence of black American culture in "How 'Bigger' Was Born." Nevertheless, in *Native Son* Wright adopted several fully developed strategies from black folk culture that have little to do with humble passivity. From his killing of a rat in the first scene of the novel until his last, bitter smile to his retreating lawyer, Bigger Thomas acts as the eternal man in revolt, a type of devil or badman hero who attempts to subvert society by refusing to heed its dictates. The burning of Mary Dalton's body and the premeditated murder of Bessie Mears are clearly the acts of a strong, Satanic figure determined, at whatever cost, to have his freedom. The moment he adopts a mask of innocence, subservience, and stupidity to allay the suspicions of detective Britten and the newspaper reporters, Bigger plays the role of the trickster. These activist strategies are quite as important as religion to black American folk culture. "How 'Bigger' Was Born" is an elucidating essay, but ultimately it tells us more about Wright's interpretation of *Native Son* than about the mysteries of the novel's creation. The author did not miss the mark in his attempt to create an appropriate representative of black folk culture, but his interpretation of his own paradigmatic creation is simply too narrow. There is, furthermore, a similar narrowness in *Black Boy.*

Innumerable passages in Wright's autobiography give a sense of black communality, a sense of fused strength, yet the narrator denies the presence of such meaningful relations in the microcosm that he sets before the reader. There is an almost querulous insistence that the narrator's is the only sensitive, artistic, struggling soul in this world. In its projection of a creative soul out of harmony with an oppressive environment, *Black Boy* is generically akin to the slave narratives, but there is more to it. In essence, Wright's attempt at a recovery of self is more a creative than an analytical act. Regarding his southern upbringing from the perspective of a successful author, Wright's memory exercised a meet selectivity; out of terror, illiteracy, and oppression emerges the young, gifted, black artist. The picture is as stirring as the autobiographer desired, for he was not reluctant to employ folk and fictional incidents in *Black Boy* for the creation of effects. Moreover, he never allows fully delineated tenderness or sentiment to distort the informing purpose of the book—to demonstrate how Richard Wright, the author, was formed. In this context, Wright's much-debated statements about "the essential bleakness of black life in America" come as no surprise. It would be virtually impossible to present a portrait of the *struggling* artist that delineated his culture as one that provided most of the essential elements an artist requires. The struggle for fulfillment would then become more an alternative than a necessity.

If we are to consider him the chronicler of his time, Wright's parenthetical statements about "the strange absence of real kindness" and "the cultural barrenness of black life" merit our concern. The following paragraph is representative:

> Whenever I thought of the essential bleakness of black life in America, I knew that Negroes had never been allowed to catch the full spirit of Western Civilization, that they lived somehow in it but not of it. And when I brooded upon the cultural barrenness of black life, I wondered if clean, positive tenderness, love, honor, loyalty, and the capacity to remember were native with man. I asked myself if these human qualities were not fostered, won, struggled and suffered for, presented in ritual form from one generation to another.[19]

Ralph Ellison regards this passage as an affirmation of black culture. Wright, according to Ellison, is pointing out that ". . . Negro sensibility is socially and historically conditioned; that Western Culture must be won, confronted like the animal in a Spanish bullfight, dominated by the red shawl of codified experience and brought heaving to its knees."[20] Dan McCall, on the other hand, feels that the passage is based on Wright's realization of the effects produced by "the terrible cultural bind of the South," which transforms the pain and desire of black life into intraracial violence. Moreover, he feels that the statement is part of the author's attempt to "find a meaning" in the bleakness, terror, lack of kindness, and violence of black life.[21]

Both critics provide useful explications, but neither seems to realize how fully Wright's perception of his relationship to the objective world (the world that had adjudged *Native Son* and its author just claimants to greatness) conditioned the writing of *Black Boy*. The reception of *Native Son* gave Wright the confidence he needed to deal with a world he viewed as tempting, fragmented, and alienating; in *Black Boy*, the intended message is one of transcendence, and in order to drive home its full significance, the author allows monochromatic or unrelieved barrenness to act as scrim and underpinning for the stage on which his narrator acts out his ascent. The total effect of *Black Boy* is magnificent; we bestow kudos where the autobiographer intends, on the hard-earned rise of Richard Wright to eminence.

Once again, however, we see the same type of paradox that confronts the reader of "How 'Bigger' Was Born." It must be kept in mind that a transcendent Richard Wright—an author who had repeatedly employed the communality, modes of adaptation, and intraracial hostility of black culture as subjects for his fiction—tells the reader of a sterile culture that can scarcely be expected to produce such an author. In short, Wright's position as some readers view it (those observers who perceive him objectively as a writer whose genius was brought to maturity by the group in which he had his genesis) is a tribute to the vitality and creativity of black culture. His position as he perceived it, however, was an altogether different thing, since he regarded himself as both subject and object. And in considering the subject of *Black Boy* he was somewhat myopic; he was unable to see his developed self as sensitive readers can. His pejorative comments on black American culture, therefore, are balanced by the reader's understanding of what Wright sought to achieve, and the fact that he chose to write what Roy Pascal designates "the story of a calling" implies an affirmation of black American culture's ability to produce outstanding authors.[22]

Impulses arising from Wright's culture conditioned his propensity for other realms of experience and influenced his definition for an authorial relationship to them. Bigger Thomas's final stance in *Native Son*, for example, is as existential as Cross Damon's primary stance in *The Outsider*. Yet it was not Wright's contact with Jean Paul Sartre and Simone de Beauvoir that shaped his existential view. The fundamental conditions of black life in America led him to see that a priori moral values could scarcely be operating in the great scheme of events; the quest for value in *Native Son* and *The Outsider*, therefore, does not extend beyond the choices of an individual man with his mind "set on freedom." In the same vein, Wright states in *Black Boy* that his choice of literary mode was not the result of overintellectualization or excessive brooding on white Western culture: "All my life had shaped me for the realism, the naturalism of the modern novel, and I could not read enough of them" (p. 274). Black life in America, which is both existential and communal, was thoroughly naturalistic for Richard Wright.

Wright sought means to order the seeming chaos of the black situation. But that chaos and the means, values, and strategies that black Americans have employed to deal with it were always integral parts of his outlook. In his first novel, he gazed steadily on the face of chaos and created a successful and enduring work, and if one holds *Native Son* alone in evidence, one must agree with Hugh Gloster that Wright, ". . . above all other American novelists, is the sensitive painter and perspicacious spokesman of the inarticulate black millions of this country."[23] In "Blueprint for Negro Literature" (published in *New Challenge*, 1937), Wright himself wrote:

> It was . . . in a folklore moulded out of rigorous and inhuman conditions of life that the Negro achieved his most indigenous expression. Blues, spirituals, and folk tales recounted from mouth to mouth, the whispered words of a black mother to her black daughter on the ways of men, the confidential wisdom of a black father to his black son, the swapping of sex experiences on street corners from boy to boy in the deepest vernacular, work songs sung under blazing suns, all these formed the channels through which the racial wisdom flowed.[24]

In recording his experiences as an orderly in a Chicago hospital in 1931, Wright tells of assisting as doctors sedated experimental dogs, stuck scalpels down their throats, and slit their vocal cords so that they would not disturb the patients. The awakened dogs, who lifted their eyes to the ceiling and attempted to cry, became for Wright symbols of silent human suffering. Wright's statement in "Blueprint" merges with his experiences in the Chicago hospital, to give a very special impact to Gloster's assessment of the achievement of *Native Son*. Richard Wright moved beyond silent suffering, far beyond inarticulateness; yet when he created it was in the tone and from the perspective of the "inarticulate" black folk of America. The racial wisdom of an accomplished cultural heritage flows through *Native Son*, one of the most dynamic novels in the black American literary tradition.

Notes

1. Blyden Jackson, "Richard Wright: Black Boy from America's Black Belt and Urban Ghettos," *CLA Journal*, XII (June, 1969). 287–309.

2. Richard Wright, *Black Boy* (New York, 1963), p. 175. All citations in my text refer to this edition.

3. Stephen E. Henderson, " 'Survival Motion': A Study of the Black Writer and the Black Revolution in America," in *The Militant Black Writer in Africa and the United States*, by Mercer Cook and Stephen E. Henderson, (Madison, Wis., 1969), pp. 63–129.

4. Wright, *Black Boy*, p. 270.

5. Richard Wright, *Uncle Tom's Children* (New York, 1963), p. 156.

6. Nathan A. Scott, Jr., "The Dark and Haunted Tower of Richard Wright," in *Black Expression*, ed. Addison Gayle, Jr. (New York, 1969), p. 308.

7. James Baldwin, "Alas, Poor Richard," in *Nobody Knows My Name* (New York, 1968), pp. 146–70; Constance Webb, *Richard Wright, a Biography* (New York, 1968). This work is at present the most definitive biography of Wright; the book is sensitive, intelligent, and well-written. It is one of the few biographical accounts from which the reader receives a genuine feeling for the subject, and I have relied heavily on it. John A. Williams's *The Most Native of Sons* (Garden City, N.Y., 1970) offers a straightforward though more elementary approach to Wright's life.

8. Webb, p. 399.

9. Richard Wright, *Native Son* (New York, 1966), p. 123. All citations in my text refer to this edition.

10. In the Signet edition of *Invisible Man* (New York, 1952), the Norton-Trueblood encounter covers pp. 46–66.

11. Richard M. Dorson, *American Negro Folktales* (New York, 1970), p. 504.

12. Dorson, pp. 134–35.

13. *Native Son*, p. 392; Wright's ellipses.

14. Quoted from *The Book of Negro Folklore*, ed. Arna Bontemps and Langston Hughes (New York, 1958). "Hyah Come de Cap'm." p. 405.

15. Robert Hayden, "Runagate Runagate," in *Selected Poems* (New York, 1966), p. 77.

16. Irving Howe, "Black Boys and Native Sons," in *A World More Attractive* (New York, 1963), pp. 100–101.

17. Richard Wright, "How 'Bigger' Was Born," *Saturday Review*, June 1, 1940, p. 4.

18. John Livingston Lowes, *The Road to Xanadu: A Study in the Ways of the Imagination* (New York, 1927).

20. *Black Boy*, p. 45. Wright's entire statement is parenthetical and occurs at the beginning of chapter two.

20. Ralph Ellison, "Richard Wright's Blues," in *Shadow and Act* (New York, 1966), p. 103.

21. Dan McCall, *The Example of Richard Wright* (New York, 1969), pp. 118–19.

22. Roy Pascall, *Design and Truth in Autobiography* (Cambridge, Mass., 1960).

23. Hugh Gloster, *Negro Voices in American Fiction* (Chapel Hill, N.C., 1948).

24. Richard Wright, "Blueprint for Negro Literature," in *Amistad II* (New York, 1971), p. 6. This is a revised and expanded version of Wright's "Blueprint."

Richard Wright: Aspects of His Afro-American Literary Relations

Donald B. Gibson*

The publication and national distribution of Richard Wright's work, beginning in 1938 with *Uncle Tom's Children*, signaled something new and different in the literature of black authors.[1] No previously published plays, poems, or fiction by a black writer bears much resemblance to Wright's work. Some reasons for this are obvious, some not so obvious; some are personal, having to do with Wright's unique character and experience; and some are historical, ensuing from historical accident or circumstance. Two questions arise immediately once Wright's relation to his black predecessors and contemporaries is considered: How specifically does his work differ? Why is it so clearly distinguished from that of others? Answers to these questions tell something about Wright, about his relation to black writers and to others, and about his place in literary history.

The most striking difference between Wright and other black writers before and during his time is in Wright's insistence that black people have power. "Freedom belongs to the strong," Reverend Taylor asserts exultantly at the conclusion of "Fire and Cloud," the fourth story in *Uncle Tom's Children*. As the stories progress in that volume, the central characters become more capable of controlling the direction of their lives. Big Boy, the chief character of "Big Boy Leaves Home," is not simply a victim of overwhelming forces. He eventually flees for his life, but twice during the ordeal he saves himself by exerting his physical strength: first, when he wrests the rifle from the man who would otherwise have shot him, and again, when he strangles the dog that threatens to expose his hiding place. In the second story, "Down by the Riverside," a man overcomes great dangers and difficulties getting his wife, who is in labor, to a hospital during a flood. He succeeds, although his wife and unborn child die. Later, he is identified as the slayer of a white man whom he has killed in self-defense. He is captured and might have been a victim had he not consciously chosen to bring about his own death by running, knowing full

*This essay was written specifically for this volume and appears here for the first time by permission of the author. Copyright © 1981 by Donald B. Gibson.

well that he would be shot. In "Long Black Song," the next tale, Silas shoots down the white man who has slept with his wife Sarah. Although he is burned to death inside his house after standing off a lynch mob, he dies defending himself with his rifle. Again the character is not simply a helpless victim. In "Fire and Cloud" Reverend Taylor chooses to defy all those who have threatened him in the past and against whom he has failed to assert himself. In so doing he declares that he has a meaningful degree of control over his destiny. In "Bright and Morning Star" the characters are organizing workers across racial lines, presumably to better their social and economic situations. Aunt Sue, the central character, is a strong, indomitable woman, hardly a victim. Her choice to sacrifice her life for the sake of the group by killing an informant before he can reveal the identity of the group's members is an act of supreme courage and a revelation of strength.

Whereas in *Uncle Tom's Children* the power of the characters is put to positive use—they exert their strength literally to save their lives, to preserve a modicum of dignity, or to uphold an ideal—in *Native Son* the power of Bigger Thomas is randomly, then intentionally, destructive. Bigger is not Big Boy, Mann, Silas, Reverend Taylor, or Aunt Sue. Rather, he is simply free-floating energy, unchanneled as are those who fulfill accepted social roles. The general he pretends to be early in the novel has perfectly acceptable means to relieve his aggressions; the pilot he wishes he were may legitimately fulfill his desire to court danger and to live adventurously and aggressively. Bigger has no program, no direction, no plan, but he has the power of his arm. It is this power that allows him to summon forth the rage, anxiety, and fear of a large, metropolitan community.

From the beginning of *Native Son*, where he kills the rat, through his bullying attack on Gus and his dismembering of Mary's body, to the calculated murder of Bessie, Bigger is depicted as assertive and aggressive. In the presence of whites he is tongue-tied, outwardly submissive, and fearful beyond normal expectation. His outward appearance, however, does not reflect his inner hostility. He is as he is because of the influence of his environment on his personality and character; had he lived in a better environment, he would have been a better person. We are not allowed, however, to see Bigger as a victim. We *know* it, but we do not *see* it. Even at the end of the novel, where Wright undoubtedly intends for us to see Bigger in a sympathetic light, we are not allowed to pity him or even to feel deep sorrow for him because of his impending execution. This is in large measure the result of Bigger's perspective on himself. His newfound awareness places him somehow above his circumstances, and his acceptance of responsibility for his past precludes his being a victim.

One way of looking at Wright's autobiography *Black Boy* is through his conception of himself during his early life: in face of a thoroughgoing, rigid system of racism and segregation, he is, even as a youth, not without power. His power lies in his consciousness of his own individuality and in his capacity to resist the attempts of persons and institutions to define who he is. His nearly unconscious inability to conform to the wishes of others bespeaks some inner strength whose presence allows him to exist with psychological and emotional integrity in the most hostile surroundings. That same quality allows him finally to escape to a less directly and personally oppressive environment.

That strength which his autobiography describes as belonging to himself belongs likewise to the central character of *The Outsider*, Cross Damon. Cross has such power that he is able to wrench himself free from his life, from a domineering mother, a nagging wife, and a pregnant mistress. He breaks away as well from a job that offers little fulfillment. Not only does he accomplish these extraordinary feats, but he creates his own new identity in a different city. No one of these things is extraordinary, but that he does them all within a short span of time is psychologically Herculean. He asserts his power when he murders two men, one a Fascist, the other a Communist. He is so powerful that he is unconstrained by ethics or morality, acknowledging only those restraints he chooses to recognize. He victimizes others, but he is not himself tyrannized or intimidated.

The central characters of Wright's first and last novels, however, are victims, powerless people who find themselves at the mercy of others as a condition of life. Jake, of Wright's posthumously published first novel, *Lawd Today*, has no control over his condition, over the character or quality of his life. Entirely controlled by forces he neither understands nor is capable of resisting, Jake has no power or influence. Society victimizes him through the people who surround him. Fishbelly and his father, Tyree—the chief characters in Wright's last novel, *The Long Dream*—are dominated and tyrannized by the chief of police in their city. Throughout the novel the two characters are controlled to the extent that Tyree has his life taken by the chief of police and Fishbelly is arbitrarily imprisoned for two years. Neither has the power to alter the circumstances, partly because both are to some degree responsible for those circumstances. They become involved with the chief of police not because of force or coercion, but because they want the money their illegal political connections bring. The chief's contempt for them is reflected in Fishbelly's contempt for himself for willingly admitting his powerlessness to his adversary. This element of the novel caused critics to feel that Wright, who was then living in Paris, had been out of the country too long and had thus lost touch with the realities of relations between black and white in the United States. The point is not that Wright reverted to earlier models. Rather, Wright did something he had previously done in no published work: he created characters who are powerless to deal with their situation. In this way Wright's last-written novel seemed to current reviewers anachronistic.[2] Its problem was, however, that Wright had taken a perspective on his characters not unlike that taken by earlier black writers, Charles Chesnutt and Paul Lawrence Dunbar, for example.

Chesnutt, the first major black writer to write extensively about black people, wrote primarily about those whose well-being depended on the attitudes and opinions of the whites around them. Uncle Julius, the central character of *The Conjure Woman*, seeks a bare modicum of control over his life by matching wits with his employer, an exercise at which he does not often succeed. Although the action takes place in the postbellum South, the relations between Uncle Julius and his employer is not unlike that between master and slave in various folk tales in which the wit and cunning of a slave is pitted against the "superior" knowledge and culture of the slaveowner.[3] The scenario acted out rests on assumptions about where power lies; otherwise, the interaction makes no sense. The only power the slave has is the cunning of his intellect, but in Chesnutt's *Conjure Woman* tales even this minimal power is denied Uncle Julius.[4]

Not unlike other tales depicting the woes of the tragic mulatto, Chesnutt's rendition, *The House Behind the Cedars*, reveals a powerless character enmeshed in circumstances beyond her control. The situation is inherent in the notion of "tragic mulatto," for such a character is by definition powerless to solve his or her greatest problem. Of the two so-called mulattos in the novel, John and Rena Walden, only one is tragic. John's problem, that he is defined by law and custom as black in his own state, is resolved when as a very young boy, he decides he will move to a state with a different legal definition of race. The matter of race is solved for him when he says early in his life, "From this time on I am white."[5] His sister, however, is discovered to be "black," and through a series of complications finally dies of race. The very definition of her personality and character—as these relate to race—means she is powerless, unable to shield her tender and vulnerable psyche from a harsh, judgemental, racially prejudiced world. An autopsy would reveal that she died of an over-refined sensibility.

In Chesnutt's second novel, *The Marrow of Tradition*, two black characters have been touched in various ways by racism. Dr. Miller is a highly trained surgeon of aristocractic bearing, and Josh Green, an uneducated working man, whose father was murdered before his eyes by nightriders. The two are objectifications of the warring impulses within black people pointed out by W. E. B. DuBois in *The Souls of Black Folk*, the impulse to identify as Americans and the impulse to identify as black, given the reality of racism. The intensity of the tension between these two characters reflects the intensity of the impulses even in the moderate Chesnutt's mind.[6] During the beginning phases of a riot in their town, Dr. Miller, the character with whom Chesnutt is most sympathetically related, counsels the militants—working-class black people who seek among middle-class professionals for leadership—to desist, to restrain themselves, for battle can only antagonize the whites. Josh Green's retort is so devastating in its implications regarding the limitations of middle class character that it calls into question Dr. Miller's integrity,[7] his strength of character, and the entire validity of his moderate stance on racial affairs.[8]

> Come along, boys! Dese gentlemen may have somethin' ter live fer; but ez fer my pa't, I'd rather be a dead nigger any day dan a live dog!

Josh Green, because he is capable of acting and because he does not have the constraints usually attendant upon middle class status, is Bigger Thomas's prototype. He differs from Bigger in that his impetus to action has a clear and definite cause—the murder of his father by McBane. He is not afraid of whites, as Bigger is, and his violence is not random and inspired by hidden motives, as Bigger's initially is. He will not abide racial insult or abuse, and he seems fearless, ready to give up his life, if need be, to maintain his dignity. In this sense he is more akin to the characters of *Uncle Tom's Children* than to Bigger. When we first meet him, Dr. Miller is treating him for wounds received when he attacked someone who had insulted him on racial terms. The end of *The Marrow of Tradition* finds Dr. Miller with a shallow moral victory over his adversaries. Josh Green's victory is complete in that he avenges the murder of his parent, though at the cost of his life. Because of his socioeconomic class, Josh may act directly to exert influence on the world; Dr. Miller, because of his, may not. Josh therefore has a certain power not available to Dr. Miller.[9] It is this power, no matter its uses or justifications—his ability to strike out—that makes him akin to Wright's characters. He exemplifies the epigraph of *Uncle Tom's Children*: "The post Civil War household word among Negroes—'He's an Uncle Tom!'—which denoted reluctant toleration for the cringing type who knew his place before white folk, has been supplanted by a new word from another generation which says—'Uncle Tom is dead!' "

Dunbar's characters, in his only novel that bears on this subject directly, are unable to do anything about their lives. For that reason he entitled this novel, which deals with Southern rural and Northern urban existence of black people, *The Sport of the Gods*. If "we are to the gods as flies to wanton boys," then we have very little power and are in fact simply victims of powerful, capricious forces. Dunbar's characters are such victims, decimated by their experience in urban New York City. The Hamilton family breaks down in the face of urban pressures: The son murders his girl friend; the mother marries a cruel man; the daughter becomes a show girl and leads, therefore, a less than proper life. At the end of the novel, after Berry, the father, has been proved innocent and released from prison, and he returns with his wife to the small Southern community of their origin, he is still powerless, for he remains dependent on the wife of his former employer for his residence and livelihood. Thus he, like most other characters of black authors prior to Wright, has the limits of his life, the range of his action and thought, and the nature of his social intercourse (especially regarding racial relations) prescribed by forces beyond his control.

Wright's fiction differs from that of other black contemporaries and predecessors because his outlook and orientation were far more akin to naturalism than to realism or romance. He was the first black literary naturalist, which, along with considerations of personality, accounts for his uniqueness. Because he was a naturalist, Wright had a range of choices not available to black writers of romance or realism, who were tied to the conventions of these genres—conventions of plot, character, theme, and language—which dictated to a great degree the limits of their fiction. *Native Son*, in the tradition of naturalism, departs radically from romance and realism. Wright could therefore choose its particular plot with fewer constraints of decorum and propriety; he could feature lower-class characters and focus on their reactions to oppression; his characters could portray sexuality in a relatively explicit manner; he could make the world of the novel correspond as closely as he was able to life as it is.

Because Wright was leftist politically and because his thinking tended toward philosophical naturalism, he analyzed the racial situation differently from other novelists. Chesnutt, along with countless others, believed that the root of racism is color prejudice. If color prejudice were eliminated, then discrimination and all its effects would disappear. Class discrimination, Chesnutt suggests in *The Marrow of Tradition*, would not be so bad, since such distinctions as it makes would apply regardless of color.[10] *The Sport of the Gods* implies that racism is, along with all other ills befalling humankind, caused by superior forces at play in the universe. If Dunbar is taken seriously regarding the implications of his title, such an analysis is worse than useless, for it suggests that racism exists out of necessity and that, therefore, nothing can be done about it. Wright opposed these two and other black writers in their literature (with the exception of Langston Hughes)[11] in interpreting the racial situation.

Wright felt that the causes of racism are more complicated than simply the attitudes of individual whites toward blacks. In the story "Fire and Cloud," for example, the local authorities withhold food not only from blacks but from whites as well, from all the poor. The Communist organizers Hadley and Green are themselves black and white, and they organize across color lines. Wright's awareness of the complex sources of racism is reflected in his understanding, as expressed in the introduction to *Uncle Tom's Children*, "The Ethics of Living Jim Crow," that an "ethics" governs the behavior of those functioning within a racist environment. Habits of response in situations involving interaction between races become part of the social fabric. In "Big Boy Leaves Home" the characters act out preexistent roles from the moment at the pond when the white woman sees Big Boy and his friends unclothed.[12] From that point on, everyone, both black and white, knows exactly how to respond, suggesting that racism causes a mode of habitual, relational response, not unlike other habits of social interaction, and consequently becomes its own cause.

Other portions of his work indicate that Wright thought racism had causes other than the attitudes of individual racists. In "Fire and Cloud" and "Bright and Morning Star" public officials act in a racist manner—making racist statements and in the latter story perpetrating a lynching. In each case, however, the official's motivation is not racial. The officials are anti-Communists, and it is implied that they are in the service of powers whose major concern is economic, not racial. In *Native Son* it is quite clear that Mr. Dalton is not personally a racist; yet his pursuit of economic goals causes him to participate in essentially racist practices. Specifically, he is a slum landlord; he profits from renting a rat-infested apartment to the Thomas family. At the same time, he is willing to give Bigger a job and to provide ping-pong tables for the black neighborhood youth center. Mr. Dalton seems unaware of the relations among his various activities; Richard Wright knows exactly what those relations are. "The Man Who Lived Underground" begins as a story about race—Fred Daniels, a black man, is accused of murdering a white woman—but by its end, when the policeman Lawson shoots him to death, the motives are other than racial. "You've got to shoot his kind. They'd wreck things," Lawson says. "His kind" has no racial referent whatsoever. Fred Daniels has to be done away with because he no longer shares belief in a commonly held system of social values.

Because Wright was a Marxist and a naturalist, he believed that existence is not predestined and that it is possible for people to effect change in the quality of their lives. Such beliefs underlie a great deal if not all his fiction. Such is not the case with Chesnutt and Dunbar. Their work implies that the social order is a fixed entity and that adjustment is the best possible way of dealing with it. The only possible victory for Rena Walden, Dr. Miller, and Berry Hamilton is a moral victory.

A further reason Wright's fiction differed from that of his predecessors around the turn of the century and before is that attitudes toward what is presentable to the public had changed. If Crane found it necessary to publish *Maggie* pseudonymously and privately, and Dreiser's *Sister Carrie* raised questions about its suitability for public presentation, then *Native Son*'s relatively explicit display of sexuality would not have been acceptable. Other aspects of the novel would likely have been found objectionable as well. The relation between black and white depicted in the novel probably required a more liberal sense of racial relations than prevailed around the turn of the century, when editors and publishers did not seem favorably inclined toward presenting the truth, presenting the issues sympathetically toward the victims of oppression. The scenes in which Bigger dismembers Mary Dalton's body and in which he brutally murders Bessie Mears would likewise have been adjudged offensive by Victorian standards. By 1940 such things could be described in literature.

Finally, Wright differed from all who came before (and after) him because of the uniqueness of his particular personality. He was a rebel, and he refused to accept any ready-made definitions of his identity.[13] Neither Dunbar nor Chesnutt was the kind of rebel Wright was. Perhaps any black man who seriously considered the pursuit of art as a profession in the nineteenth century had to be in some sense a rebel. Wright, however, unlike his predecessors, was so rebellious that he could imagine *black power*, not only as he used the term in reference to developing African nationalism, but as it could apply to black people in the United States as well. Only a rebel mind could have conceived of Bigger Thomas and Cross Damon. It was also his rebelliousness that allowed him to conceive, contrary to black culture and tradition, of a naturalistic universe. Hence, his rebellious spirit made him the first black literary naturalist,[14] no achievement per se, but an example that broadened the possibilities of literary expression for the many black writers who came after him.

Notes

1. "When Richard Wright's *Uncle Tom's Children* was published in 1938, only the least aware did not realize that a powerful new pen was employing itself in stern and terrible material; when *Native Son* appeared in 1940, even the least aware realized it." J. Saunders Redding, "American Negro Literature," *The American Scholar*, 18 (Spring 1949), 147.

2. In retrospect it is not so clear exactly what reviewers were reacting to in their responses to *The Long Dream*. There is reason to believe that the book's timing was not insignificant, published when the country had still not moved very far away from McCarthyism. The book surely has more merit than most current reviewers granted. For an account of the responses of reviewers, see Michel Fabre, *The Unfinished Quest of Richard Wright* (New York: William Morrow, 1973), pp. 464–70.

3. The best known of these tales are the so-called John tales. John the crafty slave time after time outwits his master.

4. The reason for this is that the John tales, coming as they do out of black folk experience, are insiders' tales, the sympathy of the narrator naturally being with John. Chesnutt's audience is a different one from that assumed by the John tales, and this changes the character of the tale. They become outsiders' tales because the bond of sympathy between character and narrator is less close in Chesnutt's work. Saunders Redding in "American Negro Literature," speaks of the "objectivity" of Chesnutt's tales. They were "so detached and objective that the author's race could not have been detected from a reading of them" (p. 139).

5. *The House Behind the Cedars* (London: Collier-Macmillan, 1969), p. 155.

6. *Invisible Man* shows the interaction between these two tendencies in all its complexity. Ralph Ellison knows that the issue is far more complicated than whether any given individual is a nationalist or an assimilationist. Chesnutt's handling of the tension and Ellison's too suggest that this is not an "either/or" question.

7. Dr. Miller admires Josh because he remembers the injury done him and shapes his life to the purpose of redressing it. "When his race reached the point where they could resent a wrong, there was hope that they might soon attain the stage where they would try, and, if need be, die, to defend a right. This man, too, had a purpose in life, and was willing to die that he might accomplish it. Miller was willing to give up his life to a cause. Would he be

equally willing, he asked himself, to die for it?" *The Marrow of Tradition* (Ann Arbor, Mich.: Univ. of Michigan Press, 1969), pp. 112–13. The answer seems to be negative.

8. See Addison Gayle, Jr., *The Way of the New World* (Garden City, N.Y.: Anchor/Doubleday, 1976), p. 67. Gayle discusses the class implications of Miller's position. I believe Gayle is more harsh toward Chesnutt than he should be, because Chesnutt does not see Miller as clearly right is his judgment of what should be the proper course of action. He is never quite comfortable with Miller's choices.

9. I believe Chesnutt is fully aware of the power that Josh has, and equally aware of the limitations of Dr. Miller's position.

10. See p. 61 of *Marrow*. Gayle makes this same observation in *The Way of the New World*, p. 70.

11. Hughes certainly knew about the socioeconomic implications of racism, but he did not put himself forward as a political writer. No significant collection ("significant" referring to number of poems and pages) of his social protest literature was published during his lifetime. The full nature and character of his engagement with a Marxist analysis of the racial issue was probably not fully known by most people before the publication of *Good Morning Revolution*, Faith Berry, ed. (Westport, Conn.: Lawrence Hill, 1973). Ms. Berry's introduction to the volume reveals something of the problems attendant upon discussing Hughes as political writer.

12. I think Wright intends us to see the contrast between the spontaneity, openness, and free character of the opening scene of the story and the rigidly dictated action that proceeds as soon as "the ethics of living Jim Crow" are brought into play.

13. I did not discuss Wright's relation to the Harlem Renaissance writers because I do not see his work as deriving from theirs. They were good examples because they showed it was possible for a black writer to be published, but Wright did not model himself on any Renaissance writers. Rather, he used them in an obverse way: he would interpret the situation of black people politically, and he would not see black life as exotic or as reflective of romantic primitivism.

14. When I speak of Wright as the first black literary naturalist, I mean that he was the first black writer to bring to his writing in thoroughgoing fashion the assumptions, themes, techniques, and general orientation usually associated with literary naturalism.

"... Farther and Farther Apart": Richard Wright and James Baldwin

Fred L. Standley*

> *Richard and I drifted farther and farther apart—our dialogue became too frustrating and too acrid. . . .*
>
> "Alas, Poor Richard" (1961)

Although considerable attention has been afforded the personal and literary relationship between Richard Wright and James Baldwin in a variety of essays and books, no synthesis has yet appeared that treats comprehensively the several facets of their association. Therefore, the purposes of this essay are: (1) to present a chronology of the activities and events pertaining to their relationship, (2) to specify and summarize the principal interpretations that have been thus far advanced about that relationship, and (3) to indicate the fundamental points of disagreement between the two authors.

I CHRONOLOGY OF ACTIVITIES AND EVENTS

1945 Wright and Baldwin meet for the first time in Brooklyn. Wright reads a portion of the manuscript for Baldwin's first novel and is instrumental in helping the younger man obtain a Eugene F. Saxton Memorial Trust Fellowship "to enable new and unrecognized authors to complete books."[1]

1946 Wright is visited by Baldwin before the former leaves for Paris in April.[2]

1948 Upon arriving in Paris in November as an expatriate, Baldwin meets a "surprised and pleased" Wright in a cafe and is introduced to the editors of *Zero* magazine.[3]

*This essay was written specifically for this volume and appears here for the first time by permission of the author.

1949 Baldwin's "Everybody's Protest Novel" appears in *Zero* magazine, which is edited by a friend of Wright's. Baldwin contends that the American "protest novels"—from *Uncle Tom's Cabin* to *Native Son*—"so far from being disturbing," are "a mirror of our confusion, dishonesty, panic, trapped and immobilized in the sunlit prison of the American dream. They are fantasies. . . ." He also advocates that "Bigger is Uncle Tom's descendant, flesh of his flesh," who "admits the possibility of his being sub-human," and that "the failure of the protest novel lies in its rejection of life, the human being, the denial of his beauty, power, in its insistence that it is his categorization alone which is real and which cannot be transcended."

Wright becomes incensed by Baldwin's attack upon protest literature and believes that he and all American Negroes have been betrayed by Baldwin.[4]

1950 Wright establishes the French-American Fellowship to (1) foster better relations between French and black Americans, and (2) combat job discrimination and racism in American businesses in France. Baldwin's role in the group consists of determining from the American embassy the working conditions for black Americans in Paris. Later, in 1951, Baldwin purportedly is opposed to the group's continuation.[5]

1951 Baldwin publishes "Many Thousands Gone" in *Partisan Review*. Although praising *Native Son* as "the most powerful and celebrated statement we have yet had of what it means to be a Negro in America" and calling its author the most "eloquent spokesman" for the "new Negro," Baldwin posits that the novel ultimately reinforces "that fantastic and fearful image" that "Americans hold in their minds when they speak of the Negro," for Bigger Thomas is the "incarnation of a myth." Bigger is "the monster created by the American republic," and implies that "Negro life is in fact as debased and impoverished as our theology claims," and that "black is the color of damnation, this is his only possible end."[6]

1953 Wright and Baldwin argue about protest literature in the company of Chester Himes.[7]

1956 Wright requests that "no galleys be sent to James Baldwin, Ralph Ellison or Horace Cayton, etc., these people being not independent enough to give their honest reaction to a book like *The Color Curtain*."[8] Wright introduces Baldwin to the American delegation at the Conference of Negro-African Writers and Artists in September in Paris; Wright addresses the Conference.[9]

1957 Baldwin publishes "Princes and Powers" in *Encounter* reporting on the Conference of Negro-African Writers and Artists held in

September 1956, including Wright's address. Baldwin describes portions of it as "tactless" and "strange."[10]

Wright manages to estrange himself "from almost all of the younger American Negro writers in Paris."[11]

1959 Wright's "Island of Hallucinations," an unpublished novel completed this year, satirizes Baldwin, among others; "nowhere else, with the exception perhaps of his journal in 1947, does Wright express so openly his often extremely unflattering opinions of people he knew."[12]

1960 Wright presents a polemical lecture entitled "The Situation of the Black Artist and Intellectual in the United States" at the American Church in Paris. He argues that American society reduces "the most militant" of blacks to silence whenever they want to question the racial status quo; and he uses various personal incidents as proof, among them "the quarrels which James Baldwin and other authors had sought with him."[13]

1961 "The Exile," a memoir by Baldwin after Wright's death, appears in *Le Preuve*. The author recounts several of his personal experiences with Wright, calls him "the greatest black writer in the world for me," praises *Native Son* as "the most important and most celebrated novel of Negro life to have appeared in America," acclaims his work as "an irreducible part of the history of our swift and terrible time," acknowledges his own early perception of Wright as an "idol," not a "human being," and admits that his own role as writer generated "deep and irreconcilable differences between our points of view."[14]

Baldwin publishes "The Survival of Richard Wright" in *The Reporter*. He argues that the severest shortcoming of Wright's work is its "gratuitous and compulsive" violence, having its basis in a rage generated by the sexual myths perpetrated by the guilty imaginations of "white people who invest him with their hates and longings." Nevertheless, Baldwin extols (1) Wright's "ability to convey inward states by means of externals," (2) his portrayal of the "unrelentingly bleak landscape" not merely of the Deep South or Chicago, but "of the world, of the human heart," and (3) the development in his later work of "a new tone, and a less uncertain esthetic distance, and a new depth."[15]

"Alas, Poor Richard," Baldwin's last essay treating Wright, appears in *Nobody Knows My Name*. Baldwin recalls several incidents relating to Wright, and then suggests that (1) Wright "was among the most illustrious victims" of "the war in the breast between blackness and whiteness," and (2) that he had "a tremendous effect on countless numbers of people whom he never met." Nevertheless, Baldwin argues that Wright's attitude toward both him and others was one of rejection "against anyone who seemed to threaten Richard's system of reality." This attitude was intolerable to the younger author: "I wanted to feel that he accepted me, had accepted my right to my own vision, my right, as his equal, to disagree with him."[16]

1965 "James Baldwin . . . In Conversation," an interview made in Italy, reveals some comments about Wright:

(a) " 'Everyone's Protest Novel' came out of two years of reviewing and writing for various magazines. I can see why Wright thought it was an attack. I was only trying to get at something. The essay destroyed our friendship. It did something for me too. I reread his *Native Son* and wrote another essay."

(b) "One great difference between Wright and me is what I would call my eroticism. *Giovanni's Room* is not about homosexuality. *Another Country* is about the price you pay to make a human relationship."

(c) "In the end Wright's heart was broken."[17]

1971 Baldwin and Nikki Giovanni discuss the legacy of Wright and his impact upon other Afro-American writers.[18]

II   SOME PRINCIPAL INTERPRETATIONS

For nearly two decades now critics, artists, and reviewers have surveyed the activities and events relative to Wright and Baldwin; and they have responded in a number of ways, giving emphasis to this or that issue, but ultimately tending to favor one author or the other overall.

The Sixties

Maurice Charney's "James Baldwin's Quarrel with Richard Wright" (1963) located the source of the dispute in "the large issues of the intention and aim and values of the writer;" he favored both Baldwin's rejection of Wright's "distorted artistic truth into protest and propaganda" and his belief that *Native Son*, as a protest novel, embodied the "hard, deterministic world" of naturalism, and its attendant categorization, which denied the inherent complexity, diversity, and freedom of human experience.[19]

In the same year, Irving Howe wrote in "Black Boys and Native Sons" that Baldwin's polemical essays against Wright and school of "naturalistic" protest fiction merely evaded, "through rhetorical sweep, the genuinely difficult issue of the relationship between social experience and literature." Indeed, while professing to hope to portray "the Negro world in its diversity and richness, not as a mere spectre of protest," Baldwin had either failed to register a major success in fiction (*Go Tell It on the Mountain*) or failed to get beyond protest (*Another Country*). He is widely accepted "as one of the two or three greatest essayists this country has ever produced" primarily because his essays gain "their resonance from the tone of unrelenting protest in which they are written."[20]

Responding directly to Howe's view, Ralph Ellison, in "The World and the Jug" (1963), attacked his reliance upon the adequacy of "a sociological vision of society" and his ideas that "unrelieved suffering is the only *real* Negro experience" and that the "true Negro writer must be ferocious." Ellison argued that Howe's loyalty to Wright forced him to consider Baldwin and himself as "guilty of filial betrayal" by pretending to be "American writers" who reject the path of "black boys." Ellison further suggested that no matter how strictly blacks are segregated politically and socially, on the "level of the imagination, their ability to achieve freedom is limited only by individual aspiration, insight, energy, and will." Thus, he rejects Wright's Bigger Thomas as in any sense a "final image of Negro personality."[21]

Three years later, in 1966, four separate essays fueled the increasing controversy over the relationship between Wright and Baldwin. Saunders Redding insisted in "Since Richard Wright" that with Wright's death, there was no one to take his place; other American Negro writers deviated from "the 'Negro norm' of perception and insight, or emotion, of subject matter and point of view." He argued that Baldwin had fortfeited all claim to be a successor, because "Everybody's Protest Novel" was "a stupid attack" on protest fiction. Baldwin should have known "that all good fiction, from *Pilgrim's Progress* to *Tom Jones* to *Swann's Way*, is protest fiction. All of it is against something, even when it is not for something else. The writing of novels is not solely a 'cultural' (artistic-aesthetic) activity. The novel serves a social function as well." Consequently, Baldwin had avoided in his own fiction "the very special truths that Negroes know better than anyone else"; he had thus accepted the white man's view of the "Negro reality."[22]

In a similar vein, Eldridge Cleaver in "Notes on a Native Son" castigated Baldwin's "arrogant repudiation" of some significant dimensions of black experience: his rejection of Mailer's *The White Negro*; his "grueling, agonizing, total hatred of the blacks, particularly of himself"; and his "shameful, fanatical, fawning . . . love of whites." Cleaver perceived a "decisive quirk in Baldwin's vision which corresponds to his relationship to blacks and masculinity. It was this same quirk . . . that compelled Baldwin to . . . drive the blade of Brutus into the corpse of Richard Wright." For Cleaver, Wright's work "reigns supreme for his profound political, economic, and social reference," while that of Baldwin is "void of a political, economic, or even a social reference."[23]

Taking a somewhat different approach, Albert Murray's "Something Different, Something More" proposed that Baldwin's deriding of protest fiction and of Bigger Thomas as "Uncle Tom's descendant," who betrayed the essence of black life, implied a promise that his own work would be "not only something different but something more." Yet while Baldwin's criticism of *Native Son* was valid in revealing Wright's "false assumptions about human nature itself," his own creative works had not fulfilled his promise. Indeed, the only difference discernible from his "spiritual father" was his "special interest in themes related to the so-called sexual revolution."[24]

Using still another approach, Calvin Hernton, in "Blood of the Lamb," traced Baldwin's "hang-up" with Wright not merely to the identification and idolization of the older writer, but to "the flow in the relationship between him and his father." Baldwin longed for something deeper, something he did not get from his own father—"to love and be loved"; but "what did happen was closer to denial or indifference than to love on Wright's part." Thus, having been rebuffed and angered, Baldwin "took up his pen, and with hydrochloric pathos, dealt an avenging blow to perhaps the only black man he ever really loved."[25]

The next year, 1967, Nathan Scott endeavored to explain, in "Judgment Marked by a Cellar: The American Negro Writer and the Dialectic of Despair," that Baldwin's ostensible refusal to acclaim Wright's "protest fiction" in *Native Son*, because it failed to reveal "the disquieting complexity of ourselves," was really based on "Wright's incorrigible commitment to a violent and narrow naturalism, to an aesthetic which (in its descent from Norris and Dreiser to Dos Passos and Farrell) required the artist to view the human individual as simply an epiphenomenon of social and political process. . . ." Baldwin had been so nurtured in a tradition of "Protestant sectarian pietism," with its stern and exacting ethic, that his "sense of the multi-leveled mystery of the individual human life" also inculcated "a sense of the impossibility of containing this mystery within the reductionist formulae of a Dreiser or Dos Passos—or a Wright."[26]

In "A Defense of James Baldwin" of the same year, Addison Gayle, Jr., pointed out that Cleaver's self-appointed role of "defending Negro manhood, and avenging Richard Wright" was misplaced, for the main impact of Baldwin's critical views of Wright and Bigger Thomas is that the author allows the character "to rage on, implying that he does so as a result of environmental forces beyond his control, and that for this reason he will continue to do so." Hence, Bigger's violent rebellion was inept from the beginning, because his life was "dominated by rage" having "its origin and its life in the society"; yet, this inherently limited perspective denies that even in an oppressive environment man can have "beauty, power, and life."[27]

One year later, in 1968, Jervis Anderson ("Race, Rage and Eldridge Cleaver") replied to the Black Panther leader's attitude toward Baldwin: it had been "a mean and unfair attack . . . of such sustained nastiness" as to belie its avowal of avenging Wright. Instead, it revealed its author's way of sensationally announcing "his own arrival upon the scene";

thereby, Cleaver showed he was incapable of understanding a writer "trained and rooted in a tradition of ideas" and set forth his own "impatience with ideas, a distrust of complexity, and a certain arrogance of rhetoric, feeling, and personal style."[28]

Two last articles of the sixties worthy of mention are Donald B. Gibson's "Wright's Invisible Native Son" and B. K. Mitra's "The Wright-Baldwin Controversy." Gibson's thesis was that most critics who write about Wright's *Native Son*, including Baldwin, "do not see Bigger Thomas." While Baldwin was "the critic most responsible for the perception of Bigger Thomas as a social entity" and for the advancement of some convincing arguments about the limitations of the protest novel, he too "failed to see Bigger the person" by having misread the text and having applied an inappropriate criterion of "categorization" to the novel, which was really "a prototype of the modern existentialist novel and a link between the fiction of the 1930's and a good deal of more modern fiction."[29] Mitra, on the other hand, attempted to examine objectively "the quarrel" between the maturing son and the spiritual father over protest literature in terms of the intention, aim, and values of the individual author. Each treated the rage of being a Negro differently: whereas Wright made fiction convey "the rage itself, brutal, pure, violent and unconstrained," Baldwin wanted "to penetrate and analyze the rage and convert it into a recognizable human emotion." Consequently, Baldwin saw Bigger Thomas "as a failure" because "he is presented as a monster, a being deprived of all the attributes of human experiences" and whose compulsions to violence are never analyzed by the author.[30]

The Seventies

The decade of the seventies was ushered in by Albert Murray's "James Baldwin, Protest Fiction, and the Blues Tradition," which reiterated his earlier stance, then added that despite assertions to the contrary, Baldwin as novelist, playwright, and essayist continued to resemble Wright more than any other author. Although his original critique of *Native Son* was essentially valid, Baldwin's own work, including *Blues for Mister Charlie*, had not been "something different, something more." In fact, both he and Wright had mistaken "the illusions of social science for actuality."[31]

In "Wright, Baldwin, Cleaver" (1971) Morris Dickstein espoused the view that just as Baldwin had defined his literary position by attacking Wright, so had Cleaver recently propounded his own perspective by assaulting Baldwin. Baldwin's diatribe against *Native Son* was originally based on the New Critical theory of the novel, and his subsequent fiction was rooted in "the opposite fallacy . . . an aimless assortment of characters as threadbare masks for a purely personal set of obsessions and intensities." His notion about Wright, "that the novel has intrinsically

little to do with society," emphasized his own theme of the psychological
burden, but failed to take cognizance of the fact that "there can be no
separate peace, no private accommodation" in the face of physical and
social oppression.[32]

Michel Fabre, in *The Unfinished Quest of Richard Wright* (1973),
attributed the rupture in friendship to Baldwin's "personal problems
caused by his search for an identity and his complicated relationship with
his adopted father." Baldwin was "probably hoping that Wright would
be a kind of spiritual father to him," but at the same time was fearful of
being tagged as "second generation"; hence he asserted his differences
unequivocally. Without hope of a reconciliation after his initial statement
of views in "Everybody's Protest Novel," Baldwin allowed his essay to be
reprinted in *Profils*, a magazine published by the American Cultural Service. Since the American government was openly hostile and antagonistic
toward Wright in exile, Baldwin thus appeared to be allowing himself to
be used "in an attempt to destroy Wright's reputation."[33]

In his book *From Apology to Protest: The Black American Novel*
(1973), Noel Schraufnagel used Baldwin's stress on the "fantastic" and
"subhuman" nature of Bigger Thomas as a point of departure for
generalizing about the novels of Wright and others. He viewed Wright's
essay "How 'Bigger' Was Born" as the author's explanation for his interest
"in shaping the reaction for an audience more through exaggeration and
sensationalism than by adhering to the realistic facts of the exploitation of
ghetto inhabitants." While stressing the threat to a white society of a
figure such as Bigger, the essay did not invalidate Baldwin's essential
criticism. Schraufnagel also asserted that Ellison's *Invisible Man* and
Baldwin's *Go Tell It on the Mountain* illustrate a countertrend to
Wright's fiction, namely "an interest in describing an aspect of the black
experience without using the framework of the protest novel," a use of
protagonists "representative of twentieth century man who searches for
meaning and identity in a world that tends to alienate sensitive individuals." Nevertheless, he saw Baldwin's career as illustrating the increasing militancy of black writers of the sixties, because the author's
previous revolt against protest had become transformed in *Tell Me How
Long the Train's Been Gone* (1968), which treated the nature of existence
in a racist society.[34]

The next year, two essays appeared that questioned the credence of
Baldwin's theoretical position. Kichung Kim, in "Wright, the Protest
Novel, and Baldwin's Faith," clearly sided with Wright's contention that
"all literature is protest," and also held that for many black Americans
there was nothing "mythic about Bigger." In fact, the protagonist had
been too real, and his "mono-maniacal character accurately reflects what
happens to the urban black in America whose life is overwhelmed by the
obsessive fear, anger, and frustration caused by the daily oppression he
suffers." Baldwin's views of *Native Son* and protest fiction merely

reflected "an expression of his hope and homage to what man might be"; his later works, however, have exhibited less hope and a loss of faith, the "end to another naive dream of an innocent idealist."[35]

Dan Donlan treated the views of "Cleaver on Baldwin and Wright" and disclosed clearly how Baldwin's evaluation emanated from a different philosophical position: "Baldwin is a humanist; Wright a naturalist." Cleaver, like Wright, felt that "man is a product of society," and was alienated by Baldwin's humanistic rather than deterministic orientation. Similarly, Cleaver interpreted Wright's social involvement as "a sign of virility" and lashed out against Baldwin's homosexuality, as well as his humanism as minimizing the importance of the black power struggle.[36]

A quite different assessment of the main features of the controversy was set forth by Addison Gayle, Jr., in *The Way of the New World: The Black Novel in America* (1975). While refusing to support Baldwin's argument "that the protest novel was a useless vehicle in producing societal change," he agreed with him "in the case of protest novels written by Blacks." Gayle argued that the reason for the substantial failure of black protest fiction lay in its "appeal to the conscience of whites," not in the genre. The premise of the authors, "that Americans wanted and desired an egalitarian society in which man opted for truth and beauty over narrow interests, material gain, and selfish pursuits," had proven illusory and incorrect.[37]

"Wright, Ellison, Baldwin—Exorcising the Demon," by Jerry H. Bryant (1976), evaluated the use of political and sociological concerns as criteria for judging literary works during the "hyperactive Sixties" and concluded that the effort had "connected literature with life" and was therefore positive and healthy. Bryant explained that all three writers started from the same place—the complaint that blacks had been "cordoned off from their truest and most basic emotions and the expressions of them." For Wright, fiction had become "a way of confirming his own subjective independence, of embodying emotions that were truly his, in defiance of both the black and white habit of hiding feelings." Notwithstanding that Baldwin and Ellison had questioned "the plausibility of Bigger Thomas as an accurate representation of a real black person" because of his one-dimensionality and emotional narrowness, Wright dared to create the "hitherto undepicted image" by taking the audience—black and white—inside it. The result was "an exorcism of it," bringing what was "dark and frightening into the light, making it possible for all to address it through a higher consciousness rather than the instincts we rationalize in our prejudices." He thus became the "prophet" for the contemporary black freedom movement, attacking the sins of whites and criticizing his own people. Ellison and Baldwin, whatever their differences—the former "symbolic and allegorical," the latter "impressionistic and metaphorical"—suggested the emergence of "the black culture's complexity, a greater self-awareness, and a more intense determination to embrace their blackness as a high value and as a means for changing the face of America." Thus, Ellison became the "philosopher" with a clear, detached, logical expression of vision for blacks; and Baldwin became the "poet," giving the struggle for freedom "a deeply personal touch, a special sensitivity, a set of nerves and responses he displays to the world with a candor that sometimes verges on the embarrassing." All three writers set the stage for a new variety in the work of black novelists by engaging in "the fight to break down the stereotypes."[38]

Another essay, written in the same year, explored and supported the character of Bigger Thomas. In "Wright and *Native Son*: Not Guilty," Dorothy Redden argued fervently against three false claims about the novel: that it was too emotional, the author having been "the witless instrument of wild and overpowering feelings over which he had no control"; that it was too didactic; and that it endeavored to place a burden of guilt on its intended white audience. Contrary to the attitudes of Baldwin and others, she maintained that *Native Son* was not "choked with rage, hatred, or vengefulness," but was "taut with emotion" that was continued and transcended; that the book was propagandistic about a cause, as is all literature, but not didactic; and that the thrust of the novel was not assigning or admitting guilt, but of rejecting guilt entirely and stating the facts as they were in terms of causes and consequences.[39]

The following year, Nick Aaron Ford perceptively analyzed Wright's relationship with his younger colleague in "The Evolution of James Baldwin as Essayist" (1977). Ford disputed Baldwin's claims in "Everybody's Protest Novel" and proclaimed instead (1) that Bigger's strength was the fact that he "does not understand the deeper or higher meaning of his tragedy," which "makes the whole impact of the novel the more poignant"; and (2) that Harriet Beecher Stowe's protest masterpiece, *Uncle Tom's Cabin*, had been widely acclaimed as "a powerful force in helping to inflict the mortal wound to the slavery ethic in the United States." Against Baldwin's theses in "Many Thousands Gone," Ford argued that *Native Son* "is a graphic unraveling of incidents and attitudes that molded Bigger's private and public selves and that characterized the social milieu in which such a monstrous creature was spawned and nourished." Further, Ford declared that often the "rigid isolation" of a character, as opposed to shared community experience, "is absolutely necessary in the interest of most meaningful diagnosis." Ford's criticism of "Alas, Poor Richard" consisted of (1) what he took to be Baldwin's later recognition of his mistake in not seeing "the necessity for various kinds of protest, as a socially concerned writer struggles to bring to life the compelling vision that his personal and social experiences presage"; and (2) what Baldwin failed to include in his assessment of Wright's sojourn in Paris—the harassment by the American Secret Service, the seeming conspiracy among publishers not to accept his works, the inexplicable demise of his friendship with other exiles, especially whites, and his severe financial difficulties.[40]

At the end of the seventies, Keneth Kinnamon interpreted Baldwin's conflict with Wright as the result of "psychological pressures as much as from intellectual conviction," that is, the perception of Wright as a father figure, a surrogate for the deceased David Baldwin, who by definition had to be "rebelled against in order to establish one's own identity."[41]

Similarly, Addison Gayle, Jr., has recently analyzed Baldwin's frustration at the hands of Wright as dual: "The kind of paternal attention Baldwin needed and wanted from the older man was not forthcoming," and his desire for Wright "to also accept him as an equal, to accept his right 'to disagree with him' " was not fulfilled.[42]

III POINTS OF DISAGREEMENT

After reviewing the chronology of activities and events (including the primary sources), as well as the principal interpretations of Wright and Baldwin's personal and literary relationship, a conclusion can be reached as to the main points of disagreement between the two authors. These points can be summarized within four main areas: the perceived nature of the relationship, the question of the betrayal of friendship, the definition of the term *protest literature*, and the interpretation of the character of Bigger Thomas in *Native Son*.

Whether Baldwin's motivation for the relationship with the older writer was psychological or intellectual is a moot question. Undeniably, however, Baldwin looked upon Wright as "my ally and my witness, and alas! my father"[43] and upon the two of them as "spiritual father and spiritual son."[44] Likewise, the evidence seems clear that Wright ultimately believed that the younger man, whom he had helped in several concrete ways to launch his own literary career, had "betrayed" him by attacking *Native Son* and protest literature: "But I think he liked me. I know that I liked him, then, and later, and all the time. But I also know that, later on, he did not believe this."[45] As to the concept of protest, Wright insisted upon an aesthetic base that was infused with a sociological thrust for the direct reformation of society, believing that all literature embodies protest. Baldwin's emphasis, on the other hand, that "literature and sociology are not one and the same" seemed to suggest the need for an aesthetic distancing on the part of the author in order to prevent his works from becoming "a mirror of our confusion, dishonesty, panic . . . fantasies, connecting nowhere with reality, sentimental."[46] Consequently, within that context their radically differing views of Bigger Thomas are not surprising. Wright believed that "the environment supplies the instrumentalities through which the organism expresses itself," and that Bigger Thomas, "product of a dislocated society," a "dispossessed and disinherited man," and "conditioned as organism is, [could] not become an ardent, or even a lukewarm, supporter of the *status quo*."[47] Baldwin, on the other hand, could see Bigger only as divorced and isolated from self and community and, therefore, devoid of "significance as a social (or anti-social) unit" and serving as "the incarnation of a myth" that "has led us to believe that in Negro life there exists no tradition, no field of manners, no possibility of ritual or intercourse."[48]

In each area, the contrast in attitude and perspective between Wright and Baldwin indicates undeniably the deep and irreconcilable differences in their points of view. From the time of their first conflict following the publication of "Everybody's Protest Novel," they "drifted farther and farther apart."

Notes

1. James Baldwin, "Alas, Poor Richard," in *Nobody Knows My Name* (New York: Dial Press, 1961), pp. 191–93; Fern Marja Eckman, *The Furious Passage of James Baldwin* (Philadelphia: Lippincott, 1966), pp. 102–04; Michel Fabre, *The Unfinished Quest of Richard Wright* (New York: William Morrow, 1973), pp. 290, 589; Addison Gayle, *Richard Wright: Ordeal of a Native Son* (Garden City, N.Y.: Anchor/Doubleday, 1980), p. 181.

2. Baldwin, "Alas, Poor Richard," p. 194; Gayle, p. 187.

3. Baldwin, "Alas, Poor Richard," p. 195; Eckman, pp. 114–16; Gayle, pp. 207, 224.

4. Baldwin, "Everybody's Protest Novel," in *Notes of a Native Son* (Boston: Beacon Press, 1955), pp. 13–23; Baldwin, "Alas, Poor Richard," pp. 195–97; Eckman, pp. 121–22; Fabre, pp. 362–63; 601–02; Gayle, pp. 223–24.

5. Baldwin, "Alas, Poor Richard," pp. 205–10; Fabre, pp. 357–58; Gayle, p. 218.

6. Baldwin, "Many Thousands Gone," in *Notes of a Native Son*, pp. 24–45.

7. Baldwin, "Alas, Poor Richard," pp. 197–98; Fabre, pp. 362–63, 601–02; Gayle, pp. 236–37.

8. Fabre, p. 422.

9. Baldwin, "Princes and Powers," in *Nobody Knows My Name*, pp. 36, 46–48.

10. Baldwin, "Princes and Powers," pp. 46–48.

11. Baldwin, "Alas, Poor Richard," p. 167; Gayle, p. 280.

12. Fabre, p. 479.

13. Fabre, p. 518.

14. Baldwin, "Alas, Poor Richard," pp. 190–99.

15. Baldwin, "Alas, Poor Richard," pp. 181–89.

16. Baldwin, "Alas, Poor Richard," pp. 200–15.

17. Interview with Dan Georgakas, in *Black Voices: An Anthology of Afro-American Literature*, ed. Abraham Chapman (New York: New American Library, 1968), p. 666.

18. *James Baldwin, Nikki Giovanni: A Dialogue* (Philadelphia: Lippincott, 1973), pp. 16–17; 64–65; 76–77; 80–81.

19. *American Quarterly*, 15 (Spring 1963), 65–75.

20. *Dissent*, 10 (Autumn 1963), 353–68.

21. *New Leader*, 46 (9 Dec. 1963), 22–26.

22. *African Forum*, 1 (Spring 1966), 21–23.

23. *Ramparts*, 5 (June 1966), 51–56.

24. *Anger and Beyond: The Negro Writer in the United States*, ed. Herbert Hill (New York: Harper & Row, 1966), pp. 112–37.

25. *White Papers for White Americans* (New York: Doubleday, 1966), pp. 122–47.

26. *Denver Quarterly*, 2 (Summer 1967), 5–35.

27. *Negro History Bulletin*, 20 (April 1967), 15–16.

28. *Commentary*, 46 (Dec. 1968), 63–69.

29. *American Quarterly*, 21 (Winter 1969), 728–38.

30. *Indian Journal of American Studies*, 1 (1969), 101–05.

31. *The Omni-Americans: New Perspectives on Black Experience and American Culture* (New York: Outerbridge & Dienstfrey, 1970), pp. 142–70.

32. *Partisan Review*, 38 (Winter 1970), 376–86.

33. Fabre, pp. 362–63.

34. (Deland, Fla.: Everett/Edwards, 1973), pp. 30–31; 70; 87–90.

35. *College Language Association Journal*, 17 (March 1974), 387–96.

36. *Clearing House*, 48 (April 1974), 508–09.

37. (New York: Anchor/Doubleday, 1976), pp. 217–19.

38. *Nation*, 223 (3 July 1976), 25–27.

39. *Negro American Literature Forum*, 10 (Winter 1976), 111–15.

40. *James Baldwin: A Critical Evaluation*, ed. Therman O'Daniel (Washington: Howard Univ. Press, 1977), pp. 85–104.

41. "James Baldwin," in *American Writers: A Collection of Literary Biographies*, Supplement I, ed. Leonard Unger (New York: Scribner's, 1979), p. 51.

42. Gayle, pp. 222–24.

43. Baldwin, "Alas, Poor Richard," p. 191.

44. Baldwin, "Alas, Poor Richard," p. 201.

45. Baldwin, "Alas, Poor Richard," p. 193.

46. Baldwin, "Everybody's Protest Novel," pp. 19–23.

47. Richard Wright, "How 'Bigger' Was Born," in *Twentieth Century Interpretations of "Native Son,"* ed. Houston A. Baker, Jr. (Englewood Cliffs, N.J.: Prentice-Hall, 1972), pp. 21–47.

48. Baldwin, "Many Thousands Gone," pp. 28–29.

ESSAYS ON FICTION

Many Thousands Gone

James Baldwin[*]

It is only in his music, which Americans are able to admire only because a protective sentimentality limits their understanding of it, that the Negro in America has been able to tell his story. It is a story which otherwise has yet to be told and which no American is prepared to hear. As is the inevitable result of things unsaid, we find ourselves until today oppressed with a dangerous and reverberating silence; and the story is told, compulsively, in symbols and signs, in hieroglyphics; it is revealed in Negro speech and in that of the white majority and in their different frames of references. The ways in which the Negro has affected the American psychology is betrayed in our popular culture and in our morality; in our estrangement from him is the depth of our estrangement from ourselves. We cannot ask: what do we *really* feel about him?—such a question merely opens the gates on chaos. What we really feel about him is involved with all that we feel about everything, about everyone, about ourselves.

The story of the Negro in America is the story of America—or, more precisely, it is the story of Americans. It is not a very pretty story: the story of a people is never very pretty. The Negro in America, gloomily referred to as that shadow which lies athwart our national life, is far more than that. He is a series of shadows, self-created, intertwining, which now we helplessly battle. One may say that the Negro in America does not really exist except in the darkness of our minds.

This is why his history and his progress, his relationship to all other Americans, has been kept in the social arena. He is a social and not a personal or human problem; to think of him is to think of statistics, slums, rapes, injustices, remote violence; it is to be confronted with an endless cataloguing of losses, gains, skirmishes; it is to feel virtuous, outraged, helpless, as though his continuing status among us were somehow analogous to disease—cancer, perhaps, or tuberculosis—which must be checked, even though it cannot be cured. In this arena the black man acquires quite another aspect from that which he has in life. We do not know what to do with him in life; if he breaks our sociological and sen-

[*]Reprinted from *Notes of a Native Son* (Boston: Beacon Press, 1955), pp. 24–45, by James Baldwin, by permission of the Beacon Press, © 1951, 1955 by James Baldwin. "Many Thousands Gone" appeared originally in *Partisan Review*, 18 (Nov.–Dec. 1951), 665–80.

timental image of him we are panic-stricken and we feel ourselves betrayed. When he violates this image, therefore, he stands in the greatest danger (sensing which, we uneasily suspect that he is very often playing a part for our benefit); and, what is not always so apparent but is equally true, we are then in some danger ourselves—hence our retreat or our blind and immediate retaliation.

Our dehumanization of the Negro then is indivisible from our dehumanization of ourselves; the loss of our own identity is the price we pay for our annulment of his. Time and our own force act as our allies, creating an impossible, a fruitless tension between the traditional master and slave. Impossible and fruitless because, literal and visible as this tension has become, it has nothing to do with reality.

Time had made some changes in the Negro face. Nothing has succeeded in making it exactly like our own, though the general desire seems to be to make it blank if one cannot make it white. When it has become blank, the past as thoroughly washed from the black face as it has been from ours, our guilt will be finished—at least it will have ceased to be visible, which we imagine to be much the same thing. But, paradoxically, it is we who prevent this from happening; since it is we who, every hour that we live, re-invest the black face with our guilt; and we do this—by a further paradox, no less ferocious—helplessly, passionately, out of an unrealized need to suffer absolution.

Today, to be sure, we know that the Negro is not biologically or mentally inferior; there is no truth in those rumors of his body odor or his incorrigible sexuality; or no more truth than can be easily explained or even defended by the social sciences. Yet, in our most recent war, his blood was segregated as was, for the most part, his person. Up to today we are set at a division, so that he may not marry our daughters or our sisters, nor may he—for the most part—eat at our tables or live in our houses. Moreover, those who do, do so at the grave expense of a double alienation; from their own people, whose fabled attributes they must either deny or, worse, cheapen and bring to market; from us, for we require of them, when we accept them, that they at once cease to be Negroes and yet not fail to remember what being a Negro means: to remember, that is, what it means to us. The threshold of insult is higher or lower, according to the people involved, from the boot-black in Atlanta to the celebrity in New York. One must travel very far, among saints with nothing to gain or outcasts with nothing to lose, to find a place where it does not matter—and perhaps a word or a gesture or simply a silence will testify that it matters even there.

For it means something to be a Negro, after all, as it means something to have been born in Ireland or in China, to live where one sees space and sky or to live where one sees nothing but rubble or nothing but high buildings. We cannot escape our origins, however hard we try, those origins which contain the key—could we but find it—to all that we later become. What it means to be a Negro is a good deal more than this essay can discover; what it means to be a Negro in America can perhaps be suggested by an examination of the myths we perpetuate about him.

Aunt Jemima and Uncle Tom are dead, their places taken by a group of amazingly well-adjusted young men and women, almost as dark, but ferociously literate, well-dressed and scrubbed; who are never laughed at, who are not likely ever to set foot in a cotton or tobacco field or in any but the most modern of kitchens. There are others who remain in our odd idiom, 'underprivileged'; some are bitter and these come to grief; some are unhappy, but, continually presented with the evidence of a better day soon to come, are speedily becoming less so. Most of them care nothing whatever about race. They want only their proper place in the sun and the right to be left alone, like any other citizen of the republic. We may all breathe more easily. Before, however, our joy at the demise of Aunt Jemima and Uncle Tom approaches the indecent, we had better ask whence they sprang, how they lived? Into what limbo have they vanished?

However inaccurate our portraits of them were, these portraits do suggest, not only the conditions but the quality of their lives and the impact of this spectacle on our consciences. There was no one more forbearing than Aunt Jemima, no one stronger or more pious or more loyal or more wise; there was, at the same time, no one weaker or more faithless or more vicious and certainly no one more immoral. Uncle Tom, trustworthy and sexless, needed only to drop the title "Uncle" to become violent, crafty and sullen, a menace to any white woman who passed by. They prepared our feast tables and our burial clothes; and if we could boast that we understood them, it was far more to the point and far more true that they understood us. They were, moreover, the only people in the world who did; and not only did they know us better than we knew ourselves, but they knew us better than we knew them. This was the piquant flavoring to the national joke, it lay behind our uneasiness as it lay behind our benevolence: Aunt Jemima and Uncle Tom, our creations, at the last evaded us; they had a life—their own, perhaps a better life than ours—and they would never tell us what it was. At the point where we were driven most privately and painfully to conjecture what depths of contempt, what heights of indifference; what prodigies of resilience, what untamable superiority allowed them so vividly to endure, neither perishing, nor rising up in a body to wipe us from the earth, the image perpetually shattered and the word failed. The black man in our midst carried murder in his heart, he wanted vengeance. We carried murder too, we wanted peace.

In our image of the Negro breathes the past we deny, not dead but living yet and powerful, the beast in our jungle of statistics. It is this which defeats us, which continues to defeat us, which lends to inter-racial cocktail parties their rattling, genteel, nervously smiling air: in any draw-

ing room at such a gathering the beast may spring, filling the air with flying things and an unenlightened wailing. Wherever the problem touches
there is confusion, there is danger. Wherever the Negro face appears a
tension is created, the tension of a silence filled with things unutterable. It
is a sentimental error, therefore, to believe that the past is dead; it means
nothing to say that it is all forgotten, that the Negro himself has forgotten
it. It is not a question of memory. Oedipus did not remember the thongs
that bound his feet, nevertheless the marks they left testified to that doom
toward which his feet were leading him. The man does not remember the
hand that struck him, the darkness that frightened him, as a child; nevertheless, the hand and the darkness remain with him, indivisible from
himself forever, part of the passion that drives him wherever he thinks to
take flight.

The making of an American begins at that point where he himself rejects all other ties, any other history; and himself adopts the vesture of his
adopted land. This problem has been faced by all Americans throughout
our history—in a way it *is* our history—and it baffles the immigrant and
sets on edge the second generation until today. In the case of the Negro the
past was taken from him whether he would or no; yet to forswear it was
meaningless and availed him nothing, since his shameful history was carried, quite literally, on his brow. Shameful; for he was heathen as well as
black and would never have discovered the healing blood of Christ had
not we braved the jungles to bring him these glad tidings. Shameful; for,
since our role as missionary had not been wholly disinterested, it was
necessary to recall the shame from which we had delivered him in order
more easily to escape our own. As he accepted the alabaster Christ and the
bloody cross—in the bearing of which he would find his redemption, as,
indeed, to our outraged astonishment, he sometimes did—he must,
henceforth, accept that image we then gave him of himself: having no
other and standing, moreover, in danger of death should he fail to accept
the dazzling light thus brought into such darkness. It is this quite simple
dilemma that must be borne in mind if we wish to comprehend his
psychology.

However we shift the light which beats so fiercely on his head, or
prove, by victorious social analysis, how his lot has changed, how we have
both improved, our uneasiness refuses to be exorcized. And nowhere is
this more apparent than in our literature on the subject—'problem'
literature when written by whites, 'protest' literature when written by
Negroes—and nothing is more striking than the tremendous disparity of
tone between the two creations. *Kingsblood Royal* bears, for example,
almost no kinship to *If He Hollers Let Him Go*, though the same reviewers
praised them both for what were, at bottom, very much the same reasons.
These reasons may be suggested, far too briefly but not at all unjustly, by
observing that the presupposition is in both novels exactly the same: black
is a terrible color with which to be born into the world.

Now the most powerful and celebrated statement we have yet had of what it means to be a Negro in America is unquestionably Richard Wright's *Native Son*. The feeling which prevailed at the time of its publication was that such a novel, bitter, uncompromising, shocking, gave proof, by its very existence, of what strides might be taken in a free democracy; and its indisputable success, proof that Americans were now able to look full in the face without flinching the dreadful facts. Americans, unhappily, have the most remarkable ability to alchemize all bitter truths into an innocuous but piquant confection and to transform their moral contradictions, or public discussion of such contradictions, into a proud decoration, such as are given for heroism on the field of battle. Such a book, we felt with pride, could never have been written before—which was true. Nor could it be written today. It bears already the aspect of a landmark; for Bigger and his brothers have undergone yet another metamorphosis; they have been accepted in baseball leagues and by colleges hitherto exclusive; and they have made a most favorable appearance on the national screen. We have yet to encounter, nevertheless, a report so indisputably authentic, or one that can begin to challenge this most significant novel.

It is, in a certain American tradition, the story of an unremarkable youth in battle with the force of circumstance; that force of circumstance which plays and which has played so important a part in the national fables of success or failure. In this case the force of circumstance is not poverty merely but color, a circumstance which cannot be overcome, against which the protagonist battles for his life and loses. It is, on the surface, remarkable that this book should have enjoyed among Americans the favor it did enjoy; no more remarkable, however, than that it should have been compared, exuberantly to Dostoevsky, though placed a shade below Dos Passos, Dreiser and Steinbeck; and when the book is examined, its impact does not seem remarkable at all, but becomes, on the contrary, perfectly logical and inevitable.

We cannot, to begin with, divorce this book from the specific social climate of that time: it was one of the last of those angry productions encountered in the late 'twenties and all through the 'thirties dealing with the inequities of the social structure of America. It was published one year before our entry into the last world war—which is to say, very few years after the dissolution of the W.P.A. and the end of the New Deal and at a time when bread lines and soup kitchens and bloody industrial battles were bright in everyone's memory. The rigors of that unexpected time filled us not only with a genuinely bewildered and despairing idealism— so that, because there at least was *something* to fight for, young men went off to die in Spain—but also with a genuinely bewildered self-consciousness. The Negro, who had been during the magnificent 'twenties a passionate and delightful primitive, now became, as one of the things we were most self-conscious about, our most oppressed minority. In the 'thirties, swallowing Marx whole, we discovered the Worker and realized—I should think with some relief—that the aims of the Worker and the aims of the Negro were one. This theorem—to which we shall return—seems now to leave rather too much out of account; it became, nevertheless, one of the slogans of the "class struggle" and the gospel of the New Negro.

As for this New Negro, it was Wright who became his most eloquent spokesman; and his work, from its beginning, is most clearly committed to the social struggle. Leaving aside the considerable question of what relationship precisely the artist bears to the revolutionary, the reality of man as a social being is not his only reality and that artist is strangled who is forced to deal with human beings solely in social terms; and who has, moreover, as Wright had, the necessity thrust on him of being the representative of some thirteen million people. It is a false responsibility (since writers are not congressmen) and impossible, by its nature, of fulfillment. The unlucky shepherd soon finds that, so far from being able to feed the hungry sheep, he has lost the wherewithal for his own nourishment: having not been allowed—so fearful was his burden, so present his audience!—to recreate his own experience. Further, the militant men and women of the 'thirties were not, upon examination, significantly emancipated from their antecedents, however bitterly they might consider themselves estranged or however gallantly they struggled to build a better world. However they might extol Russia, their concept of a better world was quite helplessly American and betrayed a certain thinness of imagination, a suspect reliance on suspect and badly digested formulae, and a positively fretful romantic haste. Finally, the relationship of the Negro to the Worker cannot be summed up, nor even greatly illuminated, by saying that their aims are one. It is true only insofar as they both desire better working conditions and useful only insofar as they united their strength as workers to achieve these ends. Further than this we cannot in honesty go.

In this climate Wright's voice first was heard and the struggle which promised for a time to shape his work and give it purpose also fixed it in an ever more unrewarding rage. Recording his days of anger he has also nevertheless recorded, as no Negro before him had ever done, that fantasy Americans hold in their minds when they speak of the Negro: that fantastic and fearful image which we have lived with since the first slave fell beneath the lash. This is the significance of *Native Son* and also, unhappily, its overwhelming limitation.

Native Son begins with the *Brring!* of an alarm clock in the squalid Chicago tenement where Bigger and his family live. Rats live there too, feeding off the garbage, and we first encounter Bigger in the act of killing one. One may consider that the entire book, from that harsh *Brring!* to Bigger's weak "Good-by" as the lawyer, Max, leaves him in the death cell, is an extension, with the roles inverted, of this chilling metaphor. Bigger's situation and Bigger himself exert on the mind the same sort of fascination. The premise of the book is, as I take it, clearly conveyed in these first pages: we are confronting a monster created by the American republic and we are, through being made to share his experience, to receive illumination as regards the manner of his life and to feel both pity and horror at his awful and inevitable doom. This is an arresting and potentially rich idea and we would be discussing a very different novel if Wright's execution had been more perceptive and if he had not attempted to redeem a symbolical monster in social terms.

One may object that it was precisely Wright's intention to create in Bigger a social symbol, revelatory of social disease and prophetic of disaster. I think, however, that it is this assumption which we ought to examine more carefully. Bigger has no discernible relationship to himself, to his own life, to his own people, nor to any other people—in this respect, perhaps, he is most American—and his force comes, not from his significance as a social (or anti-social) unit, but from his significance as the incarnation of a myth. It is remarkable that, though we follow him step by step from the tenement room to the death cell, we know as little about him when this journey is ended as we did when it began; and, what is even more remarkable, we know almost as little about the social dynamic which we are to believe created him. Despite the details of slum life which we are given, I doubt that anyone who has thought about it, disengaging himself from sentimentality, can accept this most essential premise of the novel for a moment. Those Negroes who surround him, on the other hand, his hard-working mother, his ambitious sister, his poolroom cronies, Bessie, might be considered as far richer and far more subtle and accurate illustrations of the ways in which Negroes are controlled in our society and the complex techniques they have evolved for their survival. We are limited, however, to Bigger's view of them, part of a deliberate plan which might not have been disastrous if we were not also limited to Bigger's perceptions. What this means for the novel is that a necessary dimension has been cut away; this dimension being the relationship that Negroes bear to one another, that depth of involvement and unspoken recognition of shared experience which creates a way of life. What the novel reflects—and at no point interprets—is the isolation of the Negro within his own group and the resulting fury of impatient scorn. It is this which creates its climate of anarchy and unmotivated and unapprehended disaster; and it is this climate, common to most Negro protest novels, which has led us all to believe that in Negro life there exists no tradition, no field of manners, no possibility of ritual or intercourse, such as may, for example, sustain the Jew even after he has left his father's house. But the fact is not that the Negro has no tradition but that there has as yet arrived no sensibility sufficiently profound and tough to make this tradition articulate. For a tradition expresses, after all, nothing more than the long and painful experience of a people; it comes out of the battle waged to maintain their integrity or, to put it more simply, out of their struggle to survive. When we speak of the Jewish tradition we are speaking of centuries of exile and persecution, of the strength which endured and the sensibility which discovered in it the high possibility of the moral victory.

This sense of how Negroes live and how they have so long endured is hidden from us in part by the very speed of the Negro's public progress, a progress so heavy with complexity, so bewildering and kaleidoscopic, that he dare not pause to conjecture on the darkness which lies behind him; and by the nature of the American psychology which, in order to apprehend or be made able to accept it, must undergo a metamorphosis so profound as to be literally unthinkable and which there is no doubt we will resist until we are compelled to achieve our own identity by the rigors of a time that has yet to come. Bigger, in the meanwhile, and all his furious kin, serve only to whet the notorious national taste for the sensational and to reinforce all that we now find it necessary to believe. It is not Bigger whom we fear, since his appearance among us makes our victory certain. It is the others, who smile, who go to church, who give no cause for complaint, whom we sometimes consider with amusement, with pity, even with affection—and in whose faces we sometimes surprise the merest arrogant hint of hatred, the faintest, withdrawn, speculative shadow of contempt—who make us uneasy; whom we cajole, threaten, flatter, fear; who to us remain unknown, though we are not (we feel with both relief and hostility and with bottomless confusion) unknown to them. It is out of our reaction to these hewers of wood and drawers of water that our image of Bigger was created.

It is this image, living yet, which we perpetually seek to evade with good works; and this image which makes of all our good works an intolerable mockery. The 'nigger,' black, benighted, brutal, consumed with hatred as we are consumed with guilt, cannot be thus blotted out. He stands at our shoulders when we give our maid her wages, it is his hand which we fear we are taking when struggling to communicate with the current 'intelligent' Negro, his stench, as it were, which fills our mouths with salt as the monument is unveiled in honor of the latest Negro leader. Each generation has shouted behind him, *Nigger!* as he walked our streets; it is he whom we would rather our sisters did not marry; he is banished into the vast and wailing outer darkness whenever we speak of the 'purity' of our women, of the 'sanctity' of our homes, of 'American' ideals. What is more, he knows it. He is indeed the 'native son': he is the 'nigger.' Let us refrain from inquiring at the moment whether or not he actually exists; for we *believe* that he exists. Whenever we encounter him amongst us in the flesh, our faith is made perfect and his necessary and bloody end is executed with a mystical ferocity of joy.

But there is a complementary faith among the damned which involves their gathering of the stones with which those who walk in the light shall stone them; or there exists among the intolerably degraded the perverse and powerful desire to force into the arena of the actual those fantastic crimes of which they have been accused, achieving their vengeance and their own destruction through making the nightmare real. The American image of the Negro lives also in the Negro's heart; and when he has surrendered to this image life has no other possible reality. Then he, like the white enemy with whom he will be locked one day in mortal struggle, has no means save this of asserting his identity. This is why Bigger's murder of Mary can be referred to as an "act of creation" and why, once this murder has been committed, he can feel for the first time that he is living fully and deeply as a man was meant to live. And there is, I should think, no Negro living in America who has not felt, briefly or for long periods, with anguish sharp or dull, in varying degrees and to varying effect, simple, naked and unanswerable hatred; who has not wanted to smash any white face he may encounter in a day, to violate, out of motives of the cruelest vengeance, their women, to break the bodies of all white people and bring them low, as low as that dust into which he himself has been and is being trampled; no Negro, finally, who has not had to make his own precarious adjustment to the 'nigger' who surrounds him and to the 'nigger' in himself.

Yet the adjustment must be made—rather, it must be attempted, the tension perpetually sustained—for without this he has surrendered his birthright as a man no less than his birthright as a black man. The entire universe is then peopled only with his enemies, who are not only white men armed with rope and rifle, but his own far-flung and contemptible kinsmen. Their blackness is his degradation and it is their stupid and passive endurance which makes his end inevitable.

Bigger dreams of some black man who will weld all blacks together into a mighty fist, and feels, in relation to his family, that perhaps they had to live as they did precisely because none of them had ever done anything, right or wrong, which mattered very much. It is only he who, by an act of murder, has burst the dungeon cell. He has made it manifest that *he* lives and that his despised blood nourishes the passions of a man. He has forced his oppressors to see the fruit of that oppression: and he feels, when his family and his friends come to visit him in the death cell, that they should not be weeping or frightened, that they should be happy, *proud* that he has dared, through murder and now through his own imminent destruction, to redeem their anger and humiliation, that he has hurled into the spiritless obscurity of their lives the lamp of his passionate life and death. Henceforth, they may remember Bigger—who has died, as we may conclude, for them. But they do not feel this; they only know that he has murdered two women and precipitated a reign of terror; and that now he is to die in the electric chair. They therefore weep and are honestly frightened—for which Bigger despises them and wishes to 'blot' them out. What is missing in his situation and in the representation of his psychology—which makes his situation false and his psychology incapable of development—is any revelatory apprehension of Bigger as one of the Negro's realities or as one of the Negro's roles. This failure is part of the previously noted failure to convey any sense of Negro life as a continuing and complex group reality. Bigger, who cannot function therefore as a reflection of the social illness, having, as it were, no society to reflect, likewise refuses to function on the loftier level of the Christ-symbol. His kinsmen are quite right to weep and be frightened, even to be appalled: for it is not his love for them or for himself which causes him to die, but his hatred and his self-hatred; he does not redeem the pains of a despised people, but reveals, on the contrary, nothing more than his own fierce bitterness at having been born one of them. In this also he is the "native son," his progress determinable by the speed with which the distance increases between himself and the auction-block and all that the auction-block implies. To have penetrated this phenomenon, this inward contention of love and hatred, blackness and whiteness, would have given him a stature more nearly human and an end more nearly tragic; and would have given us a document more profoundly and genuinely bitter and less harsh with an anger which is, on the one hand, exhibited and, on the other hand, denied.

Native Son finds itself at length so trapped by the American image of Negro life and by the American necessity to find the ray of hope that it cannot pursue its own implications. This is why Bigger must be at the last redeemed, to be received, if only by rhetoric, into that community of phantoms which is our tenaciously held ideal of the happy social life. It is the socially conscious whites who receive him—the Negroes being capable of no such objectivity—and we have, by way of illustration, that lamentable scene in which Jan, Mary's lover, forgives him for her murder; and, carrying the explicit burden of the novel, Max's long speech to the jury. This speech, which really ends the book, is one of the most desperate performances in American fiction. It is the question of Bigger's humanity which is at stake, the relationship in which he stands to all other Americans—and, by implication, to all people—and it is precisely this question which it cannot clarify, with which it cannot, in fact, come to any coherent terms. He is the monster created by the American republic, the present awful sum of generations of oppression; but to say that he is a monster is to fall into the trap of making him subhuman and he must, therefore, be made representative of a way of life which is real and human in precise ratio to the degree to which it seems to us monstrous and strange. It seems to me that this idea carries, implicitly, a most remarkable confession, that is, that Negro life is in fact as debased and impoverished as our theology claims; and, further, that the use to which Wright puts this idea can only proceed from the assumption—not entirely unsound—that Americans, who evade, so far as possible, all genuine experience, have therefore no way of assessing the experience of others and no way of establishing themselves in relation to any way of life which is not their own. The privacy or obscurity of Negro life makes that life capable, in our imaginations, of producing anything at all; and thus the idea of Bigger's monstrosity can be presented without fear of contradiction, since no American has the knowledge or authority to contest it and no Negro has the voice. It is an idea, which, in the framework of the novel, is dignified by the possibility it promptly affords of presenting Bigger as the herald of disaster, the danger signal of a more bitter time to come when not Bigger alone but all his kindred will rise, in the name of the many thousands who have perished in fire and flood and by rope and torture, to demand their rightful vengeance.

But it is not quite fair, it seems to me, to exploit the national innocence in this way. The idea of Bigger as a warning boomerangs not only because it is quite beyond the limit of probability that Negroes in America will ever achieve the means of wreaking vengeance upon the state but also because it cannot be said that they have any desire to do so. *Native Son* does not convey the altogether savage paradox of the American Negro's situation, of which the social reality which we prefer with such hopeful superficiality to study is but, as it were, the shadow. It is not simply the relationship of oppressed to oppressor, of master to slave, nor is it motivated merely by hatred; it is also, literally and morally, a *blood* relationship, perhaps the most profound reality of the American experience, and we cannot begin to unlock it until we accept how very much it contains of the force and anguish and terror of love.

Negroes are Americans and their destiny is the country's destiny. They have no other experience besides their experience on this continent and it is an experience which cannot be rejected, which yet remains to be embraced. If, as I believe, no American Negro exists who does not have his private Bigger Thomas living in the skull, then what most significantly fails to be illuminated here is the paradoxical adjustment which is perpetually made, the Negro being compelled to accept the fact that this dark and dangerous and unloved stranger is part of himself forever. Only this recognition sets him in any wise free and it is this, this necessary ability to contain and even, in the most honorable sense of the word, to *exploit* the 'nigger' which lends to Negro life its high element of the ironic and which causes the most well-meaning of their American critics to make such exhilarating errors when attempting to understand them. To present Bigger as a warning is simply to reinforce the American guilt and fear concerning him, it is most forcefully to limit him to that previously mentioned social arena in which he has no human validity, it is simply to condemn him to death. For he has always been a warning, he represents the evil, the sin and suffering which we are compelled to reject. It is useless to say to the courtroom in which this heathen sits on trial that he is their responsibility, their creation, and his crimes are theirs; and that they ought, therefore, to allow him to live, to make articulate to himself behind the walls of prison the meaning of his existence. The meaning of his existence has already been most adequately expressed, nor does anyone wish, particularly not in the name of democracy, to think of it any more; as for the possibility of articulation, it is this possibility which above all others we most dread. Moreover, the courtroom, judge, jury, witnesses and spectators, recognize immediately that Bigger is their creation and they recognize this not only with hatred and fear and guilt and the resulting fury of self-righteousness but also with that morbid fullness of pride mixed with horror with which one regards the extent and power of one's wickedness. They know that death is his portion, that he runs to death; coming from darkness and dwelling in darkness, he must be, as often as he rises, banished, lest the entire planet be engulfed. And they know, finally, that they do not wish to forgive him and that he does not wish to be forgiven; that he dies, hating them, scorning that appeal which they cannot make to that irrecoverable humanity of his which cannot hear it; and that he *wants* to die because he glories in his hatred and prefers, like Lucifer, rather to rule in hell than serve in heaven.

For, bearing in mind the premise on which the life of such a man is based, *i.e.*, that black is the color of damnation, this is his only possible end. It is the only death which will allow him a kind of dignity or even, however horribly, a kind of beauty. To tell this story, no more than a single aspect of the story of the 'nigger,' is inevitably and richly to become involved with the force of life and legend, how each perpetually assumes the guise of the other, creating that dense, many-sided and shifting reality which is the world we live in and the world we make. To tell his story is to begin to liberate us from his image and it is, for the first time, to clothe this phantom with flesh and blood, to deepen, by our understanding of him and his relationship to us, our understanding of ourselves and of all men.

But this is not the story which *Native Son* tells, for we find here merely, repeated in anger, the story which we have told in pride. Nor, since the implications of this anger are evaded, are we ever confronted with the actual or potential significance of our pride; which is why we fall, with such a positive glow of recognition, upon Max's long and bitter summing up. It is addressed to those among us of good will and it seems to say that, though there are whites and blacks among us who hate each other, we will not; there are those who are betrayed by greed, by guilt, by blood lust, but not we; we will set our faces against them and join hands and walk together into that dazzling future when there will be no white or black. This is the dream of all liberal men, a dream not at all dishonorable, but, nevertheless, a dream. For, let us join hands on this ,mountain as we may, the battle is elsewhere. It proceeds far from us in the heat and horror and pain of life itself where all men are betrayed by greed and guilt and blood-lust and where no one's hands are clean. Our good will, from which we yet expect such power to transform us, is thin, passionless, strident: its roots, examined, lead us back to our forebears, whose assumption it was that the black man, to become truly human and acceptable, must first become like us. This assumption once accepted, the Negro in America can only acquiesce in the obliteration of his own personality, the distortion and debasement of his own experience, surrendering to those forces which reduce the person to anonymity and which make themselves manifest daily all over the darkening world.

Native Son:
The Personal, Social, and
Political Background

Keneth Kinnamon*

In the fiction of social protest, of which Richard Wright's *Native Son* (1940) is surely an outstanding example, the *donnée* has an interest almost equal to that of the artistic treatment. If the concern is with the relation of literature to society, one must not be content merely to grant the novelist his materials and concentrate on his fictional technique; one must examine carefully the factual substance on which the novelist's imagination operates. If this task is preliminary to literary criticism in the strict sense, it is necessary if that criticism is not to be impressionistic or narrowly aesthetic. An examination of Wright's fiction reveals that customarily he drew from experience and observation, the condition of the society about him, and his theoretic concerns. In *Native Son*, these elements may be identified respectively as certain episodes in Wright's life in Mississippi and Chicago, the social circumstances of urban Negroes and the Nixon trial, and Communist ideology.

Charles I. Glicksberg is speaking hyperbolically when he asserts that "Richard Wright is Bigger Thomas—one part of him anyway. Bigger Thomas is what Richard Wright, had circumstances worked out differently, might have become."[1] Nevertheless, there is some truth in the assertion, and not merely in the general sense, according to the formulation of James Baldwin, that "no American Negro exists who does not have his private Bigger Thomas living in the skull."[2] The general similarities between Wright at the age of twenty and the fictional protagonist of *Native Son* are obvious enough: both are Mississippi-born Negroes who migrated to Chicago; both live with their mother in the worst slums of the Black Belt of that city; both are motivated by fear and hatred; both are rebellious by temperament; both could explode into violence.[3]

More specific likenesses were recovered from Wright's subconscious by Dr. Frederic Wertham, the eminent psychiatrist. When Wright, as a boy of fifteen, worked for a white family named Bibbs in Jackson, Mississippi, his duties included chopping wood, carrying coal, and tend-

*Reprinted from *Phylon*, 30 (Spring 1969), 66–72, by permission of the journal.

ing the fire. The pretty young daughter of the family generally was kind to him within the limits of Southern custom, but when, on one occasion, he chanced upon her in her bedroom while she was dressing, "she reprimanded him and told him to knock before entering a room." The diffident and fearful young Negro handyman, the amiable white girl, the sexually significant situation—these elements, transmuted, found their way into *Native Son.* The name of the wealthy white family for whom Bigger works in the novel, *Dalton*, may itself bear an unconscious symbolic import. In the Chicago hospital where he worked as an orderly in 1931, Wright learned of Daltonism.[3] In their fashion, the Daltons in the novel strive toward color blindness, though they fall tragically short of achieving it.

Essentially, Bigger Thomas is a conscious composite portrait of a number of individual Negroes Wright had observed over the years. In that remarkable exercise in self-examination, *How "Bigger" Was Born*, Wright sketched five such Bigger prototypes he had known in the South. All of them were rebellious defiers of the jim crow order, and all of them suffered for their insurgency: "They were shot, hanged, maimed, lynched, and generally hounded until they were either dead or their spirits broken." In Chicago, especially when Wright worked at the South Side Boys' Club in the middle thirties, he observed other examples of the Bigger Thomas type—fearful, restless, moody, frustrated, alienated, violent youths struggling for survival in the urban jungle.[4]

The slum conditions of the South Side so vividly portrayed in *Native Son* had been the daily reality of a decade in Wright's life (1927–1937). He had lived in a cramped and dirty flat with his aunt, mother, and brother. He had visited hundreds of similar dwellings while working as an insurance agent.[5] The details of the Chicago environment in the novel have a verisimilitude that is almost photographic. The "Ernie's Kitchen Shack" of the novel, located at Forty-Seventh Street and Indiana Avenue, for example, is a slight disguise for an actual restaurant called "The Chicken Shack," 4647 Indiana Avenue, of which one Ernie Henderson was owner.[6] Similar documentary accuracy is observed throughout the book.

Aside from wide personal experience, moreover, Wright was becoming increasingly more interested in sociology at the time he was writing *Native Son*. The caseworker for the Wright family in Chicago was Mary Wirth, the wife of Louis Wirth of the University of Chicago, who was in the process of conducting an enormous research project on the urban ecology of the city. In Wirth's office Wright examined the files of the project and met Horace R. Cayton, a Negro research associate who was himself to become a distinguished sociologist and a warm friend of the novelist.[7] Sociological concepts, quite as much as Marxist theories, are apparent in the novel, especially in the final part.

In New York, too, where he moved in May, 1937, Wright became intimately acquainted with the conditions of Negro ghettos. Not only did he live for almost a year in Harlem, but as a participant in the Federal Writers' Project of New York City, he wrote the Harlem sections of *New York Panorama* (1938) and *New York City Guide* (1939), two volumes in the American Guide Series. He also served during the last five months of 1937 as chief Harlem correspondent for the *Daily Worker*, contributing forty signed articles as well as numerous brief, unsigned dispatches. A fourth of the signed articles deal with hardships of life in Harlem. In one of these Wright reported on a hearing conducted by the New York State Temporary Commission on Conditions Among Urban Negroes. The questioning of Henry Dalton about his real estate policies by Boris Max in the last part of *Native Son* draws directly from this article.[8]

As if to confirm Wright's notions about the Bigger type and society's attitude toward him, when the writer "was halfway through the first draft of *Native Son* a case paralleling Bigger's flared forth in the newspapers of Chicago."[9] This case involved Robert Nixon and Earl Hicks, two young Negroes with backgrounds similar to that of Bigger. According to the first of a long series of highly sensationalistic articles in the *Chicago Tribune*, on May 27, 1938, Mrs. Florence Johnson "was beaten to death with a brick by a colored sex criminal . . . in her apartment."[10] Nixon and Hicks were arrested soon after and charged with the crime. Though no evidence of rape was adduced, the *Tribune* from the beginning called the murder a sex crime and exploited fully this apparently quite false accusation.[11] Nixon was chosen for special attack, perhaps because he was darker and ostensibly less remorseful than Hicks. He was referred to repeatedly as the "brick moron," "rapist slayer," "jungle beast," "sex moron," and the like. His race was constantly emphasized. The casual reader of *Native Son* might consider the newspaper article which Bigger reads in his cell early in Book Three greatly exaggerated in its racism;[12] in point of fact, it is an adaptation of an actual piece in the *Tribune*. Although Nixon came from "a pretty little town in the old south—Tallulah, La.," the *Tribune* reporter wrote, "there is nothing pretty about Robert Nixon. He has none of the charm of speech or manner that is characteristic of so many southern darkies." The reporter proceeded to explain:

> That charm is a mark of civilization, and so far as manner and appearance go, civilization has left Nixon practically untouched. His hunched shoulders and long, sinewy arms that dangle almost to his knees; his out-thrust head and catlike tread all suggest the animal.
> He is very black—almost pure Negro. His physical characteristics suggest an earlier link in the species.
> Mississippi river steamboat mates, who hire and fire roustabouts by the hundreds, would classify Nixon as a jungle Negro. They would hire him only if they were sorely in need of

rousters. And they would keep close watch on him. This type is known to be ferocious and relentless in a fight. Though docile enough under ordinary circumstances, they are easily aroused. And when this happens the veneer of civilization disappears.

. . . .

As he talked yesterday Nixon's dull eyes lighted only when he spoke of food. They feed him well at the detective bureau, he said. He likes coconut pie and strawberry pop. It was after a generous meal of these refreshments that he confessed two of his most shocking murders. . . . These killings were accomplished with a ferocity suggestive of Poe's "Murders in the Rue Morgue"—the work of a giant ape.

Again the comparison was drawn between Nixon and the jungle man. Last week when he was taken . . . to demonstrate how he had slain Mrs. Florence Johnson, mother of two small children, a crowd gathered and there were cries of: "Lynch him! Kill him!"

Nixon backed against a wall and bared his teeth. He showed no fear, just as he has shown no remorse.[13]

The article concludes by quoting from a letter from the Louisiana sheriff of Nixon's home parish: "It has been demonstrated here that nothing can be done with Robert Nixon. Only death can cure him."[14]

This remedy was applied almost exactly a year after the murder of Mrs. Johnson. During this year the case became something of a local *cause célebrè*. The Chicago police quickly accused Nixon of a number of other murders, and the Los Angeles police did the same.[15] Early in the case the International Labor Defense became interested, providing Attorney Joseph Roth, white, to aid Negro lawyers in representing Nixon and Hicks.[16] Public emotion ran very high, stimulated by the lurid treatment given the case by the *Tribune*. A week after the crime the Illinois House of Representatives "approved a bill sponsored by State's Attorney Thomas J. Courtney of Cook County to curb moronic attacks." In debate on this bill, Nixon was mentioned prominently.[17] A complicated series of confessions and repudiations, charges of police brutality, and dramatic outbursts of violence[18] preceded the trial, which began in late July under Judge John C. Lewe after attorneys for the youths won a change of venue because of the prejudiced atmosphere.[19] The trial itself, despite some apparently contradictory evidence, was very brief, lasting just over a week before the jury reached a verdict of guilty on the first ballot after only one hour of deliberation. The death sentence was imposed on Nixon.[20] By this time, however, leaders of the Chicago Negro community were thoroughly aroused. The National Negro Congress, which had been providing legal representation for the two youths, continued its efforts on their behalf, including the sponsorship of a fundraising dance.[21] Prominent Chicago Negro clergymen joined the struggle to save Nixon.[22] With the aid of such support, together with some irregularities in the evidence presented by the state, Nixon was able to win several stays of execution, but his struggle ceased in the Cook County electric chair three minutes after midnight, June 16, 1939.[23]

By the time Nixon was finally executed, Wright had completed *Native Son*. He did not need to wait the outcome of legal appeals and maneuvers to know the "Fate" (his title for Book Three of the novel) of Robert Nixon or of his fictional counterpart, Bigger Thomas. In any event, Wright's use of the Nixon case was that of a novelist, not that of an historian or journalist. He adapted whatever seemed useful to his fictional purpose, changing details as he wished. He followed the facts of the case fairly closely in his account of the newspaper treatment of Bigger Thomas. The inquest and trial scenes, also, resemble in certain respects their factual prototypes. Among the more significant distortions of Nixon material are those relating to Wright's polemic intent as a communist writer.

In the Nixon case the role of the International Labor Defense and its representative, Attorney Joseph Roth, was small and initiatory; it was soon replaced by the National Negro Congress. In *Native Son*, however, Wright magnifies the role of this organization (changing its name slightly to "Labor Defenders") and its radical Jewish attorney, Boris Max, who is made Bigger's sole lawyer. Another change illustrates even more vividly Wright's shift of emphasis in transforming fact to fiction. One of the murders for which Chicago police elicited confessions, later repudiated, from Nixon was that of a Mrs. Florence Thompson Castle a year before the murder of Mrs. Johnson. According to a newspaper report, in his account of this crime Nixon "told of picking up a lipstick belonging to Mrs. Castle and scrawling on the dresser mirror these words: 'Black Legion.' "[24] When Bigger in the novel wishes to divert suspicion to an extremist group, he selects leftists rather than fascists, signing the kidnap note to the Daltons in such a way as to implicate the Communist Party (p. 151).

As a fervent party member, Wright maintained a thoroughly communistic point of view in *Native Son*. The courtroom arguments of Max in the final section, of course, are patently leftist. He equates racial and class prejudice, both being based on economic exploitation (pp. 326–27). He repeats the basic party concept of the times regarding the collective status of Negroes in America: "Taken collectively, they are not simply twelve million people; in reality they constitute a separate nation, stunted, stripped, and held captive *within* this nation, devoid of political, social, economic, and property rights" (p. 333). He discerns in Bigger a revolutionary potentiality (pp. 337–38). Not all of Max's courtroom speech reflects so directly communist doctrine, but none of it is inconsistent with the party line on racial matters.

Communist material is obvious enough in the final section of the novel, but it is often implicit elsewhere. Early in Book One, for example, while Bigger and his friend Gus are loafing on the street they amuse themselves by "playing white," assuming roles of the white power structure. The youths are themselves nonpolitical, but the white activities Wright has them imitate are precisely those which he and other communists viewed as typical of the American capitalist system: warfare, high finance, and political racism (pp. 15–17). For Bigger's mother, religion is clearly presented as an opiate, as it is generally for the Negro masses. To accept the consolations of Christianity, Bigger comes to recognize, would be to lay "his head upon a pillow of humility and [give] up his hope of living in the world" (p. 215). The first movie that Bigger and a friend see in Book One, *The Gay Woman*, presents a Hollywood stereotype of a communist as a wild-eyed bomb thrower (pp. 27–28). Indeed, prejudice against communists is frequently depicted in the novel. On the other hand, party members Jan Erlone[25] and Boris Max are idealized portraits of selfless, noble, dedicated strivers toward the new social order.

These, then, are the main elements that went into the composition of *Native Son*. Much of the powerful sense of immediacy felt by the reader of the novel derives from the genesis of the work in the author's personal experience and observation. Though one may have reservations about the validity of Wright's communist ideological orientation, it provided him with an intellectual instrument with which to render meaningful the personal and social materials of the novel. The nice balance of subjective and objective elements in *Native Son* prevents the work from becoming either a purely personal scream of pain, on the one hand, or a mere ideological tract on the other. Whatever verdict one may finally reach about the artistic merits of *Native Son*, one must take into account the personal, social, and political materials out of which it grew.

Notes

1. "The Furies in Negro Fiction," *The Western Review*, XIII (Winter, 1949), 110.

2. "Many Thousands Gone," *Partisan Review*, XVIII (November-December, 1951), 678. This essay is reprinted in James Baldwin, *Notes of a Native Son* (Boston, 1955), pp. 24–45.

3. Waldemar Kaempffert, "Science in Review: An Author's Mind Plumbed for the Unconscious Factor in the Creation of a Novel," *The New York Times*, September 24, 1944, Sec. 4, p. 11. This article asserts that the Bibbs girl loaned Wright money for his junior high school graduation suit, but Wright's autobiographical *Black Boy: A Record of Childhood and Youth* (New York, 1945) says that her mother did so (p. 156). Dr. Wertham comments briefly on his experiment with Wright in "The Dreams That Heal," his introduction to *The World Within: Fiction Illuminating Neuroses of Our Time*, ed. by Mary Louise Aswell (New York, 1947), xxi.

4. *How "Bigger" Was Born* (New York, 1940), pp. 6, 28–29. See also Wright's pamphlet *The Negro and Parkway Community House* (Chicago, 1941).

5. The main source for this period of the novelist's life is Richard Wright, "Early Days in Chicago," *Cross-Section 1945*, ed. by Edwin Seaver (New York, 1945), pp. 306–42. This essay is reprinted, with minor changes, as "The Man Who Went to Chicago" in Wright's *Eight Men* (Cleveland and New York, 1961), pp. 210–50.

6. Advertisement, *The Chicago Defender*, January 8, 1938, p. 3.

7. Horace R. Cayton, *Long Old Road* (New York, 1965), pp. 247–48. Cayton gives further details in a symposium on Wright included in *Anger and Beyond: The Negro Writer in the United States*, ed. by Herbert Hill (New York, 1966), pp. 196–97. Having written the finest fictional portrayal of the South Side, Wright was the inevitable choice of Cayton and St. Clair Drake to write the introduction to their classic sociological treatise on the area, *Black Metropolis* (1945).

8. "Gouging, Landlord Discrimination Against Negroes Bared at Hearing," *Daily Worker*, December 15, 1937, p. 6. Cf. *Native Son* (New York, 1940), pp. 276–79. Parenthetical page references in the text are to this edition.

9. *How "Bigger" Was Born*, pp. 30–31.

10. "Sift Mass of Clews for Sex Killer," *Chicago Daily Tribune*, May 28, 1938, p. 1.

11. David H. Orro, a Negro reporter, wrote that police stated that Nixon and Hicks were "bent upon committing a sex crime," but that "authorities were unable to state whether the woman had been sexually attacked." " 'Somebody Did It.' So 2 Youths Who 'Might Have Done It' Are Arrested," *The Chicago Defender*, May 28, 1938, p. 24. The date as printed is an error; this is actually the issue of June 4, 1938.

12. Hubert Creekmore, the white novelist from Mississippi, charged that "the press is shown as chiefly concerned with unsubtle inspiration of hatred and intolerance. The manner and content of these newspapers exceed belief. Again Mr. Wright makes them present incidents and ideas which reflect his own mind rather than an editor's mind or the public mind." "Social Factors in *Native Son*," *The University of Kansas City Review*, VII (Winter, 1941), 140.

13. Charles Leavelle, "Brick Slayer Is Likened to Jungle Beast," *Chicago Sunday Tribune*, June 5, 1938, Sec. 1, p. 6. Cf. *Native Son*, pp. 238–40.

14. Leavelle, p. 6.

15. "Science Traps Moron in 5 Murders," *Chicago Daily Tribune*, June 3, 1938, p. 1.

16. "Robert Nixon Attacked By Irate Hubby," *The Chicago Defender*, June 11, 1938, p. 6.

17. "Pass Courtney Moron Bill In Heated Debate," *Chicago Daily Tribune*, June 8, 1938, p. 1.

18. When Nixon and Hicks were taken by police to the scene of the crime, a hostile, lynch-minded mob required police control. Then "a dramatic incident occurred just as the police were about to leave with their prisoners. Elmer Johnson, the bereaved husband . . . drove up with his two children, and his brother-in-law, John Whitton . . . Johnson said nothing, but Whitton clenched his fists and shouted, 'I'd like to get at them.' Police hurried the prisoners away." "2 Accuse Each Other in Brick Killing," *Chicago Daily Tribune*, May 30, 1938, p. 2. Perhaps Elmer Johnson was merely waiting for a better opportunity, for, at the inquest he attacked the handcuffed Nixon savagely before police intervened. Shortly after this attack, Nixon attempted to retaliate. Johnson explained his intention to a reporter: "I hoped to hit him hard enough so his head would fly back and his skull would be cracked against the wall." "Beats Slayer of Wife; Own Life Menaced," *Chicago Daily Tribune*, June 8, 1938, p. 3. See also "Robert Nixon Attacked By Irate Hubby," p. 6, Cf. the incident in *Native Son* in which Bigger is attacked at the inquest (p. 265).

19. "Brick Slayers' Trial Assigned To Judge Lewe," *Chicago Daily Tribune*, July 19, 1938, p. 6.

20. "Guilty of Brickum Gets Death In Chair," *Chicago Daily Tribune*, August 5, 1938, p. 3.

21. "Dance Profits To Aid Nixon, Hicks," *The Chicago Defender*, August 20, 1938, p. 5.

22. "Nixon Plea To Be Given To Governor," *The Chicago Defender*, October 15, 1938, p. 6.

23. "Nixon Dies In Chair," *The Chicago Defender*, June 17, 1939, pp. 1–2.

24. "Brick Moron Tells of Killing 2 Women," *Chicago Sunday Tribune*, May 29, 1938, p. 5.

25. Wright may have taken the first name from that of Jan Wittenber, a white friend who was active in the Chicago John Reed Club and served as secretary of the Illinois State International Labor Defense.

The Short Stories:
Uncle Tom's Children;
Eight Men

Edward Margolies*

Although Richard Wright's fame as an author of fiction rests chiefly on the impact of his Chicago novel, *Native Son*, he first came to the attention of the general reading public with the appearance of a collection of five of his stories about life in the rural South, *Uncle Tom's Children*.[1] The great publicity attendant on the publication of *Native Son* has obscured the fact that Wright focused so many of his fictional settings in the South—and that his "southern" stories are perhaps his best artistic achievement. Moreover, it is in these stories that the reader may find the theme, the structure, the plot, and the ideational content of all his later fictional work. Although Wright, when he wrote these stories, was a convinced Communist, it is revealing how related they are to the later phases of intellectual and political development. Here, for example, one finds Wright's incipient Negro nationalism as each of his protagonists rises to strike out violently at white oppressors who would deny him his humanity. More significantly his Negro characters imagine whites as "blurs," "bogs," "mountains," "fire," "ice," and "marble." In none of these stories do his heroes act out of a sense of consciously arrived at ideology (most of them, as a matter of fact, are ignorant of Marxism), but rather out of an innate, repressed longing for freedom—or sometimes merely as an instinctive means of self-survival. Often the act of violence carries along with it a sudden revelatory sense of self-awareness—an immediate knowledge that the world in which the protagonist dwells is chaotic, meaningless, purposeless, and that he, as a Negro, is "outside" this world and must therefore discover his own life by his lonely individual thoughts and acts. We find thus in these first short stories a kind of black nationalism wedded to what has been called Wright's existentialism—the principal characteristics of Wright's last phase of political and philosophical thinking.

Paradoxically, Wright's Marxism seldom intrudes in an explicit didactic sense (although it was to do so on occasion in his later works, even after he left the Party). Perhaps this was because he had so ingested

*Reprinted from Edward Margolies, *The Art of Richard Wright* (Carbondale: Southern Illinois Univ. Press, 1969), pp. 57–89, by permission of the publisher. Copyright © 1969 by the Southern Illinois Univ. Press.

128

the concepts of struggle and conflict as being the central facts of life that he had little need to remind himself that the strife he was describing was ideological. Although Marxist dialectic must have provided Wright with a clear-cut arena on which he could observe the struggle of the oppressed and the oppressors, the reader is left with the nagging feeling that this was not quite the same way in which the Communists saw the class struggle in the 1930's. (In this connection it is interesting to note that some years later Wright admitted some Communist officials asked him if he really wrote the book.) To be sure, Communists are viewed in a kindly light in the last two of Wright's stories, but they are only remotely instrumental in effecting his heroes' discovery of themselves and their world. Oddly enough, in three of the stories ("Down by the Riverside," "Fire and Cloud," and "Bright and Morning Star"), Wright's simple Negro peasants arrive at their sense of self-realization by applying basic Christian principles to the situations in which they find themselves. In only one ("Bright and Morning Star"), does a character convert to Communisim—and then only when she discovers Communism is the modern translation of the primitive Christian values she has always lived. There is a constant identification in these stories with the fleeing Hebrew children of the Old Testament and the persecuted Christ—and mood, atmosphere, and settings abound in Biblical nuances. Wright's characters die like martyrs, stoic and unyielding, in their new-found truth about themselves and their vision of a freer, fuller world for their posterity. Sarah, of "Long Black Song," lost in her dreams of love and simple understanding among men, stands as the primitive prototype of the madonna as she suckles her infant at her breast. The spare, stark accounts of actions and their resolution are reminiscent in their simplicity and their cadences of Biblical narrations. The floods, the songs, the sermons, the hymns reinforce the Biblical analogies and serve, ironically, to highlight the uselessness and inadequacy of Christianity as a means of coping with the depression-ridden, racist South. Even the reverse imagery of white-evil, black-good is suggestive in its simple organization of the forces which divide the world in Old Testament accounts of the Hebrews' struggle for survival.

In *Uncle Tom's Children*, unlike most modern short stories, the complexities of the narrative line, the twists and turns of the plot are essential for an understanding of the characters' feelings and the nuances of their emotions. As opposed to the stories of Chekhov or Joyce, say, a good deal "happens" in Wright's short stories. The reasons are clear when one considers the kind of characters Wright is dealing with. They are, for the most part, uneducated, inarticulate, and have had neither the time nor inclination to cultivate or verbalize their feelings in their terrible struggle for physical survival. Hence Wright must show them for what they are in terms of their reactions to certain situations—particularly in situations where violence and rank injustices cry out for immediate decisions. They are sometimes in flight after having killed a white person—and their recognition of their hatred is their first sense of freedom. Often Wright describes their mood in terms of a raging landscape or sunlit fields or the desolate sky which feeds upon their senses and draws out their hearts in the actions they perform. But more often he is successful in delineating their character by means of the dialogue they employ. Since their vocabularies are limited, they are compelled to convey meaning in terms of gesture, tone, and voice volume. Folk idiom and rhythms are maintained as much as possible (spelling is often phonetic) and conversations are rendered in dialect. To indicate shouts, significant voice emphases, or jarring revelations, Wright frequently spells out his words in upper case letters. (A Negro who has been forcibly separated from his dying wife in order to work on the flood-threatened levee shouts out his anguish, "AHM TIRED! LEMME GO WID MAH FOLKS, PLEASE!") Sounds of violence which are so much a part of their lives and consciousness are recreated onomato-poetically. Rifles "CRACK!," whips "whick," white terrorists creep up on their prey in the wet grass "cush-cush," exploding steam is rendered "Pseeeezzzzzzzzzzzzzzzzzzz . . ." Again Wright suggests the kind of characters they are by songs they sing. The raucous, bawdy adolescents of "Big Boy Leaves Home" sing snatches from the Negro "Dirty Dozens." Sarah, the mother earth figure of "Long Black Song" croons lullabies to her sleeping child and makes love to the surging rhythms of a gospel song. Sue, the mother of two adult sons, in "Bright and Morning Star" is converted to Communism because the Communist vision of a better life satisfies her deeply imbued religious nature, represented by a hymn which she sings over and over again half to herself throughout the story.

Although Wright's characters move toward a kind of inevitable doom because they have violated the impossible conditions of their caste, their tragedy, as Edwin Berry Burgum points out, is not a result of an implacable nemesis wreaking vengeance on an ungovernable pride.[2] Rather is it a kind of final irony that once they have come to a recognition of themselves and a realization of the world that made them, they are destroyed physically. Yet their "short happy lives" have not been lived in vain; the vision of a humanity at peace with itself and free to explore its potentialities completes the tone of Wright's short stories.

There is a thematic progression in these stories, each of which deals with the Negro's struggle for survival and freedom. In the first story, flight is described—and here Wright is at his artistic best, fashioning his taut, spare prose to the movements and thoughts of the fugitive. In "Big Boy Leaves Home," four truant adolescent boys are discovered naked by a white woman as they trespass in a swimming hole forbidden to Negroes. The woman's escort kills two of them, but the other two manage to overcome him and kill him. The narrative now centers on Big Boy, the leader of the group, who flees home, and is advised by the leaders of the Negro community (that is, the deacons of the Negro church) to conceal himself in a kiln on the hills outside of town until morning when a truck driver will pick him up and drive him to Chicago. The boy manages to scramble in the dark to the hiding place, and while there views the brutal burning of his comrade who had escaped with him. The following morning the Negro truck driver arrives and Big Boy escapes.

The pathos of the story lies in the precariousness of the lives of the Negro community. The story opens on an American dream setting—an idyllic country atmosphere—carrying echoes of Mark Twain and *Peck's Bad Boy* as the four boys push, jostle, wrestle, joke, and sing their way to the swimming hole. But the results of their joy and zest are the death of three of the boys, the destruction of Big Boy's house and Big Boy's lonely flight to the big city. Hence Wright sets up a situation whose simplicity and innocence ring a nostalgic appeal in the reader—and then jars the reader into a sense of horror when he comes to realize what such a situation can mean if Negroes are involved. For Big Boy and his friends are not merely simple, unassuming fellows with picturesque ways of expressing themselves. They are bawdy and vulgar; they tell inane jokes; they are neither committed nor uncommitted to a way of life; they are aware only of themselves and the limits of their own pleasure. Their fate is moving not because they are extraordinary, but because they are so commonplace. To be sure Big Boy is a cut above his companions, yet despite his developing maturity, at the moment of truth he remains a boy—and there is a skillful interplay of the boy-man aspects of Big Boy's character (perhaps his name is significant) in the latter part of the story.

Wright is particularly good at depicting terror and Big Boy's changing reactions to his situation not only by means of interior monologue but by describing Big Boy's movements as well. When, for example, Big Boy arrives at the kiln, he discovers he must first kill a snake that has ensconced itself in the depths of the pit. Somehow the startling confrontation with the snake and the methodical, impassioned manner in which Big Boy destroys it suggest at one and the same time his terror and burning hatred of the whites. Later, now safely in the hole himself, he fantasies killing whites in just the same way as he killed the snake—whipping them, stamping on them, and kicking their heads against the sand. His dreams of glory—an ironic comment on the usual order of the boys' fantasies—are headlines in which he imagines himself described as the killer of twenty white lynchers.

Although "Big Boy" is a relatively long story, the rhythm of events is swift, and the time consumed from beginning to end is less than twenty-four hours. The prose is correspondingly fashioned to meet the pace of the plot. The story is divided into five parts, each of which constitutes a critical episode in Big Boy's progress from idyll, through violence, to misery, terror, and escape. As the tension mounts, Wright employs more and more of a terse and taut declarative prose, fraught with overtones and meanings unspoken—reminiscent vaguely of the early Hemingway.

> Will pushed back a square trapdoor [of the truck] which
> swung above the back of the driver's seat. Big Boy pulled

through, landing with a thud on the bottom. On hands and knees he looked around in the semi-darkness.
"Wheres Bobo?'"
Big Boy stared.
"Wheres Bobo?"
"They got im."
"When?"
"Las night."
"The mob?"
Big Boy pointed in the direction of a charred sapling on the slope of the opposite hill. Will looked. The trapdoor fell. The engine purred, the gears whined, and the truck lurched forward over the muddy road, sending Big Boy on his side.[3]

Big Boy's escape was effected through the will of the oppressed Negro community despite obvious risks. Wright's concept of this community—extending beyond the Negro world—clasping hands with its white oppressed brothers, informs the very essence of a developing social vision in the other stories of *Uncle Tom's Children*. And though Wright's world falls far short of ever fulfilling this vision, the dream lives on ironically stronger with every tragic failure of his heroes to realize their humanity.

"Down by the Riverside," the next story in the collection, is not nearly so successful. If flight (as represented by "Big Boy Leaves Home") is one aspect of the Negro's struggle for survival in the South, Christian humility, forbearance, courage, and stoic endurance are the themes of Wright's second piece. But here the plot becomes too contrived; coincidence is piled upon coincidence, and the inevitability of his protagonist's doom does not ring quite true. The story relates the odyssey of Brother Mann, his pregnant wife, small son, and mother-in-law, who set out in a stolen boat at a time when the Mississippi is overflowing its banks, drowning villages and farms—in order to find a Red Cross hospital where his wife can safely deliver her child. One of the houses he passes on his perilous trek is owned by the proprietor (Heartfield) of the stolen boat, who tries to kill him. Mann, in self defense, shoots back and kills Heartfield. When later he arrives at the hospital, he learns that his wife is dead. He is next separated from his son and mother-in-law and conscripted to set sandbags on the levee. When the levees break down, he is sent back to the hospital, where he is put to work aiding the survivors to escape. Afterwards he is put on a small boat with another Negro to search for people who might still be inhabiting their floating homes. The first house to which he is sent belongs to none other than Heartfield whose son and wife recognize him as the killer. Mann considers killing them, but the course of events changes his mind and he ultimately rescues them. When they reach the safety of the hills, the Heartfields tell the white citizenry who he is, and he is shot.

Despite the virtuosity of Wright's prose style which lends a certain plausibility to Mann's adventures, the plot is overladen with events and symbols that appear to foreshadow Mann's doom. Brother Mann (the name is obviously symbolic), along with the others in the family sings "Down by the Riverside," at his wife's bedside just prior to their journey. Although the song rings an ironic counterpart to what happens to Mann later, the words are hardly appropriate to the occasion ("Ahm gonna lay down mah sword n shiel/Down by the riverside/Ah ain gonna study war no mo.") That Mann's boat should float past Heartfield's house is perhaps a legitimate turn of the events but that the Heartfields would recognize Mann in the darkness on the raging waters is stretching credibility. Again, that Mann should later be sent to Heartfield's home to rescue the family strikes one as contrived, as does the occasion when Mann, axe in hand, prepared to kill the family, is prevented from doing so by a sudden tilting of the house on the waters which throws him off balance. Finally, that the Heartfields should turn him in as a murderer without making some extenuating comments about him as their rescuer seems almost unbelievable even for the most rabid Mississippi white racist.

Yet, there is a certain epic quality to the piece—man steadily pursuing his course against a malevolent nature, only to be cut down later by the ingratitude of his fellow men—that is suggestive of Twain or Faulkner. And Mann's long-suffering perseverance and stubborn will to survive endow him with a rare mythic Biblical quality. Wright even structures his story like a Biblical chronicle, in five brief episodes, each displaying in its way Mann's humble courage against his fate. But if Mann's simple Christian virtues failed to save him, it was in part because the ground had not yet been laid on which these virtues might flourish. The recognition that the bourgeois ethic is incapable of providing men with the possibility of fulfilling themselves is an element of Wright's next story.

The plot of "Long Black Song" is relatively simple. A white travelling salesman seduces a young Negro farm mother (Sarah) whose husband has gone to the town to buy provisions. When Silas returns home, he discovers her betrayal and attempts to whip her. She flees, but steals quietly back to recover her infant. The following day the salesman returns with a white friend. Silas horsewhips one and kills the other. Later, Sarah, watching from a distance observes a posse of lynchers burn down the house in which Silas has entrenched himself, but not before he has succeeded in killing one or two others. The success of the story, perhaps Wright's best, lies in the successful integration of plot, imagery, and character which echo the tragic theme of Silas's doomed awareness of himself and the inadequacy of the bourgeois values by which he has been attempting to live. Silas's recognition is his death knell, but he achieves a dignity in death that he had never known in life. His sexual jealousies arouse his long repressed burning racial enmities, and he comes to realize that the sacrifices he has been making for the past ten years to buy his own farm are all meaningless in the face of a scale of values that allows for the selfish exploitation and manipulation of people. The caste system has made the bourgeois dream of owning his own farm impossible, and he is made to see the wider implications of his own life. For the past ten years he has been living an illusion; the denial of human dignity in race relations renders freedom and independence unattainable in any sphere of human activities.

> 'The white folks ain never gimme a chance. They ain never give no black man a chance! There ain nothin in yo whole life yuh kin keep from em! They take you lan! They take yo freedom! They take you women! N then they take yo life.'⁴

When he decides to fight it out, he is determined, at least, to become the master of his own death. Silas is more worldly, less instinctive than his wife. Steeped as he is in middle-class values, he regards his wife as his personal property and the sanctity of marriage as inviolable. Yet when his revelation comes, he achieves truly tragic stature.

It is Sarah, though, who is the most memorable portrayal in the story. The narrative unfolds from her point of view—and she becomes, at the end, a kind of deep mother earth character, registering her primal instincts and reactions to the violence and senselessness she sees all about her. But for all that, she remains beautifully human—her speech patterns and thoughts responding to an inner rhythm, somehow out of touch with the foolish strivings of men, yet caught up in her own melancholy memories and desires. As she moves through her lonely day she remembers Tom, her former lover, now gone from her in the war (the time is just after World War I), the only person whom she had ever really loved. Wright conveys her mood and memories and vagaries of character in sensuous color imagery—while certain cadences suggest perhaps Gertrude Stein whom Wright regarded as one of his chief influences. (Indeed "Melanctha" may have been the prototype of Sarah.) Later as she is being seduced by the salesman, Wright fuses images of the seasons, the days and nights, the lush colors, and the earth rhythm into a condensed and brilliant evocation of her nature.

> A liquid metal covered her and she rode on the curve of white bright days and dark black nights and the surge of the long gladness of summer and the ebb of the deep dream of sleep in winter till a high red wave of hotness drowned her in a deluge of silver and blue that boiled her blood and blistered her *flesh bangbangbang*.⁵

Sarah is Wright's most lyrical achievement, and Silas, her husband, Wright's most convincing figure of redemption. Yet Silas's redemption is at best a private affair—and the Negro's plight is no better as a result of his own determination to fight his oppressors with their own weapons. He is hopelessly outnumbered. A recognition that the white and black oppressed share a common human heritage is the theme of Wright's next story.

"Fire and Cloud" takes place during the Depression and deals with the efforts of a Negro minister, the Reverend Taylor, to acquire food relief for the near starving Negro community of a medium sized southern town. For some reason, not made altogether clear, the white civic leaders have been refusing help and a protest march is being planned (a number of poor whites are expected to participate) in order to make them change their minds. The march, significantly, is being organized by two Communists, a white and a Negro, who hope to persuade Taylor to join them in sponsoring the demonstration. Meanwhile the mayor, who has granted Taylor some favors in the past, the police chief, and Lowe, the chief of the industrial squad (an anti-Communist committee, presumably) are putting pressure on the minister to dissuade his followers from marching. Although Taylor refuses to sponsor the parade, he says he will march with his parishioners if they wish him to do so. The night before the demonstration is to take place, he is kidnapped by a group of whites and brutally horsewhipped. Instead of breaking Taylor's will, the lashing serves to inspire him with a new vision. God's will can best be realized by mass social action. The demonstration on an integrated basis takes place with Taylor leading his followers. The Mayor, observing its success, relents and promises the poor their food. Success

Although "Fire and Cloud' won Wright the *Story* magazine prize, it is the weakest piece in the collection. Wright too often resorts to stereotype. The individual whites in imagery and fact are all of one piece—icy, cold, hard, and malevolent; the blacks, simple, unassuming, trusting and God-fearing, but driven to their desperate actions by the hunger they feel in their bodies. Even the black Judas in their midst, the Deacon Smith, who sides with the white authorities, is motivated only by his desire to take the Reverend Taylor's place as minister of the church. The story line itself, divided into thirteen separate sections, tracing Taylor's spiritual growth from passive Christian resignation to active social participation, resembles the standard plot structure of proletarian fiction of the 1930's—downtrodden, humbled "bottomdogs" perceiving through the course of their experiences a vision of a new and better world. Taylor's socialist vision is couched in Biblical allusions, but remains, nonetheless, true to form. "Gawd ain no lie! His eyes grew wet with tears blurring his vision; the sky trembled; the buildings wavered as if about to topple; and the earth shook." Taylor cries out exultingly, "Freedom belongs to the strong."[6]

Yet despite the clichés surrounding his character, there is an authentic ring to the minister's driving ambition to be the Moses of his people. And Wright records with consummate skill the way in which he evokes responses from his congregation. Taylor's self-assumed Biblical role allows him to see perhaps better than any of Wright's previous heroes that Negro freedom depends upon Christian brotherhood. Moreover, as leader of the Negro community, he perceives that success requires that he organize mass social action. He cautions his son who, like Silas of "Long Black Song," wants to resort to the same kind of isolated violence that whites use against Negroes.

> We gotta git wid the *people*, son. Too long we done tried t
> do this thing our way n when we failed we wanted t run out n
> pay-off the white folks. Then they kill us up like flies.[7]

Wright's treatment of the relationship between the white power structure and bourgeois Negro leadership in southern cities is a theme he would develop in greater detail in his last published novel, *The Long Dream*. But it is interesting to note that Wright here for the first time reveals the extent of the corruption and moral blackmail involved. Insofar as Taylor had been acquiescent and accommodating, the white civic authorities tolerated him and even recognized him as a fine leader of his people. When Taylor discovers that he had been manipulated all along to suit their own purposes, he is beaten and discarded. Taylor's discovery that the "cordial" relationships that exist between the white and Negro communities are based ultimately on an underlying reality of terror and brute power is a key theme of *The Long Dream*. But unfortunately in *The Long Dream*, the only alternative to submitting to this humiliation is flight whereas in "Fire and Cloud" Taylor's Negroes demonstrate, protest, and succeed. It would seem that Wright had his chronology confused. In 1938 when "Fire and Cloud" was published, any Negro protest movement would have been bloodily suppressed. By 1958, the time of *The Long Dream*, the first stirrings of the Negro rebellion had already begun to achieve results. Ironically, Wright had given up hope in a dream he had visualized so accurately twenty years before.

Wright progresses from the idea of organized Negro-white protest to the specific idea of a society based on Marxist principles. Although the two chief characters of "Bright and Morning Star" are cruelly maimed and murdered, they die secure in the belief that the cause for which they had given up their lives will some day be realized. In some respects "Bright and Morning Star" is the most classical of Wright's tragedies inasmuch as Wright's scapegoats die not in vain, but for an orderly, healthy, and progressive society that will flourish as a result of their death.

The story is related in the third person from the point of view of an elderly Negro tenant farmer's widow whose two sons (one of whom is already in jail) are Communist Party organizers. As the story opens, Sue reminisces about the hardships she has undergone in her life and how her two sons have managed to convert her simple Christian beliefs of a heaven in the next world to a vision of Communist utopia on earth. In effect, the transition was not hard for her to make, since the principles underlying her old faith are the same as those of Communism. She discovers herself humming an old hymn, "Bright and Morning Star," the star signalling the new era approaching with the Resurrection. Reva, the white daughter of a tenant farmer, who loves her son, Johnny-Boy, calls on her and tells her that the sheriff and other white officials have learned of a secret Party meeting that is to be held the following evening. When Johnny-Boy returns later that evening, Sue delivers Reva's message and Johnny-Boy goes out in the rain to warn the other Party members. Shortly after Johnny-Boy's departure, the sheriff and his men break into her house and demand to know the whereabouts of her son. When she refuses to tell them, they beat her and leave. A new Party member, Booker (white) arrives (whom she distrusts instinctively) and tells her Johnny-Boy has been captured. Booker manages to get from her the names of the other Party members. Reva returns and tells her that Booker is an informer. Sue now determines to kill Booker before he can give the names to the sheriff. She takes a short cut through the woods to the place where Johnny-Boy lies bound, tortured, and mutilated by the sheriff and his men. When Booker arrives on the scene, she shoots him before he can speak, whereupon she and Johnny-Boy are shot and killed.

The story is remarkable for the intense religious fervor that informs Sue's character. Like the Reverend Taylor of "Fire and Cloud," she conceives her mission in Biblical apocalyptic terms. But here the imagery is of a higher order, the metaphors sustained in a mounting tension until an ultimate sublimity is reached that transports her suffering into a mystical unity. As she lies dying,

> Focused and pointed she was, buried in the depths of her star, swallowed in its peace and strength; and not feeling her flesh growing cold, cold as the rain that fell from the invisible sky upon the doomed living and the dead that never dies.[8]

Like the other pieces in *Uncle Tom's Children*, "Bright and Morning Star" celebrates southern Negro folk whose faith, courage, and endurance Wright regarded as easily translatable, in terms of constructive social action, with the new dispensation of Communism. Yet Wright's Negroes achieve their sense of recognition through the course of their Negro experiences, and not through any inculcation of Communist ideals. As has been already shown, Taylor and Sue arrive at their decisions as a result of their peculiar Negro folk mysticism—or, perhaps, as Wright would have it, a native Negro revolutionism. Even Sue is a Negro first, before she is a Communist. Although she presumably possesses maternal feelings toward the white girl who loves her son, she has an instinctive distrust of whites. She tells her son that the Judas among them must be a white man, and although he chides her for being a black chauvinist, her Negro instincts prove truer than his Communist training.

Hence, Wright's militant Negroes, despite their protestations to the contrary, often sound more like black nationalists than Communist internationalists. It was perhaps this facet of Wright's work, in addition to the obvious, extreme, and frequent isolated individualism of his heroes that had now begun to disturb Communist Party officials. Yet regardless of whether Wright had been at heart a Communist, an outsider, or a nationalist when he wrote these pieces, there can be little doubt that they draw a good deal of their dramatic strength from the black and white world Wright saw. There is little the reader can do but sympathize with Wright's Negroes and loathe and despise the whites. There are no shadings, ambiguities, few psychological complexities. But these are of course the weaknesses of the stories as well.

How then account for their overall success? First of all, they *are* stories. Wright is a story teller and his plots are replete with conflict, incident, and suspense. Secondly, Wright is a stylist. He has an unerring "feel" for dialogue, his narrations are controlled in terse, tense rhythms, and he manages to communicate mood, atmosphere, and character in finely worked passages of lyric intensity. But above all they are stories whose sweep and magnitude are suffused with their author's impassioned convictions about the dignity of man, and a profound pity for the degraded, the poor and oppressed who, in the face of casual brutality, cling obstinately to their humanity.

Eight Men is a posthumous miscellany of eight of Wright's prose pieces that had not previously been collected in book form.[9] Two of the stories had been written in the thirties, three in the forties, and three in the fifties. One of the pieces, "The Man Who Went to Chicago," is in reality part of an unpublished chapter of *Black Boy*. Although *Eight Men* appeared two months after Wright died, it is clear that its publication was no hasty attempt to take advantage of any publicity occasioned by his death. Wright himself had evidently been preparing the book for some time and had anticipated its publication by dedicating it to friends he had made in Paris. Unlike the pieces in *Uncle Tom's Children*, these stories are not arranged along any progressively thematic lines; instead the order in which they are assembled indicates that Wright was more concerned with showing a variety of styles, settings and points of view. To be sure, they all deal in one way or another with Negro oppression, but they do not point, as Wright's previous collection of stories did, to any specific social conclusion. With one exception—"The Man Who Lived Underground"—they are considerably shorter than the pieces in *Uncle Tom's Children*, and since they represent Wright's work over a far greater span of years, the uneven quality of some of his writing becomes more apparent.

Wright did not particularly mature as a craftsman although he experimented more in the forties and fifties trying to find appropriate prose forms to suit his post-Communist intellectual growth. The stories in *Eight*

Men are representative of the different stages of Wright's development. The pieces that he had written in the thirties ("The Man Who Saw The Flood," "The Man Who Was Almost A Man") deal with oppressed southern Negro peasants; the stories of the forties ("The Man Who Lived Underground," "The Man Who Went to Chicago," "The Man Who Killed A Shadow") employ an urban setting to depict the Negro's "invisibility," outsider, or underground status; the stories of the fifties ("Man of All Work," "Man, God Ain't Like That," "Big Black Good Man") celebrate in an odd sort of way a kind of Negro nationalism—Negro virility as opposed to the white man's flabbiness, and a proud awareness of an African identity. In the latter period too there appears now an element of humor—albeit sometimes strained or ironic—and a lessening of the fierce tensions that had characterized his fiction up until this time. These changes do not necessarily reveal any slackening in Wright's commitment to Negro equality, but they do suggest that he may perhaps have now discovered himself in the process of acquiring a more even emotional equilibrium. Possibly the success of African independence movements for which he had so long fought encouraged him to believe that a turning point in race relationships had been achieved. Whatever the reasons, the hard narrative drive of Wright's earlier work is no longer present—the stories are now more psychological, more sophisticated, perhaps even more self-consciously stories. Yet somehow one feels that these are transition pieces, that Wright was moving in a new direction toward new subject matter and new themes—and that possibly he might have found what he was looking for, had he not died so young.

"The Man Who Saw The Flood," the first of the stories in *Eight Men*, was published initially in 1938 in *New Masses* under the title, "Silt." The piece is little more than a vignette—possibly intended as a sketch for a longer story—dealing with a tenant farm family of three who return to their devastated home after a flood. Wright best evokes their sense of loss and desolation by images. As they slosh silently across their oozey floors, they observe their dresser sitting "catercornered its drawers and sides bulging like a bloated corpse. The bed with the mattress still on it, was like a giant casket forged of mud. Two smashed chairs lay in a corner, as though huddled together for protection."[10]

Wright's other story of the thirties—a far more developed piece— was first published in *Harper's Bazaar* in 1939 under the title, "Almos' A Man." It is less sensationally dramatic than Wright's other Depression pieces in that the confrontation between whites and blacks is not nearly so violent. But it may be for this very reason that the point Wright is making about the ravages of the caste system is all the more telling. For the story speaks not simply of the economic exploitation of the southern Negro, but how this exploitation affects the psyche of an adolescent Negro boy. What makes this theme particularly effective is that the boy is not especially complex or sensitive; he is neither "socially aware" nor is he like Big Boy, a leader among boys of his age. Yet it is through the relative naïveté of his nature that the reader becomes cognizant of the terrible conditions of his life.

"The Man Who Was Almost A Man" tells the story of sixteen-year-old Dave who works in the fields and dreams of owning his own gun. The gun evidently symbolizes for him self-respect, virility, strength, all of which attributes Dave sorely lacks. The other Negro field hands taunt him, his father frequently beats him, and his mother receives his wages directly from Dave's white employer, Mr. Hawkins. One evening Dave manages to persuade his mother to allow him to buy an antiquated pistol from a white storekeeper—and the following morning Dave accidentally shoots Mr. Hawkins' mule. When he is discovered, he learns that he must work two years for Mr. Hawkins in order to pay for the dead animal. Rather than submit to this final outrage, he jumps aboard a passing train travelling north—his gun still securely in his pocket.

The pathos of the story lies in the poverty of Dave's dreams. For him, as for most adolescents, manhood is the highest order of achievement—but his paucity of social and emotional experience makes him view that goal in the image of a gun. It is clear from the very beginning of the story that Dave feels himself emasculated not only by his parents and peers, but by the very conditions of his work. Hence the killing of the mule may not have been so accidental as Dave had supposed. On the one hand he may be killing the mule in himself that has been submitting to all these assaults on his dignity—at a certain point in the story Dave in a fit of pique calls himself a mule—and on the other hand he may be striking out at his white employer by destroying his property. Significantly, once the accident has occurred Dave feels free to express his hatred in fantasies of killing the white man. In any event, he is now capable of acting, of making a decision—even if the decision is to flee rather than give up his gun to his father. It is instructive to note in this respect that the general pattern of plot and action in "Almost A Man" anticipates a similar pattern in Wright's novel, Native Son, that would be published later the same year. In the novel, the accidental killing of a white girl gives the murderer a sense of freedom and manhood he had never known before. Like the pieces in Uncle Tom's Children, much of the narrative is carried chiefly by dialogue and interior monologue. This is the last fictional work employing a southern setting that Wright would publish until his Mississippi novel eighteen years later. This story too marks the end of one phase of Wright's development.

The only significant work of fiction Wright produced in the decade of the forties was his long story, "The Man Who Lived Underground." (Native Son although published in 1940 had been completed the previous year.) The history of the publication of "Underground Man" offers a suggestive link between Wright's Marxist social views and his metaphysical speculations. Originally published in Accent (Spring 1942) as two excerpts from a novel, Wright published a considerably fuller version in Edwin

Seaver's *Cross-section* two years later. In the two year interval Wright had broken with the Communist Party and had intensified his interests in philosophy and Freudian psychology. It is of course not possible to know all the changes Wright had made between 1942 and 1944—but there appears to be less emphasis on social injustice in the latter version. The ultimate impression one carries away is not merely that of social protest, but rather protest against the nature of man, the human condition—what Camus called the metaphysical protest.

The 1944 version becomes essentially a detailed expansion of Wright's earlier piece. A Negro, Fred Daniels, in flight from the police who have falsely accused him of murder, descends through a manhole on the street into a sewer. Sloshing his way through the slime and sewage of the city, he discovers an entrance to the basement of a building adjacent to the sewer. Here he finds tools, and ultimately manages to dig his way through the walls of other buildings adjacent to the sewer. In the course of his underground expeditions he visits a Negro church, an undertaker's embalming room, a movie, a butcher's shop, a radio shop, and a jewelry store. He plunders whatever strikes his fancy (watches, diamonds, a butcher cleaver, a gun, a radio, and money) and brings these back to the secret room he had discovered in one of the buildings. He finds too that, from an invisible vantage point, he can view the nefarious behavior of respectable people who imagine they are acting unobserved. He comes to understand that the nether world in which he dwells is the real world of the human heart—and that the surface world which hums above him in the streets of the city is senseless and meaningless—a kind of unreality which men project to hide from themselves the awful blackness of their souls. He is invested suddenly with a sense of pity for all mankind. All men are guilty; it does not matter whether or not he killed the woman about whom he was forced to confess. He was guilty nonetheless by virtue of his being human. He rises Lazarus-like to the surface of the city to announce his message. Charged with the zeal of a prophet, he runs first to a church where the choir is ironically chanting a hymn quite opposed to the truth he now knows:

> Oh, wondrous sight upon the cross
> Vision sweet and divine
> Oh, wondrous sight upon the cross
> Full of such love sublime

He is turned away as being disreputable. He goes next to the police from whom he had fled. They tell him that they have found the real murderer, and that he is free—but he insists on his guilt. They regard him as deranged. He leads them to the sewer in which he had been hiding, plunges in once again, and asks them to follow. But one policeman, fearing some sort of trick, shoots him, and he is swept away dead in the scummy waters that flow below the city.

No mere synopsis can do justice to the story. Here Wright is at his storytelling best, dealing with subject matter he handles best—the terrified fugitive in flight from his pursuers. Like Wright's other fugitives, Fred Daniels exercises a kind of instinct for survival that he perhaps never knew he possessed. But what makes him different from the others is that he is not merely a victim of a racist society, but that he has become by the very nature of his experiences a symbol of all men in that society—the pursuers and the pursued. For what the underground man has learned in his sewer is that all men carry about in their hearts an underground man who determines their behavior and attitudes in the aboveground world. The underground man is the essential nature of all men—and is composed of dread, terror, and guilt. Here then lies the essential difference between Wright's Communist and post-Communist period. Heretofore dread, terror, and guilt had been the lot of the Negro in a world that had thrust upon him the role of a despised inferior. Now they are the attributes of all mankind. Previously Wright's Negro protagonists had been required to discover their own values, build their own ethics in a world that denied them access to "white" morality. In a word, white denial of Negro freedom rendered the Negro free to seek his identity outside the standards of the white world. But now these standards are held to be as illusory for whites as they had always been inaccessible for Negroes. All of men's striving, activities, and ideals are simply a means of keeping from themselves the knowledge of their underground nature. When Fred Daniels attempts to educate men to this truth, he is shot and killed. The police officer who kills him says, "You've got to shoot this kind. They'd wreck things."[11] In reality what Wright is doing is transferring what he once regarded as a special Negro experience, a special Negro truth in white America, to all men, white and Negro, everywhere. If Negroes are more aware of this truth, it is because their outsider-pariah status has made it less easy for them to delude themselves.

Fred Daniels is then Everyman, and his story is very nearly a perfect modern allegory. The Negro who lives in the underground of the city amidst its sewage and slime is not unlike the creature who dwells amidst the sewage of the human heart. And Fred Daniels knows that all of the ways men attempt to persuade themselves that their lives are meaningful and rational are delusions. As he stands over his loot of the aboveground world in his darkened room, he realizes these "images with their tongueless reality were striving to tell him something." What he discovers at bottom is that all men are murderous and in love with death. Significantly Fred places a butcher's bloody meat cleaver next to a "forest" of green paper dollar bills he had earlier pasted on all his walls. But paradoxically despite Fred's new found knowledge of the savagery of the human heart and the meaninglessness of the aboveground world, he recognizes its instinctive appeal as well, and he must absurdly rise to the surface once more.

It is understandable how in 1944 young French existentialist authors must have seen in Wright's works a confirmation of their own views. The dread, the terror, the guilt, the nausea had always been basic thematic elements in Wright's fiction—and now in "The Man Who Lived Underground," they are made the explicit components of the human personality. Like Wright's heroes, the characters of existentialist authors move about in a world devoid of principles, God, and purpose—and suffer horror at their awesome godlike powers as they create their own personalities and values out of the chaos of existence. But in some respects Wright's heroes are different. They are alienated often enough not from any intellectually reasoned position (at this stage in Wright's career), but by chance happenings in their lives or an accident of birth—race, for example. (In Fred Daniels' case, for instance, he is a Negro who quite by chance happened to be near the scene of a crime.) They arrive then accidentally at their insights, and as a result of having discovered themselves outside the rules of conventional social behavior recognize that they are free to shape (and are therefore responsible for) their own lives. But this is not primarily why they suffer guilt. Wright seems to prefer a Freudian explanation; guilt is instinctively connected with the trauma of birth.

> Why was this sense of guilt so seemingly innate, so easy to come by, to think, to feel, so verily physical? It seemed that when one felt this guilt one was retracing in one's feelings a faint pattern designed long before; it seemed that one was always trying to remember a gigantic shock that had left a haunting impression upon one's body which one could not forget or shake off, but which had been forgotten by the conscious mind, creating in one's life a state of eternal anxiety.[12]

Hence, for Wright, a man's freedom is circumscribed by his very humanity. In ways he cannot possibly control, his nature or "essence" precedes his existence. But however different the routes French existentialist authors and Wright may have taken, they meet on common ground in regard to their thrilled horror at man's rootlessness—at the heroism of his absurd striving.

"The Man Who Lived Underground" undoubtedly owes something in the way of plot and theme to *Les Miserables*, and to what Camus called the "Dostoevskian experience of the condemned man"—but, above all, Fred Daniels' adventures suggest something of Wright's own emotions after ten years in the Communist underground. The air of bitterness, the almost strident militancy are gone—momentarily at least—and in their place a compassion and despair—compassion for man trapped in his underground nature and despair that he will ever be able to set himself free.

Wright's two other representations of the forties are partial reflections of "Undergound Man." "The Man Who Went to Chicago" is interesting because Wright here has chosen to depict himself living literally in an underground situation. One of Wright's first jobs after coming to Chicago was that of a hospital attendant. He had a number of menial tasks—one of which took him to the hospital basement to feed caged animals on whom certain experimental inoculations were being performed. On one occasion two of the other Negro attendants with whom Wright worked began to fight, and in the course of their quarrel pushed against and fell among some of the cages, thereby setting free some of the animals. The resulting chaos of violence, animals, and men in the cluttered basement comes to symbolize the true heartbeat of the civilization in which the hospital stands as such a deceptive example.

"The Man Who Killed A Shadow" was the first of Wright's works to be published after he had gone to Paris.[13] The story, which in some ways hearkens back to Native Son, deals with a Negro who inadvertently kills a white woman. The woman in this case is a forty year old, sexually repressed, white librarian who commands the Negro to look at her legs. When he tries to flee, she screams and he brutally hacks her to death for fear of being discovered alone with her. What makes the story something other than a restatement of the Bigger Thomas theme is Wright's use of the Negro as a symbol of libidinal abandon. The irony, of course, lies in the fact that Saul Saunders is as much a shadow of a man as the woman he kills is a shadow of a woman. Like the underground man he lives on a plane of fear, guilt, and dread. Hence the Negro man and white woman are not only shadows to one another, but shadows to themselves.

The fifties saw Wright experimenting with new subject matter and new forms. Problems of race remain the central issue, but are now dealt with from changing perspectives. For the first time there are two stories with non-American settings, and race neurosis is treated more as the white man's dilemma than as the black man's burden. This shift in emphasis from black to white is accompanied by corresponding shifts in social viewpoint. Racial antagonisms do not appear to be immediately—or for that matter remotely—traceable to compelling class interests. It is clear that Wright was trying to broaden the range and scope of his fiction—that he was trying to move away somewhat from the psyche of the oppressed Negro peasant or proletariat toward characters of varying social and ethnic backgrounds. The three novels Wright produced in this ten year period bear out this conclusion. In the first, The Outsider (1953), he wrote of his hero that though a Negro "he could have been of any race." Savage Holiday, written the following year, contains no Negro characters and deals with the misfortunes of a white, "respectable" middle-aged retired insurance executive. The Long Dream (1957) is written from the point of view of an adolescent, middle-class Negro boy.

Wright was apparently reaching for a universality he felt he had not yet achieved—but his craft was not quite equal to the tasks he had set for himself. Too often, as before, his whites appear as stereotypes, and his

Negroes are a bit too noble or innocent. In the 1930's Wright's social vision lent his stories an air of conviction, a momentum all their own; in the 1950's Wright's quieter catholicity, his wider intellectuality, perhaps removed his stories from this kind of cumulative dread tension, the sense of urgency, that made his earlier works so immediately gripping.

Nonetheless it cannot be said that Wright's new stories do not possess their own narrative qualities. Two of the stories are written entirely in dialogue with no interceding explanatory prose passages. This kind of dramatic framework has, of course, certain advantages. For one thing, pace is considerably accelerated, and the climactic confrontations are made more immediately suspenseful—if perhaps somewhat less meaningful than in the *Uncle Tom* stories. What these stories sorely lack are the charged, vibrant rhythms and vivid lyric imagery that so rounded out character and theme in his earlier works. Perhaps Wright wanted to pare his prose down to what he regarded as bare essentials—just as he may have fancied his idol, Gertrude Stein, had done. Whatever the reasons, the results are only occasionally successful.

"Man of All Work," probably composed in 1953, was inspired by an item Wright read in *Jet* about a man who dressed himself as a woman in order to find work as a domestic. In a sense this story appears to develop more fully an idea first implied in "The Man Who Killed A Shadow"—that racial antagonisms are related in some fashion to serious sexual maladjustment. Wright builds his case carefully, playing delicately but never explicitly with notions of homosexuality, transvestism, castration, and hermaphroditism. The story—the first of Wright's dialogue pieces—deals with a Negro man who informs his wife that their situation is so desperate that he intends to dress himself in his wife's clothes and seek employment as a maid. She protests, but he persists—and shortly thereafter finds himself working for a white family, the Fairchilds. It soon develops that, among his other duties (cooking, cleaning and taking care of a small child) Carl must stave off the predatory advances of Mr. Fairchild, who apparently regards all Negro maids as fair game. At one juncture Mrs. Fairchild enters while the two men are wrestling and becomes so jealous that she shoots hysterically at her husband's presumed paramour. When it is discovered that Carl is after all a man—and not very seriously wounded—they pay him two months wages and make him promise that he will not tell the authorities of Mrs. Fairchild's attempt at murder.

The story unfolds in three swiftly changing scenes: Carl's home, the Fairchild's house, and back again to Carl's home. All the reader knows of character and action is what he can infer from the dialogue. The dialogue itself sounds occasionally stiff and awkward, especially when Wright attempts to relate what the characters are doing at a particular moment, or what events have just taken place. (There is some evidence Wright had written this piece as a radio play which may in part explain the awkward transitions.) The story (or play) makes a grim little joke about mistaken identity on several levels. Because Carl cannot provide for his wife and children, he has symbolically been denied his virility long before he actually decides to appropriate the role of the woman. The Fairchilds, perhaps significantly named, also undergo a similar confusion of sexual roles. It is obvious from the moment Carl applies for the job that Mrs. Fairchild plays the dominant part in her relationship to her husband. She makes it clear to Carl (who calls himself Lucy) that she regards her husband as an irresponsible child, particularly when he drinks. Perhaps because of the brusque efficient way in which she runs her family, she has, in her way, emasculated her husband, who attempts to recover his virility in drink and Negro girls. To compound the confusion the Fairchild's little girl dominates both her parents in this white, child-centered middle-class family. The final confusion lies in the way whites look at the Negro woman as a figure both of a wild physical abandon and warm motherhood. Poor Carl-Lucy, whom American culture has effectively deprived of his sexuality, is expected to play both roles—and it is in the role of the latter, as mammy-nurse, that Wright produces one rather good ironic twist. In what amounts to a parody of Red Riding Hood, the frightening little girl cross-examines her disguised nursemaid.

> —Lucy, your arms are so big.
> —Hunh?
> —And there's so much hair on them.
> —Oh, that's nothing.
> —And you've got so many big muscles.
> —Oh, that comes from washing and cleaning and cooking.
> Lifting heavy pots and pans.
> —And your voice is not at all like Bertha's.
> —What do you mean?
> —Your voice is heavy, like a man's.
> —Oh, that's from singing so much, child.
> —And you hold your cigarette in your mouth like Papa holds
> his, with one end dropping down.
> —Hunh? Oh, that's because my hands are busy, child.[14]

Wright's other dialogue piece, "Man, God Ain't Like That," although more ambitious in that it treats of European-African relationships, is not nearly so successful or clever.[15] There are a number of reasons, but the principal one is that Wright has attempted to impose in fictional form his rather complex ideas about the psychology of imperialism. Or, put another way, plot and action issue from Wright's preconceptions about Europeans and Africans in certain situations rather than from the actual characters and situations he writes about. The story opens with a description of a journey an English painter and his wife are making through the back country of the Ashanti. John, the artist, feels that he can somehow reinvigorate himself in a primitive setting. In the course of their travels they adopt as their servant a queerly religious Ashanti boy who sings Methodist hymns publicly, but makes strange secret sacrifices to his dead ancestors when he is alone. John regards Babu as an amusing curiosity and takes him with him to Paris. Babu, who adores his white master, is overwhelmingly impressed by his civilization and disappears for a time presumably observing the sights of Paris. He returns to his master's apartment just as John is preparing to leave for a gallery that will be displaying his African paintings for the first time. Babu is convinced that John is Christ and that he, Babu, must kill him. He reasons that since white men had to kill their god to achieve such a magnificent civilization, so Babu must kill his master to achieve the same results. The artist pleads with him—but to no avail; Babu proceeds sanguinely about his task. The scene shifts to two Paris detectives who are discovered discussing a baffling murder that had occurred some five years before. They are convinced that John must have been killed by a jealous mistress—and laughingly dismiss the claims of a primitive superstitious black boy (whom they had shipped back to Africa shortly after the crime) that he had killed his white messiah.

Wright was probably attempting here another allegory on the order of "The Man Who Lived Underground." The artist and his wife are representative of the white colonial mentality that regards natives as dolts who exist exclusively for the pleasures and convenience of their white masters. Babu, on the other hand, suggests mass African man, rootless, directionless, partially detribalized—existing somewhere between the Christianity of his rulers and the paganism of his ancestors—between the modern world and the primitive. He adores his white master as a god who represents for him all strength and wisdom, and slaughters him in ritual fashion in hopes of assimilating that strength and wisdom. Possibly Wright is saying here that the white man had to kill his god—particularly those anti-worldly aspects of him—in order to build so glitteringly a materialistic civilization—and that Babu in murdering his white master god frees the black man to build a similarly developed civilization. But whatever the interpretation the allegory fails. The dialogue is wooden, the characters too contrived, and the plot, hovering somewhere between realism and fantasy, is too fantastic or not fantastic enough.

"Big Black Good Man," which first appeared in *Esquire* in 1957, is the last short story Wright published in his lifetime. Possibly it is the last he ever wrote. In any event it represents a more traditional approach to storytelling in that Wright here avoids confining himself exclusively to dialogue. On the other hand "Big Black Good Man" deviates from the usual Wright short story. For one thing, the narrative, by Wright's standards at least, is practically plotless. Scarcely anything "happens." There is no violence, practically no external narrative action, and no change of milieu. The entire story is told in terms of the emotions, attitudes and reactions of a white man, an old night-porter who sits behind his desk at a cheap waterfront hotel in Copenhagen. As the story opens, he is discovered drowsily reminiscing about his youth as a sailor when suddenly an enormous black seaman, obviously American, enters and demands a room, a bottle of whiskey, and a whore. Olaf is used to requests like these and ordinarily does his best to comply. He does not regard himself as prejudiced but feels now an almost instinctive terror and hatred for this black man who makes him feel so puny and white. Although he wants to, he finds himself incapable of refusing the Negro his demands—and, among other things, provides him with Lena, a prostitute, for the length of his stay. After six days the Negro prepares to leave, but just prior to his departure he puts his massive hands around Olaf's neck. After he leaves, Olaf is sure the black man wanted to humiliate him—to prove to Olaf how easy it would be to kill him. Consumed with hatred and shame, he fantasies the Negro's death at sea—he fancies he sees him drowning, about to be consumed by a white shark. A year later the Negro returns; Olaf cries out that there are no rooms, but the Negro replies that he does not intend to stay at the hotel this time. He thereupon presents Olaf with six shirts—one for each day he had spent with Lena the previous year—and informs him that he is going to live with Lena at her home. Olaf, in tears, confesses he feared that the Negro had intended to kill him when he measured his neck. The Negro, on his way out, laughs and calls back, "Daddy-O, drop dead!"

The story thus probes Olaf's psyche not simply in terms of his behavior, but mainly in terms of his dreams, fantasies, and memories. For the first time Wright has assumed the role of the enemy—and tells the story from his point of view. For all intents and purposes, Olaf is a normal petty bourgeois. He owns his own home, is fond of his wife and children, loves to putter about in his garden, and is not dissatisfied with his job. To be sure he is smug; there are no great depths to Olaf's passions. How then account for his sudden obsession, his terror? To Wright's credit, he does not attempt to explain, only to record. But the reader may gather insights nonetheless. Olaf's hatred is not socially conditioned; he is a Dane, and Danes are presumably relatively free of racial prejudice. Moreover, he has been a sailor and seen all parts of the world, and hence may be regarded as a cosmopolitan of sorts. Finally, it is probably true that Olaf has himself never consciously mistreated nor remembered feeling any animosity toward the other colored guests in the hotel. Are Olaf's reactions then instinctively racial? Do they suggest a repository of violent race memories buried beneath the placid exterior—of which Olaf was himself unaware?

Olaf's reactions are, of course, deep-seated sexual responses, feelings of sexual inferiority—but, perhaps, above all, feelings of terror of the raw, intense sexuality of life that the Negro represents. Olaf sees the Negro as a "huge black thing that fills the door;" he has "snakelike fingers," a neck like a bull, a voice that "booms," and "wide and flaring nostrils." In describing him thus, there can be little doubt that Wright deliberately portrayed his black giant in romantic fashion—"His chest bulged like a barrel; his rocklike and humped shoulders hinted of mountain ridges; the stomach ballooned like a threatening stone."[16] There is then something regal, something suggestive of Prester John perhaps in this magnificent figure that strides across Olaf's soul from another world.

One now senses a new element of race pride in Wright's portrayal; the tone of proud defiance has somehow been stilled and replaced by a note of contained racial triumph. It is not quite racial revenge, but it is nonetheless interesting to note that Wright has now reversed the imagery of much of *Uncle Tom's Children*. Instead of white, there are now "black shadows," "black mountains," "black clouds like a stormy sky descending"[17] on the terrified Olaf. Yet despite the black sailor's mythic proportions Wright still manages to keep him down to earth, chiefly by means of dialogue. Somehow the Negro's "Daddy-O, drop dead!" suddenly transforms him to one more cynical, jazzy American. There is to be sure bitterness in the Negro's recognition that Olaf had been hating him all along—but in the midst of the bitterness there is the almost amused observation that such hatred can no longer harm him. It would of course be impossible to say whether Wright had intended "Big Black Good Man" to be the last word on what it means and feels to be a Negro. One can only say on the basis of this story that Wright himself came, momentarily at least, to a sense of pride and self-adjustment. Ironically, though, he could only do this by imagining what the white man felt.

Notes

1. The edition I use in this study was published as the seventh printing of Tower Books by World Publishing Company (New York and Cleveland, 1946).

2. See "The Art of Richard Wright's Short Stories" in *Quarterly Review of Literature*, 1 (Spring 1944), 198–211.

3. *Uncle Tom's Children*, pp. 64–65.

4. *Uncle Tom's Children*, pp. 148–49.

5. *Uncle Tom's Children*, p. 135.

6. *Uncle Tom's Children*, pp. 210–11.

7. *Uncle Tom's Children*, p. 201.

8. *Uncle Tom's Children*, p. 250.

9. The first edition of *Eight Men* was published by World (New York and Cleveland, 1961). The edition which I use for this study was published later the same year by Avon, New York, in paper cover.

10. *Eight Men*, p. 34.

11. *Eight Men*, p. 68.

12. *Eight Men*, p. 50.

13. "The Man Who Killed A Shadow," *Zero*, 1 (Spring 1949), 45–53.

14. *Eight Men*, p. 100.

15. Neither "Man of All Work" nor "Man, God Ain't Like That," had been published

prior to *Eight Men*. It is therefore difficult to date either but the latter sounds as if it may have been written after Wright's return from the Gold Coast in the fall of 1953.

16. *Eight Men*, p. 71.

17. *Eight Men*, p. 71.

Images of "Vision"
in *Native Son*

James Nagel*

Perhaps it is understandable that a "race" novel as provocative as Richard Wright's *Native Son*[1] has evoked a critical response largely in terms of sociological analysis. Indeed, as a social document the work is a penetrating and controversial statement which has shocked the conscience of American complacency. But regardless of the accuracy of Wright's picture of the racial condition in this country, his book is not only a social study but a "novel," a work of art which transcends the limitations of sociological prose. In this work, as in all good fiction, the "art" of the novel supports the theme, and no reading of the book is complete until it has given careful attention to the relationship between "method" and "meaning."

One of the most prevalent aspects of the artistry of *Native Son* is the persistence of the images of "vision" which pervade almost every significant moment. The very frequency of these images would suggest that this book is not merely about racial violence, not only a vehicle of "chase adventure," nor a courtroom drama, nor a study of urban mechanization. It is, rather, an analysis of "perception" which documents the effect prejudice, alienation, oppression, and isolation have on one's ability to "see" and "be seen" clearly. In fact, the narrative device of this book is to relate nearly all events as they are "seen" by the protagonist, Bigger Thomas. And, further, the plot is described and developed in images of blindness, impaired vision, and "seeing" for the first time.

As several critics have already pointed out,[2] the central image in its various forms is that of blindness. Literally, blindness relates only to Mrs. Dalton who is in fact without sight, and whose disability permits and provokes the murder of her daughter. She is also blind, however, in a figurative sense (as are all the rest of the characters) in that she has virtually no insight into the realities of Negro life in Chicago. Like her husband, she sees Bigger only as a type, a generalized object of her cathartic altruism that is expected to respond to generosity with gratitude and humility, but not with any overt expressions of individualism. Thus she is blind on two counts, a condition symbolic of the depth of the "blindness

*Reprinted from *University Review*, 36 (Dec. 1969), 109–15, by permission of the author and the journal.

151

of the white liberal philanthropic community,"[3] as Edward Margolies has pointed out.

But Mrs. Dalton is not the only character whose vision and understanding have been impaired. Britten, for example, sees only "communists" and "niggers." To Dalton he says: "Well, you see 'em one way and I see 'em another. To me a nigger's a nigger" (p. 154). It should be also noted that his attitude has been carefully foreshadowed by the frequent references to the peculiarities of his eyes (see pp. 146–153), beginning with Bigger's first exposure to him:

> The white man at Mr. Dalton's side [Britten] was squinting at him; he felt that tight, hot, choking fear returning. The white man clicked on the light. He had a cold, impersonal manner that told Bigger to be on his guard. In the very look of the man's eyes Bigger saw his own personality reflected in narrow, restricted terms. (p. 146)

And Bigger's first view of Britten is no better. He sees Mr. Dalton and the investigator only in "red darkness" and as "white discs of danger" (p. 146). To Bigger he is an enemy and easily recognizable: "Britten was familiar to him; he had met a thousand Brittens in his life" (p. 154). Thus both of them are reduced to a "type" in the eyes of the other.[4]

In fact, until the first murder Bigger is as blind as anyone: he does not understand himself and plays no clear role in either his family, gang, or society. Those around him are equally sightless: Bessie, for example, is twice mentioned as being blind (pp. 132, 165) as is Reverend Hammond, who casts his gaze on a more promising vision of the promised land.

At one point he asks Bigger to "Fergit yuh's black" (p. 263). Indeed, in Bigger's mind, at least, nearly everyone is blind: "His feet were cold and he stamped them in the snow, surrounded by people waiting, too, for a car. He did not look at them; they were simply blind people, blind like his mother, his brother, his sister, Peggy, Britten, Jan, Mr. Dalton, and the sightless Mrs. Dalton and the quiet empty houses with their black gaping windows"[5] (pp. 163–64).

Perhaps Bigger's inability to see and understand the world about him precludes the possibility of his realizing that anyone is more insightful than he.[6] In some respects he is right: the newspapers reduce him to a dehumanized "ape" and the police underestimate him to the extent of suspecting an accomplice on the grounds that "the plan of the murder and kidnapping was too elaborate to be the work of a Negro mind" (p. 229). Apparently they have not "seen" him at all, a fact he senses in counting on their blindness for his escape.

Thus blindness is operative throughout the novel as a metaphor of a lack of understanding and of a tendency to generalize individuals on the basis of race. It is both a rationalization for those who are looking and a disguise for those who are being looked at. This concept is expressed in other terms as well: Wright continually refers to a "curtain" or "barrier" which prevents his characters from fully seeing and communicating with others, particularly those of another race. Because of it, Bigger is alienated from even his friends and isolated behind his symbolic "curtain." Threatened by the shame of acknowledging the living conditions of his family, he erects a protective barrier: "he lived with them, but behind a wall, a curtain" (p. 14); and, again: "All that morning he had lurked behind his curtain of indifference and looked at things, snapping and glaring at whatever had tried to make him come out into the open" (p. 31).

Sometimes the "wall" seems the result of a deterministic force which prevents him from establishing rapport with anyone. Jan, for example, tries to reach Bigger on the street after being questioned at the Daltons', but despite his intentions, circumstances prevent full communication: "In the pale yellow sheen of the street lamp they faced each other; huge wet flakes of snow floated down slowly, forming a delicate screen between them" (pp. 161–62).

Throughout *Native Son* this metaphor is reminiscent of the "veil" concept explored in *The Souls of Black Folk*,[7] by W. E. Burghardt DuBois. DuBois, of course, was writing much earlier (1903), but the meaning of the device is, tragically, much the same. The veil, he points out, not only prevents whites and blacks from seeing each other, but also deters a Negro from truly seeing himself: "After the Egyptian and Indian, the Greek and Roman, the Negro is a sort of seventh son, born with a veil, and gifted with a second-sight in this American world—a world which yields him no true self-consciousness, but only lets him see himself through the revelation of the other world" (DuBois, p. 16).

The result is an imposed self-destruction of identity, with the white-ideal constantly at odds with the reality of blackness. This dichotomy, DuBois suggests, promotes a unique duality, perpetually schizophrenic, in one's view of himself: "It is a peculiar sensation, this double-consciousness, this sense of always looking at one's self through the eyes of others, of measuring one's soul by the tape of a world that looks on in amused contempt and pity. One ever feels his two-ness—an American, a Negro; two souls, two thoughts, two unreconciled strivings; two warring ideals in one dark body, whose dogged strength alone keeps it from being torn asunder" (DuBois, pp. 16–17).

Thus the veil, like blindness, creates a sense of isolation within impregnable walls and transfers a pathological dualism from society to the oppressed individual.

What DuBois is talking about seems very close to the situation Bigger finds himself in:

> But what was he after? What did he want? What did he love and what did he hate? He did not know. There was something he *knew* and something he *felt*; something the *world* gave him and something he *himself* had; something spread out in *front*

of him and something spread out in *back*: and never in all his life, with this black skin of his, had the two worlds, thought and feeling, will and mind, aspiration and satisfaction, been together; never had he felt a sense of wholeness. (p. 225)

In addition to the images of the "veil" and "blindness," there are other metaphors of vision which relate to the central theme. For example, Bigger's view of the white world is, essentially, a simplistic re-creation of the images in the popular media. Perhaps this process is best illustrated in the "movie scene" in which Jack and Bigger attend a local double feature. Wright has selected the two pictures very carefully: *The Gay Woman* depicts the sophisticated white cocktail set whirling through social crises against a background of swimming pools and golf courses and night clubs. Bigger takes this to be an accurate reproduction of upper-class society and this misconception informs both his goals and his disappointment upon meeting the Daltons, who do not fit the pattern.

The second movie presents another hyperbole in ironic contrast to the first: *Trader Horn* shows "black men and black women dancing against a wild background of barbaric jungle" (p. 32). For all its exaggeration, this scene is, unfortunately, much closer to the primitive conditions of his own life, yet it does not replace the first. It is, rather, at least in part, the lingering portrait of *The Gay Woman* which prompts him to work for the Daltons: "He looked at *Trader Horn* unfold and saw pictures of naked black men and women whirling in wild dances and heard drums beating and then gradually the African scene changed and was replaced by images in his own mind of white men and women dressed in black and white clothes, laughing, talking, drinking and dancing. Those were smart people; they knew how to get hold of money, millions of it. Maybe if he were working for them something would happen and he would get some of it. He would see just how they did it" (pp. 35–36).

Thus his response to the movies underscores Bigger's refusal to identify himself with black society and reveals his quest for the amorphous splendor of the white world.

This fantasy of the white world, however, has a devastating effect on his thoughts and actions. "Whiteness," as an oppressive symbol, is omnipresent: there is the white world of Cottage Grove Avenue, the white cat which leaps upon his shoulder, the white snow which retards his escape, the white water which assists his capture, the white faces which glare at him in the courtroom, and the "white mountain" which demands his execution. Whiteness becomes both the coveted goal and the oppressive enemy: he goes to work for the Daltons seeking the wealth of the white world; he finds not richness, but a "white blur," symbolizing hostility, manifested in the blind Mrs. Dalton. She is an abstraction to him, a white nebulous threat, and as such she frightens him into killing her daughter:

He turned and a hysterical terror seized him, as though he were falling from a great height in a dream. A white blur was standing by the door, silent, ghostlike. It filled his eyes and gripped his body . . . Frenzy dominated him. He held his hand over her mouth . . . (p. 84)

Significantly, it is a white image which motivates each of the murders: with Mary it was the "white blur;" with Bessie it is a whiteness in nearly the same form. As he prepares to kill her he watches her "white breath" in the cold air, resentment and hostility swelling within him.

When he is about to strike, the motivating image leaves him, and he pauses for it to return, suggesting that without the whiteness there would be no killing; "he had to stand here until that picture came back, that motive, that driving desire to escape the law. Yes. It *must* be this way. A sense of the white blur hovering near, of Mary burning, of Britten, of the law tracking him down, came back. Again, he was ready" (p. 222).

Thus violence being a weapon of the weak, both murders are born of fear and are a symbolic thrust against an enormous oppressor, a futile act of self-defense.

There are also a number of consistent images involving "visions" and "dreams." Perhaps the most important of these is Bigger's haunting memory of Mary's head severed from her body.[8] The picture recurs again and again as an immediate and constant reminder of the reality of his action. He had struck out against a white blur, but it was an individual he had killed, a girl whose memory provokes a feeling as close to guilt as he is capable of.

He becomes so preoccupied with the image that in a dream he substitutes his own head for Mary's: "he stood on a street corner in a red glare of light like that which came from the furnace and he had a big package in his arms so wet and slippery and heavy that he could scarely hold onto it and he wanted to know what was in the package and he stopped near an alley corner and unwrapped it and the paper fell away and he saw—it was his *own* head—his own head lying with black face and half-closed eyes and lips parted with white teeth showing and hair wet with blood and the red glare grew brighter like light shining down from a red moon and red stars on a hot summer night . . ."(p. 156).

It is a vivid image, recalling the red glow of the furance that had frightened him during the investigation, the heat in the furance room; and it suggests, symbolically, that in killing Mary he has killed himself as well.

Perhaps it is suitably ironic that both the triumph and the tragedy of Bigger's life are realized in the same act: the murder is at once the culmination of his isolation and blindness and the inception of his ability to "see." The death scene is the pivotal point for not only the structure and theme, but for the imagery as well: it is a moment of "recognition" in the classical sense. From this moment on, the prevailing image for Bigger is one of "seeing."

He sees his home life as it really is (p. 100), and he seems to have gained a remarkable insight into character: he realizes that he has not been alone in his blindness, that ". . . Jan was blind. Mary had been blind. Mr. Dalton was blind. And Mrs. Dalton was blind; yes, blind in more ways than one . . . Bigger felt that a lot of people were like Mrs. Dalton, blind . . . Buddy, too, was blind . . . Looking at Buddy and thinking of Jan and Mr. Dalton, he saw in Buddy a certain stillness, an isolation, meaninglessness" (pp. 102–03).

Not all of his new insights are negative, however. In a splendid image, Bigger sees, for a moment, the amelioration of the racial "problem":

> Another impulse rose in him, born of desperate need, and his mind clothed it in an image of a strong blinding sun sending hot rays down and he was standing in the midst of a vast crowd of men, white men and black men and all men, and the sun's rays melted away the many differences, the colors, the clothes, and drew what was common and good upward toward the sun . . . (p. 335)

Clearly, something has happened to Bigger. The act of killing, as Max later explains, was not only destructive but "creative" in the sense of giving Bigger a life he was denied before.[9] For the first time he has a sense of his own identity: he now understands the motivation of the Daltons (p. 122); he glimpses the incredulousness of his actions and is forced to laugh at himself (p. 175); and, ultimately, through a combination of his new perception and the compassion of his lawyer, he strikes through the "whiteness" to see individual people: "For the first time in his life he had gained a pinnacle of feeling upon which he could stand and see vague relations that he had never dreamed of. If that white looming mountain of hate were not a mountain at all, but people, people like himself, and like Jan—then he was faced with a high hope the like of which he had never thought could be, and a despair the full depths of which he knew he could not stand to feel" (p. 334).

Strangely, after the murder, Bessie too sees as she never could before: she realizes that Bigger has murdered Mary (p. 168), that she is irretrievably involved with Bigger (p. 173), and that the police will charge him with rape as well as murder (p. 213). She now understands the damaging effect of her entire relationship with him (p. 215) and her former blindness (p. 216).

The change is also manifested in Jan; he and Bigger find it possible to remove the veil: "He looked at Jan and saw a white face, but an honest face . . . Suddenly, this white man had come up to him, flung aside the curtain, and walked into the room of his life . . . He saw Jan as though someone had performed an operation upon his eyes, or as though someone had snatched a deforming mask from Jan's face" (p. 268).

Of all the characters, of course, Max sees most brilliantly. In appropriate visual imagery, he explains Bigger's situation to the court: "The central fact to be understood here is not who wronged this boy, but what kind of a vision of the world did he have before his eyes, and where did he get such a vision as to make him, without premeditation, snatch the life of another person so quickly and instinctively that even though there was an element of accident in it, he was willing after the crime to say: 'Yes, I did it. I had to' " (p. 364).

In the same terms he pleads for mercy for Bigger: "But our decision as to whether this black boy is to live or die can be made in accordance with what actually exists. It will at least indicate that we *see* and *know*! And our seeing and knowing will comprise a consciousness of how inescapably this one man's life will confront us ten million fold in the days to come" (p. 369).

Unfortunately, however, Max has not seen *all*. Despite his perceptive analysis of the racial situation in general, he too has failed to see the individual in the mass. He sees Bigger as one black man among twelve million, not as a boy suddenly aware of his own identity. He understands the cause of the crime, but not what it means to Bigger; thus he cannot acknowledge the murder as a "good" act in any sense. Even though the boy says, "But what I killed for, I *am*" (pp. 391–92), and "it must have been good! When a man kills, it's for something" (p. 392), Max does not understand and gropes for his hat like a "blind" man (p. 392).

And so the novel ends, deep in the themes and images with which it began. Bigger, on the basis of his new individuality, realizes that his real tragedy is not death; it is rather the fact of never having been clearly seen by anyone. Throughout the novel the images of vision have suggested this conclusion: blindness prompting isolation, impaired vision, alienation. Thus the imagery contributes to the central theme that the denial of personal identity is the worst form of oppression. Therefore, through the techniques of his fiction Richard Wright emphasizes the role of *perception* in the racial issue and develops the depth and greatness of the "art" of *Native Son.*

Notes

1. Richard Wright, *Native Son* (A Perennial Classic: New York, 1966).

2. See, for example, Robert A. Bone, *The Negro Novel in America* (New Haven, 1968), pp. 140–152, and Edward Margolies, "Richard Wright: *Native Son* and Three Kinds of Revolution," *Native Sons: A Critical Study of Twentieth-Century Negro American Authors* (New York, 1969), pp. 65–86.

3. Margolies, p. 84.

4. In addition, although the reader grows to know Bigger intimately, Britten remains stereotypic, the effect of which is to artistically restrict the vision of the reader. Thus he too becomes, very subtly, a participant in the blindness.

5. On another occasion he sees the windows of the empty building as the "eye-sockets of empty skulls" (p. 216).

6. Bigger's fear of and resistance to the white world is frequently symbolized by his gesture of throwing his hands up in front of his face. Generally this action occurs when he is attempting to blot out some detail which does not conform to his understanding of reality. For examples, see pp. 49–50, 95, 109, 133, 236, and 307.

7. W. E. B. Du Bois, *The Souls of Black Folk* (A Fawcett Premier Book: Greenwich, Conn., 1967).

8. See pp. 108, 110, 113, 123, 126, 183, 195, 204, and 220 for examples.

9. See Margolies, p. 86.

Lawd Today:
Notes on Richard Wright's
First/Last Novel

Lewis Leary*

It seems to me a mistake to write of *Lawd Today*, the first written and last published of Richard Wright's novels, as if it were only an unsuccessful trial run for *Native Son*. I find it to stand securely on its own merits and in important ways quite to surpass the story of Bigger Thomas. One reason for its superiority may be that the people who have very much to say in *Lawd Today* are all black, so that there is none of the uneasiness in accent when crossing color lines—the kind of embarrassment which a reader may feel when confronted with people like kind Mr. Dalton, poor Bessie, or well-meaning Max who in *Native Son*, however individualized, maintain a taint of purposefulness as instruments used in fashioning a thesis. A protest novel may protest too much. Bigger did live, certainly, for Richard Wright has explained in detail how he was born, and any reader may believe that, yes, but for the grace of circumstance, he might be any underprivileged boy, Richard Wright or himself. His blackness is inescapable, and what he did was the result of terrifying pressures. But am I wrong in thinking that his blackness is superimposed? Or that I am tempted to steal a phrase from Mark Twain and say that, shucks, anyone could have done what he did. Clyde Griffith, or even me. That may be part of the great talent which was Richard Wright.

I

James Baldwin's early testimony that *Native Son* is "the most powerful and celebrated statement we have yet had of what it means to be a Negro in America" must be received with respect because it comes from a man whose own experience certifies him as an expert witness. Written twelve years before the appearance in 1963 of *Lawd Today*, it seems still fairly to represent the attitude of more recent commentators like Russell Brignano, Dan McCall, and Edward Margolies who have written of Wright in the late 1960's. But to me, like them partially disqualified as white, Jake Jackson's long, harrassed, expectant, shattered activities

*Reprinted from *CLA Journal*, 15 (June 1972), 411–20, by permission of the author and the journal.

during a single winter day in Chicago, though less celebrated than Bigger's awful experience, and less melodramatic and less productive of polemic also, nonetheless provide a powerful and terrifying insight into what it must be to be black in America, the essential bleakness of black life, the cultural barrenness. But it also, insidiously, provides glimpses into what it means to be white, colorless, ubiquitous.

Jake Jackson has only casual contacts with whites, and yet they circumfuse his world. They lurk on its outskirts, menacing his precarious occupation as a postal clerk. They form his opinions, alternately as objects of veneration ("I always said that we colored folks ought to stick with the rich white folks"), of resentment ("The white folks just ain't going to let no black man get to the top"), or of scorn ("The American white man is a natural born coward"). But Jake is no black liberationist. No Negro protest for him. He is proud of Joe Louis, but only casually dismayed that white Max Schmelling has defeated his black fighter. That is just the way things are. Whatever the wish that they might be different, sensible men simply accept the inevitable. And not as cop-outs either.

Jake's views are largely white middle class views, on communism (which is bad), on capitalism (by which he means getting lots of money quickly), on reading (it addles your brains), and on movies starring blue-eyed blondes and darkly handsome menacers of golden-haired, white-thighed womanhood. Those who do him in are of his own race, like Doc who has political connections and who, for a fee, will use them, and like Blanche whose lush flesh is a wondrous lure but a delusion. "Niggers," said Jake, "is just like a bunch of crawfish in a bucket. When one of 'em gets smart and tries to climb out of the bucket, the others'll grab 'im and pull 'im back."

What gives Jake his ultimate appeal is that he is as disillusioned and sloppy, as nitty-gritty human, as any of us. He is first seen at eight o'clock in the morning of February 12, 1936, the birthday of Abraham Lincoln, "a man . . . who bestowed the blessings of liberty and freedom upon millions of his countrymen." But not on Jake Jackson who is a rudderless derelict on what Van Wyck Brooks is quoted as describing as "a vast Sargassa Sea—a prodigious welter of unconscious life, swept by ground-swells of half-conscious emotion." Jake awakens that morning from dreams of steps which he climbs and climbs, leg weary, and never reaching their top: "*Jeeesus, all that running for nothing.*" They are the inevitable steps of which Emerson reminds us, with no beginning and no end: we find ourselves upon a stair and, willy-nilly, climb.

The gates of gifts are closed to Jake Jackson. He is what he is, what he was born to be, what he has been made, and circumstance offers little aid. As he wrenched himself that winter morning from sleep, his "piggish eyes blinked at sunlight," his "Adam's apple jumped up and down . . . like a toy monkey on a string. . . . Heat was melting tiny cakes of grease in his nappy hair. He . . . scratched at a thin stream of slickness oozing down the ebony nape of his neck." His "broad nose squatted fat and soft, its two holes gaping militantly frontward like barrels of a shotgun. Lips were full, and moist, and drooped loosely, trembling when he walked. A soft roll of fat seeped out of his neck, buttressing his chin."

Not an attractive fellow was Jake. But though perhaps a caricature, he is recognizable—as stereotype? as portrait only slightly distorted? as a victim dangling between two worlds? He had a wife who for comfort read magazines of Christian healing, and well she might. She was a sickly woman who suffered from the results of an abortion which Jake had insisted she have and for which he still owed the doctor five hundred dollars. And now she had developed a "Gawddamn tumor" and would need another operation: *"That bitch!"* A second operation would put Jake a clean thousand dollars in debt, not counting "the furniture bill and the rent bill and the gas bill and the light bill and the bill at the Boston Store and the insurance bill and the milk bill," all overdue. On top of that, Jake suspected Lil of carrying on behind his back with the milk man. So he beat on her and bad-mouthed her to keep his spirits up: *"My life is just all shot to hell!"*

But Jake was also proudly a man of property. He had ten suits in his closet, black, blue, and brown, a grey tweed and a tan, a wine reddish ensemble with pleated trousers, and a green one-buttoned sack. That morning he chose the latter, and a soft collared lavender shirt, a wide yellow tie studded with blue halfmoons into which he inserted "a huge imitation ruby that burned like a smear of fresh blood." A purple embroidered orange handkerchief peeped out of his breast pocket. Spotlessly white spats topped low cut suede shoes with high Cuban heels and toes that tapered to a point. His light grey topcoat was adorned with huge buttons of liquid pearl. Taking his mahogany-handled cane, putting on his black hat with a tiny red feather peeping jauntily from its back, he stomped down the stairs to the vestibule where he pocketed mail he wanted to keep Lil from seeing, and then into the street and the day that lay tediously before him.

II

Not Octavus Roy Cohen or Roark Bradford produced a more splendidly repulsive or more colorfully adorned character, with mind more a melange of middleclass misapprehension. No klansman, redneck, linthead, or hard-hat was more befuddled with cliches than was Jake. Headlines in the morning paper had declared that Franklin D. Roosevelt would drive the moneychangers from the temple, but what chance, thought Jake, had even the President when "old man Morgan and old man Rockefeller and old man Ford" were against him: "Why them men owns and runs the country," and more power to them. Of Germans, he recalled what they had done to "them little Beljum babies," and what happened when they "come across a French woman, no matter how old she was . . . one soljer after another getting on one poor little woman, and she just laying there and can't do nothing." And, he added with a masculine, wistful sigh, "ain't no policeman around to bother you." Will the real Jake Jackson please stand up! And gangsters: "Jeeesus, it takes nerve to be a gangster. But they have plenty of fun. Always has a lot of girls hanging on their arms. Dress swell in sporty clothes. Drive them long, sleek automobiles. And got money to throw away." But Jews!: "That's what's wrong with this country, too many Jews, Dagos, Hunkies, and Mexicans." Why don't they go back to where they belong? As for communists: "Why don't they stay in their own country if they don't like the good old USA?" Why, "over in Roosia where they in power, folks is starving to death," and if you don't do what they tell you to do, "then they lines you up against a wall and shoots you down!"

When Lil dared protest that people were starving to death in this country also, Jake confidently informed her that "Nobody but lazy folks can starve in this country." Like a woman, she continued in argument, telling him:

> "And they burned a colored man alive the other day."
> "Who?"
> "The white people in this country."
> "Shut up! you don't know what you talking about."
> "Well, they *did*!"
> "How you know?"
> "It was in the papers."
> "Aw, that was down South, anyhow."
> "But the South's a part of this country."

Jake paused over his breakfast, stopped chewing, and glared at her. "Woman, is you a *Red*?" he said, and kept on chewing.

III

Jake's day thereafter continued long and dull and dreary. It was a beautiful day, "dazzlingly bright." As he looked from his dingy living room window, that "portion of the sky he could see was marvelously blue. Tons of golden sunshine splashed the streets and houses." It was a day certainly for new beginnings, for a fresh start: "A lost spring day set like a jewel amongst the dreary winter ones," a day filled with promises of delight. Jake's "blood sogged slowly through his veins like warm milk . . . an uneasy feeling, elusive and light as a feather, played over the surface of his stomach" as there swam before him the vision of a "brown, winsome, and delicately oval-shaped" face, its eyelids drooping with languorous passion, its wet lips hovering closer and closer and closer, but unattainable, a dream not unlike the dream of lithesome, languorous young beauty which haunted George Folansbee Babbitt as some years before he had begun a dreary day in Zenith.

Jake's day also stretched bleak before him. Hours would have to be spent within the confines of the black community and his own restless unhappiness before he must report for his job on the swing-shift at the post office. He is worried, and well he might be, about Lil, about whether she will cause him to lose his job by again reporting to the postal Board of Review that he has beaten her, and about her operation and how many years he would be in debt if he paid for it. Loitering bleakly through this day with Jake, the reader discovers himself to be with a loutish, bitter, repulsive, amiable companion. He reads over Jake's shoulder as he goes through the throw-aways in his mail-box, attracted by the burlesque, being condescending perhaps toward Jake who is sceptical and at the same time tempted by the panacea promises of quick wealth or quick health which the circulars reveal, his gullibility not greatly different from anyone's susceptibility (mine, anyway) to seed catalogues, travel brochures, and book-club come-ons. He is amused at the black man's chauvinistic, male, self-approving and self-protecting reactions to invitations to purchase Speedy's Powerful Impotency Castigator. "Shucks," said Jake, "I don't need nothing like this." But he thought he might show the advertisement for Virgin Mary's Neverfail Herb and Root Tonic for Nervous and Run-down Women to Lil: "This thing might save me some money." And he tore the flyer recommending Surefire Home Treatment for Drunkards into tiny shreds and let them drop on the floor because, he muttered, *"Lil's just crazy enough to want to try this on me if she found it."* It is not difficult to forget Jake's color. He is more person than black.

But he is black certainly, confined by color. The day was February 12, a holiday in celebration of the birthdate of the Great Emancipator, but as Jake descended to the street whistling the refrain of a popular blues song, the first thing that he saw—after passing a brown-skinned girl whose luscious plumpness causes him to cock his hat to a more rakish angle and jingle the coins in his pocket more spiritedly ("how good it was merely to be alive")—was a newsstand displaying a picture, in black and white (Richard Wright seldom wastes a word), of the half-charred nude body of a black man swinging from the end of a rope. At the top of the picture, in large capitals, was the challenge: DEATH TO LYNCHERS. "Jake grunted and whistled louder," stooped to watch black children at play, then hurried down the block, turned a corner, and knocked softly at the door of the Black Gold Policy Wheel where he lost money by betting on combinations of numbers which his dream of steps should have guaranteed to be winners.

And so, slowly and tediously, Jake is followed through his tedious day. He was joined by three companions, one an uncomfortable victim of gonorrhea, another tubercular, and the third a Falstaffian, gluttonous uncletomish man who finds some release from black bondage as a member of the white man's National Guard. Their badinage, bridge games, and misunderstandings are wondrously tedious. Their conversation is often so jumbled, so quick with quip and swift reply, that it is as difficult as it would be if one were actually there always to know just who said what, and to whom. But there is little need to know, for the reader discovers that each of the four friends has been cut by white hands into the same black pattern, and they talk and blunder in fear and jealousy and worship of their creator. They are bibulous and libidinous, and they cheerfully argue, renege, and boast of conquests, their own or those of Father Divine who has even white folks believing in him, or of Joe Louis who may, just may, become their avenging redeemer.

As they moved slowly and reluctantly toward their tedious, white encircled, jobs at the post office, they stopped to watch a sidewalk pitchman who hawked Universal Herb Cureall Medicine: "A man must make a lot of money in a business like that." They watched a parade of the Allied Imperial African War Councils in which marched mythical generals of a mythical African republic whose "medals of unfought wars and unwon victories clinked across their uniforms with every rattle of the drums." On the elevated railway which takes them to their work, they gaped clumsily at the exposed white thighs of a woman who sat carelessly, whooping and hollering like good old black boys, improvising one after another, one line each:

> *Oh, Lawd, can I ever, can I ever?* . . .
> *Naw, nigger, you can never, you can never.* . . .
> *But wherever there's life there's hope.* . . .
> *And wherever there's trees there's rope.*

IV

Only Robert Pharr in *The Book of Numbers* and *S.R.O.* has written more revealingly of the degradation and feckless humanness of the black man in urban America, wretched, loutish, vulgar, a menace, even to himself, much as Jerzy Kosinski in *Steps* has written of the uncontrolled, naked degradation of any man anywhere, of the cultural barrenness and bleakness of contemporary life. "For him without concentration," Kosinski quotes *The Bhagavadgita* as saying, "there is no peace. And for the unpeaceful how can there be happiness?" Jake is a peace-loving, violent, and peaceless man, frustrated and demeaned, searching as Babbitt searched, or as Augie March or Studs Lonigan searched, for the contentment of confidence and the security of get-rich-quick wealth, but cribbed within a world enlightened only by cliches, a victim to shoddy values which the white man who patterned him has imposed.

For *Lawd Today* is a courageous book. As a communist, Richard Wright found communism wanting. As a black man, he saw the black man a victim as much of himself as of circumstance. But not too much a victim. Within what was allowed him, he did his thing, tediously perhaps, wantonly, but according to the only terms to which he was permitted. His marital life was in shambles, his financial situation was disastrous and becoming worse, his dreams were the commonplace dreams of almost all men. His day had narrow boundaries, and only other days like it stretched ahead. Meanwhile the anger of his frustration was directed, not against the enemy, but against people like himself, against Lil who dreams and Blanche who plays him for a sucker. But Jake survives, to me more powerful than Bigger Thomas as a nightmare messenger, hauntingly a reminder of what it can mean to be a black man in America—not a good black man nor a bad black man, only a person confined, doomed to live in isolation, "condemned to seek the basest goals," explained Richard Wright in *Eight Men*, yet "sharing the culture that condemns him."

<h2 style="text-align:center">V</h2>

Lawd Today is an apprentice book certainly. Echoes of Dos Passos, Gertrude Stein, Pound, Hemingway, and many another have been discovered in it. But when Richard Wright borrows, he pays interest generously. I do not find the chronicle of Jake's tedious day to be tedious. Dan McCall is right in saying, "Some of it is funny, really funny— especially if one tries to read it aloud and discovers that it begins to sound like Ionesco—Wright's point here is surely its pointlessness." Nor is Wright's humor tainted with irony. It is genuine, as Mark Twain's at his best is genuine, with bitterness showing through but not intruding. Those bridge games which Jake and his cronies play are a joy to any kibitzer, and Wright has diagrammed and explained them, hand by tedious hand. The dreary hours at the post office are the more dreary, and more real, to anyone who has stood for eight hours at a dreary job. Night club festivities move at a faster pace, as well they might, and when the facade of happiness collapses, the promise of illicit pleasure denied, what else is there for a man to do but find release from frustration by hammering on his wife?

Only small things happen during that day, things of consequence to no one except to Jake around whom the day and the world center, complacently destructive. Jake is his world, and there is none besides. No one enters it except in his vision of comfort and wealth and soft lips. More than man black, he is man isolated, and he is a man of little merit. As we remain with him during his day, we allow ourselves more than one condescending smile, and we know that it is the only day that Jake will ever have because all other days will be like it, because Jake has been doomed to tedious days. Like William Dean Howells, Richard Wright in *Lawd Today* dared the commonplace, the temperate religion, in which neither posturing nor defiance is allowed, but which André Gide has reminded us is the invariable habitation of art.

Jake longs for but is incapable of discovering the lush tropics of sensual pleasure. He has no capacity for the bold endeavor required to withstand arctic cold. There is nothing spectacular about Jake, no melodrama, no special pleading. He is commonplace and futile, his worse side is constantly on display. If Richard Wright had not shown him to us, we might have passed him by as just another irresponsible, indistinguishable dark figure in a crowd. Instead, we have him in patiently realistic tedious detail. But to say that *Lawd Today* is a Howellsian novel is to downgrade it. There are no smiling aspects to Jake's life. Though like George Babbitt and well-meaning Studs Lonigan he is caught between a badly focussed dream and a reality which zooms in mercilessly to reveal every pore and pimple, he emerges from his day neither pathetic nor tragic, only insistently, tediously alive. No man was ever like him, and yet he becomes all men whose hunger for an unidentified good life, rich in comfort and appreciation, is not satisfied by the small mouthfuls allowed them.

For Jake, if he is a caricature, is a caricature of the white world which tempts with more than it dares to offer. A mirror image, he has been called, the photographic negative which reveals what it is really like to be a black man in America. Defenses down, the white masks off, we are all Jake Jacksons. Here is black humor most relentlessly black. Jake is joke, incongruously, enduringly alive, funny in the bleakest sense. And Richard Wright, poor Richard, wise Richard, he knew what he was about. "The differences between black folk and white folk are not blood and color," he later told us in *12 Million Black Voices*, "and the ties that bind us are deeper than those that separate us." In *Lawd Today*, without flourish or fanfare he snatched masks from many faces, from all the Clarences and Charleses and Lewises who have hidden behind the anonymity of skin which has no color until the sun brightens it. Lawd, Lawd today, it may be, but probably will not.

Native Son and
An American Tragedy:
Two Different Interpretations
of Crime and Guilt

Yoshinobu Hakutani*

I

Theodore Dreiser is, among modern novelists, one of the most influential predecessors of Richard Wright. In an episode from *Black Boy*, Wright tells us how he was inspired by Dreiser's *Jennie Gerhardt* and *Sister Carrie*: "It would have been impossible for me to have told anyone what I derived from these novels, for it was nothing less than a sense of life itself. All my life had shaped me for the realism, the naturalism of the modern novels, and I could not read enough of them."[1] Such acknowledgment must have convinced critics that the primary source of his best-known work, *Native Son*, was Dreiser's *An American Tragedy*. In fact, several early reviewers of *Native Son* pointed out that the two novels shared the same theme and technique. And both novels convince their readers that the crimes they dramatize are inevitable products of American society and that both protagonists are morally free from guilt.[2]

Except for the obvious problem of race, Wright and Dreiser shared quite similar experiences before they became novelists. Since their boyhood both had been economically hard pressed; they were always ashamed that they had grown up on the wrong side of the tracks. As boys they witnessed struggling and suffering and felt excluded from society. They grew up hating the fanatic and stifling religion practiced at home. In both lives, the family suffered because of the father's inadequacies as a breadwinner; the son inevitably rebelled against such a father, and the family was somehow put together by the suffering mother. Under these circumstances, their dream of success was merely survival; they tried to hang on to one menial job after another. As a result, both had nurtured a brooding sensibility. At twelve, Wright held "a notion as to what life meant that no education could ever alter, a conviction that the meaning of living came only when one was struggling to wring a meaning out of

*Reprinted from *Centennial Review*, 23 (Spring 1979), 208–26, by permission of the author and the journal.

meaningless suffering" (*Black Boy*, p. 112). This statement indeed echoes what Dreiser recorded in his autobiography:

> In considering all I have written here, I suddenly become deeply aware of the fact that educationally speaking, where any sensitive and properly interpretive mind is concerned, experience is the only true teacher—that education, which is little more than a selective presentation of certain stored or canned phases of experience, is at best an elucidative, or at its poorest, a polishing process offered to experience which is always basic.[3]

But this close kinship between the lives of Wright and Dreiser need not necessarily have resulted in the similarities between *Native Son* and *An American Tragedy*. Although both novels are obviously concerned with the crime and guilt of a deprived American youth struggling to realize his dreams of success, the characterization of the hero fundamentally differs in the two novels. Clyde Griffiths in *An American Tragedy* is seen by Dreiser as a representative type, and the novel's psychological focus serves to delineate the frustrations of not only an individual, but a class. Bigger Thomas in *Native Son*, on the other hand, is presented as a particular individual in Wright's imagination. Wright's essay "How 'Bigger' Was Born" suggests an extension of Bigger to include all those rebels the author had known in the South, and even white victims of the system who actively fought against it. Nevertheless, within the confines of the novel itself, we find no other character remotely like Bigger once the murder triggers the creation of his personality and no similar identification between character and author. It is significant in this regard that, as *Black Boy* demonstrates, Wright always considered himself unique, an outsider, not only from whites but also from most of the blacks with whom he grew up.

It would seem that both authors, being literary naturalists, used authentic court records. Dreiser drew on the Gillette murder case in upstate New York; Wright on the Leopold and Loeb kidnap-murder as well as the Robert Nixon murder trial and conviction in Chicago. Both titles strongly imply that Clyde and Bigger are the products of American society and that society, not the individuals involved in the crimes, is to blame. But doesn't a naturalistic novel *always* create tensions in the life of the hero, growing out of an environment over which he has no control and about which he understands very little and, therefore, by which he is *always* victimized? If so, *Native Son* does not appear to fit into this genre. Bigger's transcendence of the type of defeated, determined protagonist of which Clyde in *An American Tragedy* is a good example provides the clearest distinction between the two works. Despite the obvious parallels between *Native Son* and *An American Tragedy*, the comparison is of limited value, and the purpose of this essay is to demonstrate significant differences between the two books.

II

It is true that both novels employ crime as a thematic device. In *Native Son*, the murder of Bessie is the inevitable consequence of Mary Dalton's accidental death; in *An American Tragedy*, Clyde's fleeing the scene of the accident which kills a child leads to his plotting of murder later in the story. Without the presence of crime in the plot neither author would have been able to make significant points about his protagonist. But the focus of the author's idea differs in the two books. Wright's center of interest, unlike Dreiser's, is not crime but its consequences—its psychological effect on his hero. Before committing his crime Bigger is presented as an uneducated, uninformed youth; indeed he is portrayed as a victim of white society who grew up in the worst black ghetto of the nation. We are thus surprised to see him gain identity after the murder. The crime gives him some awareness of himself and of the world of which he has never been capable before. When Bigger and his friend Jack went to see a bourgeois movie called *The Gay Woman*, they were both puzzled by certain words used in the dialogue:

> "Say, Jack?"
> "Hunh?"
> "What's a Communist?"   *Pg. 582*
> "A Communist is a red, ain't he?"
> "Yeah; but what's a red?"
> "Damn if I know. It's a race of folks who live in Russia, ain't it?"
> "They must be wild."
> "Looks like it. That guy was trying to kill somebody."[4]

We are surprised to learn that after the murder Bigger is well versed in world affairs. "He liked to hear," Wright tells us, "of how Japan was conquering China; of how Hitler was running the Jews to the ground; of how Mussolini was invading Spain" (*Native Son*, p. 110). By this time he has learned to think for himself. He is even proud of Japanese, Germans, and Italians, because they "could rule others, for in actions such as these he felt that there was a way to escape from this tight morass of fear and shame that sapped at the base of his life" (pp. 109–10).

Book I of *Native Son* is entitled "Fear," and ironically Wright's characterization of Bigger makes his stature deliberately smaller and less courageous than we might expect of a fighter against oppression. No small wonder that Mary Dalton's death is caused by Bigger's fear of whites and their world. His killing of Mary is an accidental homicide. In *An American Tragedy*, on the other hand, Clyde is placed in a situation so oppressive that only violence can provide him with the hope of dignity. But the oppression for Clyde has a corollary of hope, not fear, on his part. Clyde is an optimistic character, always seeking opportunities for success in life. While Bigger can only kill accidentally, Clyde in the same position can consciously plot murder. Even though the boat into which Clyde lures Roberta overturns when he has not planned it, and her actual death may legally prove accidental, Clyde is not entirely innocent. On this ground alone the interpretation of the death of a girl as a central episode vastly differs between *Native Son* and *An American Tragedy*.

Throughout the story Dreiser implies that Clyde's aspirations to rise in the world are not matched by his abilities. Near the beginning Dreiser makes known that Clyde, overly impressed by every sign of success in his future, "lacked decidedly that mental clarity and inner directing application that in so many permits them to sort out from the facts and avenues of life the particular thing or things that make for their direct advancement."[5] This is why whatever he does is so inept that he is easily caught after the crime. At the trial, Clyde after such a harrowing experience is called by the prosecutor "a loose, wayward and errant character" (p. 525). Before execution Clyde remains "a mental and moral coward," as his defense attorneys have presented him. Not only has he become a puppet of his own lawyers for their political purposes but he ends his life as an immature youth without a sense of remorse, let alone a conviction.

In contrast, Bigger after committing two crimes has for the first time redeemed his manhood. Max, Bigger's defense attorney, argues that the actions leading to the death of Mary and Bessie were "as instinctive and inevitable as breathing or blinking one's eyes. It was an act of *creation!*" (*Native Son* p. 366). Bigger tells Max:

> But really I never wanted to hurt nobody. That's the truth, Mr. Max. I hurt folks 'cause I felt I had to; that's all. They was crowding me too close; they wouldn't give me no room. Lots of times I tried to forget 'em, but I couldn't. They wouldn't let me. . . . (p. 388)

Bigger's earlier evasion of life has been converted to participation. The fact that he had killed a white girl, a symbol of beauty for white society, made him "feel the equal of them, like a man who had been somehow cheated, but had now evened the score" (p. 155). Bessie's murder also marks a new development in Bigger's manhood. For the first time he desires to be at peace with himself. Bigger is no longer a slave but a free man who claims his right to "create." Bessie's murder results from a willful act, a clear departure from the accidental killing of Mary Dalton.

Despite a death sentence handed down by his white rulers, Bigger now proclaims his own existence. Even Max, who has taken a sympathethic attitude towards the oppressed, is bewildered by Bigger's deep urges for freedom and independence. "I didn't want to kill," Bigger tells Max. "But what I killed for, I *am!*" (pp. 391–92). Having overcome white oppression, Bigger now stands a heroic exemplar for the members of his race. His brother Buddy, he realizes, "was blind . . . went round and round in a groove and did not see things." Bigger sees in Buddy "a certain stillness, an isolation, meaninglessness" (p. 103). His sister Vera, too, was a tired and fearful girl who "seemed to be shrinking from life in every gesture she made" (p. 104). Alcohol was what sustained his girl friend Bessie as religion was what obsessed Mrs. Thomas. All his mother could do after Bigger's capture was kneel on the floor at Mrs. Dalton's feet to beg for sparing her son's life. "Bigger," says Wright, "was paralyzed with shame; he felt violated" (p. 280). Finally, in both *Native Son* and *An American Tragedy* a preacher appears before the trial to console the accused. But in *Native Son* the black preacher is described in derogatory terms. Bigger immediately senses that the Reverend Hammond possesses only a white-washed soul and functions merely as an advocate of white supremacy. Wright offers this explanation:

> The preacher's face was black and sad and earnest. . . . He had killed within himself the preacher's haunting picture of life even before he had killed Mary; that had been his first murder. And now the preacher made it walk before his eyes like a ghost in the night, creating within him a sense of exclusion that was as cold as a block of ice. (p. 264)

During his act of liberation, too, Bigger is consciously aware of his own undoing and creation. A successful naturalistic novel often creates tensions in the life of the hero and they often crush him. To survive in this state of being, Bigger is forced to rebel, unlike Clyde, who remains a victim of the tensions. In rebelling, then, Bigger moves from determinism to freedom. Bigger knows how to escape the confines of his environment and to gain an identity. Even before he acts, he knows exactly how Mary, and Bessie later, has forced him into a vulnerable position. No wonder he convinces himself not only that he has killed to protect himself but also that he has attacked the entire civilization. In *An American Tragedy*, Dreiser molds the tragedy of Clyde Griffiths by generating pity and sympathy for the underprivileged in American society. In *Native Son*, however, Wright departs from the principles of pity and sympathy which whites have for blacks. In "How 'Bigger' Was Born," Wright admits that his earlier *Uncle Tom's Children* was "a book which even bankers' daughters could read and weep over and feel good about."[6] In *Native Son*, however, Wright would not allow for such complacency. He warns the readers that the book "would be so hard and deep that they would have to face it without the consolation of tears."[7]

The meaning of *Native Son* therefore derives not from crime but from its result. Dreiser's interest in *An American Tragedy*, on the other hand, lies not in the result of crime but in its cause. While Bigger at the end of his violent and bloody life can claim his victory, Clyde at the end of his life remains a failure. *Native Son* thus ends on an optimistic note; *An American Tragedy* as a whole stems from and ends on the dark side of

American capitalism. F. O. Matthiessen is right in maintaining that the reason for Dreiser's use of the word *American* in his title "was the overwhelming lure of money-values in our society, more nakedly apparent than in older and more complex social structures."[8] Furthermore, Helen Dreiser seems to confirm Dreiser's central thought in interpreting materialism as the cause of Clyde's tragedy. Commenting on Dreiser's choice of the Chester Gillette murder case for fictionalization, Helen Dreiser writes:

> This problem has been forced on his mind not only by the extreme American enthusiasm for wealth as contrasted with American poverty, but the determination of so many young Americans, boys and girls alike, to obtain wealth quickly by marriage. When he realized the nature of the American literature of that period and what was being offered and consumed by publishers and public, he also became aware of the fact that the most interesting American story of the day concerned not only the boy getting the girl, but more emphatically, the poor boy getting the rich girl. Also, he came to know that it was a natural outgrowth of the crude pioneering conditions of American life up to that time, based on the glorification of wealth which started with the early days of slavery and persisted throughout our history.[9]

Dreiser's fascination with this subject resulted in his treatment of Clyde as a victim of the American dream. Bigger, too, a product of the same society, cherishes a dream of his own. Like anyone else, he reads the newspapers and magazines, goes to the movies, strolls the crowded streets. Bigger is intensely aware of his dreams: "to merge himself with others and be a part of this world, to lose himself in it so he could find himself, to be allowed a chance to live like others, even though he was black" (*Native Son*, p. 226). Unlike Dreiser, Wright must have clearly recognized his hero's sense of alienation from the rest of the world. It is an alienation that Wright himself, not Dreiser, often experienced as a boy and as a man. But it never occurs to Bigger that he can pursue such a dream. Indeed, throughout the book Wright amply documents the prevailing social mores, economic facts, and public sentiments to prove that Bigger's actions, attitudes, and feelings have already been determined by his place in American life. It is understandable for James Baldwin to say of *Native Son* that every Negro has "his private Bigger Thomas living in the skull."[10] Given such a determined state of mind, Bigger would not be tempted to pursue his dreams. Ironically, the racial oppression and injustice in fact enhance his manhood. To Clyde Griffiths, however, the flame of temptation is brighter and more compelling. He is easily caught, and he thrashes about in a hopeless effort to escape the trap. Under these circumstances, "with his enormous urges and his pathetic equipment,"[11] as Dreiser once characterized the plight of such an individual in America, there is no way out for Clyde but to plot murder.

The central meaning of *An American Tragedy* thus comes from the economic and social forces that overpower Clyde and finally negate his aspirations. Where a Bigger Thomas before liberation must always remain an uninformed, immature youth, a Clyde Griffiths is the one whose mind is already ingrained with that glorious pattern of success: one must climb the social ladder from lower to middle to upper class. Money is necessarily the barometer of that success. At the beginning of the story Dreiser directly shows how the family's mission work in which Clyde is compelled to take part looks contrary to his dreams. Dreiser at once comments that "his parents looked foolish and less than normal—'cheap' was the word. . . . His life should not be like this. Other boys did not have to do as he did" (*An American Tragedy*, p. 12). A basically sensitive and romantic boy, he cannot help noticing the "handsome automobiles that sped by, the loitering pedestrians moving off to what interests and comforts he could only surmise; the gay pairs of young people, laughing and jesting and the 'kids' staring, all troubled him with a sense of something different, better, more beautiful than his, or rather their life" (p. 10). This scene functions in the story as a great contrast to a similar scene in *Native Son*. Near the beginning Bigger goes to the movies and sees double features. *The Gay Woman*, portraying love and intrigue in upper-class white society, quickly loses his attention, and *Trader Horn*, in which black men and women are dancing in a wild jungle, shows him only life in a remote world. Bigger is thus placed in no man's land; he is only vaguely aware that he is excluded from both worlds. Unlike Wright, however, Dreiser places his hero in *An American Tragedy* at the threshold of success and achievement.

Clyde is also a victim of sexual forces. Early in the story his family is confronted by his older sister Esta's elopement, pregnancy, and desertion. Although Clyde is aware that sex leads to exploitation and misery on the part of the girl, he does not blame the whole problem upon the seducer. This ambivalence in his attitude towards sex has a foreshadowing effect on his own affair with Roberta. For Bigger, sex is merely a biological force and it plays a minor role in his life. For Clyde, however, sex is not only viewed materialistically but weighed in the gradations of the economic and social scale. Clyde is first attracted to the incipient whore, Hortense Briggs, because her eyes remind him of an alcove in the hotel hung with black velvet. To her suggestion that "fellows with money would like to spend it" on her, Clyde boasts: "I could spend a lot more on you than they could" (p. 79). To win her love he must buy her an expensive fur coat beyond his means. Sondra Finchley, his ultimate love, for whom he is forced to sacrifice his second girl friend Roberta, is called "the most adorable feminine *thing* he had seen in all his days" (p. 219, italics added). Dreiser can make us feel what Clyde feels: "Indeed her effect on him was electric—thrilling—arousing in him a curiously stinging sense of what it was to want and not to have—to wish to win and yet to feel, almost agonizingly that he was destined not even to win a glance from her" (pp. 219–20). In short, sex becomes not a romantic force of love but a symbol of material success in the American dream.

Thus Clyde is presented as a helpless victim of society. Characterized by the defense attorneys as "a moral and mental coward," he is not strong enough to oppose the system, nor is he well equipped to transcend his spurious dreams. On the contrary, Bigger in *Native Son* is represented to his disadvantage by the defense attorney. A more convincing argument in that courtroom would have been for the defense to plead insanity rather than to demonstrate that Bigger is a victim of society. Such representation does not occur in Clyde's defense in *An American Tragedy*. Jephson most faithfully equates Clyde's infatuation with Sondra with a "case of the Arabian Nights, of the ensorcelled and the ensorcellor. . . . A case of being bewitched, my poor boy—by beauty, love, wealth, by things that we sometimes think we want very, very much, and cannot ever have" (p. 681). Dreiser's theme therefore becomes the baffling problem of Justice. Jephson, Dreiser's mouthpiece during the trial, tells Clyde and the court: "Clyde—not that I am condemning you for anything that you cannot help. (After all, you didn't make yourself, did you?)" (p. 675). This pronouncement is later echoed by Clyde's own reflections in the prison:

> Was it not also true (the teaching of the Rev. McMillan—influencing him to that extent at least) that if he had led a better life—had paid more attention to what his mother had said and taught—not gone into that house of prostitution in Kansas City—or pursued Hortense Briggs in the evil way that he had—or after her, Roberta—had been content to work and save, as no doubt most men were—would he not be better off than he now was? But then again, there was the fact or truth of those very strong impulses and desires within himself that were so very, very hard to overcome. (p. 784)

Other naturalists who often show their characters being destroyed by overwhelming forces always remind us how small and helpless human efforts are. "Men were nothings," says Norris towards the end of *The Octopus*, "mere animalcules, mere ephemerides that fluttered and fell and were forgotten between dawn and dusk."[12] Dreiser never does this because he is always seeking the possibility of magnitude and self-determination in human existence. No matter how small and weak a man like Clyde may prove to be, Dreiser never gives up searching for his humanity and individual worth. In an interview in 1921 Dreiser flatly stated his predilection for little men that was to explain his treatment of Clyde Griffiths: "I never can and never want to bring myself to the place where I can ignore the sensitive and seeking individual in his pitiful struggle with nature."[13]

Both Wright and Dreiser are intensely concerned with the forces in society which man must battle for survival. Most naturalist writers are clearly pessimistic determinists who observe that man is destroyed either by competition or submission. And his fate is often death. But Wright stands at the opposite end of this human struggle, for his hero is victorious over the brutal facts of experience. True, Bigger is condemned to die as a murderer, but this defeat is really a triumph for Bigger, who has rejected society's rules and values and established his own. Dreiser, on the other hand, stands between defeat and triumph. If naturalism faces the tension between will and determinism, Dreiser is content to keep the tension unresolved. Despite Clyde's destruction in the end, Dreiser refuses to indict life. Instead he has tenaciously sought its beauty and exaltation till the end.

III

The two novelists' divergent attitudes towards the problem of guilt are reflected in the style and structure of their books. *Native Son* is swift in pace and dramatic in tone, and displays considerable subjectivity, involving the reader in experiences of emotional intensity. The thirties were hard times for whites as well as blacks, and it was not possible to take a calm and objective view of the situation. Wright himself was a victim of the hard times and he could speak from his heart. Morever, Bigger Thomas is a conscious composite portrait of numerous individual blacks Wright had known in his life. As indicated in "How 'Bigger' Was Born," all of them defied the Jim Crow order, and all of them suffered for their rebellion. "So volatile and tense," Wright observes, "are these relations that if a Negro rebels against rule and taboo, he is lynched and the reason for the lynching is usually called 'rape,' that catchword which has garnered such vile connotations that it can raise a mob anywhere in the South pretty quickly, even today."[14] As in the novel, Wright had lived in a cramped and dirty flat. He had visited many such dwellings as an insurance agent.[15] In Chicago, while working at the South Side Boys' Club, he observed other prototypes of Bigger Thomas—fearful, frustrated, and violent youths who struggled for survival in the worst slum conditions.[16]

The twenties, the background of Dreiser's novel, however, had not of course erupted into the kind of social strife witnessed a decade later. Unlike the hostile racial conflicts dramatized in *Native Son*, what is portrayed in *An American Tragedy* is Clyde Griffiths' mind, which is deeply affected by the hopes and failures of the American dream. A later reviewer of *An American Tragedy* accused Dreiser of scanting, "as all the naturalists do, the element of moral conflict without which no great fiction can be written, for he fobbed the whole wretched business off on that scapegoat of our time, society."[17] But the depiction of such a conflict was not Dreiser's intention for the novel in the first place. Rather the poignancy of Clyde's tragedy comes from his helpless attraction and attachment to the dream which society had created. Dreiser defines this essential American psyche in an essay:

Our most outstanding phases, of course, are youth, optimism and illusion. These run through everything we do, affect our judgments and passions, our theories of life. As children we should all have had our fill of these, and yet even at this late date and after the late war, which should have taught us much, it is difficult for any of us to overcome them. Still, no one can refuse to admire the youth and optimism of America, however much they may resent its illusion. There is always something so naive about its method of procedure, so human and tolerant at times; so loutish, stubborn and ignorantly insistent at others, as when carpetbag government was forced on the South after the Civil War and Jefferson Davis detained in prison for years after the war was over.[18]

In contrast to Bigger's violent life, Clyde's mind can only be conveyed by a leisurely pace and undramatic tone. Dreiser's approach is basically psychological, and this allows us to sympathize with the character whose principal weakness is ignorance and naiveté. Consequently we become deeply involved with Clyde's fate. Above all, the relative calmness and objectivity in which Clyde's experience is traced stem from a mature vision of the tribulations shared by any of us who have ever dreamed.

The lack of dramatic tone in *An American Tragedy* is also due to change of setting. Dreiser's restless protagonist begins his journey in Kansas City, flees to Chicago, and finally reaches his destiny in upstate New York. In contrast, Wright achieves greater dramatic intensity by observing a strict unity of setting. All of the action in *Native Son* takes place in Chicago, a frightening symbol of disparity and oppression in American life. Wright heightens the conflict and sharpens the division between the two worlds throughout the book. In the beginning, the Thomases' apartment is described as the most abject place imaginable, while the Dalton mansion suggests the white power structure that ravages blacks and destroys their heritage. The conflict is obvious throughout, and the descriptions of the two households present ironic contrasts. Whereas everything at the Thomases' is loud and turbulent, at the Daltons' it is quiet and subdued. But the true nature of the oppressor is later revealed: Mr. Dalton, real estate broker and philanthropist, tries to keep blacks locked in the ghetto and refuses to lower the rents. During the trial, the prosecutor, the press, and the public equally betray the most vocal racial prejudice and hatred. Thus the central action of Book III is for the defense to confront and demolish this wall of injustice before Bigger could be spared his life.

The narrative pattern in *An American Tragedy* is entirely different. Although the novel is divided into three parts as is *Native Son*, Dreiser's division is based upon change of time and characters. Each part has its own complete narrative, and one part follows another with the same character dominating the central scene. Each unit is joined to the other not only by the principal character but by the turn of events that underlies the theme of the novel. Book I begins with Clyde's dreams of success but ends in an accident that forebodes a disaster. This narrative pattern is repeated in Book II, beginning with a portrayal of the luxurious home of Samuel Griffiths in Lycurgus and ending with the murder. Book III opens with a depiction of Cataraqui County, where Clyde is to be tried and executed. Clyde's defense, resting upon the most sympathetic interpretation of his character as a moral and mental coward, clearly indicates the possibility of hope but nonetheless ends on a note of despair. The death of a child caused by an automobile accident at the end of Book I does not make Clyde legally guilty, but his fleeing the scene of the accident makes him morally culpable. This pattern is also repeated at the end of Book II, where he willfully ignores Roberta's screams for help, an act of transgression for which he is tried and punished. Such a narrative pattern is not given to the death of Mary and Bessie in *Native Son*, since one murder is necessarily caused by the other. Despite the fact that Bessie's death is caused by a premeditated murder, Bigger's crime does not raise the same moral issue as does Clyde's.

There are also many other parallels that thread the three parts together in *An American Tragedy*. Esta's seduction and abandonment by a travelling actor earlier in the story foreshadows what happens to Roberta. Clyde's attraction to Hortense Briggs has a great deal in common with his helpless enticement to Sondra Finchley with her beauty and wealth. Roberta and Clyde, in fact, come from similar backgrounds, both trying to extricate themselves from the past in order to realize their dreams of social and economic success. Furthermore, the entire book is enclosed, in the beginning and in the end, by almost the same vignettes. The novel opens with Clyde and his family preaching in a street of Kansas City at dusk of a summer night and closes with an almost identical scene in San Francisco, with Russell, Clyde's nephew, now taking his place. Dreiser's implication is unmistakable: given the same temperament and circumstance, Russell will grow up to be another Clyde Griffiths and encounter another American tragedy.

Such parallels and ironies not only dominate Dreiser's narrative structure but also constitute the naturalistic detail that characterizes a Zolaesque experimentation. A literary naturalist first establishes a milieu taken from life and, into it, projects characters who then act in accordance with that milieu. In *An American Tragedy*, unlike his earlier novels such as *Sister Carrie*, Dreiser conducts his experiment with the characters not once but twice to prove the process of a natural phenomenon. What underlies the plot development in this novel is Dreiser's constant reminder for us to form our own flashbacks and reflections. In *Native Son*, Wright allows us as little interruption of the action as possible. Unlike *An American Tragedy*, Wright's book has no chapter divisions and only an occasional pause to indicate a transition or change of scene. Before Mary's murder, for example, Wright gives us only three brief glimpses of Bigger's life: his relations with his family, his gang, and his girlfriend. Before Roberta's murder, on the other hand, which occurs at the end of Book II, Dreiser provides a comprehensive background of Clyde's life: his relationship with his family including Esta, with all his friends and associates, and with all the girls with whom he has attempted to make friends. Whereas Dreiser's presentation is complete and direct, Wright's is selective and metaphorical.

In *Native Son*, Wright thus differs from the traditional naturalist who piles detail upon detail to gain verisimilitude. He is more akin to his contemporaries like Faulkner and Steinbeck in using the devices of the symbolic novel. He writes with great economy, compressing detail in small space and time; the reader must supply the rest. But his ideas are scarcely misinterpreted, because *Native Son*, as James Baldwin aptly points out, is a protest novel with the author's voice dominating the narrative.[19] Bigger is therefore meant not so much to be a character but to be a symbol, though some critics consider this a confusion in the book.[20] In *An American Tragedy*, the author's voice is relatively absent. In *Sister Carrie*, for example, Dreiser is noted for a lengthy philosophical commentary inserted at every turn of event, as well as for a strong tendency to identify with his characters throughout the story. But in *An American Tragedy* Dreiser's comments are not only few but short. Despite Clyde's resolution to work hard and steadily once he has reached the luxurious world of the Green-Davidson, Dreiser's comment is devastatingly swift: "The truth was that in this crisis he was as interesting an illustration of the enormous handicaps imposed by ignorance, youth, poverty and fear as one could have found" (p. 384).

In contrast to *Native Son*, Dreiser in *An American Tragedy* also reduces the author's omniscience by relying upon the method of indirect discourse. When Clyde is helplessly trapped between his loyalty to Roberta and his desire for Sondra, the insoluble dilemma is rendered through his dreams involving a savage black dog, snakes, and reptiles. About the possibility of Roberta's accidental murder, Dreiser depicts how Clyde is trying to dismiss the evil thought but at the same time is being enticed to it. His actual plot to murder, suggested by the newspaper article, now thrusts itself forward, as Dreiser says, "psycho-genetically, born of his own turbulent, eager and disappointed seeking" (p. 463). This crucial point in Clyde's life is explained in terms of a well-known myth:

> . . . there had now suddenly appeared, as the genie at the accidental rubbing of Aladdin's lamp—as the efrit emerging as smoke from the mystic jar in the net of the fishermen—the very substance of some leering and diabolic wish or wisdom concealed in his own nature, and that now abhorrent and yet compelling, leering and yet intriguing, friendly and yet cruel, offered him a choice between an evil which threatened to destroy

him (and against his deepest opposition) and a second evil
which, however it might disgust or sear or terrify, still provided for freedom and success and love. (pp. 463–64)

The immediate effect of such a passage for us is to create compassion for
the character whose mind is torn between the two forces with which he is
incapable of coping. Given Clyde's weaknesses, then, we are more likely
to sympathize with than despise such a soul.

On the contrary, Bigger's manhood—which is as crucial a point in
his life as Clyde's dilemma in his—is rendered through direct discourse. It
is not the narrator's voice but the character's that expresses his inner
life—the newly won freedom. His murder of a white girl makes him bold,
ridding him of the fear that has hitherto imprisoned him. In the midst of
describing Bigger's intoxication over his personal power and pleasure,
Wright shifts the tone of the narrative to let Bigger provide a lofty voice of
his own. While preparing a ransom note, Bigger utters: "Now, about the
money. How much? Yes; make it ten thousand. *Get ten thousand in 5 and
10 bills and put it in a shoe box. . . .* That's good" (*Native Son*, p. 167).
Even more remarkable is Bigger's final statement to Max:

"What I killed for must've been good!" Bigger's voice was full
of frenzied anguish. "It must have been good! When a man
kills, it's for something. . . . I didn't know I was really alive
in this world until I felt things hard enough to kill for
'em. . . . It's the truth, Mr. Max. I can say it now, 'cause I'm
going to die. I know what I'm saying real good and I know
how it sounds. But I'm all right. I feel all right when I look at it
that way. . . ." (p. 392)

Bigger's utterance, in fact, startles the condescending lawyer. At this
climactic moment Max, awe-stricken, "groped for his hat like a blind
man" (p. 392). Interestingly enough, Dreiser's presentation of Clyde in
the same predicament is given through indirect discourse:

He walked along the silent street—only to be compelled to
pause and lean against a tree—leafless in the winter—so bare
and bleak. Clyde's eyes! That look as he sank limply into that
terrible chair, his eyes fixed nervously and, as he thought, ap-
pealingly and dazedly upon him and the group surrounding
him.
Had he done right? Had his decision before Governor
Waltham been truly sound, fair or merciful? Should he have
said to him—that perhaps—perhaps—there had been those
other influences playing upon him? . . . Was he never to have
mental peace again, perhaps? (p. 811)

In contrast to this portrait of Clyde, who is largely unaware of his guilt
and his manhood, the final scene of *Native Son* gives the ending its
dramatic impact. Despite his crimes and their judgment, Bigger's final ut-

terance elicits from us nothing but understanding and respect for the emerging hero.

IV

The sense of ambiguity created by Dreiser's use of portraits, dreams, and ironies throughout *An American Tragedy* is thus suited to the muddled mind of Clyde Griffiths. Bigger Thomas, however, can hardly be explained in ambivalent terms, for he has opted for the identity of a murderer. Clyde is presented as a victim of the forces over which he has no control, and Dreiser carefully shows that Roberta's murder—the climax of the book—has inevitably resulted from these forces. The principal interest of the novel, centering upon this crime, lies in Clyde's life before the murder and its effect on him. In Book III, Clyde is depicted not merely as a victim of society but more importantly as a victim of his own illusions about life. In the end, then, he still remains an unregenerate character as Dreiser has predicted earlier in the story.

Like Clyde, Bigger in *Native Son* is presented in the beginning as an equally naive character, and his life is largely controlled by fear and hatred. He kills Mary Dalton because he fears his own kindness will be misunderstood. He hates in turn what he fears, and his violence is an expression of this hatred. But unlike Clyde, he has learned through his murders how to exercise his will. Each of the three books in *Native Son* is built on its own climax, and Book III, "Fate," is structured to draw together all the noble achievements of Bigger's life. Significantly enough, each of the changes in Bigger's development is also measured by his own language. The difference in characterization between the two protagonists is therefore reflected in the style and structure of the novels. Granted, both writers deal with similar material, but their treatments of a young man's crime and guilt in American society vastly differ in theme as well as in technique.

Notes

1. Richard Wright, *Black Boy* (New York: Harper and Row, 1963), p. 274.

2. Clifton Fadiman, for instance, wrote, "*Native Son* does for the Negro what Theodore Dreiser in *An American Tragedy* did a decade and a half ago for the bewildered, inarticulate American white," *The New Yorker*, 16 (2 March 1940), 52. Also see Peter Jacks, "A Tragic Novel of Negro Life in America—Richard Wright's Powerful 'Native Son' Brings to Mind Theodore Dreiser's 'American Tragedy,' " *New York Times Book Review*, 3 March 1940, p. 2.

3. Theodore Dreiser, *Dawn* (New York: Liveright, 1931), p. 586.

4. Richard Wright, *Native Son* (New York: Harper and Row, 1966), pp. 34–35. Later textual references are to this edition and appear in parentheses.

5. Theodore Dreiser, *An American Tragedy* (New York: The New American Library, 1964), p. 169. Later textual references are to this edition and appear in parentheses.

6. Richard Wright, "How 'Bigger' Was Born," in *Native Son*, p. xxvii.

7. "How 'Bigger' Was Born," p. xxvii.

8. F. O. Matthiessen, *Theodore Dreiser* (New York: William Sloane, 1951), p. 203.

9. Helen Dreiser, *My Life with Dreiser* (Cleveland: World, 1951), pp. 71–72, 76.

10. James Baldwin, "Many Thousands Gone," in *Notes of a Native Son* (New York: Bantam Books, 1968), p. 33.

11. Quoted by F. O. Matthiessen in *Theodore Dreiser*, p. 189.

12. Frank Norris, *The Octopus* (Garden City, N.Y.: Doubleday, 1956), p. 343.

13. Matthiessen, p. 189.

14. Richard Wright, "How 'Bigger' Was Born," in *Native Son*, p. xii.

15. Richard Wright, "The Man Who Went to Chicago," in *Eight Men* (Cleveland: World, 1961), pp. 210–50.

16. See Richard Wright, "The Negro and Parkway Community House," Chicago, 1943 [a four-page pamphlet]. Cf. Keneth Kinnamon, *The Emergence of Richard Wright* (Urbana: Univ. of Illinois Press, 1972), p. 120.

17. J. Donald Adams, "Speaking of Books," *New York Times Book Review*, 16 Feb. 1958, p. 2.

18. Theodore Dreiser, "Some Aspects of Our National Character," in *Hey Rub-A-Dub-Dub* (New York: Boni and Liveright, 1920), p. 24.

19. Baldwin argues that although this authorial voice records the Negro anger as no Negro before him has ever done, it is also, unhappily, the overwhelming limitation of *Native Son*. What is sacrificed, according to Baldwin, is a necessary dimension to the novel: "the relationship that Negroes bear to one another, that depth of involvement and unspoken recognition of shared experience which creates a way of life . . . it is this climate, common to most Negro protest novels, which has led us all to believe that in Negro life there exists no tradition, no field of manners, no possibility of ritual or intercourse, such as may, for example, sustain the Jew even after he has left his father's house." *Notes of a Native Son*, pp. 26–28.

20. Edward Margolies, for instance, in *The Art of Richard Wright* (Carbondale: Southern Illinois Univ. Press, 1969), p. 113, observes an inconsistency of tone in Book III, "where the reader feels that Wright, although intellectually committed to Max's views, is more emotionally akin to Bigger's." What Margolies regards as inconsistent might more profitably be interpreted as a thematic juxtaposition of points of view, the personal (Bigger's) and the ideological (Max's), with both of which Wright is sympathetic.

Richard Wright, French Existentialism, and *The Outsider*

Michel Fabre*

If Richard Wright's interest in existentialism was generally interpreted by American reviewers during his lifetime as a regrettable concession to literary fashion or an incongruous "roll in the hay" with "a philosophy little made to account for Negro life,"[1] critics and scholars have by now recognized and seriously examined the place and nature of the existentialist worldview in Wright's novels, if not in his entire body of writings. For a time, there even existed a tendency to overemphasize the influence of the French school of existentialism, as opposed to the German school or pre-existentialist writers like Dostoevski and Nietzsche. Partly with the aim of restoring a proper balance, I have already attempted to document the actual contacts and collaboration—mostly political—between Wright and such leading French existentialist thinkers and writers as Sartre, Camus, and de Beauvoir, while providing a more precise, if more sobering, view of possible literary influences.[2] In this article, I will reconsider this relationship, focusing upon the convergence of philosophical views and their possible impact on the shaping of Wright's only existentialist novel. I will touch as well upon the emotional and ideological coloring that the discovery of French existentialism imparted to Wright's "metaphysical decade," as we might call the years of meditation, pessimism, questioning, and self-examination that resulted in the writing and publication of *The Outsider*.

Wright's encounter with French existentialism took place in the mid-1940s at a crucial time in his career, when, having rejected Communism, if not Marxist perspectives and explanatory principles, he was for the first time without the sustenance and burden of an ideology. Also, in contemplating the possibilities left open for human values in the industrialized West at the close of World War II, he had become utterly disillusioned. His correspondence with Gertrude Stein, among others, documents his rejection of the consumerism and materialistic goals of American life—what Henry Miller described at the time as *The Air Con-*

*This essay was written specifically for this volume and appears here for the first time by permission of the author.

ditioned Nightmare. As Wright turned to Europe as a repository of humanistic concerns in the tradition of the Enlightenment, the pronouncements of the leading French intellectuals—existentialists like Sartre, Camus, and de Beauvoir (each of whom visited the United States on lecture tours and made public their reactions to the American and the European situation)—undoubtedly played a part in reinforcing Wright's own pessimistic leanings.

Wright's existentialism, however, should by no means be limited to his contacts with the French existentialist group from the mid-forties to the mid-fifties. His interest in an existential worldview both predates and postdates those contacts. On the one hand, works like *Native Son* and *Black Boy* already express an existential vision of life, couched in Dostoevskian terms, which is closely linked with the oppressed, traumatic and precarious aspects of the Afro-American experience. On the other hand, Wright's genuine interest in and knowledge of Kierkegaard and Heidegger, among the German school of existentialists, lasted throughout his later life and became just as integral a part of his *Weltanschauung* as Marxism. This paper does not deal, therefore, with all the dimensions of Wright's existential philosophy. It concentrates, rather, upon the period (roughly from 1946 to 1953) that saw the genesis of *The Outsider*, in order to emphasize possible convergences between Wright's outlook and that of the French existentialists, when it does not prove possible to speak of outright influences.

Wright had three major general preoccupations at the time: how to inject a personal philosophy into Marxist theory; how to restore morality to political action; and how to save mankind from atomic destruction through the reactivation of humanistic values.

The publication of *Native Son* and its reception by the American left-wing and Communist intelligentsia had raised for Wright the problem of how far a Marxist writer could go in presenting a humanist, or personalized, version of his ideology. Aside from all the misunderstandings, the problem arose: Did the writer who accepted Marxism enjoy the liberty of expounding a personalized philosophy? In 1937 Wright had outlined his literary program in "Blueprint for Negro Writing" in the CP-sponsored *New Challenge*, but he had not renounced ideas expressed in earlier pieces, often unpublished, like "Personalism," and he remained very much a humanist. A close analysis of Max's speech in *Native Son* reveals he is attempting to state certain ideas and concepts that are implicit in Marxist philosophy, but that, since Marx and Lenin were more interested in politics and economics than in literature, were not previously stated in humanistic terms. Wright had perceived the important failure of Marxism to treat the human personality. In attempting to remedy that, revolutionary novelists like Gorki and Malraux were compelled to use a sort of mysticism for which they were faulted by communist critics.

On another level, Wright's autobiographical essay "I Tried To Be a Communist" (1944) concerned, among other things, the morality of politics (i.e., the morality of American Communism) and how it was shaped by the nature of race relations in American society. Wright's exposure of its faults, which pointed to what was vital to the theory of (Marxist) action, was in fact an example of that morality in action. After the explosion of the atomic bomb in 1945, he felt more than ever that mankind must move to a humane, intelligent path of action or be removed from the planet. International unity was becoming, more than ever, a political necessity and a matter of life and death.

Ralph Ellison and Wright were close friends at that time, and they often discussed existentialism, especially that of Kierkegaard and Heidegger. In the summer of 1945, Ellison sent Wright, who was thinking of going to Paris, a copy of *Horizon*, the avant-garde British magazine, with an article about new literary developments in France. By this time, Ellison had become as disillusioned and disgusted by American Communist politicians, especially black ones, as Wright had, and hoped American complacency could be jostled by "speaking from a station that gets its power from the mature ideological dynamo of France and the Continent."[3] Therefore, when Ellison called his friend's attention to the achievements of the French existentialists, he did so, significantly, out of an interest in writing and commitment, not from a philosophical worldview:

> I've been reading some fascinating stuff out of France concerning plays written and produced there during the Occupation. Kierkegaard has been utilized and given a social direction by a group who have organized what is called "Existential Theater" and, from what I read, their psychological probing has produced a powerful art. France is in ferment. Their discussion of the artist's responsibility surpasses anything I've ever seen. . . . They view the role of the individual in relation to society so sharply that the leftwing boys, with the possible exception of Malraux, seem to have looked at it through the reverse end of a telescope. I am sure that over there the war has made the writer more self-confident and aware of the dignity of his craft. Sartre, one of the younger writers, would have no difficulty understanding your position in regard to the Left. He writes: "Every epoch discovers one aspect of . . . the condition of humanity, in every epoch man chooses for himself with regard to others, to love, to death, to the world (Kierkegaardian categories, aren't they?) and when a controversy arises on the subject of the disarmament of the FFI, or of the aid to be given to the Spanish Republicans, it is that metaphysical choice, that personal and absolute decision, which is in question. Thus by becoming a part of the uniqueness of our time, we finally merge with the eternal, and it is our task as writers

to cast light on the eternal values which are involved in these social and political disputes. Yet we are not concerned with seeking these values in an intelligible paradise, for they are only interesting in their immediate form. Far from being relativists, we assert emphatically that man is absolute. But he is absolute in his own time, in his own environment, on his own earth. The absolute which a thousand years of history cannot destroy is *this* irreplaceable, incomparable decision, which he makes at *this* moment, in these circumstances. The absolute is Descartes, the man who escapes us because he is dead . . . and the relative is Cartesianism, that coster's barrow philosophy which is trotted out century after century, in which everyone finds whatever he has put in it. It is not by chasing after immortality that we will make ourselves eternal: we will not make ourselves absolute by reflecting in our works desiccated principles which are sufficiently empty and negative to pass from one century to another, but by fighting passionately in our time, by loving passionately and by consenting to perish entirely with it."[4]

This letter is revealing of Ellison's own reasons for becoming interested in Sartre, whose philosophy confirmed his opinion that "man is absolute in his own time, in his own environment," i.e., that the black writer will achieve universality by concentrating on the specific, by dealing with his own experience. This restored his self-confidence and belief in the worth of his craft in the face of the political dictates clamoring for "commitment" under the banner of the CPUSA that he was forcefully rejecting.

Wright was similarly concerned with the responsibility of the artist, as evidenced by his moving answer to the South American artist Antonio Frasconi:

There is . . . beyond the boundaries of imperious politics, a common ground upon which we can stand and see the truth of the problem. . . . Out of what vision must an artist create? The question seems vague but when it is conceived in terms of political pressure from Left or Right it has vital meaning. . . . I hold that, on the last analysis, the artist must bow to the monitor of his own imagination, must be led by the sovereignty of his own impressions and perceptions.[5]

So much for the vindication of independent thinking and personal outlook. But Wright also emphasized responsibility and commitment to truth:

We must beware of those who seek, in words no matter how urgent or crisis charged, to interpose an alien and dubious curtain of reality between our eyes and the crying claims of a world which it is our lot to see only too poignantly and too briefly.[6]

In many ways, the French existentialists were addressing similar problems: the responsibility of the intellectual, the defense of humanistic values, the importance of solidarity, the relationship between truth and freedom. These are clearly the concerns and qualities that Wright so much admired in Sartre. He had found him rather reserved when he first met him at a gathering at the home of his friend Dorothy Norman, the editor of *Twice a Year* and a liberal columnist for the *New York Post*. But later, in 1946 and in 1947, when Wright lived in Paris, he often spoke and wrote of Sartre with the utmost enthusiasm and reverence: "Sartre is the only Frenchman I've met who had voluntarily made the identification of the French experience with that of mankind." "How rare a man is this Sartre," he noted in his journal after a conversation during which the French philosopher compared the plight of the colonized world to that of the French under Nazi occupation.[7] Again, after another conversation on the role of the intellectual regarding the political and human situation, Wright noted, not without a touch of delighted awe:

> Sartre is quite of my opinion regarding the possibility of human action today, that it is up to the individual to do what he can to uphold the concept of what it means to be human. The great danger, I told him, in the world today is the very feeling and conception of what is a human might well be lost. He agreed. I feel very close to Sartre and Simone de Beauvoir.[8]

Wright reiterated—somewhat naively—his respect for Sartre's intelligence and perspicacity in his "Introduction to the *Respectful Prostitute*," which presented the play to the American reader:

> Jean-Paul Sartre, principal exponent of French Existentialism, has brought his keen and philosophical temperament to bear upon the problem of race relations in America. . . . The French mind—especially French minds of the Sartre level—is rigorously logical. . . . The dismally lowered tone of personality expression in America seems ludicrous to the mind of a man who, above all modern writers, is seeking and preaching the integrity of action. . . . It took a foreign mind to see that the spirit of virgins could exist in the personalities of whores. Let us then be thankful for the eyes and mind of Jean-Paul Sartre who, in *La Putain Respectueuse*, is helping us to see ourselves. . . . Finally remember that the artist is, in the last analysis, a judge and it is the business of a judge to render judgments.[9]

Wright could not but be impressed at this time. He had hardly begun to discover French existentialist philosophy with the help of Dorothy Norman and was only relatively more conversant with the work of the German school, even though, as Ellison's letter suggests, his knowledge of Kierkegaardian categories was more thorough and anterior. This is not to say that Wright did not attempt to study French existentialism. He acquired several introductory treatises, like G. de Ruggiero's *Existentialism* (1946) and Jean Wahl's *Short History of Existentialism* (1949), as well as several books by Sartre in English translation, especially *Existentialism* and *The Psychology of Imagination*, before 1950. Yet *Being and Nothingness* was not translated until 1957, and Wright did not master French well enough to read it in the original. Sartre's metaphysics were, therefore, somewhat unclear to him and less important to his own concerns than such political and social essays as "Anti-Semite and Jew" and "What Is Literature?" and, possibly, than literary works like *Age of Reason, The Reprieve, The Diary of Antoine Roquentin*, and the short stories *Intimacy* and *Men Without Shadows*, not to mention Sartre's plays, of which he knew at least *The Respectful Prostitute, Huis-Clos, The Chips Are Down*, and *Les Mains Sales*.

I have dealt elsewhere at some length with Wright's participation in the political ventures of the French existentialists under the banner of the Rassemblement Démocratique Révolutionnaire from 1949 to 1952. I have also explained how the *Temps Modernes* group perceived Wright as a "representative man" and cast him in that role for a time.[10] It remains to be seen, however, to what extent Wright's reverence for Sartre's stance as a committed intellectual and his experiments as a *romancier à thèse* may have inspired Wright's own efforts in *The Outsider*.

Although the early pencil drafts of the novel no longer exist, the half-dozen successive versions of the manuscript are sufficient evidence that, even though it was planned and begun before Wright's first trip to Paris and his acquaintance with French existentialism, the novel was, in some limited manner, influenced by that way of thinking as well as by that style. It must be remembered that Wright apparently started to write a sort of political thriller much in the vein of his earlier naturalistic novels. Drawing on episodes of the then-unpublished *Lawd Today*, he based the experience of his new protagonist, Cross Damon, on the day-to-day, routine, oppressed, and confined existence of Jake, a Chicago postal worker. Admittedly, the sense of confinement and entrapment in a web of circumstances of such a routine recalls Antoine Roquentin's *"engluement"* and subsequent "nausea." Even more Sartrean, if one turns to the plot, is the underground railway accident that allows Cross to start again from scratch with a new, yet-to-be-defined identity. This is the "second chance" given by Sartre to one of the protagonists of *The Chips Are Down*. Yet such occurrences that allow man to "create himself out of nothing" do happen in everyday life, and Wright may have thought of the accident episode before leaving the United States. More probably, his reading the trilogy *Les Chemins de la Liberté* (at least the first volume of it) confirmed Wright in his choice of inserting long philosophical exchanges and considerations in the midst of a well-filled, detective-like plot. Perhaps the example of Sartre should not, in this case, have been followed, since his *romans à thèse* do not make very lively reading. It might have been preferable for Wright to rewrite his own novel as a first person narrative (as he nearly decided to do after reading Camus's novel *The Stranger*).

Does this mean that the influence of Camus prevailed? It would be quite hazardous to make such a statement.

If one considers the way Wright discovered Camus's writings before he met the man, chronological considerations compel us to state, first of all, that in spite of the many resemblances between *Native Son* and *The Stranger*, there never did exist any kind of contact between the two men that could account for possible influences in either direction. Resemblances are coincidental, more a result of convergence.

Wright first heard of Camus in the spring of 1946, around the time he first met Sartre. The first works by Camus he read deserve closer scrutiny than I have granted them previously, because they set the tone for Wright's perception of the Algerian-born novelist. At the end of 1946 *Twice a Year* printed a lecture Camus had given in the spring of that year in New York under the title "The Human Crisis." Strangely enough, when one considers the bulk of Camus's writings and his general outlook, the views he expressed then were exceedingly despondent and pessimistic, notwithstanding a last-minute appeal to "the best in mankind." Such views must have reinforced Wright's contemporary pessimism regarding the morality of politics and the direction of human history in postwar America, where consumerism and the cult of material success were again rampant. Camus spotted what he called "the clearest symptoms" of the human crisis. He denounced "the rise of terror following upon such a perversion of values that a man or a historical force is judged today not in terms of human dignity but in terms of success."[11] Somewhat unexpectedly, Camus was not indicting man's inhumanity to man in wartime—although he later did so—but the overshadowing of human-oriented goals by the quest for material wealth and "happiness." French intellectuals had, as a rule, leveled accusations of crass materialism against the United States in the 1920s and 1930s: the idea was far from new. Yet Camus made American materialism sound ominous and pervasive. He perceived it as the condition of modern man, as a plague coming to Europe:

> If that unhappy man, the Job of modern times, is not to die of his hurts on his dunghill, then must the mortgage of fear and anguish first be lifted, so that he may again find that liberty of mind without which none of the problems set for our modern consciousness can be solved.[12]

Wright's own categories of fear and anguish were probably more "metaphysical" (more Kierkegaardian) than "intellectual," which is the dimension Camus stresses here, but he could not disagree with Camus's second "symptom," namely, loss of "the possibility of persuasion," of appealing to an individual's feelings of humanity to get a human reaction. "For SS," Camus wrote, "were no longer men, representing men but like an instinct elevated to the height of an idea or a theory."[13] This is precisely what Wright tried to prove in *The Outsider* of Communist leaders like Blount or Blimin; and this is what he had opposed in his analysis of the Trotskyite trials in "I Tried To Be a Communist." A corollary of the lack of human response of "commissars" was indeed mentioned by Camus, who conceptualized it as "the replacement of the natural object by printed matter"—the overwhelming rise of bureaucracy—so that, in short, "we no longer die, love, or kill, except by proxy."[14] Camus ended with a discussion of the substitution of the political man for the living man: "No longer are individual passions possible, but only collective, that is to say abstract, passions"[15] in the new cult of efficiency and abstraction.

Although Damon's opponents and targets in *The Outsider* are precisely the cosmic "blocks" of fascism and political totalitarianism—both based upon an essential repudiation of individual needs and feelings—the protagonist's quest is more specifically oriented toward the creation, if not the discovery, of individual norms, which in his utterly nihilistic criticism of existing social values, he hardly manages to claim at the very end. "Man is nothing in particular": Cross's statement to Houston, which in many ways recalls Sartre's definition of man as "a vacant passion," may thus have been, in deeper ways, supported and corroborated by Wright's reading of "The Human Crisis." Indeed, Camus wrote that the cult of efficiency and abstraction explained why man in Europe today experienced only solitude and silence: he could not "communicate with his fellows in terms of values common to them all." Hence, "since he is no longer protected by a respect for man based on the values of man, the only alternative henceforth open to him is to be the victim or the executioner."[16]

Admittedly, the reasons for Cross's outright "metaphysical egotism" could be found more at the personal than at the societal level, as evidenced by his treatment of his women or comrades at the beginning. One should also consider the racial dimension that prevented him from respecting the non-values of so-called American ideals. Yet he might have adhered to the ideals of Communism, had he not discovered the ruthless authoritarianism of leaders cultivating what Camus calls "abstraction" when not seeking a sensuous enjoyment of power. It followed that Cross's espousal of Nietzschean theories of a godless, amoral universe can also be explained in the terms used by Camus: no longer protected by human norms, man believes in nothing but himself. Camus concludes:

> If we believe in nothing and nothing makes sense and we are unable to find values in anything, then anything is permitted and nothing is important. Then there is neither good nor evil and Hitler was neither right nor wrong. . . . And since we

thought that nothing makes sense we had to conclude that he who is right is he who succeeds.[17]

As a result, Wright's definition of "man as nothing in particular," which might be construed in the positive, optimistic Sartrean perspective of man as a potentiality to be actualized through existential choice, seems to come closer to Camus's more despondent view of man as neither good nor evil, and deprived of values. This is the path Cross explores as a murderer, although in his heart of hearts he wishes he were neither victim nor executioner. This reading of Camus thus sheds some added light on his final exclamation about being innocent and having experienced the utmost horror. He is innocent because he is not responsible for the human condition, which is "nothing in particular." He is crushed not only by the horror inherent in this metaphysical predicament, but by the realization that, in Camus's terms, "we knew deep in our hearts that even the distinction was illusory, that at bottom we were all victims, and that assassins and assassinated would in the end be reunited in the same defeat."[18]

Camus and Wright parted ways, however, in their unequal emphasis on politics. In spite of his condemnation of fascism and communism, or at least of the means used by the latter, Wright, like Sartre and de Beauvoir, believed that political commitment still represented a means for action, and he eagerly joined in the efforts of the Rassemblement Démocratique Révolutionnaire to reject both the United States and the USSR in the name of Europe's freedom of choice. As for Camus, he not only declared that politics must whenever possible be kept in its proper place, which is a secondary one, but also stated emphatically:

> The great misfortune of our time is precisely that politics pretend to furnish us at once with a catechism, a complete philosophy, and at times even a way of loving. But the role of politics is to set our house in order, not to deal with our inner problems. I do not know for myself whether there is or not an absolute. But I do know that this is not a political concern. The absolute is not the concern of all, it is the concern of each. . . . Doubtless our life belongs to others and it is proper that we give it to others when it is necessary but our death belongs to ourselves alone. Such is my definition of freedom.[19]

Only much later, and only half-heartedly, did Wright thus limit the role of politics in "The Voiceless Ones," a review of Michel del Castillo's *The Disinherited*.[20]

It is evident that Wright's ideology converged with that of the French existentialists, if it was not directly influenced by it at the time. The tone of their respective articles for the "Art and Action" commemorative issue of *Twice a Year* in 1948 is strikingly similar. Wright's "Letter to Dorothy Norman" ends with the declaration that politics and consumerism curtail the definition of man:

The Right and Left, in different ways, have decided that man is an animal whose needs can be met by making more and more articles for him to consume. . . . A world will be built in which everybody will get enough to eat and full stomachs will be equated with contentment and freedom, and those who will say that they are not happy under such a regime will be guilty of treason. How sad that is. We are all accomplices in this crime. . . . Is it too late to say something to halt it, modify it?[21]

On the following page, Camus's article, entitled "We Too Are Murderers," begins:

Yes, it is a fact that we have no future, and the present-day world bodes nothing save death and silence, war and terror. But it is also a fact that we ought not tolerate this, for we know that man is long in the making and everything worth living for, love, intelligence, beauty, requires time and ripening.[22]

One could believe that Wright is simply pursuing his argument. As a matter of fact, Wright's letter, sent to Dorothy Norman on 9 March 1948, was not intended for publication; and Camus's article, originally published in *Franchise* in 1946, largely developed the concepts of his lecture "The Human Crisis." At the time, such positions and ideas were in the air in existentialist circles, and it is difficult to attribute the authorship of any of them to any one intellectual. Even Stephen Spender, in "The Spiritual Failure of Europe," expressed similar views in his criticism of the Soviet Union and the United States. He found that the problems of our time were more real in Europe than elsewhere, and thus more likely to be stated and solved there:

Wherever nations and great interests are powerful, they become victims of illusions even if these illusions are euphemistically called political realism. The fundamental illusion of power politics is that freedom begins with the protection of the powerful group.[23]

To return to the similarity of Wright's and Camus's views in the late forties, it is likely that Wright's composition of his existentialist novel was influenced in subtle ways by his reading of *The Stranger* in August 1947. He read the book in the American edition at a very slow pace, "weighing each sentence," admiring "its damn good narrative prose," and remarked:

It is a neat job but devoid of passion. He makes his point with dispatch and his prose is solid and good. In America a book like this would not attract much attention for it would be said that he lacks feeling. He does however draw his character very well. What is of course really interesting in this book is the use of fiction to express a philosophical point of view. That he does with ease. I now want to read his other stuff.[24]

Wright's remarks are somewhat surprising. On the one hand, he already knew of the use of fiction to express a philosophical point of view through the novels and theories of Sartre and de Beauvoir. Thus, when he calls Camus's use "very interesting" and "done with ease," he refers to the actual blending of message and narrative—something he himself proved little capable of doing in *The Outsider*, where long political and metaphysical speeches stand out like didactic asides. On the other hand, when Wright finds a lack of passion and feeling in *The Stranger*, he refers to a lack of warmth in the style and the pace of the narration, not in the protagonist, since Meursault's indifference is precisely one of the motives for his acts. In *The Outsider* Wright's hero is never "devoid of passion" and acts more upon the compulsion of his egotistical desires than from the utter existential indifference that characterizes Meursault.

Moreover, Wright's narration is never cold or detached, not because the novelist wants to please an American audience who, he supposed, likes "feeling," but because he simply cannot write in Camus's precise but detached fashion. He needs passion and feeling to carry his narrative along. Wright noted nine days after reading *The Stranger* that he felt he ought to write his novel in the first person because "there was a certain note of poignancy missing which a first person note would supply,"[25] but he made no real attempt to do so. Either *The Outsider* had reached too definitive a stage, or Wright felt incapable of changing his own style; *The Stranger*'s influence was not enough to modify significantly the tenor of his own novel. Moreover, had Camus been a determining influence, it is likely that the scenes dealing with Damon's reactions to his mother would have been modified in light of Meursault's reactions to his own. Yet it appears that Wright's motivations for his picture of the mother and son's reciprocal rejection are to be found in idiosyncratic, personal attitudes, rather than in a detached attempt to illustrate metaphysical estrangement.

Leaving later political opinions and racial choices aside, it appears that although Wright and Camus shared a common conception of the role and responsibility of the artist and intellectual in the modern world, as well as a deep-seated pessimism, their artistic temperaments differed far more than those of Wright and Sartre. Another remark that Wright jotted down in his journal on 7 August 1947 is revealing: "There is still something about this Camus that bothers me. Maybe it is because he is the artist and Sartre and de Beauvoir are not primarily." Wright accurately perceived himself, Sartre, and de Beauvoir as less preoccupied with art and less able to achieve the perfect aesthetic adequacy to be found in Camus. He may have felt some regret, but could not and would not change his own style of writing.

Simone de Beauvoir was both more congenial and less impressive than Sartre or Camus in Wright's eyes. Not that her thinking was less vigorous than theirs, but her manners were more open and her metaphysical interest always focused upon everyday implications and applications. As a result, Wright found more in common with her than with the two men, insofar as he tended to define Sartre as the metaphysician and Camus as the aesthete.

Since de Beauvoir spoke some English and understood it fairly well, their exchanges were more frequent, too, and Wright knew more about her work and opinions than he did about any other French existentialist. Before reading *The Ethics of Ambiguity* and *The Second Sex*, in 1949 and 1953 respectively, he had been able to ponder de Beauvoir's long and important essays included in the 1948 *Art and Action*. Under the title "Literature and Metaphysics," the first essay provided a theoretical framework for precisely the problems Wright was grappling with when writing *The Outsider*, i.e., the conditions of writing a successful "metaphysical novel." De Beauvoir was convinced:

> There is no doubt that the novel cannot be successful if the writer limits himself to disguising in a more or less alluring fictional cloak a previously constructed ideological framework. . . . It is impossible to see how an imaginary story can serve ideas which have already found their proper mode of expression.[26]

She emphasized the analogous relations between novel writing and metaphysics, the role and value of subjectivity as expressing the temporal form of metaphysical experience, and the aspect of spiritual adventure to be encountered in a novel, which she saw as "an effort to conciliate the objective and the subjective, the absolute and the relative, the intemporal and the historical." Her goal was no less than an attempt to "grasp the meaning at the heart of existence; and if the description of essence belongs to the sphere of philosophy proper, the novel alone makes it possible to evoke the original outpouring of existence in its complete, singular, temporal truth."[27]

Such language was not very different from Wright's definition of a novel's aims and of what it should arouse in its readers, even though he failed to give enough concreteness to his demonstrations in *The Outsider*.

More interesting to him must have been the essay on "Freedom and Liberation," which opposed one of the main objections raised against existentialism, namely, that the precept "seek freedom" proposed no concrete plan of action. De Beauvoir reexamined the concept of freedom to restore its concrete meaning and show that it could be realized only by man's committing himself to the world and embodying his ideal in definite rules of conduct.

Positive freedom was defined as a movement to "unveil being" and turn it into existence: a movement that was constantly being transcended, since man had to "pursue the expansion of his existence and take this effort in itself as an absolute."[28] This expansion was, in many ways, what

Wright claimed for Cross Damon. Yet de Beauvoir approved of a personal movement of expansion only insofar as she grounded it in ethics, so as to condemn, in the name of theology, a sort of "happiness" that artificially expanded man's existence through consumerism, but really prevented him from transcending it. She analyzed the process of freeing oneself from oppression: there are two ways of transcending the given, to escape (to go on a journey) or to free oneself (from imprisonment), which are very different things, since the present is accepted in the one case, rejected in the other. This led her to criticize Hegel's concept of *Aufhebung*, which is the foundation of his optimism and brings him to regard the future as harmonious development, in the name of realism. She argued that revolt did not integrate itself into harmonious development, but constituted a violent disruption, which led Marx to define the proletariat in terms of a negation. Wright actually discussed the concepts and implications of alienation and freedom with Sartre and de Beauvoir. He may have been led to some of his own conclusions about man's responsibility to others and about the limits of individual freedom as incarnate in Damon's end by such assertions as this:

> Freedom need be respected only when it is directed towards freedom and not when it evades itself and falls off from its own principles. . . . And it is not true that the recognition of other people's freedom limits my own. To be free does not mean to have the power to do anything whatsoever; it consists in being able to transcend the given towards an open future; the existence of others as free defines my situation and is even the condition of my own freedom. I am oppressed if I am thrown into prison, not if I am prevented from throwing my neighbor into prison.[29]

One can easily see just how de Beauvoir's conception of other people's freedom meets Sartre's definition of "*l'enfer, c'est les autres,*" or in terms of Wright's fiction, how Damon's nihilism can be reconciled with Fred Daniels's belief that he must share his underground vision with others. De Beauvoir writes, "To be free consists in being able to transcend the given towards an open future." Damon discovers this at his own expense, when he realizes that his disregard of others blocks his capacity for change, for establishing a love relationship with Eva especially, i.e., for transcending his personal problems, even though he was miraculously able to recreate his social relationships out of nothing after the train wreck. Damon has no "open future," not because he is chased and killed, but because his egotism without norms negates the notion of openness, which is the bedrock of freedom.

It would be easy to multiply examples of interface between the theories of French existentialism and their application to literature, and Wright's own use of certain metaphysical concepts in *The Outsider*, but it may be more revealing to stress some differences.

One can regret that Wright did not pattern *The Outsider* more consistently after the simple plot, classical structure and terse style of *The Stranger*, but his idiosyncrasies oriented him more toward a mixture of melodrama and rhetorical exposition. Edward Margolies aptly points out in his comparison of Damon and Meursault that "both men kill without passion, both men appear unmoved by the death of their mothers; both men apparently are intended to represent the moral and emotional failure of the age."[30] When writing a notice for the jacket of *The Outsider*, Wright himself specified that "the hero could be of any race." He claimed, "I have tried to depict my sense of our contemporary living as I see it and feel it." He also saw the novel as his first literary effort "projected out of a heart preoccupied with no ideological burden save that of rendering an account of reality" as it struck his sensibilities and imagination. It seems, however, that the motivation and behavior of Meursault are more emblematic of modern man than those of Damon. This may be because the earlier section of the novel is patterned after the naturalistic depiction of black ghetto life in *Lawd Today*, and also because Damon's resentment is rooted in racial offense, economic oppression, and a familial atmosphere in which the male is spiritually crushed by women. Damon's "metaphysical resentment" would only come second, or even third, after his hatred for political manipulation and totalitarianism.

Many American critics have found that *The Outsider* was plagued by a problem of motivation. Yet the gratuitousness of Damon's half-dozen murders poses no problem when it is seen as a prevalent feature of French existentialist fiction and when one recalls that Sartre and Camus refrain precisely from exploring the ambiguous relationship between the condition of freedom and the desire to kill.[31] In the case of Wright's hero, his search for unlimited freedom makes him his own victim when his hatred of others turns into self-hatred. And the root of his compulsive violence must be traced back to the behavior of much earlier Wrightian protagonists like Big Boy and Bigger Thomas, those oppressed and temporarily impotent youngsters who are seized by a compulsion to "blot out" their fellow creatures as they would some insect.

This behavior must be related to the condition of social and racial oppression under which the presence of the "other" (the white man, the capitalist boss) is equivalent to torture and hell, where *"L'enfer, c'est les autres."* But Wright quickly leaves this trend of thinking whereby he might have rejoined the Sartrean perspectives of *Huis-Clos*. *The Outsider* set out to prove another existentialist theme: *"L'enfer, c'est soi-même,"* which Wright developed most completely in *The Man Who Lived Underground* before he was aware of it as an existentialist concept. In spite of its rhetoric, *The Outsider* rather aptly reveals the gloomy abysses of man's mind when he is totally outside life. Again, the problem is less the satisfaction of the desires and compulsions of the individual, than it is man's need for purification. Trapped in his *mauvaise foi* (although his inauthenticity at the beginning of the novel is rather different from Roquentin's or Meursault's), Damon does not really feel the type of nausea experienced by Sartre's hero—his *engluement* is more the condition of being unable to escape from the social trap—and, in spite of a recurrent use of phrases that may have been borrowed from the French existentialists, the reader is reluctant to believe that Cross can simply decide to be his "own little God" and follow his unrestrained desires. Even the five sections of the novel do not really correspond to Kierkegaardian categories beyond the concept of dread. The final titles, "Despair" and "Decision," are interesting insofar as they recall the mood, if not always the concepts, emphasized both in the gloomy forebodings of Camus's essay on the crisis of man and in de Beauvoir's more spirited analysis of freedom and commitment. Wright's outlook, however, is more unremittingly bleak and sombre, and also more narrowly individual than even Camus's. On the whole, the French existentialists were preoccupied with societal survival through the restoration of human values and morality, whereas Damon's trajectory is a negation of all social norms; and his final decision, at the end of his metaphysical journey to the end of night, is more the result of intrinsic dread than the outcome of clearly defined, freely made choice. In the course of Wright's narrative, a world grounded upon the freedom of existentialist choice does not seem possible. Although he symbolically slays the totalitarian and authoritarian monsters of fascism and communism (presumably for, among other reasons, the greater freedom of mankind), and although he finds in Houston a kindred spirit and an emblematic opposite, Damon never really bridges the gap between himself and others, as is made clear by Eva's suicide when she knows the "horrible truth" about her lover. If Camus's saying "Our life belongs to others but our death belongs to us alone" is true, then Damon is unable to do anything with his death, except to utter a desperate cry of horror that is just as ambiguous as that of Kurtz at the close of *Heart of Darkness*. The "horrible innocence" of Damon—a victim of inhuman society and metaphysical fate as much as of totalitarian ruthlessness—is compounded by his being one of the Nietzschean "new men," one of the godless race who suffer no obligations, since they recognize no values. At this stage, therefore, Wright seems to part ways with the French existentialists. Again, his definition of man as "nothing in particular" does not correspond to Sartre's conception of man as "anything," i.e., as a potentiality to be fulfilled and actualized through choice and action. Wright's view is far more nihilistic than Sartre's; even though Damon's final claim is for human solidarity and compassion, his murderous past and the general atmosphere of *The Outsider* leave us with the impression that this change of heart *in articulo mortis* does not suit the protagonist's previous behavior, that this is a last-minute choice inflicted upon by the novelist.

One may wonder about the reasons for these differences in mood between Wright and the French existentialists, mostly Sartre and de Beauvoir, with whom Wright had so much in common and with whom he worked for years along common political lines. Was it that, for the French intellectuals existentialism remained less visceral, more conceptual, more "intellectual," in a word, than for the man who had painfully emerged from the deprivations and insecurity described in *Black Boy*? Was it due to Wright's "American" situation—the plight of a modern man in a country of extremes, a country more urbanized than France, which could not fall back on the comfortable traditions of lay humanism to explain theoretically and vindicate what was happening to it? When they expressed their horror at a "valueless universe," the French existentialists often did so in order to excite others to a redefinition of the essential moral and human qualities of social life. When, under the brunt of political disillusionment, Wright explored the implications of a normless existence, he did so with characteristic thoroughness and impetus, with the result that he outdid even Camus's gloomiest forebodings. The results of his attempt are undoubtedly clumsier and psychologically less convincing than the novels of Sartre or Camus; yet for all its aesthetic faults and not too subtle conceptualization, *The Outsider* remains a fascinating piece of writing, and one that still speaks to our present needs. By comparison, *Les Chemins de la liberté* is best regarded as a historical testimony about the mistakes and hopes of the war generation.

Notes

1. See, among others, J. Saunders Redding, "Home Is Where the Heart Is," *New Leader*, 11 Dec. 1961, pp. 24–25: "The one thing French that caught him was Existentialism and this held him only long enough for him to write his unqualifiedly bad novel." At a 1964 symposium, transcribed in Herbert Hill's *Anger and Beyond* (New York: Harper, p. 209), Redding was of the opinion that "Existentialism is no philosophy to accommodate the reality of Negro life, especially Southern Negro life," and he agreed with Arna Bontemps, who dismissed Wright's metaphysical attempts as "a roll in the hay with the French existentialists."

2. See my article, "Richard Wright and the French Existentialists," *MELUS*, 5 (Summer 1978), 39–51; also the relevant chapter of *The Unfinished Quest of Richard Wright* (New York: William Morrow, 1973), especially pp. 320–22.

3. Ralph Ellison, Letter to Wright, 18 Aug. 1945.

4. Ellison, Letter to Wright, 22 July 1945.

5. Wright, "Richard Wright to Antonio Frasconi—An Exchange of Letters," *Twice a Year*, 12–13 (Fall–Winter 1945), 258.

6. "Wright to Frasconi," p. 251.

7. Wright, Unpublished journal, 7 Aug. 1947.

8. Unpublished journal, 7 Sept. 1947.

9. Wright, "Art and Action," *Twice a Year* (1948), 14–15.

10. See Fabre, "Wright and the French Existentialists."

11. Albert Camus, "The Human Crisis," *Twice a Year*, 14–15 (Fall–Winter 1946–47), 22.

12. Camus, p. 22.

13. Camus, p. 23.

14. Camus, p. 23.

15. Camus, p. 24.

16. Camus, p. 24.

17. Camus, p. 24.

18. Camus, p. 26.

19. Camus, p. 29.

20. Wright wrote: "May it not develop that man's sense of being disinherited is not mainly political at all, that politics serve it as a temporary vessel, that Marxist ideology in particular is but a transitory makeshift pending a more accurate diagnosis, that Communism may be a painful compromise containing a definition of man by sheer default?" See "The Voiceless Ones," *Saturday Review*, 43 (16 April 1960), 54.

21. Wright, "Two Letters to Dorothy Norman," "Art and Action," *Twice a Year* (1948), 73.

22. "Two Letters to Dorothy Norman," p. 73.

23. "Two Letters to Dorothy Norman," p. 79.

24. Wright, Unpublished journal, 7 Aug. 1947.

25. Unpublished journal, 7 Aug. 1947.

26. "Art and Action," p. 89.

27. "Art and Action," p. 92.

28. "Art and Action," p. 97.

29. "Art and Action," p. 100.

30. Edward Margolies, *The Art of Richard Wright* (Carbondale: Southern Illinois Univ. Press, 1969), p. 135.

31. See Kingsley Widmer, "The Existential Darkness: *The Outsider*," *Wisconsin Studies in Contemporary Literature*, 1 (Fall 1960), 13–21. This essay very competently addresses itself to the comparison of some of the conceptual components of the novel with those emphasized by Kierkegaard and other German existentialists on the one hand, and by Sartre on the other.

ESSAYS ON NONFICTION

Richard Wright's Blues

Ralph Ellison*

> If anybody ask you
> who sing this song,
> Say it was ole [Black Boy]
> done been here and gone.[1]

As a writer, Richard Wright has outlined for himself a dual role: to discover and depict the meaning of Negro experience; and to reveal to both Negroes and whites those problems of a psychological and emotional nature which arise between them when they strive for mutual understanding.

Now, in *Black Boy*, he has used his own life to probe what qualities of will, imagination and intellect are required of a Southern Negro in order to possess the meaning of his life in the United States. Wright is an important writer, perhaps the most articulate Negro American, and what he has to say is highly perceptive. Imagine Bigger Thomas projecting his own life in lucid prose, guided, say, by the insights of Marx and Freud, and you have an idea of this autobiography.

Published at a time when any sharply critical approach to Negro life has been dropped as a wartime expendable, it should do much to redefine the problem of the Negro and American Democracy. Its power can be observed in the shrill manner with which some professional "friends of the Negro people" have attempted to strangle the work in a noose of newsprint.

What in the tradition of literary autobiography is it like, this work described as a "great American autobiography"? As a non-white intellectual's statement of his relationship to Western culture, *Black Boy* recalls the conflicting pattern of identification and rejection found in Nehru's *Toward Freedom*. In its use of fictional techniques, its concern with criminality (sin) and the artistic sensibility, and in its author's judgment and rejection of the narrow world of his origin, it recalls Joyce's rejection of Dublin in *A Portrait of the Artist*. And as a psychological document of life under oppressive conditions, it recalls *The House of the Dead*, Dostoievsky's profound study of the humanity of Russian criminals.

*Reprinted from *Shadow and Act* (New York: Random House, 1953), pp. 77–94, by Ralph Ellison, by permission of Random House, copyright © 1953, 1964 by Ralph Ellison. "Richard Wright's Blues" appeared originally in *Antioch Review*, 5 (June 1945), 198–211.

Such works were perhaps Wright's literary guides, aiding him to endow his life's incidents with communicable significance; providing him with ways of seeing, feeling and describing his environment. These influences, however, were encountered only after these first years of Wright's life were past and were not part of the immediate folk culture into which he was born. In that culture the specific folk-art form which helped shape the writer's attitude toward his life and which embodied the impulse that contributes much to the quality and tone of his autobiography was the Negro blues. This would bear a word of explanation:

The blues is an impulse to keep the painful details and episodes of a brutal experience alive in one's aching consciousness, to finger its jagged grain, and to transcend it, not by the consolation of philosophy but by squeezing from it a near-tragic, near-comic lyricism. As a form, the blues is an autobiographical chronicle of personal catastrophe expressed lyrically. And certainly Wright's early childhood was crammed with catastrophic incidents. In a few short years his father deserted his mother, he knew intense hunger, he became a drunkard begging drinks from black stevedores in Memphis saloons; he had to flee Arkansas, where an uncle was lynched; he was forced to live with a fanatically religious grandmother in an atmosphere of constant bickering; he was lodged in an orphan asylum; he observed the suffering of his mother, who became a permanent invalid, while fighting off the blows of the poverty-stricken relatives with whom he had to live; he was cheated, beaten and kicked off jobs by white employees who disliked his eagerness to learn a trade; and to these objective circumstances must be added the subjective fact that Wright, with his sensitivity, extreme shyness and intelligence, was a problem child who rejected his family and was by them rejected.

Thus along with the themes, equivalent descriptions of milieu and the perspectives to be found in Joyce, Nehru, Dostoievsky, George Moore and Rousseau, *Black Boy* is filled with blues-tempered echoes of railroad trains, the names of Southern towns and cities, estrangements, fights and flights, deaths and disappointments, charged with physical and spiritual hungers and pain. And like a blues sung by such an artist as Bessie Smith, its lyrical prose evokes the paradoxical, almost surreal image of a black boy singing lustily as he probes his own grievous wound.

In *Black Boy*, two worlds have fused, two cultures merged, two impulses of Western man become coalesced. By discussing some of its cultural sources I hope to answer those critics who would make of the book a miracle and of its author a mystery. And while making no attempt to probe the mystery of the artist (who Hemingway says is "forged in injustice as a sword is forged"), I do hold that basically the prerequisites to the writing of *Black Boy* were, on the one hand, the microscopic degree of cultural freedom which Wright found in the South's stony injustice, and, on the other, the existence of a personality agitated to a state of almost manic restlessness. There were, of course, other factors, chiefly ideological; but these came later.

Wright speaks of his journey north as

> . . . taking a part of the South to transplant in alien soil, to see
> if it could grow differently, if it could drink of new and cool
> rains, bend in strange winds, respond to the warmth of other
> suns, and perhaps, to bloom. . . .

And just as Wright, the man, represents the blooming of the delinquent child of the autobiography, just so does *Black Boy* represent the flowering—cross-fertilized by pollen blown by the winds of strange cultures—of the humble blues lyric. There is, as in all acts of creation, a world of mystery in this, but there is also enough that is comprehensible for Americans to create the social atmosphere in which other black boys might freely bloom.

For certainly, in the historical sense, Wright is no exception. Born on a Mississippi plantation, he was subjected to all those blasting pressures which in a scant eighty years have sent the Negro people hurtling, without clearly defined trajectory, from slavery to emancipation, from log cabin to city tenement, from the white folks' fields and kitchens to factory assembly lines; and which, between two wars, have shattered the wholeness of its folk consciousness into a thousand writhing pieces.

Black Boy describes this process in the personal terms of *one* Negro childhood. Nevertheless, several critics have complained that it does not "explain" Richard Wright. Which, aside from the notion of art involved, serves to remind us that the prevailing mood of American criticism has so thoroughly excluded the Negro that it fails to recognize some of the most basic tenets of Western democratic thought when encountering them in a black skin. They forget that human life possesses an innate dignity and mankind an innate sense of nobility; that all men possess the tendency to dream and the compulsion to make their dreams reality; that the need to be ever dissatisfied and the urge ever to seek satisfaction is implicit in the human organism; and that all men are the victims and the beneficiaries of the goading, tormenting, commanding and informing activity of that imperious process known as the Mind—the Mind, as Valéry describes it, "armed with its inexhaustible questions."

Perhaps all this (in which lies the very essence of the human, and which Wright takes for granted) has been forgotten because the critics recognize neither Negro humanity nor the full extent to which the Southern community renders the fulfillment of human destiny impossible. And while it is true that *Black Boy* presents an almost unrelieved picture of a personality corrupted by brutal environment, it also presents those fresh, human responses brought to its world by the sensitive child:

> There was the *wonder* I felt when I first saw a brace of moun-
> tainlike, spotted, black-and-white horses clopping down a
> dusty road . . . the *delight* I caught in seeing long straight
> rows of red and green vegetables stretching away in the
> sun . . . the faint, cool kiss of *sensuality* when dew came on to

> my cheeks . . . the vague *sense of the infinite* as I looked down
> upon the yellow, dreaming waters of the Mississippi . . . the
> echoes of *nostalgia* I heard in the crying strings of wild
> geese . . . the *love* I had for the mute regality of tall, moss-
> clad oaks . . . the hint of *cosmic cruelty* that I *felt* when I saw
> the curved timbers of a wooden shack that had been warped in
> the summer sun . . . and there was the *quiet terror* that suf-
> fused my senses when vast hazes of gold washed earthward
> from star-heavy skies on silent nights. . . .[2]

And a bit later, his reactions to religion:

> Many of the religious symbols appealed to my sensibilities and
> I responded to the dramatic vision of life held by the church,
> feeling that to live day by day with death as one's sole thought
> was to be so compassionately sensitive toward all life as to view
> all men as slowly dying, and the trembling sense of fate that
> welled up, sweet and melancholy, from the hymns blended
> with the sense of fate that I had already caught from life.

There was also the influence of his mother—so closely linked to his
hysteria and sense of suffering—who (though he only implies it here)
taught him, in the words of the dedication prefacing *Native Son*, "to
revere the fanciful and the imaginative." There were also those white
men—the one who allowed Wright to use his library privileges and the
other who advised him to leave the South, and still others whose offers of
friendship he was too frightened to accept.

Wright assumed that the nucleus of plastic sensibility is a human
heritage: the right and the opportunity to dilate, deepen and enrich sensibility—democracy. Thus the drama of *Black Boy* lies in its depiction of
what occurs when Negro sensibility attempts to fulfill itself in the
undemocratic South. Here it is not the individual that is the immediate
focus, as in Joyce's *Stephen Hero*, but that upon which his sensibility was
nourished.

Those critics who complain that Wright has omitted the development of his own sensibility hold that the work thus fails as art. Others,
because it presents too little of what they consider attractive in Negro life,
charge that it distorts reality. Both groups miss a very obvious point: That
whatever else the environment contained, it had as little chance of
prevailing against the overwhelming weight of the child's unpleasant experiences as Beethoven's Quartets would have of destroying the stench of
a Nazi prison.

We come, then, to the question of art. The function, the psychology,
of artistic selectivity is to eliminate from art form all those elements of experience which contain no compelling significance. Life is as the sea, art a
ship in which man conquers life's crushing formlessness, reducing it to a
course, a series of swells, tides and wind currents inscribed on a chart.
Though drawn from the world, "the organized significance of art," writes

Malraux, "is stronger than all the multiplicity of the world; . . . that significance alone enables man to conquer chaos and to master destiny."

Wright saw his destiny—that combination of forces before which man feels powerless—in terms of a quick and casual violence inflicted upon him by both family and community. His response was likewise violent, and it has been his need to give that violence significance which has shaped his writings.

What were the ways by which other Negroes confronted their destiny?

In the South of Wright's childhood there were three general ways: They could accept the role created for them by the whites and perpetually resolve the resulting conflicts through the hope and emotional cartharsis of Negro religion; they could repress their dislike of Jim Crow social relations while striving for a middle way of respectability, becoming—consciously or unconsciously—the accomplices of the whites in oppressing their brothers; or they could reject the situation, adopt a criminal attitude and carry on an unceasing psychological scrimmage with the whites, which often flared forth into physical violence.

Wright's attitude was nearest the last. Yet in it there was an all-important qualitative difference: it represented a groping for *individual* values, in a black community whose values were what the young Negro critic, Edward Bland, has defined as "pre-individual." And herein lay the setting for the extreme conflict set off, both within his family and in the community, by Wright's assertion of individuality. The clash was sharpest on the psychological level, for, to quote Bland:

> In the pre-individualistic thinking of the Negro the stress is on the group. Instead of seeing in terms of the individual, the Negro sees in terms of "races," masses of peoples separated from other masses according to color. Hence, an act rarely bears intent against him as a Negro individual. He is singled out not as a person but as a specimen of an ostracized group. He knows that he never exists in his own right but only to the extent that others hope to make the race suffer vicariously through him.

This pre-individual state is induced artificially—like the regression to primitive states noted among cultured inmates of Nazi prisons. The primary technique in its enforcement is to impress the Negro child with the omniscience and omnipotence of the whites to the point that whites appear as ahuman as Jehovah, and as relentless as a Mississippi flood. Socially it is effected through an elaborate scheme of taboos supported by a ruthless physical violence, which strikes not only the offender but the entire black community. To wander from the paths of behavior laid down for the group is to become the agent of communal disaster.

In such a society the developments of individuality depends upon a series of accidents, which often arise, as in Wright's case, from conditions within the Negro family. In Wright's life there was the accident that as a small child he could not distinguish between his fair-skinned grandmother and the white women of the town, thus developing skepticism as to their special status. To this was linked the accident of his having no close contacts with whites until after the child's normal formative period.

But these objective accidents not only link forward to these qualities of rebellion, criminality and intellectual questioning expressed in Wright's work today. They also link backward into the shadow of infancy where environment and consciousness are so darkly intertwined as to require the skill of a psychoanalyst to define their point of juncture. Nevertheless, at the age of four, Wright set the house afire and was beaten near to death by his frightened mother. This beating, followed soon by his father's desertion of the family, seems to be the initial psychological motivation of his quest for a new identification. While delirious from this beating Wright was haunted "by huge wobbly white bags like the full udders of a cow, suspended from the ceiling above me [and] I was gripped by the fear that they were going to fall and drench me with some horrible liquid . . ."

It was as though the mother's milk had turned acid, and with it the whole pattern of life that had produced the ignorance, cruelty and fear that had fused with mother-love and exploded in the beating. It is significant that the bags were of the hostile color white, and the female symbol that of the cow, the most stupid (and, to the small child, the most frightening) of domestic animals. Here in dream symbolism is expressed an attitude worthy of an Orestes. And the significance of the crisis is increased by virtue of the historical fact that the lower-class Negro family is matriarchal; the child turns not to the father to compensate if he feels mother-rejection, but to the grandmother, or to an aunt—and Wright rejected both of these. Such rejection leaves the child open to psychological insecurity, distrust and all of those hostile environmental forces from which the family functions to protect it.

One of the Southern Negro family's methods of protecting the child is the severe beating—a homeopathic dose of the violence generated by black and white relationships. Such beatings as Wright's were administered for the child's own good; a good which the child resisted, thus giving family relationships an undercurrent of fear and hostility, which differs qualitatively from that found in patriarchal middle-class families, because here the severe beating is administered by the mother, leaving the child no parental sanctuary. He must ever embrace violence along with maternal tenderness, or else reject, in his helpless way, the mother.

The division between the Negro parents of Wright's mother's generation, whose sensibilities were often bound by their proximity to the slave experience, and their children, who historically and through the rapidity of American change stand emotionally and psychologically much farther away, is quite deep. Indeed, sometimes as deep as the cultural distance between Yeats' *Autobiographies* and a Bessie Smith blues. This is the historical background to those incidents of family strife in *Black Boy* which have caused reviewers to question Wright's judgment of Negro emotional relationships.

We have here a problem in the sociology of sensibility that is obscured by certain psychological attitudes brought to Negro life by whites.

The first is the attitude which compels whites to impute to Negroes sentiments, attitudes and insights which, as a group living under certain definite social conditions, Negroes could not humanly possess. It is the identical mechanism which William Empson identifies in literature as "pastoral." It implies that since Negroes possess the richly human virtues credited to them, then their social position is advantageous and should not be bettered; and, continuing syllogistically, the white individual need feel no guilt over his participation in Negro oppression.

The second attitude is that which leads whites to misjudge Negro passion, looking upon it as they do, out of the turgidity of their own frustrated yearning for emotional warmth, their capacity for sensation having been constricted by the impersonal mechanized relationships typical of bourgeois society. The Negro is idealized into a symbol of sensation, of unhampered social and sexual relationships. And when *Black Boy* questions their illusion they are thwarted much in the manner of the occidental who, after observing the erotic character of a primitive dance, "shacks up" with a native woman—only to discover that far from possessing the hair-trigger sexual responses of a Stork Club "babe," she is relatively phlegmatic.

The point is not that American Negroes are primitives, but that as a group their social situation does not provide for the type of emotional relationships attributed them. For how could the South, recognized as a major part of the backward third of the nation, nurture in the black, most brutalized section of its population, those forms of human relationships achievable only in the most highly developed areas of civilization?

Champions of this "Aren't-Negroes-Wonderful?" school of thinking often bring Paul Robeson and Marian Anderson forward as examples of highly developed sensibility, but actually they are only its *promise*. Both received their development from an extensive personal contact with European culture, free from the influences which shape Southern Negro personality. In the United States, Wright, who is the only Negro literary artist of equal caliber, had to wait years and escape to another environment before discovering the moral and ideological equivalents of his childhood attitudes.

Man cannot express that which does not exist—either in the form of dreams, ideas or realities—in his environment. Neither his thoughts nor his feelings, his sensibility nor his intellect are fixed, innate qualities. They are processes which arise out of the interpenetration of human instinct with environment, through the process called experience; each changing and being changed by the other. Negroes cannot possess many of the sentiments attributed to them because the same changes in environment which, through experience, enlarge man's intellect (and thus his capacity for still greater change) also modify his feelings; which in turn increase his sensibility, i.e., his sensitivity, to refinements of impression and subtleties of emotion. The extent of these changes depends upon the quality of political and cultural freedom in the environment.

Intelligence tests have measured the quick rise in intellect which takes place in Southern Negroes after moving north, but little attention has been paid to the mutations effected in their sensibilities. However, the two go hand in hand. Intellectual complexity is accompanied by emotional complexity; refinement of thought, by refinement of feeling. The movement north affects more than the Negro's wage scale, it affects his entire psychosomatic structure.

The rapidity of Negro intellectual growth in the North is due partially to objective factors present in the environment, to influences of the industrial city and to a greater political freedom. But there are also changes within the "inner world." In the North energies are released and given *intellectual* channelization—energies which in most Negroes in the South have been forced to take either a *physical* form or, as with potentially intellectual types like Wright, to be expressed as nervous tension, anxiety and hysteria. Which is nothing mysterious. The human organism responds to environmental stimuli by converting them into either physical and/or intellectual energy. And what is called hysteria is suppressed intellectual energy expressed physically.

The "physical" character of their expression makes for much of the difficulty in understanding American Negroes. Negro music and dances are frenziedly erotic; Negro religious ceremonies violently ecstatic; Negro speech strongly rhythmical and weighted with image and gesture. But there is more in this sensuousness than the unrestraint and insensitivity found in primitive cultures; nor is it simply the relatively spontaneous and undifferentiated responses of a people living in close contact with the soil. For despite Jim Crow, Negro life does not exist in a vacuum, but in the seething vortex of those tensions generated by the most highly industrialized of Western nations. The welfare of the most humble black Mississippi sharecropper is affected less by the flow of the seasons and the rhythm of natural events than by the fluctuations of the stock market; even though, as Wright states of his father, the sharecropper's memories, actions and emotions are shaped by his immediate contact with nature and the crude social relations of the South.

All of this makes the American Negro far different from the "simple" specimen for which he is taken. And the "physical" quality offered as evidence of his primitive simplicity is actually the form of his complexity. The American Negro is a Western type whose social condition creates a state which is almost the reverse of the cataleptic trance: Instead of his consciousness being lucid to the reality around it while the body is rigid, here it is the body which is alert, reacting to pressures which the constricting forces of Jim Crow block off from the transforming, concept-creating activity of the brain. The "eroticism" of Negro expression springs from much the same conflict as that displayed in the violent gesturing of a man who attempts to express a complicated concept with a limited vocabulary; thwarted ideational energy is converted into unsatisfactory pantomime, and his words are burdened with meanings they cannot convey. Here lies the source of the basic ambiguity of *Native Son*, wherein in order to translate Bigger's complicated feelings into universal ideas, Wright had to force into Bigger's consciousness concepts and ideas which his intellect could not formulate. Between Wright's skill and knowledge and the potentials of Bigger's mute feelings lay a thousand years of conscious culture.

In the South the sensibilities of both blacks and whites are inhibited by the rigidly defined environment. For the Negro there is relative safety as long as the impulse toward individuality is suppressed. (Lynchings have occurred because Negroes painted their homes.) And it is the task of the Negro family to adjust the child to the Southern milieu; through it the currents, tensions and impulses generated within the human organism by the flux and flow of events are given their distribution. This also gives the group its distinctive character. Which, because of Negroes' suppressed minority position, is very much in the nature of an elaborate but limited defense mechanism. Its function is dual: to protect the Negro from whirling away from the undifferentiated mass of his people into the unknown, symbolized in its most abstract form by insanity, and most concretely by lynching; and to protect him from those unknown forces *within himself* which might urge him to reach out for that social and human equality which the white South says he cannot have. Rather than throw himself against the charged wires of his prison he annihilates the impulses within him.

The pre-individualistic black community discourages individuality out of self-defense. Having learned through experience that the whole group is punished for the actions of the single member, it has worked out efficient techniques of behavior control. For in many Southern communities everyone knows everyone else and is vulnerable to his opinions. In some communities everyone is "related" regardless of blood-ties. The regard shown by the group for its members, its general communal character and its cohesion are often mentioned. For by comparison with the coldly impersonal relationships of the urban industrial community, its relationships are personal and warm.

Black Boy, however, illustrates that this personal quality, shaped by outer violence and inner fear, is ambivalent. Personal warmth is accompanied by an equally personal coldness, kindliness by cruelty, regard by malice. And these opposites are as quickly set off against the member who gestures toward individuality as a lynch mob forms at the cry of rape. Negro leaders have often been exasperated by this phenomenon, and Booker T. Washington (who demanded far less of Negro humanity than Richard Wright) described the Negro community as a basket of crabs, wherein should one attempt to climb out, the others immediately pull him back.

The member who breaks away is apt to be more impressed by its negative than by its positive character. He becomes a stranger even to his relatives and he interprets gestures of protection as blows of oppression—from which there is no hiding place, because every area of Negro life is affected. Even parental love is given a qualitative balance akin to "sadism." And the extent of beatings and psychological maimings meted out by Southern Negro parents rivals those described by the nineteenth-century Russian writers as characteristic of peasant life under the Czars. The horrible thing is that the cruelty is also an expression of concern, of love.

In discussing the inadequacies for democratic living typical of the education provided Negroes by the South, a Negro educator has coined the term *mis-education*. Within the ambit of the black family this takes the form of training the child away from curiosity and adventure, against reaching out for those activities lying beyond the borders of the black community. And when the child resists, the parent discourages him; first with the formula, "That there's for white folks. Colored can't have it," and finally with a beating.

It is not, then, the family and communal violence described by *Black Boy* that is unusual, but that Wright *recognized* and made no peace with its essential cruelty—even when, like a babe freshly emerged from the womb, he could not discern where his own personality ended and it began. Ordinarily both parent and child are protected against this cruelty—seeing it as love and finding subjective sanction for it in the spiritual authority of the Fifth Commandment, and on the secular level in the legal and extralegal structure of the Jim Crow system. The child who did not rebel, or who was unsuccessful in his rebellion, learned a masochistic submissiveness and a denial of the impulse toward Western culture when it stirred within him.

Why then have Southern whites, who claim to "know" the Negro, missed all this? Simply because they, too, are armored against the horror and the cruelty. Either they deny the Negro's humanity and feel no cause to measure his actions against civilized norms; or they protect themselves from their guilt in the Negro's condition and from their fear that their cooks might poison them, or that their nursemaids might strangle their infant charges, or that their field hands might do them violence, by attributing to them a superhuman capacity for love, kindliness and forgiveness. Nor does this in any way contradict their stereotyped conviction that all Negroes (meaning those with whom they have no contact) are given to the most animal behavior.

It is only when the individual, whether white or black, *rejects* the pattern that he awakens to the nightmare of his life. Perhaps much of the South's regressive character springs from the fact that many, jarred by some casual crisis into wakefulness, flee hysterically into the sleep of violence or the coma of apathy again. For the penalty of wakefulness is to encounter ever more violence and horror than the sensibilities can sustain unless translated into some form of social action. Perhaps the impassioned character so noticeable among those white Southern liberals so active in the Negro's cause is due to their sense of accumulated horror; their passion—like the violence in Faulkner's novels—is evidence of a profound spiritual vomiting.

This compulsion is even more active in Wright and the increasing number of Negroes who have said an irrevocable "no" to the Southern pattern. Wright learned that it is not enough merely to reject the white South, but that he had also to reject that part of the South which lay within. As a rebel he formulated that rejection negatively, because it was the negative face of the Negro community upon which he looked most often as a child. It is this he is contemplating when he writes:

> Whenever I thought of the essential bleakness of black life in America, I knew that Negroes had never been allowed to catch the full spirit of Western civilization, that they lived somehow in it but not of it. And when I brooded upon the cultural barrenness of black life, I wondered if clean, positive tenderness, love, honor, loyalty and the capacity to remember were native to man. I asked myself if these human qualities were not fostered, won, struggled and suffered for, preserved in ritual from one generation to another.

But far from implying that Negroes have no capacity for culture, as one critic interprets it, this is the strongest affirmation that they have. Wright is pointing out what should be obvious (especially to his Marxist critics) that Negro sensibility is socially and historically conditioned; that Western culture must be won, confronted like the animal in a Spanish bullfight, dominated by the red shawl of codified experience and brought heaving to its knees.

Wright knows perfectly well that Negro life is a by-product of Western civilization, and that in it, if only one possesses the humanity and humility to see, are to be discovered all those impulses, tendencies, life and cultural forms to be found elsewhere in Western society.

The problem arises because the special condition of Negroes in the

United States, including the defensive character of Negro life itself (the "will toward organization" noted in the Western capitalist appears in the Negro as a will to camouflage, to dissimulate), so distorts these forms as to render their recognition as difficult as finding a wounded quail against the brown and yellow leaves of a Mississippi thicket—even the spilled blood blends with the background. Having himself been in the position of the quail—to expand the metaphor—Wright's wounds have told him both the question and the answer which every successful hunter must discover for himself: "Where would I hide if *I* were a wounded quail?" But perhaps that requires more sympathy with one's quarry than most hunters possess. Certainly it requires such a sensitivity to the shifting guises of humanity under pressure as to allow them to identify themselves with the human content, whatever its outer form; and even with those Southern Negroes to whom Paul Robeson's name is only a rolling sound in the fear-charged air.

Let us close with one final word about the blues: Their attraction lies in this, that they at once express both the agony of life and the possibility of conquering it through sheer toughness of spirit. They fall short of tragedy only in that they provide no solution, offer no scapegoat but the self. Nowhere in America today is there social or political action based upon the solid realities of Negro life depicted in *Black Boy*; perhaps that is why, with its refusal to offer solutions, it is like the blues. Yet in it thousands of Negroes will for the first time see their destiny in public print. Freed here of fear and the threat of violence, their lives have at last been organized, scaled down to possessable proportions. And in this lies Wright's most important achievement: He has converted the American Negro impulse toward self-annihilation and "going-under-ground" into a will to confront the world, to evaluate his experience honestly and throw his findings unashamedly into the guilty conscience of America.

Notes

1. Signature formula used by blues singers at conclusion of song.
2. Italics mine.

The Self-Creation
of the Intellectual:
American Hunger
and *Black Power*

John M. Reilly*

Though the publisher of *American Hunger* observed upon its appearance in 1977 that the manuscript was printed "intact for the first time," this continuation of a narrative begun in *Black Boy* has long influenced popular understanding of Richard Wright's life. For example, the source of the image of Wright resisting political intrusion upon his artistic integrity derives from the story he told in "I Tried to Be a Communist," which he published in 1944, seven months before *Black Boy* itself was issued.[1] The account of Party experiences, constituting the last three of *American Hunger*'s six chapters, also appeared in Richard Crossman's celebrated anthology of ex-Communist testimony, *The God That Failed*.[2] As early as 1942 Wright published an account of absurdist experiences in a Chicago hospital were he and three other black men lived an underground life.[3] This recollection was then incorporated into the autobiographical manuscript as part of the three chapters that make up the opening half of *American Hunger*. The same three-chapter segment has also been published as "Early Days in Chicago" in Edwin Seaver's anthology *Cross Section, 1944*[4] and again in Wright's short story collection *Eight Men*, under the title "The Man Who Went to Chicago."[5] In each case the prior publication of early Chicago experiences has enforced for readers a sense that Wright's existentialism predates by many years the appearance of that philosophy as an overt theme in his novel *The Outsider* (1953).

To complete the record of prior publication for *American Hunger*, it must also be noted that the first chapter, describing the author's state of mind and mannerisms as a young man in Chicago, also was printed—as "American Hunger"—in *Mademoiselle*, where it must have reached an audience somewhat different than did "Early Days in Chicago."[6] On the other hand, a specialized audience has had available in some research

*This essay was written specifically for this volume and appears here for the first time by permission of the author.

libraries since 1946 the entire "intact" text of *American Hunger* in a privately circulated photo-offset pamphlet edited by Constance Webb.[7]

This history of previous publication makes it impossible to believe, as some reviewers did in 1977, that the account of Wright's life in Chicago and with the Communist Party was suppressed in 1945.[8] Whatever the reasoning was that led Edward Aswell, Wright's editor at Harper's, or the Book-of-the-Month Club, which accepted *Black Boy* as a selection for March 1945, to recommend dividing the manuscript, it is evident that Wright could agree without fear that the full story would remain unpublished. Indeed, the bibliographical record of the manuscript suggests that in reading *American Hunger* we are actually reassembling its familiar anecdotes and episodes into a continuous narrative, rather than receiving a new text.

There is one further extratextual condition to be considered before an estimate of that reassembled text is attempted. This condition results from the apparent difference between biographical fact, substantiated by other sources, and Wright's devised life in *American Hunger*. The major part of the book concerning his experiences as a member of the Communist Party reaches a climax in the final pages, where Wright describes being thrown bodily out of the 1936 May Day parade in Chicago. Earlier, he says, he had been accused of Trotskyist deviations and been found an undependable intellectual. The clear impression is that the expulsion from the parade marks Wright's break with the Party. Yet the following year he was in New York working as a staff correspondent for the Party's *Daily Worker*. In 1937 and 1938 he published regularly in *New Masses*, and in 1941 wrote for its pages "Not My People's War," an article supporting the position of the German-Soviet Nonaggression Pact, that plans for war were a capitalist threat to the survival of the USSR. Five days after the appearance of the article, the Nazis invaded Russia, and Wright turned to public statements in support of the Soviet military effort. So, while Wright was discontented with some practices of the Party as early as 1936, he nevertheless continued to work on its behalf into the 1940s and probably did not completely sever his relations with it until 1942.[9] In other parts of *American Hunger* Wright confuses the chronology of Party positions or overlooks the variations in practice that resulted from those changes.[10] Moreover, there is no indication in the autobiography that his writings, besides articles contributed to *New Masses* or the *Daily Worker*, continue after that May Day parade to show an allegiance not only to Marxism, but also to its Communist Party interpretation.[11]

These deliberate revisions of the record of experience, accidental oversights, and omissions mean that one cannot read *American Hunger* as political history, nor even as dependable biography. But, then, no one should be so inclined. Rather, these extratextual observations of the gap between objective fact and narrative will serve, like the bibliographical account of the manuscript's previous publication, to direct our attention away from its presumed reference value as an account of objective happenings and toward its salient features as a literary construction. Just as the bibliography of publication makes it clear that the episodes comprise a discontinuous text, the departures from objective fact also signal a narrative that employs the form of life-writing for a fictive purpose. We may be free to read *American Hunger* as though it were a true story of Richard Wright, but we have been advised to seek in it something else—perhaps a story of authenticity.

The narrator of *American Hunger* introduces himself in a Chicago expressionistically described as dehumanized.[12] The city seems unreal to him, its mythical houses "built of slabs of black coal wreathed in palls of gray smoke," their foundations "sinking slowly into the dank prairie." Looking about the scene, he finds nothing to relieve the impression: "only angles, lines, squares, bricks and copper wires." Evidently, though, the thoroughly bleak description results from his later recollection of subjective consciousness, for in 1927 when he first arrived in Chicago, he was preoccupied by the need for a job. Community, he says, hardly occurred to him, because "in all my life—though surrounded by many people—I had not had a single, satisfying, sustained relationship with another human being and, not having had any, I did not miss it. I made no demands whatever upon others" (p. 1).

Yet the preoccupation did not make him unfeeling. He catches the sense of insecurity in the personalities of people around him in his family, an insecurity he shared and protected with a "terse, cynical mode of speech that rebuffed those who sought to get too close to me" and a deadpan face that expressed only the nonaffective mask of controlled smiles and nods. At times he attributes his insecurity to social conditioning that led him to read Chicago in terms of his native South or that prevented his Southern ears from interpreting the broken English of his first employers. At other times, though, the compensatory superiority he felt behind his mask seems more than a strategy to deal with insecurity. Working among young white women in a North Side cafe, he was convinced that he "had a firmer grasp of life than most of them," for "they lived on the surface of their days; their smiles were surface smiles, and their tears were surface tears" (p. 12). What is the difference, one wonders, between the women's superficial expressions and his own deadpan face? A parenthetical break in the text's chronology allows Wright to use the women as exemplars of a white American culture devoted to the "trash of life." "Their constant outward-looking . . . made it impossible for them to learn a language which could have taught them to speak of what was in their or others' hearts. The words of their souls were the syllables of popular songs" (p. 14). While the tawdry values of the white waitresses characterize the dominant American culture, blacks do not escape it. In the narrator's home environment, "the highest item of value was a dime or a dollar, an apartment or a job," and "the most valued pleasure of the people I knew was a car, the most cherished experience a bottle of whisky, the most sought-after prize somebody else's wife" (p. 21). How, then, is Wright different from the people, white and black, with whom he necessarily associated in work or home? The difference lies in the fact that Wright knows that his masked persona developed a rich inner life. In the telling of experiences set in the past, he anticipates the maturity to which he will arrive by the time he comes to write his autobiographical manuscript. In anticipation he describes his personal past as prologue to the present. As for waitresses and pleasure seekers, he does not know how they turned out, nor does it matter. They are a literary device, a means to stress the singular potential of his persona.

Wright makes no claim to having felt superior to other people. "I merely felt that they had had no chance to learn differently. I never criticized them or praised them, yet they felt in my neutrality a deeper rejection of them than if I had cursed them" (p. 21). Originally this neutrality must have been part of his masked withdrawal, which is to say that it had a psychological function. In the telling, though, it has come to signify attachment to more profound sources of knowledge than others possess. Inability to express himself spontaneously, or refusal to try, no doubt intensified his isolation. In time, however, he created out of his detached state an identity no longer to be described in terms of psychological strategies of compensation or protection. It became an autonomous condition, which he can describe as characteristic of his capacity to know that Negro life is "a sprawling land of unconscious suffering" of which few Negroes knew the meaning or could tell the story (p. 7).

This dimension of Wright's persona, arising in the opening chapter of *American Hunger* as an exaggerated extension of the narrator in *Black Boy*, establishes both pattern and premise for the subsequent narrative. The pattern is a series of episodes selectively arranged to explain or to justify the identity of the isolated persona; the premise underlying the pattern is that the condition is identical with and necessary to a rationalistic stance before reality.

Wright can be ambivalent in his persona. He can confidently assert that his reading in social science enabled him to type many Negro characters and modes of behavior, while at the same time saying that he was "too subjective, too lacking in reference to social action" (p. 26). He will mock himself as a cynical wit, yet readily advance in all seriousness the idea that the pretensions of a young people's literary group result from their preoccupation with sex. The ambivalence is all in localized expression, however, because he cannot doubt for long the inner self that drives him, in ways he cannot yet comprehend, to write, to understand. It is this inviolable core of identity that becomes the reference point for the dominant persona in *American Hunger*.

A series of descriptions in the second chapter will illustrate. While working for a burial society, Wright visited the dingy flats of young black housewives to collect their insurance premiums, admittedly taking sex in lieu of cash or simply because it was offered. One illiterate young woman with whom he had had an extended relationship perplexed him because she yearned for him to take her to a circus. Of his discovery that she could not read, he writes: "I stared at her and wondered just what a life like hers meant in the scheme of things, and I came to the conclusion that it meant absolutely nothing. And neither did my life mean anything" (p. 32). Of her explanation that what attracted her to the circus, which she had never seen, was the animals, he writes: "I felt that there was a hidden meaning, perhaps, in what she had said; but I could not find it" (p. 34). And summing up his involvement with her, he characterizes her inner being: "Each time I left her I resolved not to visit her again. I could not talk to her; I merely listened to her passionate desire to see a circus. She was not calculating; if she liked a man, she just liked him. Sex relations were the only relations she had ever had; no others were possible with her, so limited was her intelligence" (p. 35).

In each comment on the woman, Wright reduces her human significance. Perhaps it is true that neither of their lives at the time had meaning in the scheme of things, but he is implicitly confident that the lack of meaning in his life is a philosophical position. Of the lack in her life he is not so sure. He possesses the categories of interpretation; she does not. Her remarks on the circus may have meaning, but it cannot be exhumed. And on the basis of an exclusively sexual relationship, he concludes that she could have no other kind, while he, of course, has a quotient of potentiality beyond her intelligence. One is tempted to say, "How dare he!" But the near-parody of rationalistic tone demands instead the observation that the insensitivity is the unconsciously ironic expression of a narrator working as a nonparticipating observer. Bodily, he was there with the woman, but his still insecure grasp on a rationalist's pose compels him to emphasize their separateness.

The same temporal duality that permits Wright to anticipate the mature identity of his persona in accounts of his past life also forestalls our criticism of his personality. Conventionally realistic life-writing so limns the career of an individual that we might very well charge him with smug self-satisfaction, but the synchronic narrative presents individual experiences and the events of specific time as stages in the emergence of consciousness. The persona obtains such privileged dominance that its environment and associations become almost entirely secondary; the dialectic of character development is contained within the self. In this respect, autobiography is less the genre than it is the guise of *American Hunger*. Psychology in Wright's text provides verisimilitude characteristic of the narrative's form, but eventually not the motive of a life. Historical and biographical detail are materials to symbolize development, rather than dependable records of fact, and the sequence of discontinuous episodes yields illustrations of authorial control but not plot.

Among other places where Wright's generic adaptation is clear, the opening pages of chapter three are noteworthy. The scene is a relief station, where Wright becomes aware that the quiet mumbling among the black men and women waiting their turns to see the professional caseworkers signifies a spontaneously generated realization of life. Listening to the talk, he "could see black minds shedding many illusions" (p. 43), community forming, and so wishes to join them that he feels his cynicism lift, his deadpan manner change. He grows open and questioning, eager to follow whatever directions for life that will emerge from the incident. Psychologically, Wright's observation seems suspiciously like a case of projection, and the mundane experience of a day in the relief station more likely to be boring or frustrating than exhilarating. The episode in the relief station, however, is a variety of conversion scene, a dramatic symbolization of achieved insight into generalized history. And in the question this experience raised for him—"Who would give these people a meaningful way of life?"—there is adumbration of a writer's mission.

As if to demonstrate how a writer might reveal life's significance, Wright places next within the text of *American Hunger* his bitterly satiric account, published in 1942, of working in Chicago's Michael Reese Hospital. This tells of three other black men and himself living in the underworld of a universe arranged strictly by race. Science and reason reign among white staff, while in the basement corridors, all but invisible to the doctors, the four black men labor to clean the building and tend the cages of experimental animals. Image after image represents the contradiction of reason by irrationality, as the anecdote moves toward climax in a pointless fight between two of the orderlies, with the audience of experimentally diseased animals leaping and whistling in their cages. Suddenly the fighters topple the tiers of cages. There is chaos as the rats and mice, dogs and rabbits race wildly around the floor, freed from confinement and from the categorical system designed to control the chaos which is nature before reason is applied. Hurriedly recaging the animals by simple numerical distribution, because they had been kept ignorant of a more scientific system of order, Wright and the others reproduce a semblance of a rational system. The scientists are as oblivious to the reorganization as they are to the orderlies. Work goes on as before.

Wright stresses the amusement of the anecdote by his tone. Was some hypothesis discarded, he wonders, or some tested principle given new refinement because of the reclassification of evidence? Yet he is also intent upon the deadly serious purpose of revealing the absurdity of Western reality:

> The hospital kept us four Negroes, as though we were close kin to the animals we tended, huddled together down in the underworld corridors of the hospital, separated by a vast psychological distance from the significant processes of the rest of the hospital—just as America had kept us locked in the dark underworld of American life for three hundred years—and we had made our own code of ethics, values, loyalty. (p. 59)

Not surprisingly, Wright produced his hospital story within a year of the manuscript of "The Man Who Lived Underground."[13] The works share an existential outlook and, much to the point of the present discussion, show a technical similarity as well. The original manuscript of "The Man Who Lived Underground" is written in a realistic style, but it was heavily revised before publication; so as we read the printed story, we are led immediately away from the mode of conventional realism. The purpose is similar to that of the ostensible autobiography, which almost as quickly subordinates events to their symbolic meaning. The difference between the fiction of novella and the nonfiction of autobiography becomes barely discernible, and as a result, we are further encouraged to describe *American Hunger* as a literary rather than historical project. In this respect, the hospital episode epitomizes the formula of Wright's persona. Assuming a distance from the world where empirical reasoners live absurdly, he observes and generalizes by means of a higher, more authentic reason that has its source in the inviolable self. By the privilege of this viewpoint his language creates a meaning that portrayal of unmediated reality, or an empirical narrator, would miss.

Though the three chapters of the manuscript that constitute "I Tried to Be a Communist" are best known as a presentation of the writer's conflict with the organized political movement of communism, when they are returned to their context in *American Hunger* they become the means of playing out the twin dramas of reason versus absurdity, and an isolated persona engaging his environment.

Here the self-representation has no ambivalence. Having shed his protective cynicism, Wright discovers in the John Reed Club of Chicago the men and women with whom he would at last form the sustained relationships, the lack of which underlined his earlier isolation. What is more, he finds there, too, a sense of personal integration. The literature of communism proves the existence of "an organized search for the truth of the lives of the oppressed and the isolated." In the relief station he had wondered "if the outcasts could become united in action, thought, and feeling. Now I knew. It was being done in one-sixth of the earth already. The revolutionary words leaped from the printed page and struck me with tremendous force" (pp. 62–63). Appropriately, this second conversion scene links with Wright's first through the medium of literature. As an immediate consequence of discovering communism's purpose, he writes a poem (probably "I Have Seen Black Hands") of unity, in the act expressing a belief that art, politics, and personal needs can be synthesized for him in the work of an engaged writer announcing new directions in historical life.

For a time Wright becomes totally accepting. He achieves office in the Reed Club, joins the Communist Party, finds personal acknowledgement among his comrades. A portent appears amidst the idyll when an escaped lunatic almost takes over internal direction of the club, causing Wright briefly to wonder if he and the rest of the club could have lost the ability to distinguish reality, but enthusiasm prevails. Disillusion is yet to come.

When it does arrive it comes in the train of criticism of his achieved identity. In his party unit (cell) he receives categorical disapproval as an intellectual, a writer who talks like a book. By definition, an intellectual means to the unit members, as it does to many of us as well, one who stands apart. Once the charge is levied, the persona begins to withdraw, as he had in earlier episodes, but the withdrawal serves a new personal function:

> The more I learned of the Negro Communists the more I found that they were not vicious, that they had no intention to hurt. They just did not know anything and did not want to learn anything. They felt that all questions had been answered, and anyone who asked new ones or tried to answer old ones was dangerous. The word "writer" was enough to make a black Chicago Communist feel that the man to whom the word applied had gone wrong. (p. 77)

His identity has been further specified as "writer," and its core significance is "man of reason," one who is required by the possession of his insight to keep the distance that will protect reason. Protect reason, not the self.

"An invisible wall was building slowly," he says, "between me and the people with whom I had cast my lot" (p. 78). Subsequent experience with the Party is further stonework. He feels repudiated and betrayed, and doubts that the Communists can in fact relate to people like the young, untutored boys he works with in a South Side club. The Party's abandonment of the John Reed Clubs as a consequence of its adopting the People's Front Policy and its efforts to supervise his writing projects represent a severing of his newly felt bond between art and politics, politics and the self. The politician, he finds, stands at a pole opposite to the artist's. The types differ not only because they approach reality differently. For Wright there is no question about it: those with responsibility for Communist political practice have lost contact with reality. The Party is ruled by fantasy. The forms of militant discipline to which he is bade to submit are vestiges of the secret movement under the czars. Enacted in an American environment, they bear no relationship to rational necessity.

Wright makes his point very clearly. The Communist Party's failing him cannot be explained by any of the reasons advanced by professional anticommunism: its hypocrisy, the manipulative and conspiratorial schemes, the allegiance it gives a foreign power, or its inadequate philosophy in comparison with capitalism in the Western democracies. On the contrary, communism possesses the highest ideals based upon historical analysis. It holds the key to the future of the world, the meaningful sense of reality for which he, and such black men and women as those in the Chicago relief station, hungered. Yet communist organizations are beset by cruel hatred, suspicion, internecine strife.

To explain the depth of the contradiction, Wright focuses upon the trial of the organizer Ross. Emotionally, he feels the trial could be his own, but in a triumph of narrative viewpoint Wright establishes his persona at the distance of an engaged observer. He is neither the defensively aloof spectator he had been in early pages of the manuscript, nor is he the enthusiast of the early John Reed Club days. Though political functionaries doubt the validity of the tentative integration he had felt in his art and political aims, his literary technique creates a mode of narration exemplifying unity. Without protecting his ego, he extends sympathy toward those from whom he differs, acknowledging the significance of the understanding of collective life he shares with them, while retaining confidence in the integrity of his own analysis of reality. The persona has completed his identity and with completion gained the means to render the climax of *American Hunger* in the most effective writing of the book.

The trial, says Wright, had "a structure that went as deep as the desire of men to live together" (p. 120); thus, it functions as a ritual, bonding the Party members in collective recognition of the significance their lives acquire through participation in a vanguard revolutionary organization. Opening in an informal way, "like a group of neighbors sitting in judgment upon one of their kind who had stolen a chicken" (p. 120), the rite proceeds through a sequence of prescribed speeches, rising in intensity as they move from description of the world situation to discussion of the Party's role among blacks of Chicago's South Side. Ross shares and accepts the vision and analysis that inform the speeches. He has given himself wholly to the vision, for the Party had given him the same map of reality his accusers use, and it had given him "new eyes" with which to see that he has violated the consensual sanctions of the group. For Ross, as for the comrades he believes he has betrayed, the penetrating analytic method of Marxism has been transformed from an instrument of thought into a system of life as deeply felt as, say, culture, a culture whose ritual affirmation is "a spectacle of glory" (p. 125).

But "a spectacle of horror," also.[14] Wright yearns as strongly as anyone for the communal world created in vision and practice by the Party, but its achievement will cost him the way of thinking and feeling he has struggled to establish as his identity and persona. Committed as he might be to the dynamics of communism, he will not equate them to the dynamics of his personality. So *American Hunger* necessarily moves to conclusion in tragedy. The splendid goal of collectivity becomes impossible for Wright. The Party must deny his independence if it is to repair his isolation, but the persona forged in solitary and independent thought cannot accept an alternate integrity.

It is to enforce this irremediable conflict that Wright has replaced the fact of his gradual withdrawal from the Party with the climactic scene of forced ostracism from the 1936 May Day parade. Invited to participate by black comrades, Wright describes himself physically expelled by two white Communists, while the other comrades, white and black, look on "with cold eyes of nonrecognition" (p. 132). Like the faith exemplified in the ritual trial, the solidarity promised by the ceremonial observation of the working-class demonstration proves to be inauthentic. Wright's rational persona is again alone.

He is not, however, imprisoned in isolation, as he was a decade before when the narrative of *American Hunger* begins. With new objectivity of vision he can see into the condition of those who are apart from him. The rational observer has achieved empathy, and with it a purpose expressive of his created self. With language he will bridge the distance between his self and "that world outside, that world which was so distant and elusive that it seemed unreal" (p. 135). He will be a writer.

Appropriately, the writer's role emerges in a narrative that controls fact with literary means. Focusing on his persona's making sense of reality and discovering an integrity, Wright creates a story of consciousness. In describing his aim when he first began to imitate the manner of imaginative literature, Wright speaks of a vanishing style. He wishes to fasten the reader's mind so firmly upon the words that they would be forgotten. "I strove to master words, to make them disappear. . . ." (p. 22) Through the realism of more or less factual life-writing, words may disappear, but at the heart of Wright's *American Hunger* language and its representational properties become the action of the self. There is no way other than language for us to know the core of self from which Richard Wright created his persona, no other way to appreciate that his movement from isolation to detached, sympathetic observer was the making of him as an artist.

Ten years after writing the manuscript about his early life, Wright again placed his autobiographical persona at the center of a narrative. This time his purpose was to present the rationalist's conclusions about the representative history of anticolonial politics in Africa. A great deal had happened to him in the meanwhile. He had taken up permanent residence in France, become internationally known as a spokesperson for American blacks, and published *The Outsider*. He had also undergone an intellectual crisis manifest in the implicitly nihilist philosophy of that novel's protagonist, Cross Damon.[15] To resolve the crisis he needed a newly compelling subject that would permit him to reaffirm his writer's identity. This he found in an investigative trip to West Africa in 1953 and through writing an account of Africa in the book called *Black Power*.[16]

In *American Hunger* he wrote of his admiration for the followers of Marcus Garvey. He could give no credence to their ideological attachment to Africa, but recognized the potential strength of American blacks in the Garveyites' resolve to live "within the boundaries of a culture of their own making" (p. 29). Thoroughly convinced that American black identity is unquestionably Western, Wright nevertheless shared recognition that the question of relationship to Africa provides a framework for exploring that identity. Consequently, the record of Wright's stay in the Gold Coast during the period when Kwame Nkrumah's Convention People's Party was building a mass base for independence as the nation of Ghana carries as its epigraph Countee Cullen's lines beginning "What is Africa to me."

Apparently, Wright was at first bewildered in the Gold Coast. He shows himself put off by a shopkeeper's asking him what part of the continent his family came from and barely suppresses his hostility in saying that the Africans who sold his ancestors and the whites who bought them did not keep records. Witnessing dancing women, funerals, and other cultural performances, he is overwhelmed by confusion at the thought that the resemblance they bear to Afro-American culture might show transcendent racial unity. He must find a rational explanation for what other observers encompass in a racial mystique.

The necessity to discover a rational explanation of all he observes is as characteristic of *Black Power* as it is of *American Hunger*, and just as much a premise of the persona. In the early pages of *Black Power* Wright exerts himself to assure readers that he is an "objective" observer. The preface, which acknowledges his past membership in the Communist Party of the United States, also announces that he intends to use the scientific categories of Marxism. Then, in the early pages of the main text, given over to an account of his passage to Africa, he enforces the image of a self-secure, rational persona by contrasting himself with a small-minded African colonial judge who is concerned mainly with preserving his position as a comprador amidst the changes sweeping Africa. Wright insists also upon his immunity to emotionalism. Off Freetown, Sierra Leone, he is impressed by the wondrous display of the sunset, but hastens to say that he remains detached, refusing to permit his feelings to drown his reason, rejecting the possibility that awe before nature—or any other grand force—should cause in him an irrational response. He is the consummate rationalist who eventually will explain the resemblance between Afro-American and African cultural forms, not as the basis of negritude, but as aspects of the traditional culture that survive when the black is prevented by racism and economic oppression from fully adjusting to a modern environment.

As the concern with African survivals indicates, *Black Power* is an intensely expositional book. Throughout the text Wright summarizes secondary sources to give readers the colonial history of the Gold Coast, records interviews he conducted among contemporary African intellectuals, and of course, offers lengthy analyses of African nationalism derived from his own political knowledge. Despite confessions to bewilderment and self-consciousness, Wright never relaxes control of his narrative.

Constantly explaining, he is constantly assimilating his subject to the persona dominating the narrative.

As we have seen, Wright was always eager to discover the general patterns of historical black experience. Once, in *12 Million Black Voices*, he had affirmed by means of a collective narrative voice that he had found the fundamental Afro-American experience. The controlling conception of that "folk history" is a representation of the passage of black American peasants from their traditional Southern life into the conditions of the industrial city. Wright terms the movement an "entry into conscious history," a process also inherent in his own personal struggle to attain a role in the modern world.[17] In *Black Power* Wright implicitly extends his analogy further. Life in the Gold Coast of West Africa during the anticolonial struggle, like the life of American blacks migrating into the Northern urban centers, like the life of Richard Wright surpassing racial and economic barriers, manifests the effort to acquire citizenship in a modern society; and qualifications for that citizenship include reconstruction of culture and personality under the direction of rational analysis.

Throughout the book Wright describes the culture of the Gold Coast and the personalities of Africans changed for all time by their historical encounter with Europe. Economic and colonial exploitation destroyed the viability of tribal life; its vestiges remain only to be used for political control by the metropolitan powers. Traditional society could not be revived, even if it were desirable. Africans can only move forward, attempting to make themselves into a modern nation. The means of such transformation lies in the syncretic politics of Nkrumah's Convention People's Party, which fuses the surviving patterns of a tribal way of life with the goals of African nationalism.

Thematically, the Convention People's Party as the agency of African self-determination becomes central to Wright's ideas about African entry into conscious history. Within the text, though, something else just as important is going on. Richard Wright, the Western rationalist, is adapting his observations of Gold Coast life to *a priori* conceptions that will explain what Africa means to him as well as to his readers. Again genre is a guise. The book is presented as a reporter's document, a type of writing normally marked by empiricism. The dynamics of the observing persona, however, produces a text that frames the facts within concepts previously created as intimate features of the writer's identity. Structurally, the book consists of short chapters that interweave observed scenes with explanatory passages of recorded conversation or background description. For example, Wright describes the activity and color of a funeral observance, stressing the notion that at first its meaning escapes him. He cannot follow the procession physically or mentally, because he is not disposed to the cultural anthropologist's search for significance by imaginative participation. His language is controlled to exclude inexplicable emotion in himself or those he observes. He then records the explanation of the funeral given by a Westernized Africa and concludes, "Yes, if you accepted the assumption, all the rest was easy, logical. . . ." (p. 132) The sequence of style from detailed description by outside observer, to explanation by authority, to reflection thus confirms the power of rational comprehension and affirms the narrator's inherent mastery of mystery.

Similarly, Wright's portrayal of the Convention People's Party testifies to its great emotional force from a distance that denies, or prohibits, an appeal to innate Africanness he might be presumed to possess. What he actually possesses and applies to his subject is the previously developed character of *American Hunger*. In that character Wright observes Nkrumah, generalizes about the place of spirit in African life, and interviews Africans who can comment on Gold Coast politics according to the categories of Western practice. All this he does in the way of the persona finally created in *American Hunger*, resisting uncontrolled emotional participation, but engaging rather than turning from the experiences of others.

Within the setting of Wright's career this engaged attitude has immediate personal significance. The despairing outlook that marked his reflection on modern life in *The Outsider* is nowhere in evidence in *Black Power*. He writes with an enthusiasm previously matched only by the description of his discovery of Communism in *American Hunger*, for what Africa has come to mean to him is positive renewal of his faith in the possibility of human reconstruction. From renewed faith follows affirmation of the role he has created for himself as an intellectual and writer who advises and fosters this reconstruction.

Black Power concludes with a startling letter recommending that Kwame Nkrumah militarize the life of his people and "be merciful by being stern" in moving Africans rapidly from their tribal past into the twentieth century. Wright hopes to distinguish such a path from dictatorship and to indicate it is an alternative both to communism and to the recommendations that will come from Western democracies; yet the reader cannot overlook the fact that the discipline, and the justification for it, that Wright now proposes for West Africa are almost precisely those he found unacceptable in the American Communist Party. There is a contradiction to be sure, but at the risk of paradox one must say it is merely a logical contradiction, for despite the insistence upon his persona's rational powers, Wright's narratives of his self in the world operate finally on other levels.

American Hunger tells of the creation of an adequate persona, one for whom rationality is first defensive and then a means for discovering an authentic role as a writer. Secure in his identity by the time he visits Africa, Wright's investigations focus more surely on their object. The persona having been created, the task at hand is to find it useful work. The thrill of liberation from colonialism and from the irrational dependencies of traditional culture satisfy Wright's taste for politics and confirm the accuracy of his progressive interpretation of historical and autobiographical experience. No longer feeling a personal threat from deliberate efforts to sustain collective unity, because he has assured himself and the world around him that he has created an independent self, Wright can concentrate on glory and disregard the horror he had seen in the American left.

The open letter to Nkrumah must have been received as presumptuous. Wright was still speaking in the tone of the detached intellectual. He knew, however, that the intellectual is a figure created in the circumstances of modern life. Isolation and alienation are painful conditions to be overcome, but the intelligentsia's detachment is a function of role. The transformation of isolation into a stance appropriate to the intellectual marks Wright's achievement of authentic identity, and *Black Power* as one of its accomplishments.

Wright's stay in West Africa ended with a visit to the seventeenth century castles built by European slave traders. The visit symbolizes a return to the beginnings of the journey into the modern world for Africans and Europeans both. For Wright personally, the visit to the castles enacted a feeling of solidarity that we receive through his written text. His language provides us our connection with the event and the author. Richard Wright wished to build a bridge of words between his self and the world. He succeeded, and we acknowledge the accomplishment by discovering within the constructions of his language the prerequisite endeavor to create his expressive self.

Notes

1. "I Tried to Be a Communist," *Atlantic Monthly*, 174 (Aug. 1944), 61–70; (Sept. 1944), 48–56.

2. Richard Crossman, ed., *The God That Failed* (New York: Harper, 1949).

3. "What You Don't Know Won't Hurt You," *Harper's Magazine*, 186 (Dec. 1942), 58–61.

4. Edwin Seaver, ed., *Cross Section, 1944* (New York: McClelland, 1945), pp. 306–54.

5. Richard Wright, *Eight Men* (Cleveland: World, 1961).

6. "American Hunger," *Mademoiselle*, 21 (Sept. 1945), 164–65, 299–301.

7. "A hitherto unpublished manuscript by Richard Wright being a continuation of *Black Boy*," with "Notes preliminary to a full study of the work of Richard Wright by Constance Webb," privately circulated, 1946. Princeton University Library holds copy No. 56.

8. See, for example, Robert Kirsch, *Los Angeles Times*, 29 May 1977, pp. 1, 71; and Darryl Pinckney, "Richard Wright: The Unnatural," *Village Voice*, 4 July 1977, pp. 80–82.

9. Michel Fabre, *The Unfinished Quest of Richard Wright* (New York: Morrow, 1973), pp. 228–31.

10. For a notation of these details of Party politics, see George Breitman, *International Socialist Review*, supplement to *The Militant*, 38 (5 Aug. 1977), 12; rpt. in John M. Reilly, ed., *Richard Wright: The Critical Reception* (New York: Burt Franklin, 1978), pp. 389–92.

11. See, for example, Richard Wright, "Blueprint for Negro Writing," *New Challenge*, 2 (Fall 1937), 53–65.

12. Richard Wright, *American Hunger* (New York: Harper, 1977). Page citations appear parenthetically in the body of the article.

13. "The Man Who Lived Underground" was apparently first conceived as a short novel. In highly abbreviated form it appeared in *Accent*, 2 (Spring 1942), 170–76. In a longer version, but still shorter than the original typescript, it was published in Edwin Seaver, ed., *Cross Section 1944* (New York: McClelland, 1945), pp. 58–102. This last version appears in Wright's *Eight Men*. An original typescript bearing evidence of revision is held by the Princeton University Library.

14. The working title of the complete autobiographical manuscript was "The Horror and the Glory."

15. For brief discussion of the intellectual crisis in relation to *Black Power* and *The Outsider*, see John M. Reilly, "Richard Wright's Discovery of the Third World," *Minority Voices*, 2 (Fall 1978), 47–53. Fuller treatments of the philosophical problems of the novel can be located through the bibliographical essay on Wright in M. Thomas Inge, Maurice Duke, and Jackson R. Bryer, eds., *Black American Writers*, Vol. 2 (New York: St. Martin's Press, 1978), pp. 29, 41–43.

16. Richard Wright, *Black Power: A Record of Reactions in a Land of Pathos* (New York: Harper, 1954). Citations appear parenthetically in the body of the article.

17. Richard Wright, *12 Million Black Voices: A Folk History of the Negro in the United States* (New York: Viking Press, 1941). For discussion of the book's conception of conscious history in relation to other works see John M. Reilly, "The Reconstruction of Genre as Entry into Conscious History," *Black American Literature Forum*, 13 (Spring 1979), 3–6.

Richard Wright
and the Third World

Nina Kressner Cobb*

Richard Wright is best known for his searing portraits of black life in the United States, but after leaving America in 1947 to live in exile in Paris, Wright turned his attention to the Third World. In *Black Power* (1954), *The Color Curtain* (1956), and *White Man, Listen!* (1957), Wright expressed his concern for and attitudes toward the emerging nations of Asia and Africa. An advocate of national independence, Wright was also a ruthless Westernizer. Although he did not use the term, Wright was an avid proponent of modernization, believing it to be both beneficial and inevitable.

In 1980, we are no longer certain about the benevolence or the inevitability of modernization, but in the 1950s, modernization theory was just coming to the fore. In response to the international situation after World War II, American social scientists directed their efforts toward those areas of the world that were seeking independence—Asia, Africa, and Latin America. In key works like Daniel Lerner's *The Passing of Traditional Society* (1958), W. W. Rostow's *The Stages of Economic Growth* (1960), Seymour Martin Lipset's *The First New Nation* (1963), and C. E. Black's *The Dynamics of Modernization: A Study in Comparative History* (1966), to mention only a few, anthropologists, sociologists, political scientists, and economists developed an analytical mode in which to understand the vast changes in these societies as they took on the trappings of Western industrial societies.[1]

Modernization theorists, for the most part, see traditional and modern societies as polar opposites. While traditional societies are described as ascriptive, particularistic, and diffuse, modern societies are achievement-oriented, universalistic, and specific. In addition, modern societies are characterized as secular, rational, industrial, and urban. Modernization itself is a process of transition that a traditional society undergoes as it develops into a modern one.

The first attacks on modernization theory came in the late sixties and were fueled by the Vietnam War. As early as 1967, Reinhard Bendix

*This essay was written specifically for this volume and appears here for the first time by permission of the author.

228

pointed out in "Tradition and Modernity Reconsidered," that the concepts "traditional" and "modern" were terribly oversimplified. Both Bendix and Robert Nisbet revealed the theory's indebtedness to Western sociological thinking in what was to be a precursor of the major critical thrust against modernization theory—its ethnocentrism.[2] In a major critique, "Modernization Theory and the Comparative Study of Societies: A Critical Perspective," Dean C. Tipps charged that the concept of modernization was based on a fundamental complacency toward American society.[3] According to Tipps, modernization theorists viewed the United States as a consensual society that combined unparalleled economic growth with political stability within a democratic framework—thus making American society an appropriate model to be emulated by less fortunate societies.[4]

Richard Wright in no way shared such a complacent view of American society. How, then, did he come to be such a firm believer in the benefits of modernization? To answer this question, we will trace Wright's attitudes toward the Third World, as found in his nonfiction, and examine them against the background of his conception of Western civilization in general. For the key to Wright's views of the Third World lies in his vision of Western civilization.

Wright left the United States in July 1947 to escape the confines of race and concentrate on more universal themes in his writing. Speaking of his exile to black expatriate writer William Gardner Smith in 1953, Wright said, "The break from the United States was more than a geographical change. It was a break with my former attitudes as a Negro and as a communist."[5] His interest in the Third World had been stimulated by George Padmore, a leader of the Pan-African movement whom he met in London in 1947, and by his association with the international black elite on the influential journal *Présence Africaine*.[6] Though the Communist Party had emphasized the kinship between America's oppressed black minority and colored colonial peoples, Wright had not been touched by these appeals to black nationalism.[7]

He had considered going to Africa as early as 1947, but it was not until he received a visit from Dorothy Padmore in Paris in 1953 that he mobilized himself for the trip. In many ways, Wright's exploration of Africa was a voyage of self-discovery. As a result, *Black Power*, the record of that journey, is the most complex of Wright's travel books.

> One does not react to Africa as Africa is. . . . One reacts to Africa as one is, as one lives; one's reactions to Africa is one's life, one's ultimate sense of things: Africa is a vast, dingy mirror and what modern man sees in that mirror he hates and wants to destroy. He thinks, when looking into that mirror, that he is looking at black people who are inferior, but, really, he is looking at himself. . . .[8]

Wright tried out several titles for the book, which, taken together, show his ambivalence toward Africa—*What Is Africa To Me?, O, My People,* and *Stranger in a Strange Land.*[9]

Of the titles Wright was mulling over before he thought of *Black Power, Stranger in a Strange Land* most aptly described his feeling of discomfort in Africa.[10] Much of what he saw he did not understand. "I'm of African descent and I'm in the midst of Africans, yet I cannot tell what they are thinking and feeling," he wrote (p. 137). His first impression of Africa was somewhat unsettling. "The kaleidoscope of sea, jungle, nudity, mud huts, and crowded market places induced in me a conflict deeper than I was aware of: a protest against what I saw seized me" (p. 37).

Wright's attitude toward Africa combined hostility, sympathy, repugnance, and condescension. His hostility was aroused when he was asked what part of Africa his family came from. He replied that the Africans who had sold their brethren as slaves failed to keep records. Wright tried to ward off feelings of condescension by understanding the underlying assumptions of African beliefs. Although he warned Westerners against seeing the African as irrational, he was not entirely successful in this himself, for Africa revealed the extent to which he was a product of Western culture.

> One did not leave the past behind; one took it with one; one made the past the present. I could not get beyond that, for it was alien to me; it was intriguing but beyond the bounds of my feelings. I could understand it, but I couldn't experience it . . . faced with the absolute otherness and inaccessibility of this new world, I was prey to a vague sense of mild panic. (p. 175)

Wright described himself as an uneasy member of the Western world, but little of his discomfort surfaced in this book. Instead, he proved a staunch rationalist who would salvage nothing of native customs and traditions if they stood in the way of modernization. In Wright's eyes, these aspects of African culture were impediments that had to be destroyed for Africa to become free of white domination. He advised Nkrumah to be hard: African life would have to be "militarized in order to be able to leap into the twentieth century" (pp. 345–49).

> A military form of African society will atomize the fetish-ridden past, abolish the mystical and nonsensical family relations that freeze the African in his static degradation; it will render the continued existence of those parasitic chiefs who have too long bled and misled a naive people. (p. 348)

Wright seemed to see no irony in recommending that Africa become more like the West in order to rid itself of Western influence. In a section of *Black Power* addressed to Nkrumah, he wrote:

> There will be those who will try to frighten you by telling you that the organization you are forging looks like Communism,

Fascism, Nazism; but, Kwame, the form of organization that you need will be dictated by the needs, emotional and material, of your people. The content determines the form. Never again must the outside world decide what is good for you. (p. 349)

Although Wright had never actually been a nationalist, he was not insensitive to Africa's appeal to many American blacks. But he was skeptical of the popular notion that his kinship with Africans gave him special insight into Africa and its customs. He rejected anthropological notions about the survival of African traits in the Afro-American and was unsympathetic to the idea that blacks had "a special gift for music, dancing, rhythm, and movement. . . ."[11]

While Wright did not believe that life could be explained in racial terms, he was puzzled by the similiarity he observed between the dancing of African women and the dancing in store-front churches and Holy Roller Tabernacles in the Deep South. He resolved this conundrum by concluding that "African survivals" were cultural rather than racial— nothing more than "the retention of basic and primal attitudes toward life" (p. 266). Wright believed that an African, like other peoples, would take on the characteristics of another culture to the degree that he had been allowed to assimilate:

To the degree that he fails to adjust, to absorb the new environment (and this will be mainly for racial and economic reasons!), he, to that degree, and of necessity, will retain much of his primal outlook upon life, his basically poetic apprehension of existence. (p. 266)

Thus, he thought that the social scientist should be concerned with the causes for the persistence of primal attitudes.

Wright claimed to follow a Marxist analysis in *Black Power*, but this was true only to the limited degree that his explanation of Western colonialism was predicated on economic motives. Much of the analysis is social psychology, focusing on the impact of religion, colonialism, and nationalism. Wright dealt briefly with the psychology of the oppressed, but not as prominently as in his later books. According to Wright, the greatest crime that took place under the aegis of imperialism was not economic exploitation, but the creation of a servile personality structure in the native population. As a result, he believed that the most important task facing Nkrumah was the creation of confidence at the core of the African personality, rather than the establishment of a strong economy—although certainly both were necessary.[12]

In this book Wright described nationalism as "politics *plus!*" (p. 56). Nkrumah filled the void that the British missionaries left when they smashed tribal culture. He "tapped the abandoned emotional reservoir" that Christianity had no use for. His genius lay in fusing politics with tribalism, combining tribal rituals such as the oath with twentieth-century politics. Nkrumah took the millions of detribalized Africans, people living in two worlds—part of neither, believing in neither—and gave them a politics that bordered on religion. Politics *plus* "involved a total and basic response to reality; it smacked of the dreamlike, of the stuff of which art and myths were made. . . ." It was not the cold, unemotional religion that the missionaries had given the African; nor was it Communism, which Wright said was "above all, ideological." What he had seen was "the quintessence of passion," a "smattering of Marxism and the thirst for self-redemption." Thus, Wright dubbed Nkrumah an "agent provocateur to the emotions of millions."[13]

Wright's political stance in *Black Power* was somewhat ambivalent. He explained that his use of Marxism did not commit him to policies or programs commonly associated with communism. Indeed, he was explicitly anti-Soviet.[14] Yet, he did advocate the same techniques of modernization that he had condemned in the USSR because they had crushed freedom. Despite the fact that Wright claimed he had written this book to warn the West that it would lose Africa to communism if it remained blind to the causes of revolution on that continent, politically *Black Power* was almost as anti-Western as it was anti-Soviet. Wright was addressing himself to the African elite, imploring them to modernize as quickly as possible. Ironically, many Africans were offended by Wright's portrayal of African life: they found him condescending and scornful.

Shocked by his reaction to Africa, in his later trips Wright probed for the factors that distinguished Western societies from the rest of the world. For that reason, *Pagan Spain* (1957), while neither an examination of a nation in the throes of modernization nor a study of a former colonial area, has a central place in Wright's thinking about these subjects. Wright's book on Spain which was his inquiry into the meaning of Western civilization shows quite definitely that for him the West was not defined geographically, but culturally.

To the extent that *Pagan Spain* was more than a travelogue, it was a discussion of the sociology of religion. Wright hypothesized that Catholicism, by shaping the Spanish personality, was the key factor responsible for the course of Spanish development. In an analysis similar to Max Weber's in *The Protestant Ethic and the Spirit of Capitalism*, Wright explained that there was a causal relationship between Protestantism and the dynamic societies of Western capitalist countries on the one hand, and between Catholicism and a more traditional society on the other.

In Wright's determination, the major difference between the two religions was the essentially spiritual nature of Protestantism and the sensual nature of Catholicism: Protestantism emphasized individual conscience, while Catholicism relied on external factors such as symbols and music.

> To Catholics, the hierarchy of Christianity was external, unspeakably beautiful, powerful, and yet miraculously accessible through the intercession of others. . . .

To Protestants this whole process had been psychologically internalized. . . . Protestants had to conjure up out of their imagination, their longings, their fears. . . . Protestants had to make severe demands on themselves; Catholics submitted to what had already been arranged.[15]

Wright's belief that religion permeated every aspect of life in Spain—in short, that the secular sphere had not emerged independent—was his basis for differentiating Spain from Western civilization. Clearly, Wright's view of Western civilization was teleological, a development culminating in the emergence of a secular, rational civilization.

Returning from Spain for the Christmas holidays in 1954, Wright read for the first time of the Bandung Conference to be held in Indonesia that spring. Twenty-nine independent African and Asian nations were meeting to discuss the problems of racism and colonialism. Wright assessed the conference as a gathering of the despised, dispossessed, and rejected of the earth: the victims of Western racism. Furthermore, almost all the nations attending the conference were deeply religious.

Feeling himself uniquely qualified to report on the conference, Wright applied to the Congress for Cultural Freedom, which he believed had the indirect backing of the State Department and actually was financed in part by the CIA, for financial support.[16] He obtained it, but not without making sure that it would not restrict his freedom of speech. Officially, Wright covered the conference as a freelance writer.

The Color Curtain, his report on the conference, was a frankly subjective work. Wright described his trip as a search for the emotional landscapes of Asia. He was not as interested in politics per se as he was in the psychological bases for politics. In Asia, he found that both religion and race, "two of the most powerful and irrational forces in human nature," were key factors in shaping the people's psyches.[17]

Religion was no longer a delicate relationship of a people of the world in which they lived, a relationship wrought through centuries and embodied in ritual and ceremony, but a proof of one's humanity, something to defend and cling to (even if one did not believe in it!) passionately, for the sake of one's pride, to redress the balance in the scales of self-esteem. (p. 74)

While religious diversity divided the nations represented at Bandung, race unified them. Black, brown, or yellow, they all were colored in the eyes of the West. Their unity had been forged over centuries at the hands of a common oppressor.

"Race" was no longer a simple designation, nonscientific, of a people and their physiological differences, but an instrument of subjection, a badge of shame, a burning and concrete fact that was instantly proved by the color of one's skin. . . . (p. 74)

Wright hypothesized that in Asia race and religion had combined into

> *a racial and religious system of identification manifesting itself*
> *in an emotional nationalism which was now leaping state*
> *boundaries and melting and merging. . . .* (p. 40, italics in
> original)

He feared that this shared racial consciousness might evolve into a
virulent racism.

Wright believed that the political significance of Bandung was enormous, despite the ridicule that the conference often received in Western
newspapers. He cautioned the West against viewing these national
movements within the context of Left or Right or as an episode in the Cold
War. Race and religion, the two major forces and issues in Asia, were
beyond these categories. Wright called Bandung "THE LAST CALL OF
WESTERNIZED ASIANS TO THE MORAL CONSCIENCE OF THE
WEST!" (p. 202, capitalized in original). The Asian elite was more
Western than the West. Yet their attitudes toward the West were highly
ambivalent. They were taught Western law, ethics, and finance, and encouraged to develop a taste for Western goods. They made their revolu-
tions in terms of Western values. Although they needed Western technical
knowledge, they feared the aid of the West because it might result in a
return of Western domination. Thus, much of the language at the conference was frankly anti-Western, manifesting Asian bitterness over centuries of humiliation.

The West would have to exercise extreme caution to avoid throwing
these nations into the arms of the communist camp. The Asian masses
were psychologically predisposed to collectivism and hierarchy, Wright
felt. "The Asian seemed to have a 'picture' of life and wanted to find out
where and how he fitted into that 'picture.' He sought no separate,
unique or individual destiny" (p. 74). These attitudes made it more likely
that the masses would be attracted to communism than to Western
individualism.

Still the apostle of Western values and modernization, Wright
predicted that men who are given a choice between the bonds of their
traditions and new horizons will choose the latter. Modernization was inevitable. The only questions still open were when and by what means. He
advised the West to do all in its power to bring about a rationalized Asia.
The secular base already existed in the Asian elite. Otherwise, the tenuous
rational strands in these societies would be subsumed by racial and
religious passions.

In *White Man, Listen!*, a collection of speeches that Wright had
given in Europe between 1950 and 1956, Wright's pro-Western bias
shows most blatantly, particularly in those speeches given after his trip to
Bandung.[18] In "The Psychological Reactions of Oppressed People," he
baldly expressed his disdain for the cultures indigenous to Asia and Africa
when he wrote that Europeans should not be too proud of their conquests
in these areas; such victories were not indications of white racial

superiority, but of the inferiority of native culture and mental habits (p. 1).

This rather unusual argument against white supremacism certainly could not have pleased black nationalists. Another speech, entitled "Tradition and Industrialization," which was given at the Congrès des Écrivains et Artistes Noirs sponsored by *Présence Africaine* in Paris in September 1956, could hardly have resulted in huzzahs from the audience. Considering the setting, his words were strange indeed.

> [The] teeming religions gripping the minds and consciousness of Asians and Africans offend me. I can conceive of no identification with such mystical visions of life that freeze millions in static degradation, no matter how emotionally satisfying such degradation seems to those who wallow in it. (pp. 48–49)

Wright called any white man who argued in favor of preserving native customs a racist, for he believed that such a stance was tantamount to advocating white dominion over these peoples. Despite the fact that Wright believed that colonialism had fostered a psychology of the oppressed he deplored in the native populations, he assessed the overall effects of imperialism positively. By smashing the ties of custom, religion, and tradition, European colonialism had liberated Asia and Africa.

To African and Asian leaders, Wright recommended the same method of accelerating the long, drawn-out process of modernization that he had recommended to Nkrumah in *Black Power*—dictatorship. Only in this way could the nations of Asia and Africa preserve their independence from the West and the USSR that Wright so desired.

Wright wanted the West to understand the necessity for such political developments in the Third World. He tried to convince Western leaders not to fear that these nations were courting communism if they established dictatorships to attain their goals. Nationalist leaders like Nkrumah, Sukarno, and Nasser, he felt, should have carte blanche in their efforts at modernization; otherwise, the West would risk alienating these nations even further. It had already lost a large part of the Third World to communism through selfishness and racism. His greatest fear was that the racism of the West would blind its leaders to its true interests.

> Never have so few hated and feared so many. What I dread is the Western white man, confronted with an implacably militant Communism on the one hand, and with a billion and a half colored people gripped by surging tides of nationalist fanaticism on the other, will feel that only a vengeful unleashing of atom and hydrogen bombs can make him feel secure. (pp. 42–43)

Wright pinned his hopes for the triumph of those Western values that he regarded so highly on the Westernized elite in the developing nations, to whom he had dedicated *White Man, Listen!* To him, these men were the freest men in the world because they were not burdened by the weight of the past. Their Western education had cast them adrift from their own culture. Inculcated with Western values, but then denied the privileges and equal treatment that these values should have accorded, they gained a critical perspective toward the society that excluded them. They represented the only bastions of Western thought beyond the confines of the West, the only chance for rationality to prevail over the forces of racism and religion in these areas of the world.

Wright had spoken of this elite in his earlier treatments of the Gold Coast and the Bandung conference, but they assumed a more significant place in his thinking in the later essays. A glance at the dedication to *White Man, Listen!*—to "the Westernized and Tragic Elite of Asia, Africa, and the West Indies—the lonely outsiders who exist precariously on the clifflike margins of many cultures . . ." (p. xxiv)—reveals the reason: Wright not only sympathized with the Westernized elite, but identified his plight with theirs. His trips to the Third World made him realize that he was far more Western than he had known; yet at the same time, he grew ever more despairing of and alienated from the West.

When writing about the Negro situation in the United States, Wright had always been concerned with vast social changes and the psychological dislocations that they brought in their wake. His earliest fiction, *Uncle Tom's Children* and *Lawd Today*, contrasted the life of rural and urban blacks, respectively. While the characters in *Uncle Tom's Children* were at one with their environment, Jake Jackson, the protagonist of *Lawd Today*, left Mississippi to lead a life of frustration, tedium, meaninglessness, and brutality in Chicago. Wright's insights on the difference between rural and urban cultures and mentalities and the disruptions involved in adjusting from the former to the latter were formulated in two works of the early 1940s: *12 Million Black Voices* (1941), a folk history of the American Negro; and the introduction to St. Clair Drake and Horace R. Cayton's *Black Metropolis* (1945). The rebellion of Bigger Thomas in *Native Son* was another response to the dislocation of a hostile urban environment. In *The Outsider* (1953), Wright considered the problem of alienation as a phenomenon of twentieth century modernization. These processes caught his imagination, and he found similar situations again in the Third World, which he described as societies in ferment. Wright's interest in the Third World thus represented a change in locale rather than a shift in subject matter.

The basic concepts that unified his later works, *Black Power*, *Pagan Spain*, *The Color Curtain*, and *White Man, Listen!*, echoed his earlier fascination with industrialization, urbanization, and secularization. The underlying themes, attitudes, and prescriptions of these accounts of non-Western societies revealed the influence of Wright's experience as a black man in America. Race, religion, and the psychology of the oppressed were *leitmotifs* that reflected Wright's background. As in his earlier works, Wright's subject was still himself.

The analytical role that industrialization and secularization played in Wright's thinking is not as surprising as the prescriptive role that he assigned to them. Wright explained that his pro-Western outlook was based on his belief in the separation of church and state, individualism, and empiricism. In what could be called his credo, he wrote:

> I feel that man—just sheer brute man, just as he is—has a meaning and value over and above all sanctions or mandates from mystical powers, either on high or from below. I am convinced that the humble fragile dignity of man, buttressed by a tough-souled pragmatism, implemented by methods of trial and error, can sufficiently sustain and nourish human life, can endow it with ample and durable meaning. . . . I hold human freedom as a supreme right and good for all men, my conception of freedom being the right of all men to exercise their natural and acquired powers as long as the exercise of those powers does not hinder others from doing the same. (*Black Power*, pp. 50–51)

He gave voice to the liberal's faith in the free circulation of ideas as a way of finding truth. Furthermore, he approved of the autonomy of both art, "independent of the spheres of political or priestly power or sanction," and science, existing "without any a priori or metaphysical assumptions," that prevailed in Western civilization (p. 51).

The roots of Wright's faith in Western civilization become clearer when we examine his attitudes toward religion. Although on the surface Wright appeared to be hostile to religion, in fact, he was ambivalent. His antagonism toward religion or quasi-religious movements was determined by the degree to which he believed that they stifled individualism and, concomitantly in his view, human progress.[19] In discussing the Gold Coast, Wright approved the use of religious fervor in politics. Yet his condemnation of the Communist Party was partly based on his perception that it was analogous to the church.

The basis of Wright's ambivalence is revealed more sharply in his fiction. In his early short stories "Fire and Cloud" and "Bright and Morning Star," his heroes were religious, and their religious energy had been channeled to strike out against an oppressive society. But Bigger Thomas and Cross Damon, the protagonists of *Native Son* and *The Outsider*, respectively, had to rebel to attain any measure of freedom from a repressively religious mother who preached submission and self-denial.

Clearly, Wright's views were strongly influenced by his own experience. The Seventh Day Adventism practiced in his grandmother's house was harsh and punitive, denying self-actualization. As he had rebelled against such strictures in his youth, so he rejected religious zeal that suppressed freedom when he was an adult. But just as clearly Wright was not able to extricate himself from his religious background fully. The starkness of Protestantism, as he described it in *Pagan Spain* above, created psychological strength, emotional independence, and a stance of detachment, just as the bleak environment that he described in *Black Boy* had fostered the growth of his imagination and intellectual abilities.[20]

The militance of Wright's pro-Western attitude can only be accounted for by reference to his autobiography. Wright believed that he would have remained a helpless victim of the cruel environment of his youth had he not applied reason to question the whys and wherefores of the society in which he lived. The rural, religious milieu that he rejected spelled poverty and degradation. As Wright tells us in *Black Boy*, he attained freedom by breaking the bonds of tradition, refusing to accept his place as a "nigger" in a Jim Crow society. To Wright, the West was synonymous with urbanization, industrialization, and secularization—processes that led to individualism, freedom, and human progress—whereas tradition, religion, and race-consciousness hampered man's mastery of his world.

Notes

1. Other important formulations of modernization theory include David Apter, *The Politics of Modernization* (1965), S. N. Eisenstadt, *Modernization: Protest and Change* (1966), and Samuel Huntington, *Political Order in Changing Societies* (1968).

2. Bendix, "Tradition and Modernity Reconsidered," *Comparative Studies in Society and History*, 9 (April 1967), 292–346; Robert Nisbet, *Social Change and History* (New York: Oxford Univ. Press, 1969).

3. Dean C. Tipps, "Modernization Theory and the Comparative Study of Societies: A Critical Perspective," *Comparative Studies in Society and History*, 15 (March 1973), 199–226.

4. Tipps' critique of modernization theory is similar in thrust to the critiques launched against the consensus school of American history in the mid-1960s by John Higham and others.

5. William Gardner Smith, "Black Boy in Paris," *Ebony*, 8 (July 1953), 40.

6. *Présence Africaine*, founded by Jean-Paul Sartre, Albert Camus, André Gide, Emmanuel Mounier, Leopold Senghor, Alioune Diop, and others, was the major voice of "negritude," a doctrine of cultural nationalism formulated in the 1930s in Paris by Senghor, Aimé Césaire, and Leon Damas. Heavily influenced by surrealism and Marxism, negritude insisted on the unique poetic attractions of the black race.

7. As a result of policy set at the Sixth World Congress in 1928, the American Communist Party was instructed to foster nationalism leading to self-determination and national liberation. This policy was changed in 1934 during the Popular Front era. Wright joined the Party in 1932 or 1933. Wilson Record, *The Negro and the Communist Party* (Chapel Hill: Univ. of North Carolina Press, 1951), pp. 54–119.

8. *Black Power* (New York: Harper & Bros., 1954), p. 158. Further page citations appear parenthetically in the body of the article.

9. Richard Wright to Paul Reynolds, 4 Oct. 1953, Richard Wright MSS in the possession of Michel Fabre, Paris (hereafter referred to as Richard Wright MSS).

10. "The title: *Black Power* means political and state power. I did not have in mind any racial meaning." Richard Wright to Margrit de Sablonière, 8 June 1955, Richard Wright MSS.

11. *Black Power*, p. 5. The idea of African survivals in Afro-American culture was first forcefully argued by anthropologist Melville Herskovitz in *The Myth of the Negro Past* (New York: Harper & Bros., 1941).

12. "African culture has not developed the personalities of the people to a degree that their egos are stout, hard, sharply defined; there is too much cloudiness in the African's mentality, a kind of sodden vagueness that makes for a lack of confidence, an absence of focus that renders that mentality incapable of grasping the workaday world." *Black Power*, p. 343.

13. *Black Power*, pp. 91–92. It should be noted that in this context Wright is quite sanguine about a quasi-religious movement of this kind; nor does he seem to be concerned about the similarity between his description of Nkrumah here and his description of Hitler in the introduction to *Black Metropolis*.

14. See "Apropos Prepossessions," *Black Power*, pp. xi–xv.

15. *Pagan Spain* (New York: Harper & Bros., 1957), pp. 226–27.

16. Richard Wright to Paul Reynolds, 4 Feb. 1955, Richard Wright MSS.

17. *The Color Curtain* (New York: World Publishing Co., 1956), p. 140. Further page citations appear parenthetically in the body of the article.

18. "The Literature of the Negro in the United States" was the earliest essay. A copy of a very similar speech appears in the Webb Collection of the Schomburg Collection, New York. It is entitled "Speech for a White Audience" and was written shortly after World War II. The essay also appeared in *Les Temps Modernes* in August 1948. "The Psychological Reaction of Oppressed People" was written some time after Wright attended the Bandung Conference in 1955. It seems likely that "The Miracle of Nationalism in the African Gold Coast" was also prepared at this time. "Tradition and Industrialization" was the latest essay, delivered at the Congrès des Écrivains et Artistes Noirs in September 1956. Citations from *White Man, Listen!* are taken from the 1964 Anchor Books edition and appear parenthetically in the body of the article.

19. See my article, "Richard Wright: Individualism Reconsidered," *CLA Journal*, 21 (March 1978), 335–54.

20. *Black Boy* reveals that Wright believed he had escaped his devastating environment by developing a fantasy life: "Because I had no power to make things happen outside of me in the objective world, I made things happen within. Because my environment was bare and bleak, I endowed it with unlimited potentialities, redeemed it for the sake of my own hungry and cloudy yearning." *Black Boy* (New York: Harper Perennial Editions, 1966), pp. 82–83.

ESSAYS ON POETRY

Richard Wright: Proletarian Poet

Keneth Kinnamon*

Richard Wright is best known as a writer of fiction and autobiography, but like a number of other American novelists, he tried his hand at poetry.[1] His first real public recognition came from the seventeen poems he published in radical little magazines. At the very end of his life, in the fourteenth year of his expatriation in Paris, he again turned to poetry, though this time to *haiku*, a far cry from the agitprop verse with which he began his literary career more than a quarter-century before. If Wright's chief importance is clearly as the interpreter of the agony of Black America in such prose works as *Uncle Tom's Children*, *Native Son*, and *Black Boy*, his early poetry nevertheless has its own interest, both intrinsically and as an instructive example of some of the problems and opportunities faced by a young writer deeply committed to the ideological left.

Wright's first exposure to leftist writers took place in the fall of 1933, when he attended a meeting of the Chicago John Reed Club, which had been operating as a cultural instrument of the Communist Party for somewhat more than a year. The welcome that Wright received at the club was warmly courteous and uncondescending. He was encouraged to sit in on an editorial meeting of *Left Front*, the organ of the club. He was given back issues of *New Masses* and *International Literature* to take home. For all his defensive skepticism about white motives, he could detect no insincerity in the behavior of his new friends. "The members," he recalled of the club after he had left the Party, "were fervent, democratic, restless, eager, self-sacrificing." Even more revelatory was the impact of the magazines he was given to read. Sitting up until dawn reading them, he "was amazed to find that there did exist in this world an organized search for the truth of the lives of the oppressed and the isolated." To this search he knew that he could make a contribution from his own bitter experience as a black man, an experience which he was beginning to learn was similar to the experience of exploited classes around the globe. If a unity of suffering existed between black and white, could not unity be achieved between them in revolutionary activity to

*Reprinted from *Concerning Poetry*, 2 (Spring 1969), 39–50, by permission of the author and the journal.

correct that suffering? His evening at the club suggested that it could, and the pages of the radical magazines provided confirmation. As dawn neared he "wrote a wild, crude poem in free verse" to express this new vision.[2] This poem must have been "I Have Seen Black Hands," the last section of which speaks hopefully of black and white uniting to fight:

> I am black and I have seen black hands
> Raised in fists of revolt, side by side
>   with the white fists of white workers,
> And some day—and it is only this which
>   sustains me—
> Some day there shall be millions and millions
>   of them,
> On some red day in a burst of fists on a new
>   horizon!

For the most part, one must accept Wright's own adjective, "crude," in describing his proletarian poetry. Through this poetry he hoped to humanize Communist propaganda, to effect a *rapprochement* between Communist intellectuals and the masses, to interpret each to the other: "The Communists, I felt, had oversimplified the experience of those whom they sought to lead. In their efforts to recruit masses, they had missed the meaning of the lives of the masses, had conceived of people in too abstract a manner. I would try to put some of that meaning back. I would tell Communists how common people felt, and I would tell common people of the self-sacrifice of Communists who strove for unity among them."[3] But often the revolutionary hope is grafted to the trunk of black experience in a much too arbitrary fashion. In "I Have Seen Black Hands," for example, the final section quoted above is immediately preceded at the end of the third section by a description of lynchings:

> And the black hands fought and scratched and
>   held back but a thousand white hands
>   took them and tied them,
> And the black hands lifted palms in mute and
>   futile supplication to the sodden faces
>   of mobs wild in the revelries of sadism,
> And the black hands strained and clawed and
>   struggled in vain at the noose that
>   tightened about the black throat,
> And the black hands waved and beat fearfully
>   at the tall flames that cooked and
>   charred the black flesh . . .

The transition to black and white fists raised in the Communist salute is abrupt, to say the least. In the first section of the poem the childhood and adolescence of blacks—a subject with which Wright's touch was always sure—are rendered effectively through synecdoche, the black hands first reaching for "the black nipples at the black breasts of black mothers," then holding "wineballs . . . and sugared cookies in fingers sticky and gummy," then holding marbles and slingshots, then coins, then "rulers . . . and books in palms spotted and smeared with ink," and finally "dice and cards and half-pint flasks and cue sticks and cigars and cigarettes in the pride of new maturity." In the second session, however, as the black hands "jerked up and down at the throbbing machines massing taller and taller the heaps of gold in the banks of bosses," the poem degenerates into political slogans, as it does in the final section. Part of the problem is that Wright's newly found political conviction has not been successfully assimilated into his stock of experience and his sensibility. Another part is the didactic exigencies of his genre, for in agitprop poetry everything had to be subordinated to the communication of a clear revolutionary message.

Perhaps the most complete failure of the agitprop poems is "I Am a Red Slogan," an embarrassing effort indeed unless one reads it as a deliberate parody of the genre. The sincerity of Wright's adherence to the Party at this time,[4] however, precludes that possibility. "Red Leaves of Red Books" is little better. His first two published poems, "Rest for the Weary" and "A Red Love Note," rely on an irony so heavy and obvious as to diminish greatly its effect. In the former, the "panic-stricken guardians of gold" are told that their burdens of wealth and pride will be removed by the "brawny hands" of the workers. "A Red Love Note" is another threat to the exploiters from the proletariat, somewhat more effective because it sustains the metaphor of a billet-doux to "my dear lovely bloated one" threatening the violent end of bourgeois civilization in amorous slang: the recipient is addressed as "honey," "darling," "sugar-pie," and "dumpling." But here again the irony is heavy. The same is true of "Child of the Dead and Forgotten Gods," in which the innocent and naive liberal is ridiculed—the days of the popular front had not yet arrived—for failing to understand the revolutionary urgency of the moment:

> . . . the pounding of police
> clubs on the skulls of strikers
> and the scream of the riot-siren to dis-
> perse the unemployed
> And the noise and clamor of slaughter and
> rapine and greed
> drowns out your soft talk of peace and
> brotherhood!

Published in the same issue of *The Anvil* as "Child of the Dead and Forgotten Gods" was "Strength," a pedestrian and highly didactic statement of the futility of individual effort "against the legions of tyranny" contrasted to the inevitable success of collective action.

Less bald is the statement of the revolutionary message in "Everywhere Burning Waters Rise," which attempts to express it through a metaphor of cumulative power and violence. This poem certainly does achieve a sense of developing momentum from the stasis of an arrested economy through the swelling revolutionary impulse to the purgative destruction of the old order. Here too, however, pamphlet slogans intrude. Furthermore, the success of the effort to achieve geographical scope in the first seven lines is immediately vitiated by the artificial and self-conscious conceits which follow: "tenemented mountains of hunger," "ghetto swamps of suffering," "breadlined forests of despair," and "peonized plains of hopelessness." The poet is trying to show the human suffering resulting from the economic stagnation indicated in the preceding lines while maintaining the sense of spatial amplitude, but the metaphorical conjunction of urban ("breadlined"), geographical ("forests"), and abstract ("despair") elements is much too contrived. These quasi-metaphysical conceits are not integrated into the essentially Whitmanesque tone of the entire poem. The sudden transformation of the flood into "waters of fire" is likewise unhappy; the change is effected "strangely" indeed.

If poetically unsuccessful, however, the combined fire-water imagery is biographically explicable. Fire and flood were the images of violence most deeply embedded in Wright's imagination. The opening pages of *Black Boy* relate an incident of his setting a house afire at the age of four. The fire-motif recurs often in his work, as in the fateful furnace of *Native Son* and the catastrophic inferno of the blazing dancehall in *The Long Dream*.[5] Living in the Mississippi valley, often in towns actually on the river, during his childhood and youth, he had long been conscious of the destructive power of floods. In his last year in the South, he had witnessed from the central vantage point of Memphis the terrible devastation of the great flood of 1927. Two of his most successful short stories, "Down by the Riverside" and "Silt," deal directly with floods. Furthermore, the Biblical associations of "Fire and Cloud"—to use the title of another of his short stories—had been thoroughly assimilated in his youth. It is understandable, then, why he would use flood imagery in "Everywhere Burning Waters Rise" to represent the accumulation of revolutionary resentment among the dispossessed and why he would shift to more vivid fire imagery to depict the apocalyptic fury of revolutionary violence and destruction.

Destructive violence recurs over and over in Wright's early poetry and remains a dominant motif throughout his entire writing career. At times the violence is masochistic, as in "Rise and Live," where the downtrodden are incited to a suicidal rebellion:

> Let's feel in our flesh the rip of their steel!
> Let's feel in our throats the burn of their gas!

More often the violence is aggressive. In "Everywhere Burning Waters Rise" the last two lines seem distinctly an afterthought; the violent destruction of the old order gripped the poet's imagination more forcefully than the construction of a new world possibly could. In "A Red Love Note" no mention is made of a new world, but rather of "a red clap of thunder rising from the very depths of hell" to destroy the old. The same is true of "Strength," where the revolution is once more envisioned as a natural force:

> a raging hurricane vast and powerful
> wrenching and dredging by the roots the rottening husks of
> the trees of greed.

The fiery violence of Wright's most successful early poem, "Between the World and Me," is not an almost impersonal force resembling a natural phenomenon, but an all too malevolently human mob action, particularized in its depiction of a sadistic lynching. Almost intolerable in its savage intensity, the violence in this poem is nevertheless strictly controlled by the emotional movement shared by the speaker and the audience. Through a kind of shock therapy both the "I" of the poem and the reader are brought to an identification with the lynch victim. At the beginning of the poem the speaker comes by chance upon the scene of a lynching. Shocked by the sight, he manages to remain calm enough to notice with accuracy each of the grisly concrete details, including "peanut shells," which suggest the festive spirit of the lynch mob, and "a whore's lipstick," which suggests, to one familiar with Southern mores, the ostensible motive of the lynching.[6] The catalog of details culminates in the tenth line: "And through the morning air the sun poured yellow surprise into the eye sockets of a stony skull. . . ." Here the skull is passive, receiving the sunlight. Shocked fascination now gives way to fear, then to a reenactment of the lynching so powerfully immediate as to become more real than vicarious. The observer of the scene now becomes the victim in the actual event, and the observed details, previously static or dead, leap luridly to life: "The gin-flask passed from mouth to mouth; cigars and cigarettes glowed, the whore smeared the lipstick red upon her lips," and the lynching takes place again. In the last line of the poem the image of the tenth line is repeated, but with a significant difference: "my face a stony skull staring in yellow surprise at the sun. . . ." The sadistic-masochistic frenzy of the description of the lynching in the preceding lines might have seemed too wildly sensational without this return at the very end of the poem to a kind of calm. On the other hand, since the observer—and the reader—have become the victim, detachment and passivity are no longer possible, not even in death. For this reason the skull does not now passively receive the sunlight, but becomes, in a sense, active, "staring in yellow surprise at the sun. . . ." "Between the World and Me," then, is an intensely felt and potently realized poem in which the theme of human solidarity in suffering goes far beyond the excessive subjectivity of another lynching poem, "Obsession," or the Marxist sloganeering of some of the other early poems.

Wright was not incapable of a lighter touch. "Spread Your Sunrise!"

is an exuberant mixture of comic exaggeration in the American folk tradi-
tion, Whitmanesque geographical sweep, and modern American slang.
The vision in the poem is of "a bushy-haired giant-child" striding from
Russia across Europe and the Atlantic into America:

> Hoooly Chriiist!
> What is that he's got in his hands?
> By George, in one he's holding a bucketful
>   of sunrise,
> And in the other he's swishing a long tall
>   broom,
> And, Jeeesus, the fool's splashing crimson
>   everywhere,
> Just painting the whole world red!

At times a cliché-ridden and incongruous seriousness intrudes into the
poem, as when the giant figure called

> a man-child of the Revolution:
> Seed of fiery workers' loins
> Fruit of October's swollen womb!

but the dominant effect is of an editorial cartoon by William Gropper or
Hugo Gellert with the unaccustomed added ingredient of a boisterous
humor.   This   ingredient   is   unfortunately   missing   from
"Transcontinental," a long, ambitious poem indebted to Louis Aragon's
"Red Front" in which the progress of the revolution across North America
is expressed through the metaphor of an automobile journey. The concep-
tion is arresting, but Wright's execution of it is heavy and labored.
"Hearst Headline Blues" contains humor, but of a grim and sardonic
kind, similar in tone to that of "A Red Love Note" and "Rest for the
Weary." The poem, in five rimed quatrains, consists entirely of Hearst-
type headlines revealing the social unrest and the official hypocrisy of
Depression America. The final two stanzas are typical:

> "Woman Dynamites Jail to Free Her Lover"
> "Starvation Claims Mother and Tot"
> "Roosevelt Says the Worst Is Over"
> "Longshoremen Picket; Two Are Shot"
>
> "Father Butchers Son With Axe"
> "Many Gold Voices to Be Heard on Air"
> "Attorney Dodd Uncovers Facts"
> "The Right Reverend O'Connell Urges Prayer"

The last two poems published during Wright's Chicago period are
"Old Habit and New Love" and "We of the Streets." The first of these uses
rather confused imagery to attempt with indifferent success to show the
new love of revolutionary creativity growing out of the old habit of in-

dustrial drudgery. The theme of the second is the quality of the collective consciousness of the urban masses, but the poem's statement of this theme seems too self-conscious. Wright's poetic idiom is uncertain in these two ambitious poems, but they do show him moving away from the facile oversimplifications of the agitprop formula.

None of the poems discussed thus far is racial in idiom. "I Have Seen Black Hands" deals with racial experience, but in a straightforward, nonracial way. "Hearst Headline Blues" is not really a blues at all except in the loosest popular sense. Three of Wright's poems, however, deal with racial experience in a racial idiom. Among his poems they come closest to satisfying the critical precepts expressed in his essay "Blueprint for Negro Writing," where he prescribes the use of Negro folk material within the context of an advanced (i.e., Marxist) social understanding and a militant class consciousness. "Ah Feels It In Mah Bones," written entirely in dialect, presents the effects of the Depression on a young lower-class black man, who is transformed from a thoughtless hedonist devoted to wenching and gambling into an incipient revolutionary. The dialect rings true throughout, often achieving a vivid, highly poetic folk locution: "An' long-lopin' mah old proud sweet stuff like a greyhound pup!" The didactic message of revolutionary awareness is artfully implicit; slogans are absent from this poem. "Ah Feels It In Mah Bones," however, does not entirely escape the danger inherent in all black dialect poems—serving to confirm white prejudices and stereotypes. A razor-totin' black dice shooter, the white readers of *International Literature* must have felt, would be a questionable candidate for party membership even after he had reformed. Stereotype of some degree would seem virtually inevitable in dialect poetry, and this poem does not escape it. "Ah Feels It In Mah Bones" does suggest, in any case, that if its author had cared to cultivate this genre, he would probably have attained a skill equal to that of its most able practitioners—Paul Laurence Dunbar, James Weldon Johnson, Sterling Brown, and Langston Hughes.

Hughes collaborated with Wright on "Red Clay Blues," which was recorded, Hughes recalled,[7] by Josh White. Alone Wright wrote another blues song, "King Joe,' recorded by Paul Robeson with the Count Basie Orchestra. These two blues appeared in 1939 and 1941, well after the seventeen proletarian poems of the middle thirties. Wright's interest in the blues continued for the rest of his life. Blues songs, of course, are proletarian poems in a quite different sense from the Marxist one. A real difficulty in dealing with blues as poetry is that, perhaps more than most other folk music, they are inseparable from their performance. "Red Clay Blues," a song expressing the nostalgia of the migrant to the city for the physical environment of his rural past and also his resentment against the tenant system, was probably fairly well rendered by Josh White, who is a skillful performer tasteful in his popularization of folk music. The recording of "King Joe," however, is a dismal and unqualified failure. Robeson's bass voice, so richly resonant in singing spirituals, is painfully lugubrious and the incongruously sophisticated music of Count Basie is disastrously slow. The total effect is ludicrous in the extreme. To judge effectively this blues song about the prowess of Joe Louis, one would need to hear it from the lips of such an authentic blues singer as Leadbelly or Lightnin' Hopkins.

Wright's apprenticeship did not lead to a later major achievement in poetry, but it did bring him much needed recognition and encouragement. It also gave him experience in dealing with subjects, themes, and metaphors, especially those involving racial conflict, that he was to exploit more fully in his prose. And it produced one poem of unmistakable merit, "Between the World and Me."

It has long been fashionable to deplore the literary consequences of Communist ideology. To the extent that the fashion has been an expression of New Criticism or McCarthyism (social phenomena not without some inter-relationships), it is probably now outmoded. Nevertheless, the case of Richard Wright suggests that some distinctions are in order. One thing seems quite clear and must be readily conceded to conservative critics: political slogans broadcast wholesale do not make for good poetry. On the other hand, radical political commitment is not necessarily stultifying for a young writer. By giving Wright a coherent world view, Marxism perhaps did more to liberate and stimulate his literary imagination than to restrict and rigidify it. Without his radicalism, Wright might well have floundered about for years writing such puerilities as the short story "Superstition," which appeared three years before his first poems. More likely still, he might have given up writing altogether. Art and ideology are seldom if ever perfectly fused in either Wright's poetry or his prose, but the ideology of his proletarian poems was a basic, even essential, motive force of the first—and major—phase of his literary career.

Notes

1. The following list includes all of Wright's published poems, except *haiku*:
"Ah Feels It in Mah Bones," *International Literature*, No. 4 (April 1935), p. 80.
"Between the World and me," *Partisan Review*, 2 (July–August 1935), 18–19.
"Child of the Dead and Forgotten Gods," *The Anvil*, No. 5 (March–April 1934), p. 30.
"Everywhere Burning Waters Rise," *Left Front*, 1 (May–June 1934), 9.
Haiku (eight poems), *Ebony*, 16 (February 1961), 92–93.
Haiku (four poems), *Richard Wright: A Biography*, by Constance Webb (New York, 1968), pp. 393–394.
"Hearst Headline Blues," *New Masses*, 19 (12 May 1936), 14.
"I Am a Red Slogan," *International Literature*, No. 4 (April 1935), p. 35.
"I Have Seen Black Hands," *New Masses*, 11 (26 June 1934), 16.
"King Joe," *New York Amsterdam Star News*, 18 October 1941.
"Obsession," *Midland Left*, No. 2 (February 1935), p. 14.
"Old Habit and New Love," *New Masses*, 21 (15 December 1936), 29.
"Red Clay Blues," *New Masses*, 32 (1 August 1939), 14 (With Langston Hughes).
"Red Leaves of Red Books," *New Masses*, 15 (30 April 1935), 6.

"A Red Love Note," *Left Front*, 1 (January–February 1934), 3.

"Rest for the Weary," *Left Front*, 1 (January–February 1934), 3.

"Rise and Live," *Midland Left*, No. 2 (February 1935), pp. 13–14.

"Spread Your Sunrise!" *New Masses*, 16 (2 July 1935), 26.

"Strength," *The Anvil*, No. 5 (March–April 1934), p. 20.

"Transcontinental," *International Literature*, No. 1 (January 1936), pp. 52–57.

Untitled poem, *Richard Wright: A Biography*, by Constance Webb (New York, 1968), p. 357.

"We of the Streets," *New Masses*, 23 (13 April 1937), 14.

2. Richard Wright, "I Tried to Be a Communist," *The Atlantic Monthly*, 174 (August 1944), 61–62, 63.

3. "I Tried to Be a Communist," p. 63.

4. Arna Bontemps recalls that "Communism was like a religion to him . . . and he was as grim about it as some other people I have known were about fundamental religious dogma." Letter to Keneth Kinnamon, 5 April 1965.

5. In his review of *The Long Dream*, Henry F. Winslow comments briefly but perceptively on this fire-motif. See "Nightmare Experiences," *The Crisis*, 66 (February 1959), 122.

6. One is reminded of Wright's account in *Black Boy* of the lynching in 1924 of the brother of a friend because he had been discovered with a white prostitute. The presence at a lynching of the white woman whose black lover was the lynch victim was not uncommon. To save face, such a woman often cried rape and incited the mob to action. Erskine Caldwell gives extended treatment to such a situation in his novel *Trouble in July*, which Wright reviewed in *The New Republic*, 102 (11 March 1940), 351–352.

7. Letter to Michel Fabre, 25 April 1963. I have not been able to locate this recording.

The Poetry of Richard Wright

Michel Fabre*

Widely recognized as the father of the contemporary Afro-American novel, Richard Wright is now also beginning to find his place in the history of contemporary ideas. In Europe, perhaps even more than in America, he is remembered as the passionate observer of the birth of Ghana and of the Bandung Conference, and his newspaper contributions and lectures enlightened the Western world about the problems and struggles of the colonized peoples long before the emergency of the Third World became a political reality and a fashionable concept.

Less well-known, in fact veritably unknown, is his poetry. Except for the readers of a handful of anthologies,[1] only a limited public has come in contact with his work. His early poems, few in number and not yet republished, first appeared in leftist magazines all of which, except for *New Masses*, were of short duration and narrow circulation. Encouraged by the success of *Uncle Tom's Children*, he soon turned to the novel and almost abandoned poetry after the triumph of *Native Son*. And yet the prose of *12 Million Black Voices* is deliberately poetic, and lyric couplets convey the wonder of childhood in Wright's autobiographical *Black Boy*. Ten years later, as shown by the notes for an unfinished work, he still saw poetry as the complementary form of the dramatic prose of his novels. Finally, on the eve of his premature death, he composed several thousand haiku whose publication would enhance his literary fame. From a purely esthetic point of view, their publication would also justify a study which, in the present circumstances, mostly seeks to uncover the major tendencies of Richard Wright's imagination by examining the evolution of his poetry.

Although symbolic, the genesis of "I Have Seen Black Hands," one of Wright's earliest poems, is significant:

> Towards dawn, I swung from bed and inserted paper into the typewriter. Feeling for the first time that I could speak to listening ears, I wrote a wild, crude poem in free verse, coining images of black hands playing, working, holding bayonets,

*Reprinted from *Studies in Black Literature*, 1 (Autumn 1970), 10–22, by permission of the author and the journal.

stiffening finally in death. I felt that in a clumsy way it linked white life with black, merged two streams of common experience.[2]

At that time his literary vocation, awakened by reading Mencken, only seemed to manifest itself in interminable stylistic exercises; under the influence of Gertrude Stein's "Melanctha," he would rewrite finely-wrought phrases, skillfully balancing the sounds of a picturesque language: "The soft melting hunk of butter trickled in gold down the grooves of the split yam," or "The child's clumsy fingers fumbled in sleep, feeling vainly for the wish of its dream," or "The old man huddled in the dark doorway, his bony face lit by the burning yellow in the windows of distant skyscrapers."[3] Lacking in these phrases (the necessary steps towards a mastery of language) is the element of inspiration, which would flow from image to image binding impressions and ideas into a vivifying whole.

It was the discovery of Communism during the most terrible winter of the Depression that provided the indispensable catalyst. Returning home after a meeting of the John Reed Club, Wright composed several poems which "blended two currents of common experience." He had just discovered an audience eager to hear his message: the great proletarian family. The Marxist demystification of the society which oppressed him racially justified his personal revolt and gave him reasons for persevering. His poetry found its inspiration in this social crusade and received its political orientation. However, as his quarrels with some leaders soon proved, Wright did not docilely conform to the party orthodoxy; his work joined the stream of proletarian literature only because it was guided there by his sense of mission.

Was Wright influenced by the numerous examples around him? As editor of *Left Front*, he read the works of Sam Gaspar or Normal McLeod; in the pages of *New Masses*, he discovered the earlier generation: Kenneth Fearing, Langston Hughes, Archibald MacLeish. At the meetings of the John Reed Club, the members criticized the works of William Carlos Williams, discussed those of T. S. Eliot and analyzed the revolutionary message of Walt Whitman. They read aloud John Reed's "America 1918." Wright's poems, however, generally do not show signs of evident imitation. On the contrary, he seems original in comparison with the secondary writers of the left.[4] His political engagement never made him lose sight of his art nor of his desire to be linked to that rebirth of Negro poetry which is associated with the Harlem Renaissance.

From 1935 to 1937 a group of black writers met every Sunday at the Abraham Lincoln center in Chicago. The members of this "South Side Club" criticized each other's latest works and discussed the relationship between literature and the racial situation. Fenton Johnson and Frank Marshall Davis were considered the "deans" while Margaret Walker, Russell Marshall and, of course, Richard Wright were among the promising young writers. Wright attended the meetings as assiduously as those of the John Reed Club, often giving talks on the authors of the previous generation like Langston Hughes and Arna Bontemps. His belonging to a dual movement—black nationalist and revolutionary—led him to merge the two major themes of his poetry, just as the Negro's fate and the class struggle were in fact intertwined. Published side by side in the February 1935 issue of *Midland Left*, the poems "Obsession" and "Rise and Live" seem to symbolize in their juxtaposition the coexistence within Wright of an obsessional terror of lynching and a vital impatience for revolt.

The first of these two major themes is that of the suffering of the black American. One of Wright's most beautiful pieces, "Between the World and Me," ends with a cry of pain from the author who identifies with the Negro who has been lynched, and through a miracle of poetic sympathy, the reader is led to share this pain:

> Panting, begging, I clutched childlike, clutched
>   to the hot sides of death,
> Now I am dry bones and my face a stony skull
>   staring in yellow surprise at the sun . . .

Wright does not give in to the temptation of facile pathos; he quickly links the fate of the Negro to that of the white proletarian, his comrade in alienation. In "Red Leaves of Red Books" he asks the pages which bear the Marxist gospel to "turn under white fingers and black fingers." The sharecropper of "Red Clay Blues" who has migrated to the hard-sidewalked city, wants to return to Georgia as much from a desire to see his former landlord overturned by the agrarian revolution as from a feeling of nostalgia for the soft clay beneath his toes. The tramp of "Ah Feels It in Mah Bones" has a coanesthesiac awareness of the social upheaval and becomes the barometer for it. The more successful "I Have Seen Black Hands" traces, in long lines of free verse, the evolution of the black community; the baby reaching with chubby hands for his mother's breast, the child with sticky and ink-spotted fingers, the adolescent able to throw dice and wield the billiard cue. In terms which foreshadow the finale of *12 Million Black Voices*, Wright then describes the calloused hands of the worker producing objects whose poor sales will bring on the War, while for himself there will only be poverty, street fighting, and repression. In opposition to "Between the World and Me," here there is hope in the solidarity of those who are oppressed:

> I am black and I have seen black hands
> Raised in fists of revolt, side by side with the
>   white fists of white workers,
> And some day—and it is only this which
>   sustains me—
> Some day there shall be millions and millions
>   of them,
> On some red day in a burst of fists on a new
>   horizon!

Thus the theme of black suffering, in its celebration of an interracial unity, joins that of the triumph of socialism.

Out of some twenty poems written between 1933 and 1939, a dozen, in fact, sing of this triumph while others exalt the virtues of the workers. "Hearst Headline Blues" provides us with a convenient summary of the themes of these poems. Its stanzas quote headlines taken from the pages of the Hearst press and show the decomposition of American society. Immorality and senseless violence reign; social problems are treated ineffectively or brutally. Counterpointing the famine which is decimating America, the Soviet Union suppresses rationing. This propaganda piece brings us back to the unprecedented atmosphere of the Depression years which, thanks to the editorship of the Harlem Bureau of the *Daily Worker*, provided Wright with a good opportunity to chronicle.

The other poems systematically probe the failure of capitalism: "Rest for the Weary," on a note of false pity, condescendingly addresses the financiers ruined by the 1929 panic. It is also the failure of liberal Christianity incapable of pacifying "the bitter and irreconcilable waters of class struggle" in "Child of the Dead and Forgotten Gods." "A Red Love Note," using the analogy between a love letter and an eviction notice, is an artistic failure. But the choice of its imagery is inspired by the daily scenes of eviction, the furniture spread out on the sidewalk and the neighbors' demonstrations of solidarity; with tender words the poet takes his leave of capitalism whose lease on American society has long run out.

If the poems which sing of the fall of the old order can be seen as the first panel of the revolutionary diptych, those which celebrate the unity of the workers and the rise of socialism can be said to form the second. The education and unity of the masses are set down by the poet as the essential prerequisites: "Red Leaves of Red Books" praises those who devote their hours of leisure to deciphering the volumes of new theories. "Strength" opposes mass action to solitary protest, the latter seen as destined for defeat. The unity of the oppressed (which, as we learn in "I Am a Red Slogan," it is the poet's mission to accelerate) will be realized through demonstrations, for the slogans chanted during a political march do not only express particular demands, they also serve to guide the masses, "lingering as a duty after my command is shouted." This theme of the mass demonstration, part of the traditional May First ("Premier Mai") literature, offers little that is original.[5] However Wright treats the end of "We of the Streets" in an interesting way, focusing on the exhilarating sense of strength which comes from a crowd, and this treatment is reminiscent of the ending of his novella "Fire and Cloud." The street thus becomes the organic milieu in which the worker grows conscious of his belonging to History and of his own immortality.

Enthusiasm for the Russian Revolution inspired Wright to compose "Spread your Sunrise" and "Transcontinental." In the first of these odes, he hails the arrival of a young Communist giant, applauding the liberties taken with the established order and urging him to paint the Statue of Liberty red and to frighten the millionaires cowering in their mansions.

A long fresco dedicated to Louis Aragon in praise of "Red Front," the poem "Transcontinental," published early in 1936 by *International Literature*, sings of the coming of better days in America. This six page symphony blends various themes: a criticism of the American dream, the rehabilitation of the exploited minorities, the wealth of the New World that will appear with the institution of the Soviets. These themes, evoked by a profusion of images, are carried forward by an epic inspiration.

In addition to such propaganda pieces, Wright's poetry at this time, and especially after 1937, centered on a description of the world of the workers and the poor. "We of the Streets" exalts the dignity and generosity which lie hidden in the slums; in "Old Habit and New Love" the worker is the salvation of humanity: not satisfied with just increasing the world's riches, he restores its soul, he delivers it from its fragmentation:

> There is an ache for marriage, for the sight
>   of halves grown whole, for cactus land to
>   blend with dingy dreams, for the welding of
>   irons and bleeding palms.
> It is for fusion of number and nerve we
>   strain . . .

> Breathing life back into the machine and
>   tuning its music to the harmony of the celes-
>   tial spheres, the worker becomes the Demi-
>   urge, an artist like the poet:

> O Creators! Poets, Makers of Melody! Some
>   first-shift dawn shall find us on equal ground,
>   holding in our hands the world's tools,
>   drafting the hope-prints of our vision on
>   canvases of green earth!

Although these poems were not inspired by a particular political event, their ideological content is closely linked to Wright's Communist faith, and yet both his sincerity and his originality emerge more clearly in the manner than the themes.

One is first struck by the fact that Wright is as realistic in his poetry as he is in his novels: lynching, financial failures, strikes and police repression, bread lines, are all news items from the columns of the *Daily Worker*. His realism—often visionary realism—extends even to urban scenes sketched effectively in a few words:

> We have grown used to nervous landscapes,
>   chimney-broken horizons, and the sun dying
>   between tenements . . .
> Our sea is water swirling in gutters; our
>   lightning is the blue flame of an acetylene

> torch, . . . we hear thunder when the "L"
> roars, our strip of sky is a dirty shirt.[6]

Here we find the Chicago of Dreiser, of Farrell, of Algren, the blizzard on the outskirts of Michigan and the pale glow of the street lights in *Native Son*. There is realism in the grounding of collective lyricism on Wright's personal experiences; however, the real world, naked and violent, is never incorporated in its everyday form: either the Marxist interpretation transforms it into a significant universe or else the author's imagination recreates it through a religious, elemental, or mythical symbolism.

At this stage of its development, Wright's art already rests on a solid cultural base in which we can distinguish several distinct sources: a Protestant tradition swallowed unwillingly under the aegis of his intransigent grandmother; wide and eclectic reading; a vital knowledge of American folklore; a keen sensitivity to nature and a truly elemental imagination.

A wealth of Biblical references, paradoxical component of these Communist poems, produces a two-sided effect: at times the aim is to parody, underlining the state of confusion in American society, as when the spectator who observes the Socialist Messiah painting the belfry cross red utters a series of pious exclamations.[7] At times the satire is directed at Christ's liberalism; the descendant of obsolete divinities, he is shown in "Child of the Dead and Forgotten Gods," to be incapable of repeating his miracles. At times the metaphor is required for reasons of form: the Marxist books become the Bible, and in "A Red Love Note" the final notice of the proletarian to the capitalist echoes the Creator's curse on Cain; the deluge and the destruction of the Temple are the principal symbols of "Everywhere Burning Waters Rise." Wright constantly harks back to Christian formulas which seem the most appropriate for his political designs. Above all, it is in following his inspiration that Wright, as we can see in this passage from *Black Boy*, delves into a religion-bound black culture:

> The elders of the church expounded a gospel clogged with images of vast lakes of eternal fire, of seas vanishing, of valleys of dry bones, of the sun burning to ashes, of the moon turning to blood, of stars falling to the earth, . . . While listening to the vivid language of the sermons, I was pulled towards emotional belief . . .[8]

The adolescent refused the dogmas of this religion, but its images remained engraved in his mind.

Linked to the Biblical references, the natural elements in "Everywhere Burning Waters Rise" become symbols of destruction. The blood haze that covers the empty silos and deserted workshops of the Egypt of the New World is the beginning of the deluge which, in the middle of the poem, is curiously transformed into a torrent of fire. The first section restates the theme of the water cycle: icy, viscous fog condenses into pools of water, flowing in thin streams and then in heavy torrents, to swell into a tidal wave. Water turns to fire—the transition facilitated by the ambiguity of the word "boiling"—and suddenly the glowing coals burst into flame, fanned by the poet's prophetic malediction:

> Sweep on, o red stream of molten anger
> surge and seethe like liquid lava
> into every nook and cranny of this greed-reared
>   temple
>   reared temple
> and blister the rottening walls with your hot
>   cleansing breath!
> Lick and lap with your tongues of flame
> at the golden pillars of oppressive privilege . . .

Wright seems to be fascinated by the element of fire. We have no intention here of analyzing his exploits as a four year old incendiary, nor those of his hero Bigger who burns the body of his boss's daughter in a basement furnace, nor the fire by which Cross Damon effaces his identity, nor the blaze which destroys the dancers in *The Long Dream*. But it is important to mention that in the poems under discussion, the element of fire already appears in all its destructive and purifying aspects. In "Spread Your Sunrise" the Reichstag fire is symbolically evoked by a splash of red paint. In the numerous lynching scenes, the flames blend with the water and the blood of the Negro burning at the stake:

> Then my blood was cooled mercifully, cooled by
>   a baptism of gasoline.
> And in a blaze of red I leaped to the sky as pain
>   rose like water, boiling my limbs . . .[9]

Along with his orchestrations of warring elements, the more benign aspects of nature are occasionally invoked. In "Strength" the image suggesting individual action, "a gentle breeze ineffectually tearing at granite crags," is just as successful as the sonorous metaphor for mass revolt:

> . . . a raging hurricane, vast and powerful,
> wrenching and dredging by the roots the
>   rottening husks of the trees of greed.

Similarly the urban landscape of "We of the Streets" is transposed into natural terms. Wright frequently borrows from nature and nature is the touchstone of his poetic sensitivity: it was the Mississippi country that restored his strength during a childhood of struggle and deprivation. We are therefore all the more prepared for the lyrical tirades of *Black Boy* when the writer sings of his renewed wonder before the scenes of nature.

The two odes to the revolution, which represent a sharp break with his other compositions, celebrate the exploits of a mythical character or narrate a symbolic adventure. Eager to communicate the appeal of the new ideology, Wright personifies it in the giant of "Spread your Sunrise." This incarnation was perhaps suggested by some of the illustrations of *New Masses*,[10] but in fact is rather in the tradition of the rough and ready hero of American folklore:

> a bushy-haired giant child,
> Big-limbed and double-jointed,
> Boisterous and bull-headed,
> With great big muscles bursting through his
>   clothes.

Compound words, alliterated consonants, the exaggerations of popular speech make him a mixture of Johnny Appleseed and John Henry. Wearing not the seven-league boots of the fairy tale but the shoes of the Five Year Plan, this "tall man" of the steel mills seems to come from certain pages of *The People, Yes* and clearly belongs to the legends of the Frontier.

The same informal and enthusiastic tone graces the poem "Transcontinental" in which Wright has painted the chariot of Time, slightly renovated as the automobile of History. The key to this symphony lies in the use of the idea of speed. At first a group of young men and women, enviously observe the glittering world of the rich:

> Across the ceaseless hiss of passing cars
> We hear the tinkle of ice in tall glasses
> Clacks of crocket balls scudding over cropped
>   lawns
> Silvery crescendos of laughter
> Like in the movies
> On Saturday nights
> When we used to get paychecks . . .

Then the desire to penetrate this inaccessible world, to ride in the rich man's limousine, takes on the convincing form of reality: time is telescoped and the rigid structure of the first stanzas comes alive in a wild race of moving images. Leaving behind them a social upheaval similar to that created by the Communist giant, these new horsemen of the Apocalypse, casting down the oppressors, lifting up the oppressed (Indians, Negroes, proletarians) cross the United States in their symbolic automobile.[11]

Lyricism plays a privileged role in these early poems; it can be shaded with humor or with anger but it always assumes one of two principal forms: that of the song, and particularly the blues ballad—as in "Red Clay Blues," "Ah Feels It in Mah Bones," or "Hearst Headline Blues"[12]—or, more frequently, that of large spans of free verse modeled on Whitman's *Leaves of Grass*.

The terms used by Wright always correspond to a definite aim. At times the Negro dialect is adopted:

> It's done got so bad Ah can't even beg a dime
> An' mah bread-basket's a-swearing mah
>   throat's been cut.[13]

At times, the language is that of popular speech, racy and coarse, which contrasts with the affected and somewhat hysterical phrases of the society women:

> But Dear America's a free country
> Did you say Negroes
> Oh I don't mean NEEGROOES
> You wouldn't want your DAUGHTER
> and they say there's no GOD
> And furthermore it's simply disgraceful how
>   they're discriminating against the children
>   of the rich in Soviet schools.

The above passage from "Transcontinental" is characteristic in many ways. It fits into the context like the fragments of polite conversation which Eliot scatters through "The Love Song of J. Alfred Prufrock." In fact Wright owes as much to "The Waste Land" as to Aragon's "Front Rouge," although it is to the latter that "Transcontinental" is dedicated. Similar to Eliot's synthesis of fragments of Western civilization (quotations, songs, references, bits of dialogue), Wright's composition incorporates all the socially significant elements of American civilization. Setting aside the lyrical movement of "Transcontinental," we would be left with a static fresco, halfway between the cubiest collage and the stream of consciousness, composed of the solidified English of the upper class, the slang of the worker, the materialized language of the road sign, blended with a litany of slogans, loudspeaker addressed lines from the "Internationale" and even a radio communique. The lyricism which binds all these diverse materials to the canvas starts out as a kind of a *parte*, a tender evocation soon embittered in reproach, which then expands and reverberates throughout the poem into a glorification of America reborn.

In his quest for a distinctive style, Wright seems to be torn at that period between two conflicting tendencies. On the one hand he admires the lyrical and rhetorical gifts of poets like MacLeish or Eliot, from whom he borrows his abrupt transitions from the serious to the trivial, his use of free association in place of a logical continuity, his succession of images without explanatory metaphors. On the other hand the robust simplicity of a Carl Sandburg or a Whitman also attracts him. Drawn both ways, he tries to create a special language:

> My purpose was to capture a physical state or movement that carried a strong subjective impression . . . I strove to master words, to make them disappear, to make them important by making them new, to make them melt into a rising spiral of emotional stimuli, each greater than the other, and all

ending in an emotional climax that would drench the reader
with the sense of a new world.[14]

With this purpose in mind, Wright sometimes coins new terms like
"hope-print" or "five-year boots." Words explode into phonetic transcrip-
tions, and letters are lengthened into words. These inventions aim to do
more than surprise the reader. When, for example, the poet gathers all
the colors of the rainbow into one line in "I Have Seen Black Hands," it is
not from a love of enumeration but rather in order to give the counter-
balanced color black the same value as all these shades added together.
Like the circumvolutions of Gertrude Stein's poetic line, the unfolding of
Wright's verse tries to exhaust all the resources of literary expression.
However, more than in these typographical or structural experiments, the
young poet's originality shines forth in the series of images enriched by
their emotional message. We see this process at work in "Between the
World and Me" where the splendor of dawn yields to the horror of a
lynching:

> And through the morning air the sun poured
>   yellow surprise into the eye-sockets of a
>   stony skull . . .
> And while I stood my mind was frozen with
>   a cold pity for the life that was gone.
> The ground gripped my feet and my heart
>   was circled by icy walls of fear
> The sun died in the sky; a night wind mut-
>   tered in the grass and fumbled the leaves
>   in the trees; the wood poured forth the
>   hungry yelping of hounds; the darkness
>   screamed with thirsty voices and the wit-
>   nesses rose and lived:
> The dry bones stirred, rattled, lifted, melting
>   themselves into my bones
> The grey ashes formed flesh firm and black
>   entering into my flesh.

This passage alone makes "Between the World and Me" one of the most
beautiful poems written by a black American.

Having made poetry the vehicle of his enthusiasm or his indignation,
Wright then turned to fiction where his gift for dialogue and for tragedy,
his sense of realism, enabled him to rapidly master its forms. If these
qualities hinder the reader, too often fascinated by the unwinding of the
plot, from paying sufficient attention to the lyric or intimate climate of
certain passages, the poetry of *12 Million Black Voices* cannot fail to strike
him.

Although Wright was beginning to detach himself from a Communist movement that then made little of the Negro's interests, his

historical point of view was that of a Marxist. *12 Million Black Voices*, subtitled "a Folk History of the Negro in the United States of America.," eliminated the privileged element, the so-called "talented tenth," as not representative of the fate of the black majority, which Wright wanted the reader to feel and share intimately.

In order to create the atmosphere necessary for this empathy, the author must avoid a language that is either too erudite or too picturesque. Wright therefore translated most of his concepts into easily accessible metaphors. One of the most evident examples is the use of the opposing symbols "Lords of the Land" (landed capital of the South) and "Bosses of the Buildings" (industrial capital of the North) as characters in a mystery play surrounded by all their attributes. Elsewhere the metaphor of a shoal of fish symbolizes the rising of the black masses against the current of racial prejudice; the island represents the Negro's psychological isolation; and the state of a soldier echoes the vicissitudes of the Negro's existence. These stylistic techniques avoid the use of concepts which would destroy the poetic climate but they do not create it. Nor can this climate be evoked by the colorful idiom of the Southern Negro; even in a popular history, particularities of speech would create too much distance between the reader and the black community. Also, to make a white and a black man speak the same language is to resist the force of stereotypes as it is to demand true racial equality. The prose of *12 Million Black Voices* must be situated mid-stream between the picturesque Negro dialect and the concision of the historian so that the reader will open his eyes to the realities hidden by custom and ignorance and feel that pity and indignation requisite to all sincere action.

This work is poetic, therefore, because of its wealth of simple and carefully chosen images and because of its tone, at times epic, at times lyric, which links this narrative to the blues tradition. The special atmosphere of *12 Million Black Voices* is often the result of imagery which flowers spontaneously in the turn of a phrase: "Like black buttercups our children spring up on the red soil of the plantations" (p. 59) or "The sand of our simple folk-lives runs out on the cold city pavement" (p. 136). Simple in appearance only, these images create a continuous metaphor and give color to the prose. More essential, however, are the passages where rhythm, emotion, and lyricism harmonize into large symphonic units. This description of the seasons, for example, paired with an admirable photograph of a team of mules toiling under a lowering sky, should be read aloud to be fully appreciated:

> In summer the magnolia tree fills the countryside with sweet scent for long miles. Days are slumberous, and the skies are high with clouds that ride fast. At midday the sun blazes and bleaches the soil. Butterflies flit through the heat; wasps sing their sharp straight lines; birds fluff and flounce, piping in querulous joy. Nights are covered with canopies, sometimes

blue and sometimes black, canopies that sag low with ripe and
nervous stars. The throaty boast of frogs momentarily drowns
out the call and countercall of crickets. (p. 32)

Here evocation and image are one; the lyricism springs from an open sympathy long considered the distinctive trait of Negro sensitivity and the
psychological foundation of negritude. It is in the childhood memories of
the author that this lyricism has its root, memories that will be revived in
the autobiographical *Black Boy*

The text modulates like the voice of a narrator reciting a four-act
play: "our strange birth," "inheritors of slavery," "death on the city
pavements" and "men in the making." The rhythms and sonorities
predominate over the visual element which might have distracted from
the photographs placed opposite the text. This is a narrative meant to be
read aloud, recited, chanted, or declaimed. By the constant use of the
pronoun "we," the chorus of the black community traces for a universal
public the vicissitudes of a minority about to enter the promised land of
democracy. Like the spirituals, this text is a sort of plea which ends with
the Biblical verses or Whitman-like couplets of a stirring hymn of hope.

A condensed version, in verse "12 Million Black Voices," published in
Coronet magazine, resembles a Negro folk song. It is a succession of
couplets which introduce some thirty photographs and which describe the
conditions and perspectives of Negro life in the big city ghettos. The
ballad opens with a nostalgic recall of the family atmosphere on the
plantation:

> Gone are de days when Negro hearts
> Were ever light as air
>
> Now we ain't got nobody
> And no one gives a care
>
> Gone de black old mammies
> A-bossin' o'er the roost
>
> Gone de old plantation
> For a filthy kitchenette . . .[15]

Here the poet is clearly addressing a black audience. This explains
the abundance of idiomatic expressions and the characteristic pronuncia-
tion. Moreover the regularity of the lines, the assonances and rhymes,
help to create the rhythm of folk ballads. In the middle of the poem the la-
ment changes into a lullaby as the mother muses on the hard future
awaiting her son:

> Sleep my kinky-headed babe
> You've stormy days ahead

> You'll grow up doing nigger work
> In dust and dirt and grime
>
> Your bones'll ache from toting loads
> On shoulder sorely bent.

But Wright allows her a pious hope:

> So on bended knees she prays de Lord
> To give you half a chance
>
> To play a bigger part than she
> In America's advance.

After his break with Communism which had nourished his inspiration for some ten years, Wright devoted himself to his now world-famous autobiography. In *Black Boy* the lyrical vein is no longer collective but personal, and in two different places, free verse provides a formal contrast with the rest of the style. One passage lists the numerous superstitions which charmed the magic world of Wright's childhood:

> Up or down the wet or dusty street, indoors or out, the days and nights began to spell out magic possibilities.
> If I pulled a hair from a horse's tail and sealed it in a jar of my own urine, the hair would turn overnight into a snake.
> If I passed a Catholic sister or mother dressed in black and smiled and allowed her to see my teeth, I would surely die. (p. 63)

A second, more important passage describes the way the world affected his sensitivity, and the link that his imagination forged between an event and its meaning:

> There was the wonder I felt when I first saw a brace of mountainlike, spotted, black-and-white horses clopping down a dusty road through clouds of powdered clay. . . .
> There was the vague sense of the infinite as I looked down upon the yellow, dreaming waters of the Mississippi River from the verdant bluffs of Natchez.
> There were the echoes of nostalgia I heard in the crying strings of wild geese winging south against a bleak autumn sky. . . .
> There was the languor I felt when I heard green leaves rustling with a rainlike sound.
> There was the incomprehensible secret embodied in a whitish toadstool hiding in the dark shade of a rotting log. (p. 7)

Here we find an echo of the experimental phrases of the young writer and especially of the hymns to nature in *12 Million Black Voices*. But in this passage the description is less important than the relationship between the child and the scene, or that between the sensation and the feeling it awakened, for: "Each event spoke with a cryptic tongue. And the moments of living slowly revealed their coded meanings" (p. 7). The symbolism leads to the discovery of a metaphysical reality in the scene before the poet's eyes. Poetry no longer appears as a creation—as it did in "Old Habit and New Love"—but as a revelation. The poetic moment becomes an epiphany.

Perhaps because it is a question here of childhood experience remembered, the relationship between the event and the message is made explicit as well as suggested by the poetic context. Nostalgia is openly associated with the cry of wild geese (similar to the cries which, in *As I Lay Dying*, filled Addie Bundren with the desire for an impossible flight) and, at the same time, the line of monosyllables represents the birds with their shrill recurrent sound. This nostalgia rises from the immensity of the sky and from the opposition between the gloom of autumn and the warmth of the summer that only the geese will see again. The sense of universality is suggested by simply the sight of the birds' flight. This is exactly what will occur in the haiku that Wright composed in the final stage of his poetic evolution.

Ten years more will elapse before Wright comes back to the poetic form. During the period when he considered poetry the complement of his novels' dramatic prose, it was used more as a foil for an ideology than a vehicle for the expression of his personal emotions. In July 1955 he sent a thirty-page letter to his friend and editor Edward C. Aswell in which he outlined a future work concerning the relationship between the individual and society:

> That problem poses for me many paradoxes: society and man form one organic whole, yet both, by the very nature of their relationship are in sharp conflict . . . I have no solution to that problem. I just want to pose it in as many ways as possible, that is why I have chosen *Celebration* as the general title of the work which I hope to do . . . (p. 8)

Eager to avoid a repetition of the criticism which his work *The Outsider* attracted because philosophical commentary occasionally marred the artistic unity, Wright adopts a different method:

> I want to assume an attitude that places me wholly on the side of feeling in life. To inject this into the work without the author speaking in his own name, in order to remain outside of the work, I've invented a device which I'd call an *impersonal mood*, which would, by implication, give the reader the above ideas. This mood rendered in terms of a kind of free verse prose says yet to all forms of experience which seek an outlet when the environment balks it . . . (p. 3)

For Wright the interest of this mood was its dual effect, both poetic and impersonal. Its form would distinguish it from the dramatic prose of the novel, its tone would contrast it with the feelings of the characters, its content would be a commentary on the novels that preceded or followed it. It is the monologue of a diffuse cosmic power which both participates in and transcends the human comedy. The following extracts from this work give an idea of its remarkable breadth:

> For the fullness of time is every day and
>   every hour; and if time I sing, time that .
>   seeks fulfillment.
> And yet no song am I; my music is unheard;
>   there is no pulse that can feel my rhythms;
> And yet nearer to music am I than to anything
>   amidst the millions of whirling suns;
> And no flesh am I, and no blood;
> And though I am of myself persuaded to
>   swell for swift moments in the breathing
>   temples of men, I am not man, and with his
>   ways I have I am not to be confounded.
> Yet I live; yet I have my being; yet I haunt the
>   whole of this and other worlds without
>   number and without end;—
> At home in the rock's deep heart, in the still
>   cold depths of the ocean's sand, on the
>   trembling leaves of tossing trees,
> In the icy stretches of stellar spaces, on the
>   stream of nodding flowers, in the falling
>   columns of light imprisoning mote and
>   beams, in the darkness and silence of
>   swamps—
> I was, I am, I will be,
> Everywhere, and nowhere, visible and invisi-
>   ble, felt and unfelt, there and not there, in
>   all and in nothing, I hover, seeking to
>   enter . . . (p. 4)

This hymn to the eternal and multiform force of life is reminiscent with its *recueillement* and its lyricism of certain passages of the Psalms although its human incarnation is celebrated with greater vigor:

> . . . Controlling the fluttering of a baffled and
>   curious child's eyelids,
> Relating the heart's beats, each to each,
> Structuring the bones of men and women,
> Breathing in laughter that leaps from singing
>   lips,
> Exulting in flexed and tensed flesh,
> And equally,

Suffering I am, pain, the compulsive rasping
   in the choked throat,
Flowing warm and red out of the fresh and
   stinging wound,
Bleeding in sweat on pallid brows,
. . . .
Restlessly I come and go, timing myself by
   my time, judging by my own harshly loving
   standards,
Indifferently regarding life and death, joy
   and sorrow,
Entering all things, reshaping life and death,
   joy and sorrow,
Entering all things, reshaping, spreading,
   scattering, dissolving, coming forth again in
   dying, being born at will. (p. 5)

Although this is only "a very rough first draft version," it is evident that the lyricism with which the poet once glorified Communism is now serving the cause of a universal transformation. For Wright, it is in harmony with Nature that man will most fully realize his humanity. The comic and physiological manifestations of the life spirit are the very source of this humanity paralyzed or destroyed by our present materialistic society. The mood conveys the poet's message: if alienated society desires to be liberated from its sclerosed forms, this mutation will be achieved when the individual, thanks to the umbilical cord organically attaching him to nature, has established a meaningful relationship with the objective world.

Wright may have preferred to use his lectures or his prose works to explore the question of man's relationship with society, yet we find this question reappearing in the intimate poems composed near the end of his life.

He discovered the Japanese haiku by chance, although there are many traces of this poetic form in the Western literature of early twentieth century. In 1905 Paul Louis Couchoud founded a French haiku movement; in America, Ezra Pound was one of the first poets to become interested in these tercets where a landscape may comment on the whole human fate.

The haiku goes back as far as the thirteenth century to poetry contests at the Heian court. The competitors took turns composing, in a witty or amusing style, the initial tercet or the final couplet of the *tanka*, a thirty-one syllable verse. The *hokku* (the first line) soon became a poem in itself composed of seventeen syllables and named a haiku or comic piece; paradoxically it flourished several centuries later as a philosophical and sèrious form. Three great masters gave it successively different orientations: in the seventeenth century the bonze Matsuo Basho evoked the delicate and tranquil scenes suggested by Zen Buddhist meditation; the eighteenth century painter Taniguchi Buson brought to the haiku the impressionism of his engravings; finally the poet Issa accentuated the realism of this form and enriched it with personal experiences. Wright who scrupulously studied the history and technique of the haiku in the four volumes of R. H. Blyth, was aware of all these aspects.

He made a particular effort to follow the rules: three lines, neither rhymed nor stressed in Japanese, number respectively five, seven, and five syllables; an implicit or explicit reference links the poem to the mood of one of the seasons; the symbolic meaning of the painting is expressed in the association of all these elements. Whereas neither the French school nor the haikuists writing directly in English generally bother about the number of arrangement of syllables within each line,[16] Wright seems to accumulate difficulties for himself. Not only does he usually follow the prescribed syllabic scheme, but he also, in the Japanese manner, condenses the essence of the poem in its first two lines. Here is an excellent example:

> The crow flew so fast
> That he left his lonely caw
> Behind in the fields.[17]

The crow which suggests autumn (as the frog, the spring, and different insects the other seasons according to the Japanese tradition) seems to symbolize by its carefree and rapid flight the selfishness of the male who, devoting all his attention to his personal ideal, leaves to his mate the drudgery of everyday life.

The painting may be more impressionistic, in the style of Buson, and the meaning less immediately accessible, as in:

> The spring lingers on
> In the scent of a damp log
> Rotting in the sun.

The seasons seem to be telescoped: spring dwells on in the summer sun and in the autumn decay. Is this the perfume of youth lingering on in old age? The association is less vague in the hurried race of the spring rain, unaware of its origin and its destination, a prey to youth's oblivious and imprudent haste:

> What town did you leave
> O wild and drowning spring rain
> And where do you go?

With this rhetorical question Wright renders a characteristic of the Japanese model which is almost untranslatable: the *kireji*. This word indicates the author's state of mind and that which is desired for the reader. Thus *yara* corresponds to this answerless question and *ya* to the emphatic mode of this haiku:

> Keep straight down this block
> Then turn where you find
> A peach tree blooming

or, even more closely, to the wonder of this one:

> With a twitching nose
> A dog reads a telegram
> On a wet tree trunk.

Is this a surrealistic scene? The poem seems more humorous than symbolic, in the tradition of the witty poet Issa. Wright's sympathy for animal and insect can be found also in this poem:

> Make up your mind snail
> You are half inside your house
> And halfway out.

Even more often, it seems, the author prefers the serious and more personal mode of the *kana*, this nostalgic sigh of man confronting his destiny!

> I am nobody
> A red sinking autumn sun
> Took my name away.

Here is a real cry of despair, the recognition that the individual can no longer define his being when the star of light and meaning disappears with his name. We are even more moved by the anguish of the writer ill on his fifty-first birthday, trying with familiar thoughts to recover his desire to write:

> It is September
> The month when I was born
> And I have no thoughts.

Rereading these poems, one finds a special quality in the evocations which at first seemed only to yield a general significance. Thus in our initial contact with the following poem,

> In the falling snow
> A laughing boy holds out his palms
> Until they are white

we feel a child's joy in receiving the gifts of nature. But does not the insistence on "until they are white" suggest that this child is black? His laughter takes on a deeper meaning if we consider it as an affirmation that there is no natural barrier between black and white. Also, the suggestion of a racial conflict gives poignancy to the innocent laughter of childhood.

It is important to underline the distinctive sensibility and particular atmosphere of Wright's haiku: the indulgent smile of the humorist, the restraint of the mature adult, the delicacy of the direct intuition of nature, the freshness of an unstaled receptivity. If he chose to obey the strict requirements of this form it is because it corresponds to an important facet of his inspiration. In some of the experimental phrases of the 1930s he was unwittingly already composing haiku.[18]. Even more significant are certain descriptions from *12 Million Black Voices* and the quotation from *Black Boy* already discussed above: "There were the echoes of nostalgia I heard in the crying strings of wild geese winging south against a bleak autumn sky." Without changing the word order or the meaning of the image, we can feel the suggestion of nostalgia in these three lines:

> Crying strings of wild geese
> Winging south against
> A bleak autumn sky.

Nothing is missing, not even the indication of the season. The same procedure could be used as successfully with other sentences. Wright therefore did not have to twist his inspiration into the haiku form; all the necessary elements were already there: word paintings, scenes rapidly sketched, and universal emotions. At the final stage of his evolution, at a moment when nature and the individual played an increasingly important part in his thinking, the poet developed a taste for these intimate tercets in which he could condense the quintessence of his art.

Wright fell in love with the haiku at first sight, and began composing in the fall of 1959 at the beginning of his illness—the consequence of a trip to Africa five years earlier. By March 1960 he had written four thousand tercets which he began to group for publication. He wrote to Margrit de Sablonière:

> I've so far selected 1500 haikus. I think now that I ought to boil them to about 800 and leave them. The problem of selecting them is agonizing. I'm trying to figure out a scheme.[19]

How deeply involved he had become in this phase of his poetry is somewhat surprising:

> I'm now through with the haikus. You know, I cannot let anything out of my hands as long as I feel and know there is something else to do with it. But now, for better or worse, I'm giving the ms. to the typist. Maybe I'm fooling around with these tiny little poems. But I could not let them go. I was possessed by them . . . There are 811 in all and they will make a ms. of some 80 pages.[20]

In September 1960 Wright was to declare:

> I've finished nothing this year but those damned haikus, and I've not even looked at them since my friends in New York

looked at them. I'll sit down one of these days and go over them, that is, reread them and see how they sound.[21]

Death prevented him from making this volume his poetic testament.

We hope that this volume will soon be published. It reveals a talent very different from that of the well-known vigorous novelist, but in perfect harmony with the deeper manifestations of his sensibility.

The distance separating the revolutionary poems of the 1930s, vibrant with indignation and brutal imagery, from the intimate symbolism of the haikus may seem great indeed. But the road travelled from the awkward enthusiasm of the young militant to the serene mastery of the mature artist is the sign, in the case of a writer as politically engaged as Wright, of a certain detachment. On the eve of his death, the novelist's interest in human affairs, his struggle against racism and injustice, had by no means faltered. It was rather that he had gradually reserved the poetic form, initially the sole vehicle of his social and political message, for the expression of feeling. Poetry served to paint scenes at once more personal and more universal, while his prose works reflected his ideological stands. Futhermore, it must not be forgotten that his poetic gifts, which shine most brilliantly in his final compositions, were manifest all along the course of his career. Often masked by the hard honesty or biting realism of the novelist, this poetry never stopped appearing in his prose works. At times lyrical, at times offended, at times outraged, his poetic sensibility vibrated in harmony with an imagination solidly rooted in the naturalness and wonder of childhood. Let us remember that *Native Son* was dedicated "To my mother who taught me to revere the fanciful and the imaginative."

The study of Wright's poetry brings to light an often neglected aspect of the writer's personality: his intimate sense of the universal harmony, his wonder before life, his thirst for a natural existence, all these tendencies which nourished, as much as did any ideology or faith, his courageous and incessant battle against all that prevents an individual from fully belonging to the world.

Notes

1. Like *The Negro Caravan*, ed. Sterling Brown et al. (New York, 1941); *The Poetry of the American Negro* (ed. Arna Bontemps and Langston Hughes, New York, 1949) or *Black Voices* (ed. Abraham Chapman, New York, 1968). For a complete list of these poems, see Michel Fabre and Edward Margolies, "Richard Wright: A Bibliography," *Bulletin of Bibliography*, 24 (January–April 1965), 131–137.

2. "I Tried to Be a Communist," *Atlantic Monthly*, 174 (August 1944), 63.

3. "American Hunger" (unpublished sequel to *Black Boy*), p. 18.

4. See the reviews and chronicles in *New Masses* from March 1934 to February 1936.

5. See Meridel LeSueur's "I Was Marching" (*New Masses*, 12 September 1934, p. 16) or Clara Weatherwax's piece which won the *New Masses* competition the following year, as instances of this type of literature.

6. "We of the Streets," *New Masses*, 23 (13 April 1937), 14.

7. "Spread Your Sunrise," *New Masses*, 16 (2 July 1935), 26.

8. *Black Boy*. New York. Harper, 1945, p. 89. All future references are to this edition.

9. "Between the World and Me," *Partisan Review*, 2 (July–August, 1935), 19.

10. See "I Tried to Be a Communist," *op. cit.*: "I stared at a cartoon drawn by a Communist artist; it was the figure of a worker clad in ragged overalls and holding aloft a red banner. The man's eyes bulged, his mouth gaped as wide as his face, his teeth showed, the muscles of his neck were like ropes." Wright admired *The People, Yes* and Carl Sandburg, but these lines also strangely resemble "Tempo Primo" of Melvin Tolson's "Dark Symphony" which reads: "The New Negro,/Hard-muscled, Fascist-hating, Democracy-ensouled/Strides in seven-league boots." The opening lines of "Everywhere Burning Waters Rise" also recall the rhythms and associations of concrete and abstract terms in "Tempo di Marcia." "Dark Symphony" was published in 1940 only, and we could not determine when it was written and whether it influenced Wright's early poetry.

11. Aragon used the image of a red engine pulling the train of revolution. Railway imagery also appealed to Wright who, as a boy, worshipped Casey Jones.

12. Wright wrote about twenty blues at different dates. The best known is "King Joe," in praise of Joe Louis, which was recorded by Paul Robeson and Count Basie in 1941.

13. "Ah Feels It in Mah Bones," *International Literature*, 4 (April 1935), 40.

14. "American Hunger," *op. cit.*, p. 20–21.

15. *Coronet*, April 1942, p. 77–93.

16. See, for instance, Miyamori Asataro's *Haiku Poems, Ancient and Modern*, Tokyo, Marazen & Co. 1944.

17. In "The Last Days of Richard Wright," Ollie Harrington quotes a number of Wright's haikus (see *Ebony*, February 1961, 82). All poems reprinted here are quoted with the permission of Mrs. Ellen Wright.

18. Wright had also shown interest in Imagist poetry. He had read Genevieve Taggard's article on William Carlos Williams in *New Masses* ("Poet Among Imagists," *New Masses*, 3 April 1934, p. 43–45) and Williams' "Red Wheelbarrow" with the poet's commentary as to why he considered it a perfect piece.

19. Unpublished letter to Margrit de Sabloniere, 8 April 1960.

20. Unpublished letter to Margrit de Sabloniere, 29 May 1960.

21. Unpublished letter to Margrit de Sablonière, 23 Sept. 1960.

The Where, the When, the What: A Study of Richard Wright's Haiku

Robert Tener*

I

While several writers have told the story of how Richard Wright became interested in writing haiku, only Michel Fabre has made any attempt to comment about their merits.[1] Part of this general neglect lies in the fact that only twenty-three of some four thousand haiku written by Wright have been published.[2] Some of the neglect lies in misunderstandings about haiku as a form of poetry. Perhaps most springs from certain misconceptions about why the novelist and essayist began to write haiku in 1959, the year before he died, as if attempting to regenerate his creative spirit. Michel Fabre has at least suggested a reasonable view when he asserts that for Wright the writing of haiku was "the rediscovery of his own deep powers, and, above all, a sign that his literary sensitivity had not been in the least dulled by his polemical and political activities."[3] Russell C. Brignano finds that the haiku resulted from Wright's turning away from man and society to find in nature the themes to renew his poetry.[4]

The answer, I think, to why Wright began writing haiku lies between those two statements of Fabre's and Brignano's. It is dependent on Wright's desire for an orderly universe, one in which black people could live with dignity free from fear, despite the dominance of white people;[5] it lies in his efforts to rediscover a common unifying factor for his four worlds: black America, white America, the Third World just emerging, and the world of nature. Most of all, it comes out of that mental and physical state which came upon him because of his sickness and loneliness when as a poet he could lose himself in the "ah-ness" or moment of nature, intuitively becoming one with the object of his vision and wanting to express that straightforward view of things without metaphor or symbol. For Wright, the act of writing haiku must have been equivalent to finding a new, powerful way to express what he had felt and yearned for

---

*This essay was written specifically for this volume and appears here for the first time by permission of the author.

all his life, a belief in the unity and harmony of all things, the sense that man and nature are one and that the point of knowledge is to abolish the division between them. In studying haiku, he surely must have identified those yearnings with some of the Taoist and Zen ideas that permeate the works of the great haiku writers. Russell C. Brignano has acutely observed that Wright lived out two views of himself through his works: one, his reaction to a hostile world; and two, his self image of a moral, intellectual man trying to turn chaos into an Eden.[6] A happy and contented Wright might never have written those haiku. For that matter, the Japanese themselves "claim that haiku are written when one is bored and lonely, not when happy or busy,"[7] Surely in the mood generated by the events of the 1950s, he had already turned to nature and his early responses to her. That mood or yearning for harmony with life was reinforced by the spirit in the haiku Wright had recently discovered, which began to express itself in his own attempts to write haiku. During those days, as Constance Webb reminds us, Wright began to look "forward to a summer in the country."[8]

It is that sense of yearning for the natural world and its order that expresses one of Wright's major motifs in both his life and his poetry. It reflects a way Wright had of looking at nature, which under the impact of discovering haiku and how Japanese artists Basho, Buson, and Issa had experienced nature, found a form of expression that appealed also to his artistic sense. Perhaps he had discovered that haiku "belongs to a tradition of looking at things, a way of living, a certain tenderness and smallness of mind that avoids the magnificent, the infinite and the eternal."[9]

Always conscious of his negritude and his creativity, Wright certainly had a way of looking at things.[10] This is reflected in the repetition of specific words and images that provide insight into his vision; terms like *sun, black, white, sky, blood red, black hands, white feathers*, and even references to *red clay, kittens, rats, bloodhounds, grasshoppers* and allusions to man's activities in the natural setting abound in Wright's works. Even his favorite line of poetry from Whitman reflects his reaction to nature, "Not till the sun excludes you do I exclude you."[11] As early as 1935, when he composed "Between the World and Me," he identified with aspects of nature and borrowed images from his natural environment, as in the line "And in a blaze of red I leaped to the sky as pain rose like water, boiling my limbs." As "dry bones" and a "stony skull," he stares in "yellow surprise at the sun. . . ."[12] The setting for these images is a "grassy clearing" with oaks and elms. Here are the remains of a black boy burned to ashes and "white bones." The "sooty details" thrust themselves "between the world" and the speaker, who is Wright himself. In this early poem the black man is an intruder in the world of nature, a theme often reflected in his writings that he could never break away from, not even in his haiku. The black and white polarities repeat themselves constantly throughout his haiku, a black boy catching snow-flakes in his hand, black trees in winter, white pillows in a sick room, night time contrasted with white bread. Part of that attitude is the sun that catches his complex response to himself, to white America, to Africa, to nature, to a "red sinking" sun that took his name away. The evidence of Wright's identification with nature and his use of its motifs stretches from "Big Boy Leaves Home," with its rural events around the swimming hole, to *Black Boy*, and culminates in the haiku. In *Black Boy* he reveals his delight "in seeing long straight rows of red and green vegetables," or his nostalgia when he heard "the crying strings of wild geese winging south against a bleak, autumn sky." He even wished to "imitate the petty pride of sparrows" and found an "incomprehensible secret embodied in a whitish toadstool hiding in the dark shade of a rotting log." Most reveal-ing, perhaps, is his yearning for identification when he saw "a solitary ant carrying a burden upon a mysterious journey."[13] The evidence is a record of his early childhood days and sensations transformed beyond the more expansive symbolism of *Black Boy* into those patterns from the days in Mississippi when Wright learned to identify his mood and self with specific aspects of nature. The domain of nature was a world he wanted to live in. Perhaps he did for a while when with his wife and daughter he lived from 1947 to 1960 on his farm in Ailly, Normandy. There, he liked to work afternoons in his garden.[14]

Fabre has pointed out Wright's "insatiable longing" to find unity and identity through his heritage and "to contemplate America from a distance."[15] His kinship with "marginal men" was not just a reflection of his being "torn between two worlds," America and Africa, feeling that he belonged to two cultures.[16] That kinship also reflected his need for unity with nature. His artistic and social activities during the 1950s suggest some of these aspects of his life. That he wanted a worldwide humanism is evident. As Russell C. Brignano points out, Wright desired "an orderly and rational universe, created by man out of the concept of his own ra-tional and humane image."[17] But in the twentieth century humanism means more than a brotherhood of human beings, which is not possible in the biology of the chain of life without an awareness of what mankind shares with all living creatures. To have a "humane image" is to be in a state of harmony with life in its broadest ranges. Michel Fabre makes much the same point about Wright when he explains that "for Wright, it is in harmony with Nature that man will most fully realize his humanity."[18]

In 1955 Wright attended the Bandung Conference of the Third World; two years later he was a member of the First Congress of Negro Artists and Writers, which met in Paris in September. During that same period he liked to work in his garden on his Normandy farm.[19] The decade of the fifties was rich in possibilities for Wright. The Third World was coming into its own artistically, socially, and politically; though still holding it, Wright was gradually shedding his romantic belief that in denying men the chance to act on the basis of their feelings, social institutions cause the individual to destroy such feelings.[20] But set against this positive mood were the effects of his financial and personal problems. His works were not bringing in much money, nor had he written anything else that was financially successful within the last few years. In addition, by the beginning of 1959 he was sick and often confined to his bed. He was approaching the end of the decade in an ambivalent mood ready for union with that which lies beyond man. Exhausted by his financial problems, sickness, and the polemic drain on his rational powers, Wright was mentally and emotionally receptive to the ideas, beauty, and form of haiku. Under these conditions he seemed to be liberated from the restrictions of rationality and to enjoy his intuitive responses to other powers and images latent within him.

Sometime during the summer of 1959 he had been introduced to haiku by a young South African friend who loved its form.[21] He borrowed R. H. Blyth's four volumes on the art of haiku and settled down to rediscover his old dream of oneness with all life. By 19 March 1960 he was so captivated by its form, content, and beauty that he was already in the midst of composing what was to turn out to be almost four thousand separate haiku. In response to his friend and Dutch translator Margrit de Sablonière, he said that he had returned to poetry and added, "during my illness I experimented with the Japanese form of poetry called haiku; I wrote some 4,000 of them and am now sifting them out to see if they are any good." In his discussion of this event, Michel Fabre notes that Wright's interest in haiku involved his research into the great Japanese masters, Buson, Basho, and Issa; he ignored the European and American forms that were then becoming popular. Fabre notes further that Wright made "an effort to respect the exact form of the poem," but adds that it was curious for Wright to become interested in haiku at a time when he was fighting his illness. As Fabre reasons, "logically he should have been tempted to turn away from 'pure' literature and to use his pen instead as a weapon."[22] Just as curiously, Constance Webb refers to none of this material. She merely says that Wright had lost his physical energy and that "while lying against the pillows one afternoon he picked up the small book of Japanese poetry and began to read it again." Apparently, it had been given to him earlier, and he read and reread it under the excitement of its style. She comments that Wright "had to study it and study to find out why it struck his ear with such a modern note." Then she adds that Wright "would try to bring the life and consciousness of a black American" to its form. Again according to her, the haiku "seemed to answer the rawness he felt, which had, in turn, created a sensitivity that ached. Never had he been so sensitive, as if his nervous system had been exposed to rough air." In a letter to Paul Reynolds, his friend and literary agent, Wright explained that he had sent to William Targ of the World

Publishing Company an eighty-page manuscript of haiku. After a few comments about Targ, Wright went on to say that "these poems are the results of my being in bed a great deal and it is likely that they are bad. I don't know."[23] That manuscript of eighty pages has never been published to the best of my knowledge. Until we can look at those pages and his other haiku, we will probably never know the real reason why Wright turned to haiku during the last years of his life. But that knowledge, while helpful, is not necessary to enjoy his published haiku. What is necessary, both to the enjoyment and to the understanding of Wright's haiku, is some knowledge about haiku as the great Japanese writers developed the genre.

II

As an American and a poet, I approach any discussion of the origin and development of haiku with caution, as it is a form of poetry rooted deeply in Japanese tradition and culture, which reflects the intimate Japanese relationships not only with nature, but also with the philosophies of Zen, Buddha, and Taoism. Thus, I am heavily indebted for my own knowledge of haiku and their history to the works of R. H. Blyth and Joan Giroux.[24] A haiku is "actually the first part of a *waka*, a highly conventionalized syllabic verse of five lines arranged in a sequence of 5–7–5–7–7 syllables, also known as a *tanka* or *uta*; the *tanka* and *uta* date back to" a poetry anthology from the eighth century. During the Kamakura period, from 1185 to 1333, the *waka* declined in popularity, and a form of group poetry known as *renga* became dominant. *Renga* is a poetic dialogue in linked verse composed of "a succession of *waka* in which the first three lines of 5–7–5 syllables are composed by one person, the next two of 7–7 by another person, the following three lines of 5–7–5 by a third person, and so on" through small groups of four or five people. The result is that *renga* turn out to be long poems of a hundred or more verses, whose first three lines often became the best known and most important. These lines were called *hokku*.[25]

The *renga* were popular at the Emperor's court, but declined in popularity during the sixteenth and seventeenth centuries because they tended to follow the conventions and "stilted *waka* rules" that permitted only the use of a specific vocabulary and excluded humor. The rebellion against the *renga* took the form of increasing the range of permissible vocabulary and introducing some humor, keeping in effect the *renga* form, but rejecting the older *waka* spirit. The result produced an earthier verse that came to be called *renku*. *Renku* still maintained the form of *renga*, and the first three lines were still called *hokku*. The new *renku* came to be called *haikai renga*, while the term *haikai* came to mean the *hokku*. Some of the better poets would compose their *hokku* ahead of time in order to be ready for a "linked-verse party." Of these Matsuo Basho

(1644–1694), one of the best poets, succeeded in making *haikai* literature, for in his hands it came to express "a meaningful reaction to reality beyond simple wit and humor." Before the time of the poet Masaoka Shiki (1867–1902), haiku were thus called *hokku* or *haikai*.[26]

According to Toshiko Miyazaki, "the word 'haiku' comes from *haikai renga no hokku* (the introductory lines of light linked verse)." But the actual term was coined by the modern poet Masaoka Shiki in the late nineteenth century.[27] The spirit and content of haiku, however, derive from the major haiku poets who came to write them. Of these Matsuo Basho wished to taste deeply of nature and life. From this desire he perfected a subjective haiku "noted for their melancholy content" and "quiet tone," and having "the subdued elegance found in old, worn things." The principal belief in his poems is that nature is the best subject for haiku. The second great poet was Taniguchi (or Yosano) Buson (1715–1783), whose love of painting and desire for experimentation reveal themselves in his "picturesque, objective imagery," which also suggest his belief that the poet need not "reveal his own emotions." The third contributor to the history of haiku was Kobayashi Issa (1763–1827). Out of his "sense of kinship with small animals and insect life," he developed a personal quality that rejected "poetic and religious convention" while stressing simple diction and the "depiction of ordinary human affairs." The last of the great haiku writers was Masaoka Shiki, who from his sickbed renewed and improved the haiku form and content. Influenced by Buson, he increased the variety of subject matter and the objective description.[28]

Throughout this period of the four great haiku poets, when haiku was a beginning in a chain of thought about poetical images, ideas, humor, and insight, it appeared in a variety of forms, often in strings of 8–8–5 or 10–7–5 or even 5–10–5 and 6–8–5 syllables. Verses of more than 17 syllables were common; those of less than 17 were not. What seems to have emerged as the more common form of haiku is the 5–7–5 pattern of 17 syllables.[29] A generalized definition offered by Joan Giroux is that "a haiku is a 17-syllable poem arranged in three lines of 5, 7, and 5 syllables, having some reference to the season and expressing the poet's union with nature." The 17-syllable form fits the evolved sense of brevity; the 3-line form seems appropriate to support the imagery, often indicating the *where* of the elements; the implicit or explicit reference to the season adds a complete atmosphere or mood indicating the *when* and permitting the necessary brevity; and of course the *what* or point of the poem is "to express the poet's union with nature, his flash of intuition concerning the objects which his senses perceive."[30]

During the eighteenth century a satirical form of haiku called *senryu* was developed by Karai Senryu (1718–1790) as a kind of "mock haiku" with humor, moralizing nuances, and a philosophical tone, expressing "the incongruity of things" more than their oneness, dealing more often with distortions and failures, not just with the harmonious beauty of nature, as can be seen in the following *senryu*:

> When she wails
> At the top of her voice,
> The husband gives in.

Senryu tend to appeal more to one's sense of the logical than to the intuition.[31] The result is that much of what Europeans and Americans write as haiku turns out actually to be *senryu*.

As R. H. Blyth points out, haiku can be understood primarily from the Zen point of view. And this must be thought of as having two meanings: one, that "body of experience and practice begun by Daruma" in the sixth century; and two, "that state of mind in which we are not separated from other things, are indeed identical with them, and yet retain our own individuality and personal peculiarities." It is the second meaning that is important in a discussion of Wright's haiku. In addition, the term "haiku" has two meanings. In a plural sense it stands for the poems themselves; in a singular sense it means "the poetical attitude of mind of the haiku poets, their way of life, their 'religion.' "[32] For Blyth they are a "kind of *satori*, or enlightenment, in which we see into the life of things." The poet grasps "the inexpressible meaning of some quite ordinary thing or fact hitherto entirely overlooked." The result, according to Blyth, is that "haiku is the apprehension of a thing by a realization of our own original and essential unity with it, the word 'realization' having the literal meaning here of 'make real' in ourselves. The thing perceives itself in us; we perceive it by simple self consciousness. The joy of the (apparent) re-union of ourselves with things, with all things, is thus the happiness of being our true selves. It is with 'all things' because, as Dr. Suzuki explains in his works on Zen, when one thing is taken up, all things are taken up with it."[33] In looking at Wright's haiku, one must, therefore, not only consider both meanings of the term, but also Blyth's comment.

Michel Fabre says that when Wright began to compose haiku he "made an effort to respect the exact form of the poem—three unrhymed lines composed respectively of five, seven and five syllables." In addition to trying to reproduce this syllabic form, Wright "tried to condense the essence of the poem into the first two lines, and to include in them an implicit or explicit reference to the chosen season of the year, designed to join emotional tone to the symbolic meaning of the description."[34]

While one might disagree with some of these statements or with their phrasing—as to whether or not Wright followed the seventeen-syllable form exactly or did condense the essence into the first two lines or did create symbolical meanings, none of which are essential or integral to haiku—one can only wonder why in his excellent discussion of Wright's poetry, Fabre fails to consider seriously the nature of haiku and Wright's basic themes.[35] Despite Fabre's admission that "it is important not to restrict the image of Wright to that of a polemicist,"[36] that is essentially what he seems to do. On the other hand, it would seem that in turning to haiku, Wright was following a pattern, perhaps unconsciously, that he had begun back in 1927, when he left Memphis for Chicago. As Russell C. Brignano described that act, Wright wanted to "learn who . . . [he] was, what . . . [he] might be."[37] In short, Wright needed to know where he was going in life, when he would find his place, and what his place would be. When he turned to haiku, he was implying the same set of questions and finding intuitive answers. He felt his negritude as deeply as he sensed his creativity and relationship to nature. But his place in life seemed at times to rest more in a hostile cultural world than in the harmonious world of nature. In "Blueprint for Negro Writing," Wright wrote that "the Negro writer who seeks to function within his race as a purposeful agent has a serious responsibility. In order to do justice to his subject matter, in order to depict Negro life in all of its manifold and intricate relationships, a deep, informed, and complex consciousness is necessary; a consciousness which draws for its strength upon the fluid lore of a great people, and moulds this lore with the concepts that move and direct the forces of history today." Despite the context of that idea, drawn from a discussion of "Social Consciousness and Responsibility," the concept of an individual consciousness dependent on the "fluid lore" of a people raises, as Wright noted, "the question of the personality of the writer. It means that in the lives of Negro writers must be found those materials and experiences which will create a meaningful picture of the world today." Wright felt that in his new role the black writer must "create values by which his race is to struggle, live and die." In his discussion of "The Problem of Theme," he adds that "this does not mean that a Negro writer's sole concern must be with rendering the social scene"; instead, he must have a sense of "the *whole* life" that "he is seeking" and that needs to be "vivid and strong in him."[38]

What was "vivid and strong" in Wright, and had been from childhood on, was the haiku moment, the *where*, the *when*, and the *what*, not that he in his early years would have called it that. Being a responsible agent for his people meant that Wright had to draw on the materials of his own life, much of which was deeply involved with his feelings about nature. To have a sense of "the whole life" and "create values" for his people meant that Wright had to contend with his deepest yearnings about a harmonious union between man and nature. In haiku he must have found echoes of all he believed in and desired, both in the form, pleasurable and challenging to him as an artist, and in the content, so strongly appealing to his inner self. In the moment he found his best self.

The haiku moment "may be defined as an instant in which man becomes united to an object, virtually becomes the object and realizes the eternal, universal truth contained in being." In quoting from the poet Yasuda's point of view about the moment, Joan Giroux adds that the writer of haiku " 'in a brief moment . . . sees a pattern, a significance he had not seen before.' "[39] In his own discussions about Richard Wright's poetry, Michel Fabre points out, while commenting on the "hymns to nature" in *12 Million Black Voices*, that "the symbolism leads to the discovery of a metaphysical reality in the scene before the poet's eyes. Poetry no longer appears as a creation—as it did in 'Old Habit and New Love'—but as a revelation. The poetic moment becomes an epiphany."[40]

III

Wright's "poetic moment" may not be as sharply and traditionally defined as it is for the great Japanese writers of haiku, but it grew out of his childhood relations with nature as Fabre has gone to some pains to reveal. To the themes of black suffering, desire for interracial unity, and the triumph of socialism, Wright added "a keen sensitivity to nature," grounding his lyricism in personal experiences. In his early work, such as "Everywhere Burning Waters Rise," the references to nature focus on its destructive aspects. But in "We of the Streets," Wright borrows from nature and begins, according to Fabre, to use nature as the "touchstone of his poetic sensitivity: it was the Mississippi country that restored his strength during a childhood of struggle and deprivation." His tendency to see himself set against the background of nature was strongly influenced by his love for Carl Sandburg's and Walt Whitman's poetry. Thus he made his own poetry "the vehicle of his enthusiasm or his indignation." In *12 Million Black Voices*, however, for the first time he began to use an imagery that links the individual with nature, comparing children to black buttercups. As Fabre comments, "Here evocation and image are one; the lyricism springs from an open sympathy long considered the distinctive trait of Negro sensitivity and the psychological foundation of negritude. It is in the childhood memories of the author that this lyricism has its root, memories that will be revived in the autobiographical *Black Boy*." That all of this is important in leading up to the writing of the haiku Fabre clearly understands. In his discussion of *12 Million Black Voices* he refers to the nostalgia that Wright developed in the lines, and then observes, "The sense of universality is suggested by simply the sight of the birds' flight. This is exactly what will occur in the haiku that Wright composed in the final stages of his poetic evolution."[41]

The haiku moment is the heart of haiku because it links complementary and antithetical qualities, that is, directness and paradox, austerity and joy, love of nature and the ordinary. It is an expression in words of "the instant of intuition uniting poet and object."[42] At his best Wright achieves that rare quality, the haiku moment, as in

> From across the lake
> Past the black winter trees
> Faint sounds of a flute.[43]

The visual image of blackness, trees, lake, and winter is joined with the aural image of a man-made sound from the flute. Two kinds of life become one in the setting placed in the distance. Everything is muted by the adjective "faint," which seems to stress quietness as the natural condition of man and trees with the lake and winter providing a sense of place and time. All is unified with man through the perception and expression, while the poet himself is almost imperceptible. The quality of the haiku cannot bear too much sound or thought, either of which would increase the tone of the flute and force man and his philosophizing to dominate the scene. At his worst as in

> Standing in the field
> I hear the whispering of
> Snowflake to snowflake

Wright forces the poet-speaker to be an intruder in the scene and attaches a sentimental anthropomorphism to the snowflakes. In this example Wright has not captured or at least communicated through words the essential unity of the perception, the instantaneous awareness of all things including the speaker being one for a second. The choice of the verb "hear," the participle "standing," and the gerund "whispering" contribute to the effect of isolation. The poet-speaker stands because he senses that he is not a part of the field and falling snow. He stands, perhaps from arrogance, from a sense of intellectual or rational superiority, or from a sense of deliberately keeping the self ready to flee from what is becoming a white world. Nor are the snowflakes talking or whispering to the speaker, sharing themselves. Instead, they whisper to each other. The entire event produces the effect that the poet-speaker is an intruder, almost a voyeur, and the snowflakes are forced to whisper in order not to be overheard. Nor can one separate the color of the snowflakes from Wright's color. In both these poems Wright deliberately evokes a specific color, in the first instance black and in the second white. But black is not intrusive in the first poem, despite its explicit statement. In the second poem the repetition of the word "snowflake," with its obvious color, imposes nuances about the color white that become intrusive.

As Joan Giroux says, quoting from Kenneth Yasuda, " 'the intent of all haiku and the discipline of the form' is to render the haiku moment, to express the 'ah-ness.' "[44] In expressing this the 17-syllable form has turned out to be an ideal length. Of Wright's published haiku, 14 have the 17 syllable pattern; 5 have 16 syllables; 3 have 18 syllables; one has 19 syllables. In those instances where he departed from the convention, Wright was apparently experimenting, trying to understand the brevity of the form. Within the historical variation of the number of syllables, there is little significance, it seems to me, to be attached to this divergence. Among his best, "From across the Lake" has only 16 syllables, and "Coming from the Woods" has 18.[45]

In linking directness and paradox, the essential aspects of haiku indicate that the poet needs to look straight at things and to transform the perception into words that do not depend upon metaphors or symbols.[46] Haiku are traditionally opposed to the use of symbols and metaphors, both of which suggest a clever use of logic or wit, characteristics that appeal more to Europeans and Americans than to the Japanese. Rather, the poet should present the event or object nude so as to form a doorway for the mind. The paradox results from the simultaneity of two different things being perceived as one through the response of the poet, an effect that cannot be expressed solely through individual words. But the ability to reject metaphor and symbol did not come easily to Wright. Much more at hand was his own preoccupation with the black and white symbolism in his life, a concern that became intrusive in his haiku and at times prevented them from communicating that special moment. In

> Merciful autumn
> Tones down the shabby curtains
> Of my rented room

as in "Standing in the Field," and in

> I am nobody
> A red sinking autumn sun
> Took my name away

Wright interjects such anthropomorphic characteristics and metaphors as personified autumn, snowflakes, and sun, making them elements of a natural world that either oppose or sympathize with the speaker who intrudes on the natural scene. Indeed, in the first example the speaker makes autumn compassionate, but in the latter he turns the red autumn sun into a symbol, perhaps of a Western world, America, that has deprived the speaker of his name and identity, perhaps that of a black African?

Neither in these haiku nor in "Standing in the Field" does the poet identify with nature or communicate a sense of harmony with her. While he supplies the *where* and *when*, a field, a room, a vague place in autumn or winter, he offers no *what*. The approach is indirect, interposing between the speaker and the scene the poet's habit of subscribing meanings to an event. But the meanings come from within the poet; they are not part of the event and its things. Behind symbol and metaphor Wright tries to hide the depth of his personal feelings, as he does in

> In the falling snow
> A laughing boy holds out his palms
> Until they are white.

Although the speaker is not directly in the scene, the poem presents an ambiguity through the emphasized use of the word "white," indirectly through reference to snow and directly through a description of the boy's hands. But the effect of describing the boy as laughing creates a question. Why is he laughing? The possible answers drive one to consider the possibility that the boy's hands are not originally white. In either case, whether the boy is white or black and is laughing because of sheer delight or because he has become white for a moment, the term "white" has symbolic overtones not present in "snow," "falling," "boy," or "palms." There is indeed no moment of intuition in which boy, snow, whiteness, and poet become one. In "From across the Lake" the poet clearly has not allowed symbols or metaphors to intrude. The description of the lake, the black trees in winter, the faint sounds of a flute do not contain symbols anchored to Wright's preoccupation with his negritude or with his social concerns. The three lines work together without hiding behind symbols.

As for paradox, again the haiku are uneven. In

> Why is the hail so wild
> Bouncing so frighteningly
> Only to lie so still[47]

there is presented no paradox. The wild and frightening quality of the hail are not aspects of hail. Instead, they reside in the poet's mind, are qualities dependent on the poet's experiences, and are imposed not too successfully on the hail. Between those mental states and the last description that the hail lies still appears no paradox. On the other hand, Wright captures the paradox of color and shape of two separate things, one a cocklebur and one a black boy, in an excellent haiku,

> The green cockleburs
> Caught in the thick wooly hair
> Of the black boy's head.

The two things, disparate in shape, size, and color are held together by one quality both share: the texture of the boy's hair matches that of the cocklebur as perceived by the poet. By chance in a moment of intuition, two aspects of nature, two forms of life, are seen as one without the poet's having to naturalize the boy or humanize the burr. In this haiku Wright has presented in direct statement the paradox of union, expressing the desire to be a part of nature while simultaneously maintaining one's separate identity. Although the *where* is vague, some place in nature, the *when* is summer before the time of ripeness and the *what* is the sense of complete harmony with nature.

As for austerity and joy, Wright as an artist must have struggled to develop these characteristics in his haiku. Austerity refers to the absence of philosophical or metaphysical comment, the absence of intellectualization or imposition of an excessive rationality. It calls for a simplicity of language, thought, and image, a lack of complication often revealed in the spontaneous joy of union. As R. H. Blyth says, the joy comes from the "(apparent) re-union of ourselves with things. . . ." It is the "happiness of being our true selves. . . ."[48] Austerity is not only a lack of intellectualization, it is almost a wordlessness, a condition in which words are used not to externalize a poet's state of feeling, but to "clear away something," according to Blyth, "that seems to stand between" the poet and real things. Because the real things are not actually separate from the poet, they "are then perceived by self-knewledge [sic]." Certainly, haiku ideally remove as many words as possible, stressing nonintellectuality, as thought like passion must depend upon and not substitute for intuition. The joy lies in the humor, the lightness, the lack of sentimentality. "It goes down to something deeper than the unconscious where repressions wait with ill-concealed impatience. It goes beyond this into the realm where a thing is and is not at the same time, and yet at the very same time *is*."[49]

In a good haiku that presents a Zen kind of humor,

> With a twitching nose
> A dog reads a telegram
> On a wet tree trunk

the austerity and joy are central. The language is simple. Except for "telegram," all are native English words. There are only 12 one-syllable words, 1 two-syllable word, and 1 three-syllable word in the poem.[50] Perhaps the only characteristic that prevents this haiku from being excellent is the use of the metaphors "telegram" and "reads." These are the sole detractions in a poem that has a simplicity unadorned with sentimentalism or sententious comment. It is the season of rain in a place of dogs and trees. Ironically, the metaphor "telegram" unites the elements of nature, the tree, and the dog, with a construction of man, a telegram through the personification embodied in "reads." Despite the obvious metaphorical quality of these two terms, Wright maintains at least some kind of intellectual distance by refusing to elaborate, to go beyond the idea of a telegram with its sense of a code in communication, chemical for the dog, and electrical for man. Unfortunately, the use of the metaphors not only violates the otherwise fine austerity of language, but also interferes with the paradoxical union of the elements of place, season, and poet. The poet is imposing his rationality upon the scene. On the other hand, the humor lies in the visual image of the dog twitching his nose, especially in "twitching," which carries a double meaning: one, visual, suggesting how the dog comes in contact with, that is reads, his message; the other, also visual, but suggesting a sense of the sharpness of the message, the odor, that causes a slight physical movement. Thus the key terms "telegram" and "reads," the latter anthropomorphizing the dog, are central to the poem, but their function depends on their metaphorical quality, not on that inherent in their literal meanings.

If Wright was not successful in eliminating the metaphor in this poem, he was able to prevent his own sentimental identification, because the poem contains a relatively impersonal response to the images on the surface. In addition, again suggesting some idea of the slight imperfection the poem bears, there seems to be no overall unifying relationship between the poet and the total event, neither in the poet's being an element of the scene nor in his perception. It is the dog that performs the territorial act, learning the boundaries of some other animal or marking his own. In that sense the dog learns his place, where he is. That such an image grows out of Wright's concern to learn his own place in time, to mark his own creative and individual territories, is possible. In this view there resides a possible limited paradoxical union for Wright, as the words "reads" and "telegram" could suggest his own view of himself transferred metaphorically to the animal. If so, then a feeling of sentimentality creeps in almost unconsciously. The same interpretation, however, does not apply to the tree. Once again the state of oneness and objectivity are imperfect. Animal and vegetable life are linked by a metaphorical object and process from the life of human beings. But the process is not total, despite the humor in the image of the dog performing a natural act that human beings themselves would find dehumanizing. Although in effect the dog has been humanized, the tree has not.

On the other hand, in a parallel poem that also focuses on a dog,

> The dog's violent sneeze
> Fails to rouse a single fly
> On his mangy back

there is even less objectivity and simplicity, despite the humor, because of an intrusive sentimentality. Only 4 of the words are not from the basic English stock ("violent," "fails," "single," and "mangy"); 11 are one-syllable, 2 are two-syllable, and 1 is three-syllable. There seems to be no indication of *where* the visual image occurs; the *when* appears vaguely to be summer. As for the subject, the poem presents a series of visual and aural images involving a dog, his sneezing, his mangy back, a fly, and the effect of that sneeze on the fly. The humor that emerges is mixed with pathos because it develops from the inability of the dog to get rid of the fly. That image is set beside the implicit sense of the dog's poverty. He cannot free himself either from the mange or the other parasites and pests of nature. Into the humor generated by the words "fails" and "mangy," the poet has injected his moral comment, which clouds the humor of the visual image. The poem loses austerity in that it fails to offer the paradoxical union between dog, fly, sneeze, back, and poet; instead, it implies a possible identification of the poet-speaker with the dog. The verb "fails," with its strong evaluation, seems to suggest that the poet has transformed his mood to the dog. As the dog's "violent" acts have failed to improve his condition, so have the poet's efforts failed to eliminate his own sickness or affect white America.

The last major characteristic of the haiku moment is the love of nature that is inseparable from the ordinary. The love of nature without humanizing or sentimentalizing it stems from a Taoist belief in the unity and harmony of all things, in a sense of kinship between all things, amounting at times to a compassionate irony derived from the paradox that the more one learns, the more that knowledge tends to abolish the arbitrary division between man and nature.[51] For R. H. Blyth this characteristic is explained in terms of selflessness, meaning that the poet has identified with nature. The loss of his individuality within the union involves a generalized melancholy aspect or loneliness as an underlying rhythm. It represents a state of Zen, of "absolute spiritual poverty in which, having nothing, we possess all." We rejoice with those who rejoice, weep with those who weep, are moved as all things in nature are by the same forces, the inevitability of nature.[52] Such concepts are also part of the idea of materiality that suffuses haiku, in which the material or the concrete is emphasized without the expression of any general principles or abstract reasoning. Animate and inanimate lose their differences to such an extent that one can say that haiku are about things. In this almost stoical sense, the ordinary thing and the love of nature are reduced to a detached love of life as it is, without idealistic, moralistic, or ethical attachments. Things are equal to human beings; both exist through and because of each other.[53]

These ideas are apparent in Issa's famous haiku,

> *Katatsumuri*
> *Sorosoro nobore*
> *Fuji no yama*
>
> O snail
> Climb Mount Fuji
> But slowly, slowly![54]

The ordinary and lowly snail has become one with the mountain and the poet through the perception of the visual image. From the repetition of "slowly" comes a compassionate wry humor, an implicit awareness that all life climbs its mountains slowly and inevitably. Wright also has a haiku on the snail. It is one of his better ones, though it comes closer to being a *senryu* than a true haiku.

> Make up your mind snail!
> You are half inside your house
> And halfway out!

In contrast with Issa's poem, Wright's presents no compassionate irony. There is humor; there is a consideration of a simple living thing from nature; there is also a perception of the visual scene coming through the poet. On the other hand, there appears to be some identification on the poet's part with the snail, but not union. It is as though the poet-speaker senses that he, like the snail, is half in and half out of his house or place. The word "house" implies more than where one lives; it suggests one's place or position within life. In addition, within the context of the total poem, it suggests further some sense of dissatisfaction with one's place. One neither totally belongs nor is totally outside. The first line reinforces this quality through the imperative "Make up," which introduces an intellectuality and evaluation far removed from the objective, dispassionate love and acceptance of nature as it is. The poem presents through indirection the poet's self-evaluation in all of his dissatisfaction, saying in effect, make up your mind. The poet has imposed a different, more rational, pattern on nature, as though the rhythm in nature were a logical process to be decided by rational means. By that quality of intellectualization the poem is weakened as a haiku.

It is, however, much more likely that the poem is a mock haiku, a *senryu*, with its humor and philosophizing comment. Rather than express the total selfless love and acceptance of nature with its consequent loss of individuality, it suggests a sense of the incongruity of things in nature when man reflects through comparisons. As with man in his cultural world, so with the snail in his natural world; he just has to vacillate, cannot make up his own mind about his body. In dealing with the particular distortion that bothers the poet, the poem stops short in communicating the joyful beauty in the harmony of nature.

Despite the large number of haiku that he wrote, it was clearly difficult for Wright to master in such a short time, a year perhaps, the complexities of haiku. The editors of the *Richard Wright Reader* say that Wright's haiku "represent some of his best efforts at writing poetry." Some of them surely are that. But I cannot totally agree with the editors when they imply that Wright had learned the discipline of writing haiku and that he had also acquired the ability to separate his political ideas from "*the sensitive lyricism of this intimate poetry.*"[55] He came close to mastering the form and to eliminating his political and personal attitudes, but he needed more time. Apparently, the need for publication and subsequent remuneration drove him to cease working with the form and to try to get some of them published before he had mastered his art. To that extent Constance Webb is correct in saying that to this uniquely Japanese form of poetry Wright was trying "to bring the life and consciousness of a black American." He was not only writing out of his themes and desires that filled his earlier work, but he was writing out of his loneliness. He explained to his friend Margrit de Sablonière, "I'd like to be alone, as much alone as possible. Have you taken solitude for your friend? I have. When I'm alone and wake up in the morning, with my world of dreams close by me, I write without effort. By noon, I've done a day's work. All else, after that, is gravy, as the Americans say."[56] Apparently, Wright never learned how to separate his two dreams, of black union with white and of his personal symbolical union with nature. Nor could he merge both dreams into a selfless, impersonal identification with nature. Haiku is a way of life, of thinking and feeling. Far too often Wright's negritude and bitterness had to intrude. Not yet had he learned the arduous task in poetry of eliminating that which does not fit.

Michel Fabre has phrased the evolution of Wright as a poet with fine insight when he says, "The distance separating the revolutionary poems of the 1930s, vibrant with indignation and brutal imagery, from the intimate symbolism of the haiku may seem great indeed. But the road travelled from the awkward enthusiasm of the young militant to the serene mastery of the mature artist is the sign, in the case of a writer as politically engaged as Wright, of a certain detachment."[57] The significant words in this evaluation, however, are "symbolism," "serene mastery," and "certain." These are expressions of attitudes or qualifications that in the first and last instances helped prevent Wright's mastering the form. Whether he did not understand that haiku are not poems with symbols—that the detachment must not be a certain part but total, that haiku represent a way of life—or whether he was unable in such a short time to develop the necessary skills is for the moment not answerable. It would require a study of all his haiku to determine this with some degree of certainty. It also seems to me, on the basis of the twenty-three haiku that are available, that he had not achieved a "serene mastery." He seemed not to be serene in those moments of writing. Indeed, Fabre almost implies this lack of serenity with his haste to add, in the next sentence following the passage I have just quoted, that "on the eve of his death, the novelist's interest in human affairs, his struggle against racism and injustice, had by no means faltered."[58] Perhaps it was failure to achieve serenity in nature (since it could not be in human affairs) that denied Wright the necessary state of mind to write the best haiku that he was capable of.

He was an artist and he was very good at his craft. But most of his published haiku fail by their amount of symbolism and inability to accept life with the loss of personal identity to meet the requirements of great haiku. The major themes in his haiku reveal this failure to attain the necessary austerity and selfless love of the ordinary. Frequently, he focuses in the *what* of the moment on either the passivity of the poet-speaker or the intrusive aspects of the speaker in a white world. In the following haiku, for example,

> It is September
> The month in which I was born
> And I have no thoughts[59]

he offers the *when*. It is September, a time that has special meaning for the poet-speaker. It not only is his birth month, but is associated with specific behavior that is supposed to occur on one's birthday or during that month. There seems to be no *where*, no place, no concept of nature. Instead of focusing on the union with simple things and a consequent harmony, it anchors itself to a rational process that can be summarized by saying, It is my birthday; one has thoughts (about the past or oneself?) on his birthday; but I have no thoughts. Thus, instead of a harmonious union with September (a weak suggestion here of season), the relationship is to the word itself, "September," conceived as a symbol for a special event in a person's life and loaded with sentiment, especially nostalgia. Exhibiting little imagination, the poem makes a commonplace identification between the symbol and his birth month, a process that implies the passivity of the poet. He feels that the event should be momentous enough to generate thought. On the other hand, what does seem to emerge from the poem is a sense of the passing of a creative mood in which his creativity is associated with the fall season with its cyclical overtones. Both the poet and the year seem to be in a quiescent phase, a cycle preparing for sleep or death.

Similary, in

> An empty sickbed
> An indented white pillow
> In weak winter sun

the theme of the poet-speaker as a passive intruder in a white world emerges strongly. The *where* and *when* are clear, a room for the sick (at home or in a hospital) and in winter. But the *what* is obscured. The two statements providing the visual images of the empty bed and the pillow are connected only by syntactical position to the third line. Nor is it clear that the absent patient is the poet-speaker. What is certain is that the patient is out of bed, but had been in it once. The first two lines emphasize the important terms "empty," "sick," "indented," and "white." Of these "white" seems out of place, despite the fact that conventionally pillow cases are white, especially in sick rooms. But one wonders why it is emphasized by position and alliteration. Why did Wright not say a white bedspread or sheet or merely an indented pillow? He was a good enough poet not to have added "white" just to fill out the rhythm. The word is there; it nags the thought; it suggests, perhaps, that again Wright's polarity between white and black emerges at an unconscious level. There seems to be no other poetic rationale for the word. The complete visual scene is now seen in the light of a winter sun described as "weak." The effect of the qualification is to reinforce the sense of "empty," "sick," "white" and to reflect a rhythm of nature as well as the poet-speaker's mood. The sun is not weak; it is the observer. He has externalized his mood through the term "weak" and transfers it to the sun. The purpose appears to be to suggest that the source of warmth and health is now weak. What rises from this context, however, is the observer's feeling of sadness and isolation, as though he is sorry for himself and thus identifies his self-image with the sun and with the other elements in the scene. Instead of revealing the submergence of self in nature, the poem leaves one with the impression that the speaker, like the sun, is an intruder in a white world where all that remains of the former inhabitant of the bed is an indentation.

A second major theme is the relationship between nature and man based on nostalgia for a lost past, a transference of feeling from poet to nature, or the desire for a quest. Sometimes in relating nature to man, Wright draws on man's domestic world for his images, as in

> Winter rain at night
> Sweetening the taste of bread
> And spicing the soup.

The visual images of rain, night, and winter reveal a time of nature that is cold and unpleasant for an indoor person. The second and third lines move into ambiguity. It is not clear whether the speaker is indoors or outside, close to a building. What is evident, however, is that the gustatory image of "taste of bread" and "soup," as man's domestic activities, create an effect opposed to that of the first line. Through contrast, the first image intensifies the second, providing the psychological effect of the season on one's enjoyment of cooking. Again in this poem, there is no harmonious union of the poet with nature. Instead, with a touch of nostalgia for such gustatory memories, the poet uses nature like a dust of flour to season the domestic image. In effect, the poem reveals the separation of man and nature and a movement into memory.

The same sense of separation coupled with nostalgia or an unstated desire occurs in

> Whose town did you leave
> O wild and drowning spring rain
> And where do you go?

The *when* is spring; the *where* is not clear. The *what* reflects that the poet has transferred his mood to the spring rain, which he humanizes. The visual image of wild rain is set within a frame of questions that immediately separate the poet-speaker from the scene. The questions spring from Wright's own intellectualization and mood, apparently of nostalgia for his past when he had left a town and knew not where to go. The image and questions generate the quality of loneliness as Wright associates his feelings with nature. There is also a lovely though sad feeling, even if romantic, that emerges from "wild and drowning spring rain," emphasizing not a destructive, but a creative aspect of things. It is as though the poet were saying that creativity or creative things cannot remain very long in a particular town, but they do not know where they will go.

Often Wright identifies himself closely with some aspect of nature directly or indirectly. More commonly, he selects an element of nature whose characteristics he emphasizes in the haiku resemble similar ones in him. For example, in one of his better haiku,

> The crow flew so fast
> That he left his lonely caw
> Behind in the fields

Wright creates the impression on the surface of a pastoral setting with fields and a crow. The bird's characteristics are blackness and flight coupled with the quality "fast" and his caw, which is "lonely." The poem thus reveals color, sound, and movement. The seasonal time is vague, perhaps summer or early autumn. But the term "lonely," being applicable to the crow only if one anthropomorphizes the bird, suggests that Wright has externalized his state of mind and memory through the crow, seeming superficially to identify with the crow in terms of color, movement (Wright's living in various places especially during his childhood), and loss of something, the caw or voice, that is lonely. Just as the crow outflew his caw, so Wright outstripped his childhood voice in nature, his own sense of what he was in rural Mississippi. But as it is the fault of the crow for flying so fast, so the loss of voice would seem to be the poet's fault. The result is ambiguous because of the transference of mood to the crow. Because the crow is a part of nature, nature too seems to be partly at fault. For Wright the identification is only symbolic; it is not complete as a union, because the poet moves from humor into an intellectualization that makes the haiku imperfect.

Part of the nostalgic and sentimental identification with nature finds meaning as a lost desire or quest, as in

> An autumn sunset
> A buzzard sails slowly past
> Not flapping its wings.

The *when* is fall; the *where* seems to be the country. The visual yet abstract image of the cessation of two different time sequences, the end of day and the end of the year, provides a temporal background for the second image, the sailing buzzard. While the first image has the typical nuances of a double cycle of time, suggesting the end of a process or of things, the second emphasizes the negation also of a process. The buzzard, as part of nature's disposal system, is a scavenger; it is black, as opposed to the color of the sunset; and it moves not from its own efforts, by flapping its wings, a process that has ceased, but as though the air supports it. In effect, the two images come together, the end of a cycle of time and the eater of dead meat, as part of natural processes on earth. Again, there does not seem to be any sudden intuitional insight that unifies poet, nature, and event. Instead, the poet seems to identify his internal state through transference with the buzzard and the cycle of time, as in "The Crow Flew So Fast." If so, then the poem is diminished as a haiku by precisely that amount in which the poet uses the events of nature to symbolize his inner states of feeling. The buzzard, in other words, is there not as part of an experience, but as part of the system of images or symbols that Wright could use to define his self-image and its polarities. As part of a picture, it reveals Wright's desire for, but failure to achieve, union with nature.

A related nostalgia for something in the past, like a lost desire, emerges in

> I would like a bell
> Tolling this soft twilight
> Over willow trees.

Both the time and place are vague, "willow trees" with "soft twilight," suggesting perhaps summer or spring. The visual image is again the end of the day with willow trees framed in the scene, all muted by the adjective "soft." Into this setting the poet has deliberately placed himself through his use of the strong personal pronoun "I" and the statement of his desire in a mode of thought contrary to reality. The use of the modal "would" raises a series of questions, admits an intrusive intellectuality. In this muted setting the poet would like an aural image, the tolling of a bell. Why alter the scene as it is? Obviously, the poet is not submerged harmoniously in nature at this point. Instead, he needs to impose something man-made on the event: in one sense the sound from a bell, in another sense an intellectualization or association. The speaker-poet sees nature as something separate from himself that he would like to alter. But perhaps his mood is derived from a series of associations. Twilight reminds the poet either of a bell sound or something else. If it is something else, that is associated with a tolling bell. In either case the key word is "tolling," whose sonorousness, as well as image, suggests that the twilight needs to be reinforced. What emerges as a dominant mood is a note of sadness or regret within the poet, a sense of an ending for him, a biblical overtone of death caught in the tolling of the bell for something. For a moment the poet almost slips into sentimentality, trying (or wishing to try) to create a scene that would regenerate a specific mood he once had. The poem departs from Wright's better haiku to the degree that the modal "would" detracts from its simplicity.

Lost desire, nostalgia, or sense of defeat as a mood imposed on the image of nature dominates

> For you, O gulls
> I order slaty waters
> And this leaden sky.

Again the *when* is vague: late fall or winter? The place is equally so. The visual image contains gulls, water, sky, and poet. The poem begins with an address to the gulls and the poet's asserting that he has ordered the water and sky and their colors within the scene. As a result, there is no harmonious union between the poet, the gulls, the water, and the sky. Yet the poet-speaker apparently associates his mood with the gulls, externalizing through them his responses, which he intellectualizes as being related to color, the second external symbol of his state of feeling. Color dominates the poem and creates the mood. The waters are slaty, the sky leaden; both are dull or mat grays sliding off into dirty blues. The mood is one of sadness; something is past or something vital is gone or lost, as though the sky and water reflect in their color the vitality drained from the gulls and the speaker. Although Wright uses the gulls as external devices to which he attaches his feelings, he also imposes a human choice upon the elements of nature. The mode of thought is transference while trying to maintain a sense of personal identification. Because the effect of sadness does not develop from the union with nature, the haiku reveals a sense of loss, whether it be of physical vitality or intellectual creativity.

At his best Wright is quite capable of separating his social and political responses to his own life from his reaction to nature. He can remain detached while becoming one with nature to create a moment of "ah-ness." For example, in

> The spring lingers on
> In the scent of a damp log
> Rotting in the sun

he has written one of his best haiku. The *when* and *where* are apparent without being overly obvious as to place. Three different kinds of images come together through and in the poet, who is not himself part of the visual setting. The visual images of the damp log and of the sun, along with the vague image of spring, are closely related through prepositional patterns with the thermal image of warmth from the sun and the rotting log, as well as with the olfactory image from the odor of the log. The *what* of the haiku is the poet's intuitive perception of spring; it is the interaction of all five images. Within this occurs no intrusive element or abstraction from the world of human beings. The perception given poetic life by the poet reveals the paradoxical union of three seemingly disparate processes of nature with a fourth one: man, the moisture in the log (whether from dew or rain or its own sap is of no consequence), the warmth given off by the sun, and the rotting process. In effect, spring is suddenly perceived as being part of decay, not death but a creative process. The important operating word is "rotting," which creates a slight smile or twist, not really intellectualized, for the stereotyped response to what is spring. What emerges strongly is that life comes from decay. From this comes a slight but necessary sadness in the recognition of the transitory but dynamic relationship of all life. Because things change and the ways of things alter, even the poet senses that he is part of this pattern called life or spring.

Wright is equally creative and objective in his other fine haiku, such as "From across the Lake" and "The Green Cockleburs." These rank among his best. One not quite as fine as these is

> Just enough of rain
> To bring the smell of silk
> From the umbrellas.[60]

Again, Wright maintains his objectivity and refuses to admit his sentiments, personal griefs or desires. The *when* is apparently spring, perhaps autumn; the *where* is vague, somewhere outside. Three images come together in the poet's perception. The image from nature is rain, which is not destructive in this poem. Instead, it is mild, even gentle as qualified by the phrase "just enough." Within the image of rain is set an image from the world of man, an umbrella. What unifies the two disparate images is the third olfactory image, the smell of wet silk. The total visual-olfactory image is sharp and strong, each part growing out of and related to the other. The light drizzle causes human beings to open their umbrellas; the material of the umbrellas is silk, a product from nature like the rain. When wet the silk produces an odor perceptible to the human nose. In this poem the world of nature, consisting of a process and the work of an insect, is joined with and through the world of man, with a man-made object and through the poet's perception. This poem seems to me not to rank among his best haiku, but to miss the mark by the slight amount in which it suggests the dominance of the human world. In its own right, however, it reveals a direction toward which Wright might have taken his interest in haiku had he not died.

Humor is also a part of Wright's theme in his relationship with nature, as evidenced in "The Dog's Violent Sneeze," "With a Twitching Nose," and "Make up Your Mind Snail!" Perhaps one of his best haiku, which creates the gentle whimsical Zen humor of the best Japanese haiku, is

> Coming from the woods
> A bull has a sprig of lilac
> Dangling from a horn.[61]

In this poem the *when* and *where* are clearly apparent; it is springtime for lilacs and a farm for the woods and bull. But the *what* or moment lies in the harmonious union of the images and their paradoxical relationships through the poet's sudden perception. There are three visual images, the woods that provides a vague, generalized sense of nature, the bull that provides a sense of the strong, vital male animal, and the lilac sprig that provides a sense of spring and of nature associated with flowers, beauty, and sadness. The important words that provide the perceptive unity in the poem are "bull," "lilac," and "dangling from a horn." In the background the terms "bull" and "horn" focus on the potential danger or destructive quality of a powerful animal in nature associated more with woods than with lilacs. But the image of the woods, being part of the life of the lilac, relates these two seemingly incongruous elements, bull and lilac, danger and beauty. In effect, the harmonious union associates the bull with other forms of life, such as trees and flowers. Its danger is lessened through the humor in the visual image of the flower dangling from a horn. The casualness of the word "dangling" suggests that the sprig is not in danger. What Wright has done is to perceive suddenly and intuitively how the danger or destructive quality in nature can become harmless and humorously casual in relationship to other aspects, such as the beauty of the lilac and the sense of chance operating. It is not a human being who has placed the sprig on the bull's horns; it was apparently torn by chance from its main stalk.

Like the Japanese poet Basho, Wright had achieved in some of his haiku the quiet tone, the sense of sad oneness in nature, coupled with a slight smile of joy and compassion. At his best Wright was clearly capable of perceiving the peaceful and temperate aspects of nature and of avoiding the confused and violent elements both in man and in nature. He could create, as it were, his own Wordsworthian "spots of time," seeing into the life of things. In September 1960, Wright declared that he had "finished nothing this year but those damned haiku. . . ."[62] But that was enough, because in the few fine haiku that emerged from his thousands, he had found his moment, his time, his place, his union, peaceful and complete, with some aspect of life. Even if it was not with a white America, it was with a nature that had dominated his childhood and had remained forever powerful in all of his work, appearing only during the last two years of his life as a dominant theme. On 28 November 1960 he died at the age of 52. His daughter Julia wrote a haiku for him as an appropriate good-bye,

> Burning out its time,
> And timing its own burning,
> One lonely candle.[63]

The major image does not come from nature, which Wright had sought unconsciously and consciously all his life; it comes from the word of manmade things. Like all things, it is subject to the changes of nature, and like man, it is also capable of speeding up the process. Haiku, Julia's poem, and those Wright himself wrote reveal more clearly than his great novels or his polemical tracts his sympathetic awareness of the complex relationship between man and nature when man needs to know where he is or is going, when he will get there, and what he will be when that happens.

Notes

1. Michel Fabre, "The Poetry of Richard Wright," *Studies in Black Literature*, 1 (Autumn 1970), 10–22; reprinted in this volume, pp. 252–72.

2. Eight first appeared in Ollie Harrington, "The Last Days of Richard Wright," *Ebony*, No. 16 (Feb. 1961), pp. 93–94; four more appeared in Constance Webb, *Richard Wright* (New York: G. P. Putnam's Sons, 1968), pp. 393–94; fourteen were published in Richard Wright, "Fourteen Haikus," *Studies in Black Literature*, 1 (Autumn 1970) 1, of these three being from Webb; ten were published in the Wright Issue of *New Letters*, 38 (Winter 1971), 100–01, of these two being from Webb and nine from *Studies in Black Literature*;

four, three from the *Ebony*, one from Webb, in Michel Fabre, *The Unfinished Quest of Richard Wright*, trans. Isabel Barzun (New York: William Morrow & Co., 1973), pp. 506, 513; and finally, all twenty-three in the *Richard Wright Reader*, ed. Ellen Wright and Michel Fabre (New York: Harper & Row, 1978), pp. 251-54. According to Fabre, Wright had selected some 811 of his some 4000 haiku for an eighty-page manuscript that he wanted to publish (*Unfinished Quest*, p. 508). As far as I know, those haiku have not been published as of the date of this study.

3. Fabre, *Quest*, p. 508.

4. Russell C. Brignano, *Richard Wright: An Introduction to the Man and His Work* (Pittsburgh: Univ. of Pittsburgh Press, 1970), p. 166.

5. See Brignano, p. ix.

6. Brignano, p. 122.

7. Joan Giroux, *The Haiku Form* (Rutland, Vt.: Charles E. Tuttle Co., 1974), p. 113.

8. Webb, p. 394.

9. R. H. Blyth, *Haiku* (Tokyo: Hokuseido, 1949), I, iv.

10. See Brignano, p. x.

11. Fabre, *Quest*, p. xix.

12. Richard Wright, "Beteen the World and Me," *Partisan Review*, 2 (July–Aug. 1935) 18-19.

13. Richard Wright, *Black Boy: A Record of Childhood and Youth* (New York: Harper & Bros. 1945), p. 7; see also Fabre, "Poetry," p. 17.

14. Fabre, *Quest*, p. 447.

15. Fabre, *Quest*, p. 274.

16. Fabre, *Quest*, p. 319.

17. Brignano, p. 119.

18. Fabre, "Poetry," p. 19.

19. Fabre, *Quest*, pp. 375, 447.

20. Fabre, *Quest*, p. 481.

21. Fabre, *Quest*, p. 505.

22. Fabre, *Quest*, pp. 505-06.

23. Webb, pp. 387, 393-94.

24. See R. H. Blyth, *Haiku*; Joan Giroux, *The Haiku Form*.

25. Giroux, p. 16.

26. Giroux, p. 17.

27. Giroux, pp. 15-16.

28. Giroux, pp. 18-21.

29. Blyth, I, 373.

30. Giroux, p. 23.

31. Giroux, pp. 22-23.

32. Blyth, I, i-iii.

33. Blyth, I, vii-viii.

34. Fabre, *Quest*, pp. 505-06.

35. See Fabre, "Poetry," p. 19. He devotes one paragraph to a description of the form.

36. Fabre, *Quest*, p. 506.

37. Brignano, p. 3.

38. Richard Wright, "Blueprint for Negro Writing," in the *Wright Reader*, pp. 43-44, 46.

39. Giroux, p. 46.

40. Fabre, "Poetry," p. 17.

41. Fabre, "Poetry," pp. 13–16, 18.

42. Giroux, pp. 45–47.

43. All of Wright's haiku are quoted from the *Wright Reader*, pp. 251–54. In those instances where an earlier publication of a haiku differs from that in the *Wright Reader*, I have so noted, but in general have followed the earlier reading.

44. Giroux, p. 76.

45. Line 2 varies in its phrasing. In *New Letters* (1971) it reads, "A bull has a sprig of lilac"; in *Studies in Black Literature* (1970), it reads, "A bull has a lilac sprig," as it does in the *Wright Reader* (1978).

46. Giroux, pp. 50–51.

47. Line 1 varies in its phrasing. In *New Letters* (1971) it reads, "Why is the hail so wild"; in *Studies in Black Literature* (1970) and in the *Wright Reader* (1978) it reads, "Why is hail so wild."

48. See Giroux, pp. 55–59; Blyth, I, viii.

49. Blyth, I, 190, 192–204, 214–17.

50. As a matter of fact, in his 23 haiku Wright used 242 one-syllable words, that is, 78% of the total number of words used are only one-syllable; 56 are two-syllable, or 18% of the total; 11 are three-syllable, or 3% of the total; and 1 is four-syllable, or less than 1% of the total. In addition, out of 310 total words used in the 23 haiku, only 12 (to the best of my knowledge) are from languages other than the native English stock. In those instances where there are variations in reading, I have based my count on the reading that I quote in this study.

51. Giroux, pp. 63–67.

52. Blyth, I, 168–72.

53. Blyth, I, 247–56.

54. Giroux, p. 66.

55. "Poetry," *Wright Reader*, p. 243.

56. Webb, pp. 393–94.

57. Fabre, "Poetry," p. 21.

58. Fabre, "Poetry," p. 21.

59. Line 2 varies in its phrasing. In Fabre, *Quest* (1973) it reads, "The month in which I was born"; in the *Wright Reader* (1978) it reads, "The month when I was born."

60. Line 3 varies in its phrasing. In *New Letters* (1971) it reads, "From the umbrellas"; in *Studies in Black Literature* (1970) and in the *Wright Reader* (1978) it reads, "From umbrellas."

61. See note 45, where I indicate the variations in line 2.

62. Fabre, "Poetry," p. 21.

63. Webb, p. 400.

INDEX